T0099194

CENTER FOR GLOBAL DEVELOPMENT

MILLIONS SAVED

NEW CASES OF PROVEN SUCCESS
IN GLOBAL HEALTH

CENTER FOR GLOBAL DEVELOPMENT

MILLIONS SAVED

NEW CASES OF PROVEN SUCCESS
IN GLOBAL HEALTH

Editors and Authors
AMANDA GLASSMAN and MIRIAM TEMIN

Millions Saved Team
Case authors: Rachel Silverman, Yuna Sakuma, Lauren Post, Alix Beith
Economic evaluation estimates: Andrew Mirelman

Advisory Group
Elie Hassenfeld, Priscilla Idele, Ruth Levine, Rachel Nugent, Richard Skolnik, Damian Walker

In cooperation with *Disease Control Priorities,* 3rd edition

Library of Congress Cataloging-in-Publication data

Glassman, Amana L.
  Millions Served: new cases of proven success in global health / Amanda Glassman, Miriam Temin
    p. cm.
Includes bibliographic rferences and index.
ISBN: 978-1-933286-88-4
LCCN: 2016936346

*Dedicated to public health workers around the world
who save lives every day.*

Contents

Foreword

The world is healthier than ever. For the first time in human history, Africa recorded no polio cases at all in 2015. Deaths from malaria, AIDS, tuberculosis, pneumococcal disease, and meningitis are down significantly. And child mortality has been cut in half in the last 25 years.

What's enabled these global health successes? At the highest level, a combination of scientific advances; innovative financial interventions designed to address market failures; and effective collaboration among developing countries, the private sector, and government and philanthropic funders.

In each instance, there are valuable insights to be learned from what has worked well—and not so well—in global health. That's what this book is about. *Millions Saved* shows, through 22 rigorously evaluated case studies, exactly what worked and why.

It is a refreshing reminder of our ability to take on some of the biggest global challenges. And it underscores the incredible impact development aid can have—and why it's so important that we continue to support poor countries in lifting themselves out of poverty.

From the virtual elimination of meningitis A in 15 endemic countries in Africa, to providing universal healthcare in Thailand, to extending antiretroviral treatment to thousands in Botswana, *Millions Saved* shows how—with the right tools and support—even the poorest countries are able to respond to difficult challenges. In an engaging and readable way, this book chronicles important global health initiatives and illuminates valuable lessons that can be applied elsewhere.

While every case study is unique, *Millions Saved* identifies some common attributes. Successful programs started with ambitious but achievable goals. They targeted efforts to the people who would gain the most. They drew on the best evidence available, measured results, and used that information to do better. The outcome was large gains in public health at stunningly low cost.

Importantly, *Millions Saved* also looks at what didn't work. In Gujarat in western India, for example, a program to pay private doctors to offer hospital childbirths to poor women failed to increase the number of hospital deliveries or reduce birth-related complications—because it never reached the poorest mothers. What this case showed is that good intentions need effective, targeted delivery systems to make a real difference. There is as much to learn from a health program that did not reach its goals as from one that did.

That's why our foundation helped fund the research, writing, and publication of *Millions Saved*—because the more information we can gather and share, the better decisions we can make and the more impact we can have. This is crucial because nearly 6 million children under the age of five are still dying every year—mostly from causes that we can prevent or treat.

The Center for Global Development has done a great job—and provided a great service—with this book. There are few organizations that apply economic research to global health and development policy with such forensic scrutiny.

I encourage global health experts, policymakers, funders, and anyone else interested in helping create a better world to read *Millions Saved*. I am confident you will come away with a clearer sense of what the world has learned about fighting some of our biggest health challenges—and how we can use that knowledge to save even more lives.

Bill Gates
Co-chair, Bill & Melinda Gates Foundation

Acknowledgments

This new edition of *Millions Saved* would not have been possible without the success of the two editions that came before it. We are therefore grateful for the efforts of the original What Works Working Group and to the authors of the earlier editions, Ruth Levine and Molly Kinder. We are also thankful for colleagues and loyal readers who encouraged us to write about a new set of global health success case studies to show what works in global health and how the right kinds of programs can continue to improve the health of people around the world.

We offer profound gratitude to our advisory group members—Elie Hassenfeld, Priscilla Idele, Ruth Levine, Rachel Nugent, Richard Skolnik, and Damian Walker—who shared candid feedback from the earliest stages of the project to the last draft of the manuscript.

A small group of internal reviewers advised us on the case selection process and methods. We are thankful for the insights and guidance of Victoria Fan, Willa Friedman, Charles Kenny, Mead Over, David Roodman, and Justin Sandefur. We are also grateful to the editors of *Disease Control Priorities,* 3rd edition, who helped ensure that the cases in this book are supported by rigorous evidence and analysis.

Thanks are due to our case authors, who read countless journal articles, conducted informant interviews, and survived multiple rounds of editing and review. For their role in the case study writing team along with Miriam Temin, we offer sincerest appreciation to Alix Beith, Lauren Post, and Yuna Sakuma. Particular thanks go to Rachel Silverman, who wrote the first versions of many of the cases in this book and suggested edits on all of the cases. Thanks also to Andrew Mirelman for his excellent work in calculating economic evaluation estimates for many of the cases and for his contributions to the methods chapter; a background working paper summarizing the full extent of this work is available on the Center for Global Development website (cgdev.org).

We are indebted to the numerous reviewers who helped us accurately express the core elements of the cases as well as the more nuanced details. Reviewers included Paul Arora, Monazza Aslam, Ava Avalos, Sebastian Bauhoff, Jere

Behrman, Monique Berlier, Carla Bonahora, Christian Borja-Vega, Joanne Bosworth, Jennifer Bryce, Peter Carrasco, Fanny Chabrol, Mariam Claeson, Michael Clemens, Brenda Colatrella, Luis Carlos Corral, Alejandro Cravioto, Ayesha de Costa, Jacqueline Devine, James Goodman Dobbins, Erin Eckert, Shams El Arifeen, Caroline Fiennes, Willa Friedman, Cui Fuqiang, Sun Gang, Frederico Guanais de Aguiar, Stephen Hadler, Ashu Handa, Gonzalo Hernández Licona, Pablo Ibarraran, Prabhat Jha, Mark Kane, Michael Kremer, Marc LaForce, Lisa Lee, X. Liang, Luis Gerardo Mejía Sánchez, Manoj Mohanan, Patience Musanhu, Nico Nagelkerke, Jonathan Passmore, Siriwan Pitayarangsarit, Dhushyanth Raju, Ferdinando Regalia, Martin Sabignoso, Michael Samson, Deviariandy Setiawan, Yehude Simon, Agnes Soucat, Jeffrey Sturchio, Yot Teerawattananon, Luis Tejerina, Alix Zwane, and the Evidence to Action staff. A special thanks to Paul Gertler, who reviewed and provided input on several case chapters.

Our colleagues at the Center for Global Development (CGD), particularly CGD president Nancy Birdsall, generously provided suggestions, constructive critiques, and moral support. We would also like to thank CGD's communications team—Rajesh Mirchandani, vice president of communications and policy outreach, and John Osterman, director of digital communications—for their guidance throughout the publication process. Thanks also to Kate McQueston and Jenny Ottenhoff for their contributions, and to Rebecca Forman and Claudia Calderon, who dedicated their internships to this project.

Finally, we are grateful for the financial support and technical feedback of the Bill & Melinda Gates Foundation and of Good Ventures.

The case details presented in this volume are based on the best available information at the time of writing. We apologize for any omissions. All errors are our own.

Disclosure

The Bill & Melinda Gates Foundation provided most of the funding for the writing, publication, and dissemination of this book as well as for several of the programs it highlights. Foundation staff also played a role in the book's production by participating in the review of evidence around a short list of cases put together by the Center for Global Development team and by providing advice and feedback on the overall project. However, the cases were selected independently, and each chapter was written and edited by individuals with no involvement or direct interest in the programs discussed.

The Center for Global Development is an independent and nonpartisan research institution. No conditions or limitations on CGD's independence in research, findings, conclusions, or resultant publications are attached to any funding received. Where appropriate, CGD welcomes and considers comments or views from donors, but CGD retains total discretion and final decision-making authority regarding programs, project research topics, speakers, participants in activities, and contents of reports.

Glossary

Bill & Melinda Gates Foundation (BMGF) The largest private foundation in the world, founded by Bill and Melinda Gates in 2000. The goals of the foundation are to enhance healthcare and reduce poverty worldwide, and to expand educational opportunities and access to information technology in America.

civil society Aggregate of nongovernmental, not-for-profit organizations and institutions that represent and express the interest of the public.

Cochrane Reviews Systematic reviews of primary research in health and health policy.

cost-benefit analysis A systematic process to calculate and compare costs and benefits, in dollar value, of a program, decision, or policy.

cost-effectiveness analysis A systematic process to calculate and compare costs and benefits, by key outcomes, of a program, decision, or policy.

counterfactual The situation in which the intervention did not occur.

Department for International Development (DFID) A UK government department responsible for administering overseas aid to end extreme poverty.

difference-in-differences A method to estimate treatment effects from observational data by comparing the pre- and post-treatment outcome differences between a treatment and a control group.

disability-adjusted life year (DALY) A metric used to quantify disease burden. One DALY can be thought of as one year of "healthy" life lost. DALYs combine the years of life lost (YLLs) due to premature mortality in the population and the years lost due to disability (YLDs) for people living with a disease or its consequences.

Expanded Program on Immunization (EPI) A World Health Organization–initiated program established in 1974 to vaccinate children throughout the world.

Gavi, the Vaccine Alliance A public-private global health partnership that was founded in 2000 with the goal of creating equal access to new and underused vaccines for people living in the world's poorest countries.

Global Fund to Fight AIDS, Tuberculosis and Malaria (Global Fund) An international financing organization founded in 2002 to accelerate the end of AIDS, tuberculosis, and malaria as epidemics.

Global Goals for Sustainable Development A set of 17 goals that aim to end extreme poverty and hunger, fight inequality and injustice, combat climate change, and more (the Global Goals replace the Millennium Development Goals). Starting on September 25, 2015, the leaders of 193 United Nations member states will use the Global Goals to frame their agendas and political policies. The 17 Global Goals and their targets for 2030 are described at globalgoals.org.

gold standard A measure of comparison used to describe the best available method or procedure.

herd immunity Indirect protection from an infectious disease because a large proportion of the community is immune to that disease.

human immunodeficiency virus (HIV) A virus spread through certain bodily fluids that weakens the immune system by destroying T cells or CD4 cells. HIV can progress to acquired immune deficiency syndrome (AIDS), the last stage of HIV infection.

intent-to-treat (ITT) An analysis of the results of a randomized controlled trial based on initial treatment assignment rather than treatment actually received. It is used to avoid the effects of factors such as noncompliance or dropout.

Joint United Nations Programme on HIV/AIDS (UNAIDS) A partnership that serves as the leading advocate for global action against HIV/AIDS and seeks to lead, strengthen, and support an expanded response to HIV and AIDS. UNAIDS is a member of the United Nations Development Group.

Millennium Development Goals (MDGs) Goals established in September 2000 to rally the world around a 15-year agenda to tackle measurable, universally agreed-upon objectives for eradicating extreme poverty and hunger, preventing deadly disease, and expanding education opportunities to all children.

Pan American Health Organization (PAHO) The specialized health agency of the Inter-American System. Founded in 1902, PAHO serves as the World Health Organization's regional office for the Americas.

pay for performance (P4P) See *results-based financing*.

President's Emergency Plan for AIDS Relief (PEPFAR) A US government initiative established in 2003 to help save the lives of those suffering from HIV/AIDS around the world.

President's Malaria Initiative (PMI) A US government initiative, launched in 2005, designed to cut malaria deaths in half in target countries in sub-Saharan Africa.

product development partnerships (PDPs) Partnerships created when nonprofit organizations bring together multiple stakeholders from both the private and the public sector to research, develop, and support access to new health technologies.

results-based financing (RBF) Any program whereby a financial reward is given based on the delivery of an agreed-upon output or outcome, after the results are verified. In global health, a program is considered to employ RBF when money or goods are transferred to a national or subnational government, manager, provider, payer, or consumer once a predefined performance target (for example, a reduction in the child mortality rate) is achieved and verified.

Sustainable Development Goals (SDGs) See *Global Goals for Sustainable Development*.

time-series analysis Use of a mathematical model to understand quantitative observations made over time.

treatment-on-the-treated (ToT) The effect of a treatment on those who received the treatment. Calculated as the intent-to-treat divided by the difference in the proportion treated.

UNITAID A global health initiative established in 2006 that provides funding for scaling up access to treatment and diagnostics for HIV/AIDS, malaria, and tuberculosis, primarily for people in low-income countries.

United Nations Children's Fund (UNICEF) A United Nations program founded in 1946 that provides humanitarian and development assistance to children and mothers in developing countries.

United Nations Population Fund (UNFPA) A United Nations organization that works to ensure universal access to reproductive health, including family planning and sexual health, to all couples and individuals. UNFPA supports population and development strategies, promotes awareness of population and development issues, and advocates for the mobilization of the resources and political will necessary to accomplish its goals.

United States Agency for International Development (USAID) The US government agency primarily responsible for administering civilian foreign aid.

World Health Organization (WHO) Agency of the United Nations specializing in international public health, founded on April 7, 1948 (now celebrated as World Health Day). Its primary role is to direct and coordinate international health within the United Nations system.

World Health Organization prequalification A World Health Organization–led process to ensure that diagnostics, medicines, vaccines, and immunization-related equipment and devices for high-burden diseases meet global standards. The outcomes of the process are used by the United Nations and other procurement agencies to make purchasing decisions.

Global Health Revolution

Since the turn of the 21st century, people in low- and middle-income countries have experienced a health revolution, one that has created new opportunities and brought new challenges. It is a revolution that keeps mothers and babies alive, helps children grow, and enables adults to thrive through and beyond their working lives.

Yet that same health revolution has left many people behind, particularly those who are disadvantaged by the circumstances of their births. The urgent task ahead is to sustain and deepen health improvements in all regions of the world while finding creative ways to support better health among people who still suffer from exclusion and deprivation.

Economic conditions have sparked the health revolution. Low- and middle-income countries' economies have grown faster than those of their wealthier counterparts, and even the worst-off families have seen their living standards rise as national incomes have grown. Aid has also played a role. Foreign aid for health from public and private sources expanded fivefold between 1990 and 2013.[1] Furthermore, the arrival of new global health funders has fostered innovation and enabled delivery of health technologies even in the most impoverished and conflict-prone places in the world.

This edition of *Millions Saved* chronicles the global health revolution from the ground up, showcasing 22 of the local, regional, and national health programs that have been part of this global change. The first edition of *Millions Saved*, published by the Center for Global Devel-

opment in 2004, described 17 large-scale global health successes, and in the second edition this number was expanded to 20.[2] This new edition, however, profiles both major achievements and a few crushing disappointments. Each case demonstrates how much effort—and sometimes luck—is required to fight illness and sustain good health in challenging settings. Sometimes technology can be the game changer, but far more often success emerges from wise strategic choices, quality analysis, and sound leadership. Together, the cases offer lessons about what it takes to bring good health to all.

This edition provides new stories of global health impact over the past decade; however, the gains profiled in the first *Millions Saved* endure. Three examples illustrate the durability of those gains against specific diseases: guinea worm, smallpox, and iodine deficiency. The global health community has brought guinea worm to the verge of eradication without the aid of a vaccine or medicine; according to the Carter Center, only 22 cases were reported in four countries in 2015.[3] Smallpox remains safely eradicated—the last wild case occurred in Somalia in 1997—although the threat of bioterrorism demands sustained vigilance. Iodine deficiency, whose symptom is goiter, was most prevalent worldwide in China. Now, since more than 90 percent of the country enjoys access to iodized salt, goiters have become rare in China, and remaining efforts now stretch to provide iodized salt to nomads and rural dwellers in the country's remote mountainous regions.[4]

Global health priorities have also shifted since the original case studies were compiled, most obviously in the transition from the Millennium Development Goals to the Global Goals for Sustainable Development.[5] First, noncommunicable diseases have risen in prominence on the global health agenda, surpassing other types of disease and causes of death in all but the very poorest countries. Second, the global health community has rallied behind the promise of universal health coverage as a strategy to improve population health and prevent families from falling into poverty as a result of sky-high medical expenses. Third, results-based funding has proliferated around the globe, and evidence is growing that—designed well—this approach can help improve health outcomes and increase access, quality, and efficiency. And fourth, health experts now give serious attention to the importance of social determinants—especially gender inequality—in shaping health outcomes. The cases selected for this new edition reflect these major shifts.

About This Volume

This new edition of *Millions Saved* contains 22 case studies and a chapter on methods. Each case profiles an at-scale program that aimed to improve health. There are four main categories of programs: those that involve (1) rolling out medicines and technologies, (2) expanding access to health services, (3) targeting cash transfers to improve health, and (4) promoting population-wide behavior change to decrease risk. The book is divided into four parts, one for each category.

Together, the 22 cases (see Box 1) showcase a diversity of strategies to improve health in low- and middle-income countries.

The cases show that health success is possible anywhere, given the right strategies. Most of the world's regions are represented: seven from sub-Saharan Africa, six from Latin America and the Caribbean, five from East and Southeast Asia, and four from South Asia. The cases also come from an economically diverse range of countries, including some of the poorest countries and regions in the world.

As in the first edition of *Millions Saved,* programs were selected based on four key criteria developed by the original What Works Working Group and updated for this edition. The key criteria included the following:

1. **Importance.** The intervention was designed to solve a problem of public health significance. Mortality, morbidity, or another standardized measure such as disability-adjusted life years (DALYs) was used to indicate importance; other indicators, such as equity or demand on health system resources, were also considered.

2. **Impact.** Interventions or programs demonstrated a significant and attributable impact on one or more population health outcomes based on currently available evidence. Evidence of impact was judged along a continuum from most to least convincing, based on study designs that used experimental or quasi-experimental methods.

3. **Scale.** Interventions were implemented on a significant scale—primarily national, but regional was also considered. Programs were characterized as national if they had strong national-level commitment even if targeting a limited area or subgroup.

4. **Duration.** Interventions functioned at scale for at least five years.

The updated selection criteria gave preference to programs that could show cost-effectiveness in implementation, global relevance, or improvements in equity or financial protection.

The "impact" criterion proved especially tricky to apply (see the discussion in "Methods Used in Selecting and Analyzing *Millions Saved* Cases," the book's final chapter). All but 4 of the 22 programs had significant impact on one or several health outcomes; this is our core definition of success. The four disappointments represent valuable opportunities to learn; the programs were large and rigorously evaluated but failed to demonstrate significant health benefits.

In the push to get the biggest health bang out of every health buck, information on the costs and effects of programs is an essential resource for donors and governments. In 11 of the 22 cases, we include a measure of the cost-effectiveness of the programs, mostly the result of our own calculations.[6] Some cases include a cost-effectiveness estimate while others do not. This is because some approaches, such as medicines and technologies, lend themselves more easily to this type of analysis than others. Efforts to increase access to care generate multiple benefits—protection from impoverishing out-of-pocket spending on health, greater access to needed care, or simply peace of mind—and quantifying this impact would require cost-benefit analysis along many more dimensions than health.

There are costs to employing such rigorous selection criteria. For example, two of the most influential small-scale programs on the impact of early nutrition inter-

Box 1. Cases in *Millions Saved*

Rolling Out Medicine and Technology
- Beginning of the End: Eliminating Meningitis A across Africa's Meningitis Belt
- Making the Impossible Possible: Botswana's Mass Antiretroviral Therapy Program
- Reducing Cancer Risk in China: Equalizing Hepatitis B Vaccine Coverage
- One Mosquito at a Time: Zambia's National Malaria Control Program
- A Solid Foundation for Child Health: Mexico's Piso Firme Program
- A Fresh Start for a Bright Future: Kenya's School-Based Deworming Program
- An Outbreak Halted in Its Tracks: Eliminating Polio in Haiti
- Learning from Disappointment: The Integrated Management of Childhood Illness in Bangladesh

Expanding Access to Health Services
- Health Access for All: Thailand's Universal Coverage Scheme
- Paying for Provincial Performance in Health: Argentina's Plan Nacer
- Tackling Disease at its Roots: Brazil's Programa Saúde da Família
- Motivating Health Workers, Motivating Better Health: Rwanda's Pay-for-Performance Scheme for Health Services
- Learning from Disappointment: Reducing the Cost of Institutional Delivery in Gujarat, India

Using Targeted Cash Transfers to Improve Health
- Giving Vulnerable Children a Fair Shot: Kenya's Social Cash Transfer Program
- Protecting Childhood: Punjab's Female School Stipend Program
- A Step Up for the Children Apartheid Left Behind: South Africa's Child Support Grant
- Learning from Disappointment: Honduras's Programa de Asignación Familiar II

Changing Behavior Population-wide to Reduce Risk
- Cracking Down on Lighting Up: Thailand's Campaign for Tobacco Control
- Improving Road Safety: Vietnam's Comprehensive Helmet Law
- A Persuasive Plea to Become "Open Defecation Free": Indonesia's Total Sanitation and Sanitation Marketing Program
- Empowering Communities to Tackle HIV: India's Avahan Program
- Learning from Disappointment: Peru's Handwashing Initiative

ventions, in Guatemala and Jamaica, are excluded by the scale and duration criteria, despite their considerable importance in shaping understanding of the long-run impact of early childhood intervention.[7] Also notable is that no study is included on the role of information technology in improving health, despite an explosion of studies on this topic, in this case because of scale and duration.

The new cases selected for this edition of *Millions Saved* were rigorously evaluated and documented. Yet there is no such thing as perfect knowledge; evidence on many programs is evolving thanks to longer periods of implementation, replication studies, new survey methods, and maybe even a "data revolution." What we do know is that this collection of case studies represents the best evidence available at the time of writing, and shows

that all but four of these experiences fall close to the "success" end of the evidence continuum.

In truth, some of the cases are not without controversy—three, in particular: Kenya's school-based deworming program, India's Avahan HIV control program, and Indonesia's program to reduce open defecation. Doubts regarding each program's impact arise from different factors. In the case of school-based deworming, a global systematic review and a replication study found that although worm loads dropped as a result of deworming, anti-anemia and education effects have not been comparable to those published in the original Kenya study, resulting in a debate that some have termed "worm wars."[8] In Avahan, the impact estimates are modeled on a counterfactual and vary widely depending on how it is defined.[9] And Indonesia's program to reduce open defecation, based on an approach first implemented in Bangladesh, yielded a significant health benefit but used tactics that many considered problematic.[10] These cases were included because the disagreements about the programs have important lessons for global health policymakers and underscore the importance of rigorous impact evaluation, local context, and systematic reviews of the range of evidence available.

Millions Saved "Wows": Four Common Features, Seven Key Lessons

Although each case is unique and context-specific, all the cases have four features in common. First, wise choices were made about the interventions or tactics to be deployed, based on the best available scientific evidence. Second, partnerships and coalitions were formed to mobilize needed technical, financial, and political resources, domestically and internationally. Third, political leaders, not one but many, sometimes across political cycles, sustained efforts over time. And fourth, the programs used data, results, and evaluation in their particular settings and countries, and parlayed this information to improve health. In this they were distinct from many other health programs.

Seven key lessons emerge from this experience.

1. *Millions Saved* **shows that global health works.**
   Global polling finds that 64 percent of adults believe that when today's children grow up, they will be worse off than their parents.[11] High-profile disease outbreaks, natural disasters, corruption, and economic woes sometimes seem to conspire to create an atmosphere of pessimism. But the global health revolution writ large, and the *Millions Saved* cases in particular, show that this pessimism has little place when it comes to global health. With the right tactics—reaching the right people at the right time—health can improve rapidly, even in the poorest countries and among the poorest people. Just a few of the programs featured in *Millions Saved* together saved more than 18 million years of life that would otherwise have been lost to preventable causes of death and disability.[12] Furthermore, these huge gains have come at a remarkably low cost; life-sustaining antiretroviral treatment, a service provided in Botswana's Masa ("New Dawn") program, comes at an estimated average cost of US$480 per patient annually. Likewise, the cost of one routine pediatrician visit in a wealthy country, about US$53,

buys enough bed nets to save 10 Zambian children from dying from malaria in a year.

2. **Focusing on the worst-off yields the biggest health gains.**
   Many of the new group of *Millions Saved* programs focused on people who live in poverty or belong to high-risk groups. Programs that were better able to reach the groups most in need achieved a larger health impact. This makes intuitive sense: more health progress is possible where baseline conditions are worse. But good targeting comes in many forms. Brazil's Programa Saúde da Família allocated more funding to poorer municipalities, adjusting the budget envelope according to the poverty level in each community. Kenya's cash transfer program used both geographic and community-based targeting, asking village leaders to identify families in need that met the program's eligibility criteria. And India's AIDS programs made a difference by focusing on key population groups that were most affected by AIDS: female sex workers, men who had sex with men, transgender people, people who used drugs, and groups that worked along major trucking routes.

   Other interventions were universal in scope—and "universal" means everyone. For example, the enforcement of Vietnam's helmet legislation affects the poor and wealthy alike. Even within universal approaches, however, dedicated efforts are often needed to reach people in the most excluded communities, via targeted outreach, subsidies, and community monitoring.

3. **Governments can do the job; aid helps.**
   In nearly all the cases, governments in low- and middle-income countries have led the hard work of reaching populations in need, making policies, and forming strategies. Brazil's Programa Saúde da Família expressed the government's commitment to equity when it brought primary healthcare to people living in poverty. In South Africa, the post-apartheid government used the Child Support Grant as a central spoke in its strategy to undo the legacy of the past. And in Thailand, advocates convinced the government to take on Big Tobacco with far-reaching legislation and a new health promotion fund financed by tobacco taxes. Even in countries that some label "failed states," health authorities have managed to work effectively. Three cases—elimination of polio in Haiti, cash transfers in Pakistan, and vaccination in Africa's meningitis belt—

show that weak governance in general does not preclude effective government-led health-service delivery when the right external support is available.

Indeed, the partnerships described in the cases show that success results from shared responsibility; all do their part and no one partner foots the bill alone. Most cases feature external cofinancing or technical cooperation (see Table 1). Many programs were critically aided by the contributions of global partnerships, bilateral and multilateral aid agencies, and foundations. The private sector can also play a role: pharmaceutical companies donated medicines in Botswana, copper companies delivered malaria control programs in Zambia, and a plastics company dreamed up handwashing stations in Peru.

4. **Incentives matter for health results.**
The cases clearly show that incentives matter for health, and that incentives can take many shapes and forms. For providers, incentives can help motivate greater effort and productivity. They might include the amount of money health workers receive for their services, the nuts and bolts of that payment, or steps to promote accountability and to monitor and reward performance, to name a few. Similarly, incentives can help motivate individual beneficiaries of interventions to adopt healthier behavior, seek healthcare services, and adhere to treatment.[13] Paying households (via cash transfers) and providers in a way that is consistent with desired health outcomes, and measuring what matters, can make a major difference in health outcomes.

In Rwanda, paying for and tracking health facilities' provision of quality health services improved provider motivation and children's nutrition. In Brazil and Argentina, paying subnational governments for each additional family enrolled in primary care motivated health workers to track down those in need and ensure that they received key services. In Thailand, people living in poverty were issued a gold card that guaranteed them access to health benefits, which incentivized families to seek care more often and improved their health. In Vietnam, stronger police enforcement of motorcycle helmet use increased the costs of going without, creating a strong new incentive for people to protect their heads.

Incentives are powerful, so it is important to ensure that they make sense and do not induce harmful unintended consequences. Honduras's cash transfer program may have unintentionally created an incentive for women to have children earlier, or more quickly, than they might have done absent an external incentive. Similarly, Indonesia's rural sanitation program was able to achieve an impact on diarrhea by stigmatizing people who defecated in the open. That powerful social incentive led to better health, but at the cost of shaming and penalizing those who could not afford to build or buy latrines.

5. **What works: efficacy is not the same as effectiveness.**
In everyday English, "efficacy" and "effectiveness" might seem to have similar meanings. In the field of public health, however, there is an important distinction between the two terms. Efficacy is an intervention's proven impact in laboratory or trial settings, whereas effectiveness is how a particular intervention fares in real-world situations. In this book we are most concerned with effectiveness.

In the field of global health, conventional wisdom often suggests that good technologies—those proven to be efficacious, to work in a small-scale trial—are enough to get the job done. Historically, the global health community has focused on buying vaccines and medicines for countries that cannot afford them, assuming that those products will make their way to those who need them most. Indeed, the main raison d'être of global partnerships such as Gavi, the Vaccine Alliance; the Stop TB Fund; UNITAID; and others is to purchase health products, on the implicit assumption that the main barrier to health impact is the lack of efficacious and affordable medicines.

This lack is certainly part of the problem, but it takes far more than an efficacious and affordable technology to improve health at scale. Efficient delivery, appropriate use, and adherence to treatment directives are equally important ingredients of effectiveness. The drop in AIDS mortality in Botswana stems not just from donated medicines but also from health providers' ability to identify people living with HIV and to support their adherence to treatment. Similarly, researchers in Bangladesh found that providing efficacious interventions on their own was not enough to improve health, given families' own counterproductive health-related behaviors as well as broader economic changes.

Taken together, the cases also show that despite our knowing "what works" in terms of health technology, we still have a lot to learn about how to scale up delivery and uptake in specific settings. Several pro-

Table 1. Program Implementers and Funders

PROGRAM	MAIN IMPLEMENTERS	LEAD FUNDERS
African Meningitis Belt's Meningitis A Vaccine Program	Meningitis Vaccine Project (led by PATH and WHO), US Food and Drug Administration's Center for Biologics Evaluation and Research, Serum Institute of India Ltd., SynCo Bio Partners, UK's National Institute for Biological Standards and Control	Meningitis Vaccine Project (PATH, WHO), BMGF, USAID, Dell Foundation, Gavi, Ministries of Health (Burkina Faso, Mali, Niger)
Botswana's Mass Antiretroviral Therapy Program	Government of Botswana, BMGF, Merck Foundation (via the African Comprehensive HIV/AIDS Partnership)	Government of Botswana; Merck Foundation; BMGF; PEPFAR; Global Fund to Fight AIDS, Malaria and Tuberculosis
China's Program to Equalize Hepatitis B Vaccine Coverage	Chinese Ministry of Health, Gavi	Government of China, Gavi
Zambia's National Malaria Control Program	Zambian Ministry of Health, UNICEF, US President's Malaria Initiative, Roll Back Malaria	USAID; US President's Malaria Initiative; Global Fund to Fight AIDS, Malaria and Tuberculosis; World Bank; PATH (funded by BMGF)
Mexico's Piso Firme Program	Government of Mexico	Government of Mexico
Kenya's School-Based Deworming Program	Kenyan Ministries of Health and Education, Deworm the World	World Bank, Deworm the World, Children's Investment Fund Foundation, END Fund
Haiti's Polio Elimination Campaign	Government of Haiti, Pan American Health Organization, US Centers for Disease Control and Prevention	Government of Haiti, Pan American Health Organization, WHO, Canadian International Development Agency, USAID, UNICEF, Rotary International, World Bank
Bangladesh's Integrated Management of Childhood Illness	Government of Bangladesh; ICDDR,B; WHO	Government of Bangladesh, UNICEF
Thailand's Universal Coverage Scheme	Government of Thailand	Government of Thailand
Argentina's Plan Nacer	Argentina's federal and provincial Ministries of Health, World Bank	Government of Argentina (federal and provincial), World Bank
Brazil's Programa Saúde da Família	Government of Brazil	Government of Brazil
Rwanda's Pay-for-Performance Scheme for Health Services	Government of Rwanda	Government of Rwanda
Gujarat's Program to Reduce the Cost of Institutional Delivery	Government of Gujarat, India	Government of Gujarat
Kenya's Social Cash Transfer Program	Government of Kenya, UNICEF	Government of Kenya, UNICEF, World Bank, UK Department for International Development
Punjab's Female School Stipend Program	Government of Punjab, Pakistan	Government of Punjab, World Bank, UK Department for International Development, Canadian International Development Agency
South Africa's Child Support Grant	Government of South Africa, Lund Committee on Child and Family Support	Government of South Africa
Honduras's Programa de Asignación Familiar II	Government of Honduras	Government of Honduras, Inter-American Development Bank
Thailand's Campaign for Tobacco Control	Government of Thailand, Thai Anti-smoking Campaign Project, Thai Health Promotion Foundation	Thai Health Promotion Fund
Vietnam's Comprehensive Helmet Law	Government of Vietnam, WHO, Asia Injury Prevention Foundation	Government of Vietnam, Asia Injury Prevention Foundation
Indonesia's Total Sanitation and Sanitation Marketing Program	Government of Indonesia, World Bank Water and Sanitation Program	Government of Indonesia, World Bank Water and Sanitation Program, BMGF
India's Avahan Program	BMGF, Family Health International, CARE International, WHO	BMGF
Peru's Handwashing Initiative	Government of Peru, World Bank Water and Sanitation Program, Public-Private Partnership for Handwashing	World Bank Water and Sanitation Program

Source: See case chapters.
Note: BMGF = Bill & Melinda Gates Foundation; ICDDR,B = International Centre for Diarrhoeal Disease Research, Bangladesh; PEPFAR = US President's Emergency Plan for AIDS Relief; UNICEF = United Nations Children's Fund; USAID = United States Agency for International Development; WHO = World Health Organization.

grams profiled in this volume—Piso Firme in Mexico, cash transfers in South Africa, pay-for-performance in Rwanda—led to improvements in children's nutritional status, yet each employed a different technology and delivery strategy to achieve its goals. While taking on board the lessons of these particular cases, we must carefully evaluate alternative technologies and delivery strategies in different country contexts to figure out in each case the best way to graduate an efficacious technology to effectiveness at scale.

6. There's an evaluation revolution, too.

Many health programs are judged on their intermediate outputs—the number of children vaccinated, the number of vaccine doses purchased, or the number of people treated or trained—without any direct assessment of health impact. At the same time, many low- and middle-income countries are seeing rapid improvement in other drivers of health status, such as girls' education, urbanization, and economic growth. Why is this important? Because if we had known that health would have improved even without a given health intervention, the money could have been better used elsewhere.

The cases in the first edition of *Millions Saved* described evidence that at-scale health impact was largely attributable to specific public health efforts rather than to broader economic and social improvements. Now there is an even better evidence base that illustrates the feasibility and affordability of rigorous evaluation for at-scale health programs. Over the past decade, there has been tremendous growth in the number of such evaluations in low- and middle-income countries, from 10 in 1995 to more than 300 in 2014.[14]

Of the 22 new cases in this book, 14 used experimental study designs that allowed for the unambiguous attribution of health impact. Some governments stepped forward to involve themselves in commissioning or carrying out evaluations. In Argentina, South Africa, Thailand, and Mexico, government evaluation agencies have been set up to assure rigorous evaluation methods and the translation of results into policy, such as the scale-up of a successful program or the move away from a disappointing one.

In some cases, attributable impact is evident even without rigorous evaluation. Zero smallpox cases is zero smallpox cases, and we need only a high-quality disease surveillance system, not an experiment, to understand program results. However, an impact evaluation might still be useful, say, to help us learn about effective immunization delivery strategies in rural areas. And in countries where other transformations are taking place, such as changes in the economy or in weather patterns, it is helpful to understand whether trends in disease are most affected by a program or by some other factor.

Despite the real progress that has been made in the world of impact evaluation, many needed types of data are unavailable. For instance, cost-effectiveness is important to many donors and policymakers. They want to know if the health gained is worth the cost of the program, and they need help in prioritizing where scarce public resources should be deployed. Yet few studies report empirical estimates of cost-effectiveness. Only two cases in this book did so; we had to derive the other estimates from modeling and secondary sources.[15] And some categories of intervention—for example, those against noncommunicable diseases—remain woefully underevaluated, with only a handful of trials and little evaluation at scale.

7. Evidence requires its own advocacy.

Policymakers do not always act on evaluation results, positive or negative. In Gujarat, a program to incentivize births in health facilities continued with an unchanged design despite disappointing results. Inertia, often coupled with political or other considerations, makes it hard to stop something once it starts. Further, policymakers may not even know about failure, thanks to publication bias. Less than half of randomized controlled trials in healthcare reach publication, and those that do tend to be heavily biased toward statistically significant results—that is, toward results that suggest a drug or program was successful.[16]

In an ideal world, policymakers absorb evaluation results, nicely synthesized in a quality systematic review, and adjust their programs to enhance their effectiveness. In reality, it is not enough to evaluate a program; evidence requires its own advocacy. In some settings, such as Mexico and South Africa, public institutions directly commission the evaluation of public programs and promote action to be taken based on the results. There is also a special role for aid; Levine and Savedoff[17] have argued that donors are "uniquely suited" to finance evaluations because of the small relative size of donor monies as domestic finance grows, as well as donors' ambitions of disproportionate influence, sensitivity to being used for illicit purposes, ability to bridge several communities, and aspirational role in advancing public-sector accountability.

The Challenges Ahead

Much has changed in global health since the first edition of *Millions Saved*, but much remains the same. In 2004, the original *Millions Saved* declared: "Ancient problems remain unsolved, such as the differentials in health between the rich and the poor. Newer ones—from the AIDS pandemic to the prevalence of tobacco-related diseases to the growing toll of cardiovascular disease— threaten future generations."[18] Although the intensity of these challenges has lessened, thanks in part to some of the programs described in this book, they do persist, and they continue to require the attention and commitment of the global health community.

In particular, it is disappointing that few noncommunicable disease (NCD) programs made the cut for inclusion in this new edition a full decade later. Although many small-scale trials have shown that NCD interventions are cost-effective, our research turned up few large-scale programs in low- and middle-income countries to reduce or treat NCDs, and even fewer with a proven impact on health status. The list is short: China's hepatitis B vaccination program to prevent liver cancer, Vietnam's motorcycle helmet laws to reduce head injuries, Thailand's tobacco control program, and Brazil's Programa Saúde da Família, which curbed heart disease. Turning global momentum on NCDs into effective at-scale programming is an imperative that cannot be ignored; the World Health Organization predicts that NCDs will cause more than three-quarters of all deaths by 2030.[19] Even in sub-Saharan Africa, cardiovascular disease is already the number one killer of adults older than 30.

Nonetheless, the "old" Millennium Development Goals agenda remains unfinished. Preventable maternal, infant, and child mortality; undernutrition; and infectious diseases are still too common, even in countries where most of the population has completed the epidemiological transition from infectious diseases and reproduction-related risks to NCDs, injuries, and other causes of death. Emerging drug resistance and the threat of malaria resurgence—as well as emerging viruses like Ebola and Zika—oblige us to remain vigilant and sustain efforts, even where specific threats are dormant.

Finally, global health headlines, like the title of this book, focus on lives saved. But many cases in *Millions Saved* are most notable for their impact on alleviating disability, not averting death—a benefit that can extend even into the next generation. Nonfatal diseases can have both immediate and long-term consequences. Among girls, for instance, anemia, human papilloma virus, HIV, and other untreated sexually transmitted infections precede a cascade of health problems for them at older ages as well as for their future children. Treatment of intestinal worms also has both short- and long-term benefits: in Kenya, women who had received deworming pills were, a full 10 years after receiving them, less likely to miscarry than others who had not received the treatment. Reducing disability and increasing the number of healthy years lived is the next generation's global health challenge, and the result on which we need to measure success going forward.

The health sector is still searching for answers, and finding some. The next edition of *Millions Saved* is likely to be quite different from this one. It will cover a new generation of programs, both within and outside the health sector. It is our hope and expectation that those programs will reflect the sea changes we are already seeing, particularly the growing use of rigorous impact evaluations and cost-effectiveness analysis as tools for health policy. The gains of the previous decade give grounds for optimism that in the next decade, better health policies will mean many more millions saved.

REFERENCES

Abdul Latif Jameel Poverty Action Lab. 2011. "The Price Is Wrong: Charging Small Fees Dramatically Reduces Access to Important Products for the Poor." *J-PAL Bulletin,* April. http://www.povertyactionlab.org/publication/the-price-is-wrong.

American Thyroid Association. 2014. "China: Leading the Way in Sustained IDD Elimination." *IDD Newsletter* 42 (2): 1–5. http://www.thyroid.org/idd-newsletter-3/.

Carter Center. 2015. "Guinea Worm Disease: Worldwide Case Totals," September 8. http://www.cartercenter.org/health/guinea_worm/case-totals.html.

Cochrane Collaboration. 2015. "The Deworming Debate," November 17. http://www.cochrane.org/news/deworming-debate.

Dwan, Kerry, Douglas G. Altman, Juan A. Arnaiz, Jill Bloom, An-Wen Chan, Eugenia Cronin, Evelyne Decullier, et al. 2008. "Systematic Review of the Empirical Evidence of Study Publication Bias and Outcome Reporting Bias." *PLoS ONE* 3 (8): e3081. doi:10.1371/journal.pone.0003081.

Evans, David. 2015. "Worm Wars: The Anthology." *Development Impact* (blog), World Bank, August 4. http://blogs.worldbank.org/impactevaluations/worm-wars-anthology.

Gertler, Paul, Manisha Shah, Maria Laura Alzua, Lisa Cameron, Sebastian Martinez, and Sumeet Patil. 2015. *How Does Health Promotion Work? Evidence from the Dirty Business of Eliminating Open Defecation.* Working Paper 20997. Cambridge, MA: National Bureau of Economic Research. http://www.nber.org/papers/w20997.

Glassman, Amanda, Victoria Fan, Mead Over, and Working Group on Value for Money in Global Health. 2013. *More Health for the Money: Putting Incentives to Work for the Global Fund and Its Partners.* Washington, DC: Center for Global Development. http://www.cgdev.org/sites/default/files/More-Health-for-the-Money.pdf.

Grantham-McGregor, S.M., S.P. Walker, S.M. Chang, and C.A. Powell. 1997. "Effects of Early Childhood Supplementation with and without Stimulation on Later Development in Stunted Jamaican Children." *American Journal of Clinical Nutrition* 66 (2): 247–53.

Hoddinott, J., J.A. Maluccio, J.R. Behrman, R. Flores, and R. Martorell. 2008. "Effect of a Nutrition Intervention during Early Childhood on Economic Productivity in Guatemalan Adults." *Lancet* 371 (9610): 411–16. doi:10.1016/S0140-6736(08)60205-6.

IHME (Institute for Health Metrics and Evaluation). 2014. *Financing Global Health 2013: Transition in an Age of Austerity.* Seattle, WA: IHME.

Levine, Ruth. 2007. *Case Studies in Global Health: Millions Saved.* Sudbury, MA: Jones and Bartlett Publishers.

Levine, Ruth, and William Savedoff. 2015. *The Future of Aid: Building Knowledge Collectively.* CGD Policy Paper 050. Washington, DC: Center for Global Development. http://www.cgdev.org/sites/default/files/CGD-Policy-Paper-Levine-Savedoff-Future-Aid.pdf.

Levine, Ruth, What Works Working Group, and Molly Kinder. 2004. *Millions Saved: Proven Successes in Global Health.* Washington, DC: Center for Global Development.

Mirelman, Andrew, Amanda Glassman, and Miriam Temin. 2016. *Estimating the Avertable Disease Burden and Cost-Effectiveness in Millions Saved Third Edition.* CGD Working Paper. Washington, DC: Center for Global Development.

Ng, Marie, Emmanuela Gakidou, Alison Levin-Rector, Ajay Khera, Christopher J.L. Murray, and Lalit Dandona. 2011. "Assessment of Population-Level Effect of Avahan, an HIV-Prevention Initiative in India." *Lancet* 378 (9803): 1643–52. doi:10.1016/S0140-6736(11)61390-1.

Pickles, Michael, Marie-Claude Boily, Peter Vickerman, Catherine M. Lowndes, Stephen Moses, James F. Blanchard, Kathleen N. Deering, et al. 2013. "Assessment of the Population-Level Effectiveness of the Avahan HIV-Prevention Programme in South India: A Preplanned, Causal-Pathway-Based Modelling Analysis." *Lancet Global Health* 1 (5): e289–99. doi:10.1016/S2214-109X(13)70083-4.

Stokes, Bruce. 2015. "Around the World, Dissatisfaction with Economy and Concern for Its Future." *Fact Tank: News in the Numbers* (blog), Pew Research Center, July 23. http://www.pewresearch.org/fact-tank/2015/07/23/around-the-world-dissatisfaction-with-economy-and-concern-for-its-future/.

WHO (World Health Organization). 2011. *Global Status Report on Noncommunicable Diseases 2010.* Geneva: WHO. http://www.who.int/nmh/publications/ncd_report_full_en.pdf.

ENDNOTES

1. IHME (2014).
2. Levine, What Works Working Group, and Kinder (2004); Levine (2007).
3. Carter Center (2015).
4. American Thyroid Association (2014).
5. The 2015 Millennium Development Goals—targeting poverty, education, gender equality, child mortality, maternal health, disease, environment, and global partnership—have been replaced by the Global Goals for Sustainable Development, a new set of universally acknowledged goals, targets, and indicators that

ENDNOTES, continued

United Nations member states are expected to use in framing their agendas and political policies until 2030.

6. Mirelman, Glassman, and Temin (2016).
7. Hoddinott et al. (2008); Grantham-McGregor et al. (1997).
8. Cochrane Collaboration (2015); Evans (2015).
9. Ng et al. (2011); Pickles et al. (2013).
10. Gertler et al. (2015).
11. Stokes (2015).
12. The sum of the Botswana antiretroviral therapy, MenAfriVac, hepatitis B, deworming, malaria, Piso Firme, Plan Nacer, helmets, sanitation, tobacco, and Avahan programs comes to 18.1 million disability-adjusted life years averted. See Mirelman, Glassman, and Temin (2016) and chapter 23 of this volume.
13. Abdul Latif Jameel Poverty Action Lab (2011).
14. Levine and Savedoff (2015).
15. Mirelman, Glassman, and Temin (2016).
16. Dwan et al. (2008).
17. 2015.
18. Levine, What Works Working Group, and Kinder (2004, 10).
19. WHO (2011).

The Structure of This Book

Case studies are grouped into four parts: Part I, "Rolling Out Medicine and Technology"; Part II, "Expanding Access to Health Services"; Part III, "Using Targeted Cash Transfers to Improve Health"; and Part IV, "Changing Behavior Population-wide to Reduce Risk." Each part has an introductory section listing the cases discussed and the way they fit with the "wows" highlighted in the introduction.

Each case's story is structured similarly: the facts of the policy or program are set out at a glance; the target health problem is defined and the approach discussed; the health impact and the strength of the evidence are described; the cost of achieving that impact is assessed; the keys to lasting success are summarized; and finally, the case's implications for global health more broadly are analyzed.

The book ends with a chapter on the *Millions Saved* process and methods.

PART I

Rolling Out Medicine and Technology

In medicine and public health, small-scale randomized controlled trials establish the efficacy of medicines, technology, and other interventions. But efficacy in a limited setting is not the same as effective delivery at scale. How can a technology that worked on a small scale translate into health gains writ large? The cases described in this section try to answer this question.

Efficacy can translate into effectiveness in even the poorest countries and among the poorest populations. In Botswana, antiretroviral therapy to combat AIDS reached almost 90 percent of the eligible population, with only 10 percent lost to follow-up in 2013, making the country a leader in the region. In the seven countries of Africa's meningitis belt, where the disease is hyperendemic, health authorities reached more than 153 million people with a new vaccine—MenAfriVac—over a three-year period. Meningitis A subsequently fell to its lowest levels in a decade, nearing zero in some countries. And when a poliovirus emerged in Haiti, the national response contained the outbreak after just eight cases of paralytic polio.

But efficacy does not necessarily imply effectiveness. In Bangladesh, the Integrated Management of Childhood Illness set of interventions, shown to be efficacious in clinical trials, reduced stunting but did not significantly lower under-five mortality rates.

And there is much we still don't know.

Few of the technology-specific evaluations assess overall impact on the whole health system. For example, did a focus on malaria crowd out other primary healthcare interventions in Zambia? Some researchers suggest a link, but none have rigorously tested the hypothesis. In Botswana, did AIDS interventions strengthen or weaken other health system functions? Here the literature is larger, but it lacks rigor. In addition, researchers rarely assess the opportunity costs of investing time, money, and effort in a single intervention—an issue that merits greater research attention.

Unlike cases in the other *Millions Saved* categories, many evaluations in this section use disease models rather than empirical studies to estimate impact. Indeed, because many infectious disease interventions are known to be efficacious in small-scale trials, researchers and health authorities typically track progress through case reports from disease surveillance systems. But because health delivery systems vary widely in form and effectiveness, we still need to rigorously evaluate alternative delivery strategies to learn more about what does and does not work.

For certain types of disease, particularly noncommunicable diseases (NCDs), rigorous, at-scale evaluations of any kind are few and far between. As a result, this section features just one NCD intervention: a hepatitis B vaccine in China. Researchers are currently testing new low-cost NCD screening and treatment programs such as visual inspection with acetic acid for cervical cancer screening, a polypill to combat heart disease, and mental health screening by lay health workers. However, most health systems in low- and middle-income countries have not yet adopted these interventions at scale.

Beginning of the End
Eliminating Meningitis A across Africa's Meningitis Belt

The Case at a Glance

HEALTH GOAL: To prevent future epidemics caused by the bacterium *Neisseria meningitidis* serogroup A.

STRATEGY: Develop, test, license, and introduce on a mass basis across Africa's meningitis belt a meningococcal conjugate vaccine, MenAfriVac, designed to prevent group A meningococcal meningitis.

HEALTH IMPACT: Suspected meningitis cases across the meningitis belt in 2013 were at their lowest levels in a decade. No cases of group A meningitis were detected among those who received a MenAfriVac inoculation. Predicted to save 142,000 lives, avert 284,000 permanent disabilities, and prevent more than a million meningitis cases in a decade in the seven hyperendemic countries of Africa's meningitis belt: Burkina Faso, Chad, Ethiopia, Mali, Niger, Nigeria, and Sudan.

WHY IT WORKED: Creative partnerships. Technological innovation. Widespread coverage. Increased surveillance. Multipartner commitment. Program's vision and structure.

FINANCING: US$87 million from the Bill & Melinda Gates Foundation for the Meningitis Vaccine Project. US$262 million from Gavi, the Vaccine Alliance. Additional support from United States Agency for International Development (USAID) and Dell Foundation. Governments of Burkina Faso, Mali, and Niger helped fund vaccine rollout in their countries. Estimated to save US$350 million in the seven hyperendemic countries between 2010 and 2020. Cost-effectiveness ratio: US$96.36 per disability-adjusted life year averted.

SCALE: More than 217 million people vaccinated (2010–2014).

From Senegal in the west to Ethiopia in the east, a wave of meningitis sweeps across the 26 countries of Africa's meningitis belt every 5 to 14 years. One of the most feared diseases in Africa, meningitis is difficult to diagnose and swift to kill. The infection causes the protective membranes around the brain and neck to swell painfully. Common symptoms include fever, headache, and neck stiffness, yet those telltale signs are easily missed or misinterpreted, and sometimes they are never present at all. Often, infected individuals—disproportionately babies and young children—go to sleep apparently healthy and never wake up.[1] Without treatment, mortality can soar above 80 percent among those infected. Even treatment is no panacea; 5 to 10 percent of infected individuals will still die, often within hours of the onset of symptoms.

Periodic meningitis epidemics present yet one more challenge in a region already suffering from extreme poverty, food insecurity, climate risks, and a host of other health problems—and the individual and societal impacts are tremendous. Meningitis epidemics can fill hospitals and strain health sectors. Children die in droves, while scant household budgets crumble as treatment consumes every spare dollar.

The most common cause of these regional epidemics is group A meningococcal meningitis (meningitis A), caused by a bacterium, *Neisseria meningitidis* serogroup A. The deadly bacterium is carried in the throat and nose and is passed around by sneezing, coughing, and direct contact. The year 2010 saw the introduction of a vaccine dubbed MenAfriVac, created and priced specifically for an extremely poor African population. It became the first effective vaccine able to counter this age-old killer.[2]

Shortly after MenAfriVac was developed, countries across the meningitis belt rolled out the vaccine at scale. Vaccination campaigns began in 2010 in Burkina Faso, Mali, and Niger, followed shortly thereafter by Camer-

This case was originally authored by Alix Beith.

oon, Chad, and Nigeria. Vaccination across all 26 meningitis belt countries will be complete by 2016. The results are clear: meningitis A incidence has dropped dramatically, and no cases have been reported in areas where mass vaccination campaigns took place. Hopes are high that the meningitis A scourge will soon be no more than a bad memory.

The Toll of Meningitis A

More than one million meningitis cases have been reported in Africa since 1988, 80 to 85 percent of which are caused by the meningococcal serotype A bacterium.[3] Major meningitis epidemics affect up to 1 in 100 people.[4] In 1996–97, the largest epidemic on record sickened over 250,000 people and killed 25,000. Incidence is highest in the meningitis belt's seven "hyperendemic" countries (locations with a high and continuous incidence of a disease), which are home to approximately 240 million people (see Figure 1).

Even though prompt use of antibiotics can treat meningitis A, treated infections can have serious long-term consequences. Up to 20 percent of survivors live with permanent disabilities, including epilepsy, deafness, brain damage, paralysis, or amputations. Affected individuals can be shunned. One victim said, "People think you are crazy. It is like you don't exist anymore."[5] Often victims are unable to work.

All seven hyperendemic countries are extremely poor, and their populations depend heavily on subsistence farming for survival.[6] When meningitis prevents family members from tending to the crops, the amount of food on the table can drop precipitously. Taking care of ill family members can add to the strain. In Ghana, households lose an average of 29 days of work per meningitis case.[7] In Burkina Faso, households spend as much as US$90 per case—more than a third of annual gross domestic product per capita. In some cases, long-term complications can increase the cost to more than US$150 per case.[8] For households struggling to make ends meet under normal circumstances, these costs may make care and treatment impossible.

Figure 1. Africa's Meningitis Belt

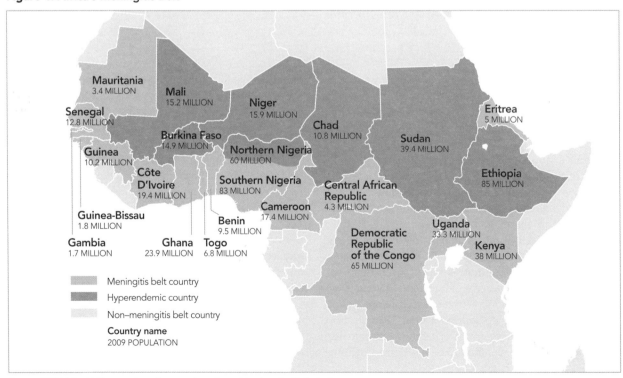

Source: PATH / David Simpson: http://www.path.org/menafrivac/meningitis-belt.php.

Putting an Idea in Motion: A New Partnership Develops a New Product

Following the devastating 1996–97 epidemic, it became clear that the current approach to meningitis management was neither effective nor efficient. Governments were responding to outbreaks with reactive polysaccharide (PS) vaccination campaigns and antibiotics, actions that saved some lives.[9] However, the PS vaccine had drawbacks: it provided just two to three years of protection, offered little protection to babies and young children, failed to prevent transmission within the general population, and cost more than many countries could afford. In 2007, Burkina Faso spent 5 percent of its entire healthcare budget on epidemic management using the PS vaccine.[10] Frustrated and determined to find a better solution, African health leaders approached the World Health Organization (WHO) for help.[11]

The WHO got to work exploring whether a new and better "conjugate" vaccine might be feasible.[12] Conjugate vaccines work by stimulating immunological memory and are more potent and durable than PS vaccines. In western Europe, a conjugate vaccine for meningitis Chad all but eliminated the disease in several countries.[13] A WHO-commissioned feasibility study suggested that the road to a meningitis A conjugate vaccine could be long but fruitful. Development would be slow—3 to 7 years. Yet once created, the conjugate vaccine was likely to radically reduce infection and transmission for at least 10 years.

Meanwhile, WHO staff concluded that a development and delivery partnership was needed to develop the new vaccine.[14] The WHO and the nongovernmental organization PATH requested US$70 million from the Bill & Melinda Gates Foundation to make the partnership a reality. In 2001, the Meningitis Vaccine Project (MVP) was born with the mandate to develop, test, license, and introduce a low-cost meningococcal conjugate vaccine.

Beyond its founders, the MVP umbrella fostered open and flexible collaboration between a broad network of partners: the US Food and Drug Administration's Center for Biologics Evaluation and Research, the Indian vaccine manufacturer Serum Institute of India Ltd., the Dutch biotech company SynCo Bio Partners, and the UK's National Institute for Biological Standards and Control.[15]

During the MVP's first eight months, the partnership's director, Dr. Marc LaForce, and his colleagues traveled across the meningitis belt to learn "what [the potential vaccine] customers wanted and the realities in delivery."[16] They met with African health officials to determine an affordable vaccine price and estimate the level of likely demand—feedback that informed the target product profile and vaccine specifications.[17]

By 2005, a product was ready to be tested for safety and efficacy. When the results came in a few years later, developers breathed a sigh of relief: the new vaccine was safe and far more effective than the existing PS product.[18] In 2010, the new vaccine, which its producer, the Serum Institute, named MenAfriVac to identify both the target disease and the target population, received WHO's fast-track approval for rollout.[19] With the vaccine receiving WHO's stamp of approval for safety and immunogenicity, United Nations agencies such as the United Nations Children's Fund (UNICEF) received the green light to buy and distribute MenAfriVac in bulk. Many governments soon followed suit. But the challenge ahead remained daunting: an estimated 25 million vaccine doses would be needed every year over the decade to come.[20]

Leaders in the affected-country governments had long stressed they would not be able to afford MenAfriVac if the vaccine cost more than US$1 per dose. "Please don't give us a vaccine that we can't afford," Hassane Adamou, secretary general of Niger's Ministry of Health, told LaForce in 2001.[21] The MVP ultimately set the maximum price at US$0.50 per dose to ensure sustainable vaccine uptake. In the end, Serum Institute did even better: the company agreed to sell MenAfriVac at US$0.40 per dose, with any future increases tied to the rate of inflation.[22]

At the country level, ministers of health from all 26 meningitis belt countries signed the Yaoundé Declaration in the capital of Cameroon in September 2008, solidifying their commitment to stamp out meningitis A.[23] As soon as the vaccine hit the market, they were ready to act.

MenAfriVac's Rollout in Action

The MenAfriVac rollout began in 2010. To determine which country would be first, a subcommittee of experts from WHO's regional African office and Gavi, the Vaccine Alliance, assessed disease burden, epidemic risk, and country preparedness.[24] To be eligible for the program, country governments also had to commit to covering half the operational costs of mass vaccination from their domestic budgets.[25]

Burkina Faso, the country most affected by meningitis, was chosen to be the first to introduce MenAfriVac. In a strategic effort to establish herd immunity—meaning that a substantial proportion of the population is immune to a disease—the campaign first targeted people under age 30, about 70 percent of the population. The Ministry of Health deployed more than 10,000 health workers and 650 supervisors across the country to reach this population. Starting with schoolchildren, the country's team succeeded in vaccinating 11 million young Burkinabè in just 10 days, finishing before the onset of the 2011 dry season. This was timely: epidemics take place during the dry season, which runs from January to June and creates an environment that irritates throat mucus and thus increases meningitis risk.

Introduction of the vaccine was phased in across the belt, with Mali and Niger following Burkina Faso, and then Chad, Cameroon, and Nigeria.[26] Special campaigns targeted specific populations such as nomadic and refugee groups. In some cases, the introduction of MenAfriVac was integrated with other vaccination campaigns. By the end of 2014, more than 217 million people in 15 countries had been vaccinated.

Thorough communication plans and solid campaigns helped facilitate successful MenAfriVac introduction. In Burkina Faso, communication efforts began as early as 2007 to raise public awareness that a new meningitis vaccine was coming. Efforts intensified in the months prior to the campaign, including outreach by community-level "town criers" and volunteers. Starting on December 1, just five days before the first MenAfriVac vaccines were administered, media outlets urged the population to turn out for vaccination, emphasizing that an end to meningitis epidemics was within reach.

Tracking progress was central to the vaccine campaign's success. From its inception, the MVP worked closely with country governments to enhance monitoring and strengthen laboratory capacity. By 2003, the Multi-disease Surveillance Center, based in Ouagadougou, Burkina Faso, was producing weekly meningitis surveillance updates on the spread of the disease for the entire region.[27]

Babies in the meningitis belt received a boost in early 2015, when the WHO finally prequalified a lower-dose formulation for infants. This allowed policymakers to include MenAfriVac within the WHO's Expanded Program on Immunization schedule.[28]

The Payoff: Immunity Replaces Infection

The MenAfriVac vaccine prevents meningitis A and inhibits the transmission of the bacterium. So far, not a single case of the disease has been reported among the 153 million individuals who have received a dose of MenAfriVac under the MVP program.[29] In some countries in the region, infection rates were already falling when the vaccination rollout began.[30] There, the vaccine dramatically accelerated positive trends (see Box 1).

In Burkina Faso, in the year following mass vaccination, no cases of meningitis A disease were detected and no local outbreaks were reported.[31] And during the 2013 epidemic season, the WHO reported that suspected cases caused by all the bacterium's serotypes had fallen to their lowest levels in a decade across the entire meningitis belt.[32]

Even more definitive proof of the vaccine's effectiveness comes from Chad, where a 2013 study found that MenAfriVac not only stopped meningitis A in its tracks but also led to a significant decrease in the prevalence of the bacterium that causes it.[33] No meningitis A cases were reported in the campaign's target areas, even with the enhanced surveillance. In fact, meningitis cases of all types dropped dramatically in the three districts where mass vaccination took place, while the epidemic raged on unabated elsewhere, leading to an incredible 94 percent difference in incidence (see Figure 2).

Figure 2. Incidence of Reported Cases of Meningitis in Chad, 2009–2012

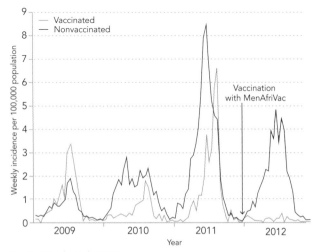

Source: Daugla et al. (2014).

Box 1. Strength of the Evidence

The WHO approved MenAfriVac because of its demonstrated safety and immunogenicity—it succeeded in provoking the desired immune response. Later, a Burkina Faso–based study confirmed its efficacy.[35] Researchers used national surveillance data to measure meningitis disease and deaths both before and one year after introduction of the vaccine. Novak and colleagues calculated a 71 percent reduction in risk of the disease and a 64 percent reduction in fatal disease as a result of the vaccine rollout, both significant results. Although this was an observational study, the number of probable cases sank below the numbers of even the lowest-epidemic years, suggesting that the result showed the impact of the vaccine and not a natural fluctuation in incidence.

In 2013, a second study assessed the impact of MenAfriVac in three regions of Chad. Using data on meningitis inci-

dence pre- and postvaccination, it found that MenAfriVac successfully halted the spread of the epidemic.[36] However, in neither the Chad nor the Burkina Faso study did the researchers randomize the selection of treatment districts, meaning that the findings might stem from systematic differences in disease incidence. The study by Daugla and others discounts this limitation, noting similar preexisting trends in both vaccinated and nonvaccinated areas.

Daugla and colleagues also suggest that their findings are likely to underestimate the actual impact in Chad for two reasons. First, MenAfriVac areas benefited from more surveillance than areas that had not received the vaccine, meaning that cases there were more likely to be detected. And second, previous reactive vaccination had likely already reduced cases of meningitis A in control areas, decreasing the observed difference between the two areas.

The positive impacts add up: in the seven countries where meningitis is hyperendemic, MenAfriVac is expected to save 142,000 lives, avert 284,000 permanent disabilities, and prevent more than one million meningitis cases over a period of 10 years.[34] And fortunately, as of this writing, no adverse results of the vaccine have been reported.

Gains at What Price?

Bringing a human vaccine to market typically costs between US$200 million and US$900 million. MenAfriVac was developed for less than one-fifth the average cost—just US$70 million.[37] Thereafter, the mass vaccination campaigns locked in a cost of about US$1.40 per person, including the vaccine and injection materials, infrastructure, and operational expenses.[38]

The MVP's initial US$70 million grant covered operational and vaccine development costs. Later, the Bill & Melinda Gates Foundation contributed an additional US$17 million to support clinical trials of the infant vaccine and to study the duration of protection after a single vaccine dose. USAID and the Dell Foundation also provided support. The first three countries to introduce MenAfriVac—Burkina Faso, Mali, and Niger—contributed to the operational costs of vaccine rollout,

and Gavi, the Vaccine Alliance, covered subsequent country costs.[39]

Since 2009, Gavi has committed US$262 million for meningitis A campaigns in Africa, which has been enough to meet the needs specified by the affected countries. By the end of 2013, 12 countries had conducted MenAfriVac campaigns; by 2016, a further 14 countries are expected to introduce the vaccine with Gavi support. Additional funding for the remaining mass campaigns will be made available on the basis of country requests.[40]

In a calculation undertaken for *Millions Saved,* researchers estimated that the vaccine likely prevented 12,469 deaths in Chad, which translated to 875,844 disability-adjusted life years (DALYs) averted over the entire three-year study period, 2010 to 2013.[41] The calculation determined that MenAfriVac offered a cost per DALY averted of US$96.36, confirming that its low cost and large health impact reflect good value. The estimate is based on the premise that mass inoculation with MenAfriVac results in herd immunity, which inhibits meningitis transmission, a benefit that the PS vaccination does not provide. Another analysis estimated that the introduction of MenAfriVac could save US$350 million or more over a decade in the seven countries where meningitis is hyperendemic, mostly by eliminating the need to continuously buy and deliver the PS vaccine.[42]

The Keys to Lasting Success

The MVP benefited from several essential ingredients, some good luck, and shared goodwill. Creative partnerships, technological innovation, widespread coverage, and strengthened surveillance all provided a foundation for the vaccine's success. Leadership from African governments—including the Yaoundé Declaration, sustained funding, and regular announcements in the media—has also been critical.

The MVP's innovative vision was fundamental to the successful development of the vaccine, as was initial funding from the Bill & Melinda Gates Foundation and Gavi. The MVP network's elastic organizational structure enhanced collaboration and fostered trust among the partners.[43] Partnership director LaForce stated that the MVP's initial country visits were "seminal in terms of starting things [and] made the equation more likely to succeed."[44]

The MVP's use of a public-private product development partnership also proved essential to its ultimate success.[45] When approached by the MVP, large pharmaceutical companies expressed their lack of interest in developing a meningitis A conjugate vaccine at a price point of US$2 or less per dose.[46] Instead, the MVP brought lower-profile, less traditional partners on board to create the product development partnership network, making MenAfriVac the first vaccine to be developed by nontraditional pharmaceutical companies.[47] These smaller companies took a gamble—one that eventually paid off. The MVP also held firm on its price ceiling of US$0.50 per dose. A higher cost would have made the vaccine useless to African governments. The lesson is clear, says LaForce: "If you do it the way somebody wants and at the price that will work, chances are it will work."[48]

Implications for Global Health

All signs point to the end of meningitis A in the worst-affected region of the world. Successful future meningitis A control is dependent on securing country and donor funding to vaccinate new generations with the infant formulation of MenAfriVac. A promising development came early in 2015 when the WHO opened the door to make MenAfriVac part of countries' routine immunization programs.[49]

The duration of the vaccine's protection, which will affect its cost-effectiveness, remains to be seen. Policymakers hope that it will prevent future epidemics, but they also worry that other meningitis strains might fill the void left by the virtual eradication of meningitis A. Only time and careful surveillance can provide answers.

In the meantime, a recent study in Benin suggests that MenAfriVac is the first meningitis vaccine to maintain its effectiveness in warm ambient temperatures, retaining full potency for up to four days without refrigeration even in temperatures of 102° Fahrenheit or hotter.[50] This enables vaccine administration outside the traditional "cold chain" delivery system, which could cut administration costs in half.[51]

If the MenAfriVac rollout can maintain its current intensity and momentum, universal access and protection could soon be a reality. But LaForce has his eyes on an even loftier ambition: an affordable, heat-stable, pentavalent conjugate meningococcal vaccine targeting all meningitis strains in Africa.[52] This improved vaccine is under development, with clinical trials scheduled to begin in 2016. With continued hard work, dedication, and a little bit of luck, a meningitis-free Africa could be within reach.

REFERENCES

Akweongo, Patricia, Maxwell A. Dalaba, Mary H. Hayden, Timothy Awine, Gertrude N. Nyaaba, Dominic Anaseba, Abraham Hodgson, Abdulai A. Forgor, and Rajul Pandya. 2013. "The Economic Burden of Meningitis to Households in Kassena-Nankana District of Northern Ghana." PLoS ONE 8 (11). doi:10.1371/journal.pone.0079880.

André, F.E. 2002. "How the Research-Based Industry Approaches Vaccine Development and Establishes Priorities." Developments in Biologicals 110: 25–29.

Bishai, David M., Claire Champion, Michael E. Steele, and Thompson Lindsay. 2011. "Product Development Partnerships Hit Their Stride: Lessons from Developing a Meningitis Vaccine for Africa." Health Affairs 30 (6): 1058–64. doi:10.1377/hlthaff.2011.0295.

Boisier, P., H.B. Mainassara, F. Sidikou, S. Djibo, K.K. Kairo, and S. Chanteau. 2007. "Case-Fatality Ratio of Bacterial Meningitis in the African Meningitis Belt: We Can Do Better." Vaccine 25 (Suppl 1): A24–29.

REFERENCES, *continued*

Campbell, Helen, Ray Borrow, David Salisbury, and Elizabeth Miller. 2009. "Meningococcal C Conjugate Vaccine: The Experience in England and Wales." *Vaccine* 27 (Suppl 2): B20–29. doi:10.1016/j.vaccine.2009.04.067.

Colombini, Anais, Fernand Bationo, Sylvie Zongo, Fatoumata Outtara, Ousmane Badolo, Philippe Jaillard, Emmanuel Seini, Bradford D. Gessner, and Alfred Da Silva. 2009. "Costs for Households and Community Perception of Meningitis Epidemics in Burkina Faso." *Clinical Infectious Diseases* 49 (10): 1520–25.

Daugla, D.M., J.P. Gami, K. Gamougam, N. Naibei, L. Mbainadji, M. Narbé, J. Toralta, et al. 2014. "Effect of a Serogroup A Meningococcal Conjugate Vaccine (PsA–TT) on Serogroup A Meningococcal Meningitis and Carriage in Chad: A Community Study." *Lancet* 383 (9911): 40–47.

De Wals, P., G. Deceuninck, N. Boulianne, and G. De Serres. 2004. "Effectiveness of a Mass Immunization Campaign Using Serogroup C Meningococcal Conjugate Vaccine." *JAMA* 292 (20): 2491–94. doi:10.1001/jama.292.20.2491.

Djingarey, Mamoudou, Rodrigue Barry, Mete Bonkoungou, Sylvestre Tiendrebeogo, Rene Sebgo, Denis Kandolo, Clement Lingani, et al. 2012. "Effectively Introducing a New Meningococcal A Conjugate Vaccine in Africa: The Burkina Faso Experience." *Vaccine* 30 (Suppl 2): B40–45. doi:10.1016/j.vaccine.2011.12.073.

Gordon, Rachel, John-Arne Røttingen, and Steven Hoffman. 2014. *The Meningitis Vaccine Project.* Cambridge, MA: Harvard Global Health Institute. http://caseresources.hsph.harvard.edu/files/case/files/2014_meningitis_vaccine_project_0.pdf.

Grace, Cheri. 2010. *Product Development Partnerships (PDPs): Lessons from PDPs Established to Develop New Health Technologies for Neglected Diseases.* London: DFID Human Development Resource Centre. https://www.gov.uk/government/uploads/system/uploads/attachment_data/file/67678/lssns-pdps-estb-dev-new-hlth-tech-negl-diseases.pdf.

Jódar, Luis, F. Marc LaForce, Costante Ceccarini, Teresa Aguado, and Dan M. Granoff. 2003. "Meningococcal Conjugate Vaccine for Africa: A Model for Development of New Vaccines for the Poorest Countries." *Lancet* 361 (9372): 1902–4. doi:10.1016/S0140-6736(03)13494-0.

Kristiansen, Paul A., Fabien Diomandé, Absatou Ky Ba, Idrissa Sanou, Abdoul-Salam Ouédraogo, Rasmata Ouédraogo, Lassana Sangaré, et al. 2013. "Impact of the Serogroup A Meningococcal Conjugate Vaccine, MenAfriVac, on Carriage and Herd Immunity." *Clinical Infectious Diseases* 56 (3): 354–63. doi:10.1093/cid/cis892.

Kshirsagar, Nilima, Naidu Mur, Urmila Thatte, Nithya Gogtay, Simonetta Viviani, Marie-Pierre Préziosi, Cheryl Elie, et al. 2007. "Safety, Immunogenicity, and Antibody Persistence of a New Meningococcal Group A Conjugate Vaccine in Healthy Indian Adults." *Vaccine* 25 (Suppl 1): A101–7. doi:10.1016/j.vaccine.2007.04.050.

LaForce, F. Marc, and Jean-Marie Okwo-Bele. 2011. "Eliminating Epidemic Group A Meningococcal Meningitis in Africa through a New Vaccine." *Health Affairs* 30 (6): 1049–57. doi:10.1377/hlthaff.2011.0328.

Lancet Infectious Diseases. 2011. "A Vaccine against Meningitis in Africa." *Lancet Infectious Diseases* 11 (1): 1. doi:10.1016/S1473-3099(10)70300-5.

Lydon, Patrick, Simona Zipursky, Carole Tevi-Benissan, Mamoudou Harouna Djingarey, Placide Gbedonou, Brahim Oumar Youssouf, and Michel Zaffran. 2013. "Economic Benefits of Keeping Vaccines at Ambient Temperature during Mass Vaccination: The Case of Meningitis A Vaccine in Chad." *Bulletin of the World Health Organization* 92: 86–92. http://www.who.int/bulletin/volumes/92/2/13-123471/en/.

Mirelman, Andrew, Amanda Glassman, and Miriam Temin. 2016. *Estimating the Avertable Disease Burden and Cost-Effectiveness in Millions Saved Third Edition.* CGD Working Paper. Washington, DC: Center for Global Development.

MVP (Meningitis Vaccine Project). 2015. WHO Surveillance Bulletins. Accessed August 5. http://www.meningvax.org/epidemic-updates.php.

Novak, Ryan, Jean Ludovic Kambou, Fabien Diomandé, Tiga F. Tarbango, Rasmata Ouédraogo-Traoré, Clement Lingani, Stacey W. Martin, et al. 2012. "Serogroup A Meningococcal Conjugate Vaccination in Burkina Faso: Analysis of National Surveillance Data." *Lancet Infectious Diseases* 12 (10): 757–64.

Romoser, Tracy. 2015. "Breaking the Paradigm: How an Essential Vaccine Was Fast-Tracked." *PATH Blog,* January 8. http://www.path.org/blog/2015/01/menafrivac-infant-prequal/.

Sow, Samba O., Brown J. Okoko, Aldiouma Diallo, Simonetta Viviani, Ray Borrow, George Carlone, Milagritos Tapia, et al. 2011. "Immunogenicity and Safety of a Meningococcal A Conjugate Vaccine in Africans." *New England Journal of Medicine* 364 (24): 2293–2304. doi:10.1056/NEJMoa1003812.

Trotter, Caroline L., Nick J. Andrews, Edward B. Kaczmarski, Elizabeth Miller, and Mary E. Ramsay. 2004. "Effectiveness of Meningococcal Serogroup C Conjugate Vaccine 4 Years after Introduction." *Lancet* 364 (9431): 365–67. doi:10.1016/S0140-6736(04)16725-1.

UNDP (United Nations Development Programme). 2015. Human Development Index. Accessed November 10. http://hdr.undp.org/en/content/human-development-index-hdi.

WHO (World Health Organization). 2008. *Yaounde Declaration on Elimination of Meningococcal Meningitis Type A Epidemics as a Public Health Problem in Africa.* Geneva: WHO.

REFERENCES, *continued*

———. 2013. "Meningococcal Disease in Countries of the African Meningitis Belt, 2012: Emerging Needs and Future Perspectives." *Weekly Epidemiological Record* 88 (12): 129–36. http://www.who.int/wer/2013/wer8812/en/.

Woods, C.W., G. Armstrong, S.O. Sackey, C. Tetteh, S. Bugri, B.A. Perkins, and N.E. Rosenstein. 2000. "Emergency Vaccination against Epidemic Meningitis in Ghana: Implications for the Control of Meningococcal Disease in West Africa." *Lancet* 355 (9197): 30–33.

Zipursky, Simona, Mamoudou Harouna Djingarey, Jean-Claude Lodjo, Laifoya Olodo, Sylvestre Tiendrebeogo, and Olivier Ronveaux. 2014. "Benefits of Using Vaccines Out of the Cold Chain: Delivering Meningitis A Vaccine in a Controlled Temperature Chain during the Mass Immunization Campaign in Benin." *Vaccine* 32 (13): 1431–35. doi:10.1016/j.vaccine.2014.01.038.

ENDNOTES

1. Monique Berlier, personal communication with the author, August 6, 2014.
2. LaForce and Okwo-Bele (2011).
3. Meningococcal serotypes C, Y, and W135 cause 10–20 percent of cases along the meningitis belt (LaForce and Okwo-Bele 2011).
4. Boisier et al. (2007).
5. Monique Berlier, personal communication with the author, August 6, 2014.
6. Data for 2012 (UNDP 2015).
7. Akweongo et al. (2013).
8. Colombini et al. (2009).
9. Woods et al. (2000).
10. *Lancet Infectious Diseases* (2011).
11. Djingarey et al. (2012).
12. Polysaccharide vaccines are cheap but their protection is short-term and they don't kill asymptomatic throat infections. Conjugate vaccines join polysaccharides—sugar-like molecules from bacterial membranes—with proteins to stimulate enduring immune responses and remove asymptomatic infections.
13. Campbell et al. (2009); Trotter et al. (2004); De Wals et al. (2004).
14. Gordon, Røttingen, and Hoffman (2014).
15. Bishai et al. (2011).
16. Marc LaForce, personal communication with the author, September 2014; Bishai et al. (2011).
17. Bishai et al. (2011).
18. LaForce and Okwo-Bele (2011); Sow et al. (2011); Kshirsagar et al. (2007).
19. Sow et al. (2011).
20. Bishai et al. (2011).
21. LaForce and Okwo-Bele (2011, 1051).
22. LaForce and Okwo-Bele (2011).
23. WHO (2008).
24. Created in 2000, Gavi, the Vaccine Alliance (Gavialliance.org), is an innovative public-private partnership that was established with the mission of saving lives and protecting people's health by guaranteeing equal access to vaccines in poor countries.
25. LaForce and Okwo-Bele (2011).
26. Northern Nigeria was one of the areas where meningitis was hyperendemic. The other countries covered were Cameroon (2011), Chad (2011), Nigeria (2011), Benin (2012), Ghana (2012), Senegal (2012), Sudan (2012), Gambia (2013), and Ethiopia (2013).
27. MVP (2015).
28. Romoser (2015).
29. Gordon, Røttingen, and Hoffman (2014).
30. Daugla et al. (2014).
31. Novak et al. (2012); Kristiansen et al. (2013).
32. Some countries have registered an increase in non-A serotypes (in particular W135 and X) as a result of strengthened surveillance (WHO 2013).
33. Daugla et al. (2014).
34. LaForce and Okwo-Bele (2011).
35. Novak et al. (2012).
36. Daugla et al. (2014).
37. André (2002); LaForce and Okwo-Bele (2011).
38. LaForce and Okwo-Bele (2011).
39. Mamoudou Harouna Djingarey, personal communication with the author, November 2, 2014.
40. Patience Musanhu, personal communication with the author, August 20, 2014.
41. The estimation of the disease burden averted used the incidence of meningitis A in Chad, the under-30 population, and the efficacy of the vaccine (Daugla et al. 2014). DALYs were calculated only for averted acute meningitis using WHO-recommended disability weights. The cost per person of the vaccine program comes from a study in Burkina Faso, Mali, and Niger (LaForce 2011). See Mirelman, Glassman, and Temin (2016).
42. LaForce and Okwo-Bele (2011).
43. Bishai et al. (2011).
44. Marc LaForce, personal communication with the author, September–November 2014.
45. Grace (2010).
46. Jódar et al. (2003).
47. Marc LaForce, personal communication with the author, September–November 2014.
48. Marc LaForce, personal communication with the author, September–November 2014.
49. Romoser (2015).
50. Zipursky et al. (2014).
51. Lydon et al. (2013).
52. Marc LaForce, personal communication with the author, September–November 2014.

Making the Impossible Possible
Botswana's Mass Antiretroviral Therapy Program

The Case at a Glance

HEALTH GOAL: To improve survival and quality of life for people living with HIV, to incentivize HIV testing and prevent new HIV infections, and to decrease the number of children orphaned by AIDS.

STRATEGY: Government provision of free antiretroviral therapy (ART) to all eligible citizens nationwide to halt HIV/AIDS.

HEALTH IMPACT: AIDS-related deaths decreased from 21,000 in 2003 to 5,800 in 2013, largely due to antiretroviral rollout. Estimated 144,000 deaths averted and eight million disability-adjusted life years (DALYs) averted.

WHY IT WORKED: Sustained high-level political and financial commitment from the government of Botswana. Free treatment at the point of service made possible by ART donations from the Merck Foundation. Financial support from donors. Investments in infrastructure and training. Decentralization of ART distribution.

FINANCING: Total domestic and international AIDS spending of US$374 million (68 percent from the government of Botswana) in 2011 and 2012. Estimated cost-effectiveness ratio: US$475 per DALY averted between 2002 and 2010.

SCALE: Covered ART for 223,974 people, approximately 87 percent of the eligible population (2013).

In 2000, many Batswana, as the people of Botswana are called, marked each Saturday with a dour ritual: funerals for their latest friends or family members who had died of AIDS. The staggering losses decimated their communities, debilitating adults in the midst of their productive years and leaving millions of orphaned children. Despite the country's relative wealth around this time, it was not unusual to encounter gravely ill men and women, bone thin themselves, trudging for miles to commemorate the lives of their loved ones.

That year, the raging HIV epidemic meant that a typical 15-year-old Batswana could expect to die by age 48; a decade earlier, that same teenager would have enjoyed a 65-year life expectancy.[1] In 2001 alone, an estimated 320,000 people in Botswana were living with HIV—slightly more than one in four.[2] Beyond the human toll, HIV also threatened to unravel decades of economic and social progress in this relatively wealthy country in southern Africa.

But for those still alive, 2002 brought a glimmer of hope. Word spread that the government was giving away antiretroviral therapy (ART), a combination of drugs that keep HIV infection in check. The ART pills had side effects; they could make patients feel sick, bring on pounding headaches, and sometimes cause nausea or extreme fatigue. But if patients took the pills at the same time every day, they could regain their health in just months. Within a year of starting ART, most who followed the protocol were strong enough to return to work. And as time passed, funerals became less frequent. Batswana were slowly reclaiming their Saturdays.

The government of Botswana had become the first African nation to supply universal free ART for its population. Leveraging an already functional health system, Botswana's government mobilized financial, human, and physical resources so that patients could start—and stay—on the lifesaving drugs. More than a decade later, Botswana has silenced the skeptics and given people living with HIV a chance for long and healthy lives.

This case was originally authored by Alix Beith.

The Toll of HIV and AIDS

By 2001, nearly 30 million adults and children world-wide were living with HIV, and two-thirds of the affected individuals lived in sub-Saharan Africa.[3] AIDS struck and killed the pillars of sub-Saharan communities, such as the parents of young children, healthcare providers, and teachers. By 2004, the disease had already orphaned 12.3 million African children.[4]

Despite its deadly toll, HIV infection did not need to be a death sentence. In the mid-1990s, the widespread introduction of combination ART dramatically reduced AIDS-related mortality in most high-income and some middle-income countries. For those privileged with access to ART and relatively strong health systems, HIV became a manageable chronic illness. Yet for the major-ity of people living with HIV, ART remained out of reach.

In 1966, when Botswana gained its independence from the United Kingdom, it had been one of the poorest countries in Africa. But after the discovery of diamonds in 1967, the country enjoyed economic growth for decades.[5] By the mid-1990s Botswana had become a sta-ble, flourishing democracy. With a per capita gross domestic product (GDP) of nearly US$3,000, Botswana's economy was also among the strongest and best man-aged in the developing world.

Botswana saw its first confirmed AIDS case in 1985; 15 years later, HIV had spread nationwide and threat-ened to derail the country's economic stability.[6] In 2001, 18,000 Batswana died of AIDS-related causes, and an astounding 320,000 Batswana, nearly 20 percent of the population, were living with HIV.[7] Girls and young women bore disproportionate risk. By 2004, they were three times as likely to test HIV positive as their male counterparts.[8] The skewed sex ratio reflected girls' and women's biological and economic vulnerability coupled with discriminatory gender norms. Young women often found themselves in multiple partnerships and risky sex-ual relationships with older men, which increased their potential exposure to the virus.[9]

Putting a Good Idea in Motion: Botswana Commits to Fight "Extinction"

In 2001, Botswana's president, Festus Mogae, saw the writing on the wall: "Botswana is threatened with extinc-tion," he warned. He pledged to make the fight against HIV a national priority.[10] This was a bold statement at the time, when many leaders around the world remained in denial about HIV—most conspicuously in the next-door economic powerhouse, South Africa.

President Mogae's remarks followed two decades of growing global activism that had finally started to pay div-idends at the country level. Thanks to the Accelerating Access Initiative, which increased pressure on the major pharmaceutical companies to undertake research on drugs to combat AIDS, and other changes in the AIDS landscape, more, and more successful HIV treatment programs had started in low- and middle-income countries, including Brazil, Thailand, Senegal, Zambia, Uganda, and others.[11]

The government's firm commitment to addressing the urgent situation inspired help from philanthropists and businesspeople alike. As lifesaving treatment rose up the agenda, government officials embarked on what turned into a fruitful collaboration with the international phar-maceutical company Merck, along with the Merck Foun-dation and the Bill & Melinda Gates Foundation. Together with the government, Merck and the Merck and Gates foundations formed the African Comprehensive HIV/AIDS Partnership (ACHAP). Beyond helping HIV-positive Batswana, the foundations had a broader goal in mind: to test the notion that a comprehensive approach—including attention to prevention, diagnosis, treatment, and care, supplemented by behavior change and infra-structure development—could be an effective national response to the HIV and AIDS crisis and save lives even in a relatively poor African setting.[12] Botswana, with its high prevalence of HIV, committed leader, and stable demo-cratic regime, represented a perfect candidate.

In 2000, the government's National AIDS Coordinat-ing Agency (NACA) worked on a comprehensive HIV and AIDS strategy that included a clear path forward for treatment rollout. When the government decided to make ART widely available as a central component of the strategy, Merck agreed to donate the drugs free of charge. And in 2002, Botswana was ready to launch its ambitious program.

The Government's ART Program in Action

The government christened its new HIV program Masa, meaning "New Dawn" in Setswana, one of the Bantu lan-guages spoken in Botswana. Starting in 2002, the pro-gram offered free universal ART to all those eligible. The government used a measure of how well a person's immune system was functioning, called the CD4+ count (a test of the presence of certain cells in the immune sys-tem), to determine people's eligibility for treatment under the national program. Monitoring the amount of virus in a person's blood, his or her viral load, also informed patient management.[13] The guidelines initially granted free ART access to all HIV-positive adults with a CD4+ count of 200 or below, plus anyone with an obvious AIDS-related illness.

In 2002, the program launched in four urban centers around the country: Gaborone, Francistown, Maun, and Serowe. Despite disappointing initial coverage—by the end of 2002 only 3,500 people had enrolled, far below the goal of 19,000—ART coverage grew swiftly with national rollout just two years later.

In 2004, Gaborone's Princess Marina Hospital became the single largest ART provider in all of Africa. Over time, the program expanded to all district-level hospitals, and eventually to satellite clinics throughout the country. By mid-2005, over half of the eligible population—43,000 people—had benefited from Masa.[14] And by the end of 2013, the national ART program covered more than 220,000 people, or about 87 percent of all eligible people.[15]

To help accelerate testing, the government tweaked its policy in a move that proved critical to the program's success. Testing for HIV infection had initially started with an "opt-in" system, whereby people had to request a test from health workers. In 2004, the government modified HIV testing to become an "opt-out" program, whereby providers offered everyone an HIV test as part of a routine office visit. President Mogae again showed his commitment and leadership by publicly announcing this policy shift and taking an HIV test on live television.[16] The new opt-out policy proved extremely effective. In 2005, of the 178,000 people who were offered the test as part of a routine visit, 89 percent agreed to be tested.[17]

In 2008, ART eligibility expanded to individuals with CD4+ counts of up to 250, and in 2012, to those with counts of up to 350.[18] With each change, the government extended ART access to a larger and relatively healthier population in a bid to improve their survival.

The increased testing and decentralization of ART distribution to local clinics contributed to the massive growth in coverage. The government also began collaborating with the country's private sector, outsourcing both routine HIV testing and ART provision, and by 2008, 14 percent of all beneficiaries were accessing ART from private-sector sources.[19]

The ART regimen provided by the government changed over time. More effective drugs with fewer side effects eventually came on the market and replaced their early-generation counterparts.[20] An additional motivation for changing over to new drugs was the

growing body of evidence that HIV could develop ART resistance, rendering first-line drugs ineffective (a "first-line" drug is the first choice to treat a condition; a "second-line" drug is the next choice if the first choice fails).[21] By 2010, some Batswana had stopped responding to the main ART regimen. Merck subsequently donated an alternate ART drug for some patients who required second-line treatment.[22]

Although Botswana's public health system was relatively robust, one of the program's aims was to strengthen it through health-worker training and infrastructure development. Few health workers knew how to administer ART, so training became a top priority. The Ministry of Health, ACHAP, and other international partners joined forces to recruit and train a diverse cadre of health workers, including doctors, nurses, counselors, pharmacists, pharmacy technicians, and laboratory workers. During the early years of the program, local experts joined those from the Harvard AIDS Institute and other foreign clinical "preceptors" to introduce new and existing staff to ART and patient management. Preceptors were international experts from Europe and the United States who came to Botswana to train health workers.

As for health infrastructure, the government and its partners built treatment and resource centers, laboratories for routine and specialized testing, and a network of satellite ART dispensaries. A critical component of effective patient monitoring was the procurement and distribution of machines for measuring CD4+ counts and viral loads by treatment centers and dispensing clinics. Another was the computerized patient management system that tracked patients' adherence to the ART protocol and kept track of any adverse reactions.

The Payoff: Longer, Healthier Lives

Botswana saw a dramatic drop in AIDS-related deaths, from a high of 21,000 in 2003 to 5,800 in 2013.[23] Several studies have tracked the contribution of the national ART program to mortality reduction and other health gains; all of them have identified a link between ART rollout and the drop in AIDS-related deaths. However, these are the results of studies that were observational rather than experimental, which limits their ability to confirm causality (see Box 1).[24]

Early concerns that people in low- and middle-income countries would not adhere to ART treatment regimens did not hold in Botswana. In fact, ART adherence rates in Botswana have risen higher than those observed in the

United States. In the early years of Masa, an estimated 85 to 90 percent of Batswana patients adhered to the ART regimen (as compared with 70 percent in the United States), and the Botswana rate remained at this high level.[25] As a result, most people enrolled in the program stayed alive and healthy. By 2010 the annual death rate was well under 1 percent among patients, and mean CD4+ counts steadily climbed with each passing month after ART enrollment.[26]

The Masa rollout was a tribute to equity. Prior to the launch of the public program, only a few wealthy Batswana could afford ART. Nationwide scale-up meant all eligible residents had the right to free lifelong treatment. The expansion of eligibility criteria over time has enabled many more people living with HIV to access the benefits of ART.

Yet coverage is not yet universal. After a steady rise, the proportion of eligible people receiving ART dropped from 96 percent in 2012 to 87 percent in 2013, which translated to less than 70 percent of all Batswana living with HIV.[27] And the pool of people in need continued to expand because prevention efforts lagged. Tragically, many of the people who face the highest risk of infection, including female sex workers and men who have sex with men, are not being effectively reached with prevention programs.[28] Laws that prohibit same-sex relation-ships in Botswana make it more challenging to reach this last group. The stigma of sex between men keeps many such men away from health services, yet this is a group at especially high risk of HIV infection.[29]

Gains at What Price?

By 2012, total annual spending on HIV and AIDS had reached US$374 million in Botswana, of which 68 percent was covered by the government—a remarkable sum for a sub-Saharan country but a challenge to sustain given competing bids for government resources.[33] The Bill & Melinda Gates Foundation contributed US$50 million and the Merck Foundation US$56.5 million to help the government get its program up and running. The two foundations provided an additional US$30 million each in 2010. The remainder came from international sources, including the President's Emergency Plan for AIDS Relief (PEPFAR) and the Global Fund to Fight AIDS, Tuberculosis and Malaria.

In 2014, treatment costs for the national ART program were estimated at US$480 per person.[34] Because people living with HIV often presented when already gravely ill, treating them consumed a larger per-person portion of treatment resources than was originally planned. It is

---

Box 1. Strength of the Evidence

Botswana's ART program did not include any randomized controls to provide a rigorous comparison group. Nevertheless, the large-scale nature of the program, the high quality of clinical services (based on CD4+ counts, retention, and mortality among enrolled patients), and the national reduction in HIV mortality observed after implementation suggest that the program has had a significant health impact. Three studies highlight the relationship between ART rollout and health outcomes in Botswana, consistently pointing to an impact on HIV mortality.

Stover and others[30] used surveillance, survey, and program data to estimate the effect of ART rollout. They found that higher ART coverage levels coincided with a drop in the annual number of adult deaths, from more than 15,500 in 2003 to fewer than 7,400 by 2008. The study further concluded that ART had saved an estimated 53,000 lives between 2000 and 2007. Bussmann and others[31] assessed long-term (five-year) clinical outcomes among 633 of the first patients who received ART in the country. These researchers observed high levels of adherence to the ART regimen. They also found that ART use increased CD4+ counts and decreased viral load over time, leading to low mortality among those who survived into their second year of treatment. However, the implications of these studies are limited by their observational nature, paired with their reliance on modeling and small scale, respectively.

More recently, Farahani and colleagues[32] analyzed mortality reduction in the treatment program between 2002 and 2010. The study found that annual mortality among enrolled patients decreased enormously over time, from 63 percent among the first 140 patients in 2002 to well under 1 percent by 2010 (note that not all enrolled patients were necessarily on ART). The main study limitation was the absence of a counterfactual. In addition, the authors had to assign outcomes for the 12 percent of patients lost to follow-up. If their estimation of mortality within this group was too high or too low, then the mortality estimates will not be fully accurate.

expected that the per-person costs will rise to US$600 by 2030, primarily due to the growing need for second- and third-line ART as the virus becomes more resistant to the first-line option.

Researchers assessed the treatment program's cost-effectiveness for *Millions Saved* using simple HIV prevalence estimates. The analysis indicated that the reported mortality decline led to nearly 144,000 averted deaths, which translates to more than eight million disability-adjusted life years (DALYs) averted. Pairing that estimate with government estimates of cost per patient-year, we calculated a cost-effectiveness ratio of US$475 per DALY averted between 2002 and 2010. This falls well below the World Health Organization (WHO) recommended threshold of the country's GDP per capita, which for Botswana was US$7,734 in 2011.[35]

The Keys to Lasting Success

The success of the national ART program can be credited to bold leadership, sustained political and financial commitment, and investments in human resources and health services, bolstered by increased testing to tackle HIV stigma. President Mogae's no-nonsense leadership steered Botswana to a long-term investment in the program—a concrete signal of its serious commitment—while the strong economy enabled Botswana to make good on that pledge.

The ART program benefited from Botswana's robust network of public clinics and hospitals within a functional public health system.[36] Nevertheless, the government wrestled with inadequate human and physical resources to effectively facilitate the massive ART rollout. A combination of new infrastructure, laboratory decentralization, task shifting (delegating tasks to less specialized health workers), and intensified training helped filled the gap. New infrastructure and decentralization meant fewer patients had to travel to access therapy. Task shifting, training, and the engagement of the private sector also increased the number of facilities offering ART, increased the pool of knowledgeable and qualified healthcare workers, and decreased waiting lists to start therapy.[37] To boost Botswana's domestic health workforce during the early years, the government also recruited providers from nearby African countries, Cuba, and India. Together, these efforts made possible regular viral load monitoring from the start of the program—unique among African programs at the time and a key factor that helped drive Masa's success.[38]

High levels of adherence underpinned the major health gains among Batswana. Counselors encouraged people on ART to find a treatment "buddy" and used computers to track their adherence.[39] In addition, patients received their ART medications on a monthly basis, leading to regular interaction with health workers who could reinforce the importance of adherence in helping to keep the virus at bay.[40] Given Botswana's health workforce constraints, extending the time between visits for those with an undetectable viral load may be a logical shift.[41]

Because of the stigma attached to AIDS, many people had avoided getting tested, which contributed to the initial slow uptake and prevented people from accessing treatment until they were extremely ill.[42] The government of Botswana took the lead on combating social stigma through its promotion of HIV testing. HIV testing created a virtuous cycle: as more people learned their status, more people changed their attitudes toward other people living with HIV.

Implications for Global Health

Given its relative wealth and stability, Botswana differs in important ways from most of its neighbors. In Masa's early years, some AIDS advocates feared that failure in Botswana would prevent ART rollout in other poorer and less stable countries. Yet the program turned a corner when its coverage expanded, proving skeptics wrong.

Despite differences between Botswana and other countries, the worldwide impact of the ACHAP approach has been tremendous. As Dr. Mark Dybul, the head of PEPFAR from 2006 to 2009, noted: "PEPFAR used Botswana [ACHAP] as [a] model of how a program needs to be built before it can take off. If Botswana [ACHAP] wasn't there, there would not have been the information required to propose PEPFAR."[43] In addition, the program's use of opt-out provider-initiated routine testing was pioneering; it was soon adopted by the Joint United Nations Programme on HIV/AIDS (UNAIDS), which, along with the WHO, issued a 2004 policy statement recommending provider-initiated testing for asymptomatic people "seen in clinical and community-based health service settings where HIV is prevalent and antiretroviral treatment is available."[44] "Botswana pioneered that approach and gave this to the world," confirmed Botswana's former health minister, Sheila Tlou.[45]

Many aspects of the program's success are applicable elsewhere, starting with the need for sustained political and financial commitment. Botswana's ongoing financial commitment to ART is particularly crucial given the drop in donor funding following its graduation to upper-middle-income-country status.[46] The end of 2014 also brought the end of Merck's partnership with ACHAP and its donation of three out of the four Merck antiretroviral drugs (it will continue donating the fourth until 2016). In response to a decline in resources, a technical working group was convened in 2014 to develop an investment case for strengthening Botswana's national HIV response.[47]

Based on a number of assumptions, the expert group calculated that if its recommendations in the investment case are taken forward, more than 76,000 HIV infections and 43,000 HIV-related deaths could be prevented by 2030. One key assumption is that as of 2014, 35,000 eligible people living with HIV were not yet receiving ART.[48] Yet the price tag to make this happen is large: additional funding of US$50 million to US$100 million per year through 2030.[49]

Another important challenge to the sustainability of Botswana's and other governments' treatment programs is the burden that caring for so many people on ART puts on health systems. In Botswana, the downsizing of government health staff since 2010 has hindered the national HIV response "from the ground level to the Ministry of Health."[50] This is reflected in failure rates—indicators of ART's declining ability to repress HIV—that have jumped from less than 6 percent among adults in 2012 to more than 10 percent in 2013.[51]

To stop new infections, it is of paramount importance that governments prioritize prevention alongside sustained treatment efforts, an area where Botswana is still struggling. HIV prevalence in Botswana, 18.5 per-cent, remains among the highest in the region.[52] Incidence of new infections among those at risk for HIV has also held steady since 2008, dropping only slightly, from 1.45 percent to 1.35 percent in 2013.[53] Specific groups remain particularly vulnerable, especially female sex workers. Nearly two-thirds of them are HIV positive. HIV testing rates have stagnated (reaching just 63 percent in 2012), and less than half of young people can accurately describe how to prevent HIV infection.[54] One bright spot: Botswana's treatment program may itself help prevent new HIV infections, because ART reduces the HIV viral load in blood, semen, and vaginal and rectal fluids, substantially lowering the risk of transmission, a strategy dubbed "treatment as prevention."[55]

Moving forward, the government is prioritizing the integration of HIV treatment, care, and support into routine healthcare delivery.[56] According to NACA, Botswana needs nothing less than a "re-visioning of healthcare service delivery that will require up to one-third of the entire country's population to interact with the healthcare system on a monthly basis."[57] Leadership and innovation are essential to guide future program evolution and ensure that early gains are not lost. It is encouraging that the government has published guidance to improve healthcare delivery and overcome legal and operational constraints to HIV care.[58]

Worldwide, nearly 13 million people were on lifesaving HIV treatment by the end of 2013.[59] For the other 63 percent of people living with HIV who are not on treatment, ART may seem like a distant fantasy.[60] But as Botswana's experience shows, government commitment and international partnerships can help turn that dream into a reality.

REFERENCES

amfAR. 2013. *Tackling HIV/AIDS among Key Populations: Essential to Achieving an AIDS-Free Generation.* Washington, DC: amfAR. http://www.amfar.org/uploadedFiles/_amfarorg/Articles/On_The_Hill/2013/Key%20 Populations%20Issue%20Brief%20-%20Final%20(2).pdf.

Avalos, Ava, and Keith Jeffries. 2014. *Botswana at the Crossroads: Investment Towards Sustainable Integration, Increased ART Access and Effective HIV Prevention.* Gaborone, Botswana: NACA.

AVERT. 2015a. "HIV and AIDS in Botswana." Accessed July 9. http://www.avert.org/hiv-aids-botswana.htm.

———. 2015b. "HIV Treatment as Prevention." Accessed August 6. http://www.avert.org/hiv-treatment-as-prevention.htm#sthash.blQIgazp.dpuf.

Bill & Melinda Gates Foundation. 2006. *Working with Botswana to Confront Its Devastating AIDS Crisis.* Seattle, WA: Bill & Melinda Gates Foundation. https://docs.gatesfoundation.org/documents/achap.pdf.

Bussmann, Christine, Philip Rotz, Ndwapi Ndwapi, Daniel Baxter, Hermann Bussmann, C. William Wester, Patricia Ncube, et al. 2008. "Strengthening Healthcare Capacity through a Responsive, Country-Specific, Training Standard: The KITSO AIDS Training Program's Support of Botswana's National Antiretroviral Therapy Rollout." *Open AIDS Journal* 2 (February): 10–16. doi:10.2174/18746136008020 10010.

Canadian AIDS Society. 2012. "Women's Biological Susceptibility to HIV." http://www.cdnaids.ca/files.nsf/pages/

REFERENCES, *continued*

15womensbio/$file/Women%E2%80%99s%20 Biological%20Susceptibility%20to%20HIV.pdf.

Chabrol, Fanny. 2014. "Biomedicine, Public Health, and Citizenship in the Advent of Antiretrovirals in Botswana: The Advent of Antiretrovirals in Botswana." *Developing World Bioethics* 14 (2): 75–82. doi:10.1111/dewb.12051.

Farahani, Mansour, Anusha Vable, Refeletswe Lebelonyane, Khumo Seipone, Marina Anderson, Ava Avalos, Tim Chadborn, et al. 2014. "Outcomes of the Botswana National HIV/AIDS Treatment Programme from 2002 to 2010: A Longitudinal Analysis." *Lancet Global Health* 2 (1): e44–50. doi:10.1016/S2214-109X(13)70149-9.

Fibæk, Maria. 2010. "Botswana's Modern Economic History since 1966: Has Botswana Reached the Last Stage of Modern Growth Regime?" Thesis, Department of Economics, University of Copenhagen. http://www.econ. ku.dk/okojwe/filer/UGT%20Seminar%202010/Maria_ Fibaek%20The%20modern%20economic%20history%20 of%20Botswana].pdf.

Miles, K., D.J. Clutterbuck, O. Seitio, M. Sebego, and A. Riley. 2007. "Antiretroviral Treatment Roll-Out in a Resource-Constrained Setting: Capitalizing on Nursing Resources in Botswana." *Bulletin of the World Health Organization* 85 (7): 555–60.

Mirelman, Andrew, Amanda Glassman, and Miriam Temin. 2016. *Estimating the Avertable Disease Burden and Cost-Effectiveness in Millions Saved Third Edition.* CGD Working Paper. Washington, DC: Center for Global Development.

Mogae, Festus G. 2003. "Christmas and New Year Message to the Nation." *Daily News* (Botswana), December 22.

NACA (National AIDS Coordinating Agency, Republic of Botswana). 2005. *Botswana AIDS Impact Survey II: Statistical Report.* Gaborone, Botswana: Central Statistics Office. http://catalog.ihsn.org/index.php/catalog/2048.

———. 2014. *Botswana 2013 Global Aids Report: Progress Report of the National Response to the 2011 Declaration of Commitments on HIV and AIDS.* Gaborone, Botswana: NACA. http://www.unaids.org/sites/default/files/country/ documents//file,94425,es..pdf.

Ntibinyane, Ntibinyane. 2012. "25 Years Fighting AIDS in Botswana." Open Society Initiative for Southern Africa blog, April 19. http://www.osisa.org/hiv-and-aids/ blog/25-years-fighting-aids-botswana.

PEPFAR (President's Emergency Plan for AIDS Relief). 2014. *Botswana Operational Plan Report FY 2013.* Washington, DC: PEPFAR. http://www.pepfar.gov/documents/ organization/222152.pdf.

Public Health Agency of Canada. 2012. *HIV Transmission Risk: A Summary of the Evidence.* Ottowa, ON: Public Health Agency of Canada. http://www.catie.ca/sites/ default/files/HIV-TRANSMISSION-RISK-EN.pdf.

Stover, John, Boga Fidzani, Batho Chris Molomo, Themba Moeti, and Godfrey Musuka. 2008. "Estimated HIV Trends and Program Effects in Botswana." *PLoS ONE* 3 (11): e3729. doi:10.1371/journal.pone.0003729.

UNAIDS (Joint United Nations Programme on HIV/AIDS). 2011. *Global AIDS Response Progress Reporting 2012: Guidelines: Construction of Core Indicators for Monitoring the 2011 Political Declaration on HIV/AIDS.* Geneva: UNAIDS.

———. 2014. *Gap Report.* Geneva: UNAIDS. http://www. unaids.org/en/resources/campaigns/2014/2014gapreport/gapreport.

———. 2015. "AIDS Info Visualization Tool." Accessed November 5. http://aidsinfo.unaids.org/.

———. 2016. AIDSinfo. Accessed February 12. http:// aidsinfo.unaids.org/.

UNAIDS, UNICEF (United Nations Children's Fund), and USAID (United States Agency for International Development). 2004. *Children on the Brink 2004: A Joint Report of New Orphan Estimates and a Framework for Action.* New York: UNAIDS, UNICEF, and USAID.

UNAIDS and WHO (World Health Organization). 2004. "UNAIDS/WHO Policy Statement on HIV Testing." http:// data.unaids.org/una-docs/hivtestingpolicy_en.pdf.

WHO (World Health Organization). 2005. *Summary Country Profile for HIV/AIDS Treatment Scale-Up: Botswana.* Geneva: WHO. http://www.who.int/hiv/HIVCP_BWA.pdf.

———. 2015a. Global Health Observatory (GHO) Data. Accessed November 10. http://www.who.int/gho/en/.

———. 2015b. "HIV Drug Resistance." Accessed August 5. http://www.who.int/hiv/topics/drugresistance/en/.

———. 2015c. "Realizing Nurses' Full Potential." *Bulletin of the World Health Organization* 93 (9): 596–97. doi:10.2471/BLT.15.030915.

World Bank. 2015. Country and Lending Groups. Accessed August 6. http://data.worldbank.org/about/countryand-lending-groups.

ENDNOTES

1. WHO (2015a).
2. UNAIDS (2015).
3. UNAIDS (2011).
4. UNAIDS, UNICEF, and USAID (2004).
5. Fibæk (2010).
6. WHO (2005).
7. UNAIDS (2015).
8. NACA (2005).
9. Public Health Agency of Canada (2012); Canadian AIDS Society (2012); UNAIDS (2014).
10. Ntibinyane (2012).
11. Chabrol (2014).

ENDNOTES, *continued*

12. Bill & Melinda Gates Foundation (2006).
13. Jeff Sturchio, personal communication with the author, August 6, 2015.
14. AVERT (2015a).
15. NACA (2014).
16. Mogae (2003).
17. Bill & Melinda Gates Foundation (2006).
18. NACA (2014).
19. Lule, Seifman, and David (2009).
20. Farahani et al. (2014).
21. WHO (2015b).
22. Ava Avalos, personal communication with the author, December 17, 2014.
23. UNAIDS (2015).
24. Bill & Melinda Gates Foundation (2006); Ava Avalos, personal communication with the author, December 17, 2014.
25. Bill & Melinda Gates Foundation (2006); Ava Avalos, personal communication with the author, December 17, 2014.
26. Farahani et al. (2014).
27. NACA (2014).
28. NACA (2014).
29. amfAR (2013).
30. 2008.
31. 2008.
32. 2014.
33. NACA (2014).
34. Avalos and Jeffries (2014).
35. The estimation of DALYs averted was based on HIV prevalence estimates from UNAIDS (2016), population size, and the HIV prevalence reduction from Farahani et al. (2014). DALY estimates were consistent with WHO Global Health Estimates. Costs per person were taken from government estimates of the Masa program. See Mirelman, Glassman, and Temin (2016).
36. Fanny Chabrol, personal communication with the author, March 4, 2015.
37. Miles et al. (2007); Bussmann et al. (2008).
38. Ava Avalos, personal communication with the author, December 17, 2014.
39. UNAIDS, UNICEF, and USAID (2004).
40. UNAIDS, UNICEF, and USAID (2004).
41. Jose-Antonio Izazola-Licea, personal communication with the author, September 7, 2015.
42. The 2014 "investment case" argues that this high rate of late presentation could be abated by strengthened HIV testing and pre-ART monitoring (see Avalos and Jeffries 2014, 11).
43. Brenda Colatrella, personal communication with the author, August 9, 2015.
44. Brenda Colatrella, personal communication with the author, August 9, 2015; UNAIDS and WHO (2004).
45. WHO (2015c).
46. World Bank (2015).
47. Avalos and Jeffries (2014).
48. Avalos and Jeffries (2014).
49. Avalos and Jeffries (2014). According to a 2010 World Bank study, under current projections Botswana's costs for treating people with HIV will grow from US$457 million to US$1.6 billion by 2025. Botswana's total budget as of 2013 was only US$5.4 billion (PEPFAR 2014).
50. Avalos and Jeffries (2014, 11).
51. NACA (2014).
52. For the general population, aged 18 weeks or older (NACA 2014).
53. NACA (2014).
54. NACA (2014).
55. AVERT (2015b).
56. Avalos and Jeffries (2014).
57. NACA (2014, 10).
58. NACA (2014, 201).
59. UNAIDS (2014).
60. UNAIDS (2014).

Reducing Cancer Risk in China
Equalizing Hepatitis B Vaccine Coverage

The Case at a Glance

HEALTH GOAL: To dramatically decrease hepatitis B–related deaths and hepatitis B–associated liver cancer and cirrhosis.

STRATEGY: Expand hepatitis B vaccination to reduce inequitable access in poorer, underserved areas of China.

HEALTH IMPACT: Provided additional hepatitis B coverage up to 15 percent and timely birth dose coverage up to 27 percent beyond coverage expected without a dedicated expansion program, contributing to a decrease in national hepatitis B prevalence to less than 1 percent. 520,000 infections averted, 93,000 deaths averted, and more than 22 million disability-adjusted life years (DALYs) averted.

WHY IT WORKED: High-level government commitment and financing. Removal of immunization fees. Locally produced materials. An enabling management structure leveraging domestic and international expertise. Program location within the National Immunization Program.

FINANCING: US$45 million from the government of China. US$38 million from Gavi, the Vaccine Alliance. Estimated cost-effectiveness ratios: US$28.70 per infection averted, US$160 per death averted, and US$3.36 per DALY averted.

SCALE: Of 1.87 million children eligible, 85 percent were vaccinated for hepatitis B and 75 percent received a timely birth dose.

In one of China's poorer western provinces, a middle-aged woman suffers from joint pain, nausea, fever, and bloating. Convinced she has the flu, she delays seeking medical attention. A visit to the nearest doctor would require taking a day off work, plus money for transportation, the visit itself, and medicine. By the time she receives care, it will be too late—her symptoms signal not influenza but advanced liver cancer, caused by the hepatitis B (hep B) virus. She will live just a few months, at most a few years.

Her story is far too common in China, home to the largest burden of hep B in the world. Many middle-aged people, infected at birth, unknowingly carry the hep B virus—which infects more than 350 million people worldwide—their entire lives. Called the "silent killer," the virus claims more than 780,000 lives each year.[1]

Chronic hep B infection often leads to cirrhosis and liver cancer; the latter is the most common cancer in many East Asian and sub-Saharan African countries. In China, hep B causes an estimated 66 percent of liver cancer deaths in men and 58 percent in women, and is also the leading cause of cirrhosis.[2] Treatment for the diseases caused by hep B is unavailable in many settings where it is prevalent, including most of China. Treatment is costly, and even if it is accessed it adds just a few years to life. The road to hep B control therefore lies in prevention.

Beginning in 1992 and intensifying in 2002, China mounted a hep B prevention campaign, rolling out the vaccine across the country. But a financial barrier kept the vaccine out of reach of most of the people in the poorer parts of China. The government of China partnered with Gavi, the Vaccine Alliance, to reduce this inequity, extending the reach of hep B prevention to underserved communities. By channeling funding and health system resources to those at risk, the prevention program eventually overcame numerous obstacles to achieve a tremendous impact: a nationwide decrease in childhood hep B prevalence from nearly 10 percent in 1992 to less than 1 percent in 2006.

This case was originally authored by Alix Beith.

The Toll of Hepatitis B

Chronic hep B infection occurs when a person has been infected for six or more months and the immune system cannot clear the infection. This puts the individual at risk for hep B–associated diseases later in life. A person's age at infection affects his or her long-term prognosis: the probability of developing chronic infection approaches 90 percent for those infected at birth, whereas the probability for those infected as adults is just 5 to 10 percent.[3]

Of the 350 million people living with chronic hep B infection, three-quarters reside in Asia and the Western Pacific.[4] Hep B is endemic in China, and most Chinese become infected when they are young—either through mother-to-child transmission during delivery or through bodily fluid exchange with playmates during early childhood. As a result, 93 million Chinese carry chronic hep B infection, causing 250,000 to 300,000 hep B–associated liver cancer deaths every year.[5] The burden is significant: hep B kills more Chinese each year than tuberculosis, HIV, and malaria combined.

Yet prevention is possible. A complete hep B vaccine series provides 95 percent protection in infants, children, and young adults, and that protection endures for 20 years or more.[6] For babies whose mothers test hep B positive, the vaccine is most effective when the first dose is received within 24 hours of delivery—called the "timely birth dose."[7] In parts of rural China, where home birth is common and women are unaware of hep B and the possibility of being infected, increasing the coverage of the timely birth dose posed a particularly urgent challenge.

Putting an Idea in Motion: China Seeks to Narrow a Vaccine Coverage Gap

Events on the international stage helped lay the groundwork for China's hep B program. The hep B vaccine first became available in 1982; a decade later, the World Health Assembly tasked hep B–endemic countries with rapid integration of the vaccine into routine childhood immunization programs.[8] In 2001, the World Health Assembly passed a binding resolution that compelled countries to achieve 90 percent hep B vaccine coverage by 2015. Countries now had both an effective vaccine at their disposal and a strong mandate to use it.

In 1990, as a result of massive efforts by governments, donors, and international agencies, an astounding 80 percent of the world's children had been vaccinated with the six vaccines that made up the World Health Organiza-

tion's (WHO's) Expanded Program on Immunization (EPI).[9] But during the 1990s, the global vaccine market changed: the number of vaccine manufacturers decreased, the vaccine needs of high-income and low-income regions diverged, and donor priorities shifted away from vaccines. By the late 1990s, there were shortages of vaccines.[10] Low- and middle-income countries struggled to maintain vaccination campaigns and sustain immunization levels.[11] By the end of the 20th century, children in wealthy countries could count on getting all needed vaccines, whereas children in poor countries received only half of those recommended by the WHO.[12] Access to newer vaccines, such as hep B, was especially inequitable.[13]

Momentum grew to renew the global emphasis on immunization. In 1998, the president of the World Bank, James Wolfensohn, convened a summit on how to solve the global problem of access to vaccines.[14] The next year, Bill and Melinda Gates hosted a dinner at their home with prominent scientists. The couple turned up the heat with a challenging question: "What breakthrough solutions could be introduced to overcome the barriers preventing millions of children from receiving basic vaccines?" In 2000, a meeting at the Rockefeller Foundation's Bellagio Conference Center recommended creating a new global public-private partnership to spur investments in immunization: Gavi, the Vaccine Alliance.[15]

Gavi's mission is to reduce global inequity between the rich and the poor, save lives, and protect health by guaranteeing equal access to newer vaccines in poor countries. As of 2013, Gavi had expanded vaccination to an additional 151 million children and helped reduce prices by bulk purchasing new and underused vaccines.[16] Hep B and yellow fever were two of Gavi's first disease priorities, making the fight against hep B a "de facto primary raison d'être of Gavi" from the start.[17]

Meanwhile, hep B awareness was growing in China. All major hospitals had liver cancer wards, and most doctors spent time with liver cancer patients during their medical school rotations.[18] There was emerging evidence of the link between hep B and liver cancer, increasing doctors' enthusiasm for vaccination against hep B at birth.[19] Two developments provided further motivation: the availability of a locally produced vaccine, as of 1986,[20] and a national hep B prevalence survey performed in 1992.[21] With solid backing from the minister of health, Dr. Chen Minzhang, leaders from the government, the Chinese Center for Disease Control and Prevention (China CDC), and academia created the China Hepatitis Foundation. At the top of its agenda was the urgent need to expand hep B vaccination across China.[22]

To expand coverage, the Chinese Ministry of Health integrated the hep B vaccine into the national basic EPI in 1992 and recommended that it be administered as part of routine vaccinations across the country.[23] The government assumed responsibility for vaccine administration and monitoring, and aligned the new vaccine's distribution with that of other vaccines, such as polio and measles, that are part of the EPI.[24]

But distribution occurred within a health system that charged user fees, meaning that patients themselves were responsible for the costs of health workers' fees, vaccines, and syringes. In 1999, the total cost for the three requisite doses ranged from CNY20 to CNY40 (US$2 to US$5), depending on location and income level.[25] This was particularly problematic because vaccination has immediate costs but delayed benefits—a dynamic that can lead to low utilization, particularly by poor families. The fees led to huge variations in coverage according to wealth: vaccines soon reached 80 to 90 percent of children in the wealthier northern and eastern Chinese provinces but just 40 percent or so of children in the poorer western regions.[26]

By 2001, these statistics helped motivate the government to take action. That year, China applied for Gavi support to expand hep B coverage. Because China was too large to qualify for national vaccine and safe injection support, it instead received a US$40 million grant to support hep B vaccination measures of its choice.[27] The government, Gavi, and other partners agreed that the grant would target poor and remote areas where coverage was stagnating. And the China-Gavi Program was born.

The China-Gavi Program in Action

The China-Gavi Program targeted China's 12 western provinces and the poorest counties in the 10 central provinces, a total of 1,301 counties. These areas saw an estimated 5.6 million births each year, more than one-third of the national total.[28]

With Gavi support from 2002 to 2007, the program aimed to increase coverage of a three-dose hep B vaccine (hep B3) to 85 percent (revised to 90 percent in 2008) and timely birth dose coverage to 75 percent or higher. Given evidence of poor injection-safety practices, including the reuse of disposable syringes, the China-Gavi Program also aimed to ensure that health workers administered all immunizations using auto-disable syringes, which can be used only once.[29] Finally, the program sought to educate decision makers in the health sector

and also the general population about the burden and impact of hep B.[30]

Typical of Gavi programs, the grant was administered domestically by the Chinese Ministry of Health and China CDC's EPI. However, the China-Gavi Program departed from the traditional Gavi approach in fundamental ways. Most notably, it established an in-country program office staffed by two coordinators, one Chinese and one from the US Centers for Disease Control and Prevention (US CDC).[31] The program office was located within the National Immunization Program of the China CDC, enabling the coordinators to manage the implementation with oversight of the Ministry of Health, even while the bulk of operations took place at local levels.[32] The program office procured the vaccine and auto-disable syringes for the western provinces; central provinces provided their own supplies in their program areas. Furthermore, the coordinators provided guidance to lower levels of the health system on health education activities and the importance of immunization.[33]

The government also gradually changed its policies on user fees for hep B immunization—a crucial step in reaching the poorest people. In 2002, the Chinese government capped user fees at around US$1 for all three doses and also integrated the vaccine into its EPI at the same time, which eliminated the cost to users of the vaccine itself.[34] In 2005, the government fully abolished user fees for all routine immunizations nationwide. Hep B vaccine and auto-disable syringes continued to be funded by the China-Gavi Program in program areas until 2008, when the central government took over responsibility for the costs of all 14 routinely recommended vaccines, including hep B, across the country.[35]

The Payoff: Hepatitis B Infections Plummet

In 1992, 1 in 10 Chinese children harbored the hep B infection; by 2006, that number had tumbled to just 1 in 100.[36] The China-Gavi Program contributed to this accomplishment; it built on existing government efforts to dramatically extend the reach of China's routine hep B vaccination program. By 2011, all provinces in the program exceeded the initial hep B and timely birth dose coverage targets (see Figure 1).

Although it is difficult to precisely quantify the China-Gavi Program's contribution to the decline in hep B infection, a credible modeling exercise suggests that the government vaccination program prevented about 3.8 million chronic hep B infections between 2003 and 2009 in program areas, averting roughly 680,000 future deaths.[37] Of that total, the program's dedicated efforts prevented about 500,000 chronic hep B infections and averted nearly 100,000 deaths (see Box 1).[38]

Beyond its considerable health benefits, the program influenced the health system in several ways that helped sustain the program's impact. In particular, the program trained more than five million health workers on hep B vaccination and on the use of auto-disable syringes.[39] Even in 2015, use of this kind of syringe is still significantly higher in the western provinces—likely a holdover from China-Gavi Program training. Indicating that the program also strengthened immunization program management, discrepancies between surveyed and reported coverage rates in the western provinces decreased.[40] Finally, public knowledge and awareness of hep B prevention grew considerably as a result of China-Gavi Program efforts.[41]

Gains at What Price?

Gavi and the government of China provided joint support for the roughly US$76 million investment. While the precise amounts are difficult to estimate in dollar terms given the fluctuating exchange rate, the government's national and provincial investment totaled about CNY361 million (US$61 million) over the original project time frame from 2002 to 2007.[44]

The China-Gavi Program achieved its hep B and timely birth dose coverage goals with significant cost savings. Vaccines and syringes were procured locally at lower than anticipated cost, and central government funds covered vaccine costs that were initially included in the program budget.[45] These savings allowed the program to redirect its project funds toward additional activities in its target regions, including additional catch-up vaccinations for children and adolescents up to age 15 who had missed out on routine childhood vaccination.[46]

A costing exercise over the period from 2003 to 2007 strongly supports the program's cost-effectiveness.[47] The program cost just US$28.70 per chronic hep B infection prevented and US$160 per future hep B death averted. Cost-effectiveness analysis conducted by researchers for *Millions Saved* suggests that the program averted 22.6 million disability-adjusted life years (DALYs) in total, resulting in a cost-effectiveness ratio of US$3.36 per DALY averted.[48] This estimate confirms the cost-effectiveness of the program as compared with a threshold of gross domestic product (GDP) per capita.[49]

The Keys to Lasting Success

The China-Gavi Program built on existing Chinese government hep B vaccination efforts, considerably extending the preexisting program's reach. National commitment to the China-Gavi Program and focused attention on the most underserved areas were critical to its success.[50] The government was dedicated to cofinancing from the outset; high-level political support also motivated EPI staff and fostered collaboration with other parts of the health sector, such as maternal and child health program staff.[51] Successful collaboration between the Ministry of Health and Gavi further facilitated implementation, as did the regular engagement of international partners such as the WHO, United Nations Children's Fund (UNICEF), and PATH, among others, in the design of the China-Gavi Program and the provision of ongoing advice.[52]

The program's management setup also helped. The program office and dual coordinator structure ensured access to knowledge and technical

Figure 1. Change in Hepatitis B3 and Timely Birth Dose (TBD) Vaccination Coverage Rates for Project and Nonproject Areas

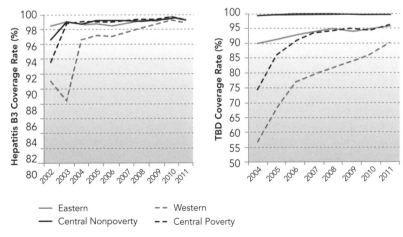

——— Eastern   – – – Western
——— Central Nonpoverty   – – – Central Poverty

Source: Chee, Xie, and Nakhimovsky (2012).

Box 1. Strength of the Evidence

The hep B vaccine was provided free of charge nationwide from 2008 onward, and the China-Gavi Program was carried out in the target areas within the context of the national program. To attribute health impact to the program alone thus required separating the effects of the targeted program from the effects of the national one. Hadler and others modeled averted chronic hep B infections and related deaths, based on vaccine coverage rates and the efficacy of the vaccine, to estimate the incremental impact of the program on coverage in underserved areas.[42] The researchers used estimates of coverage based on data from systematic population-based surveys.

Overall, the model suggested that China's nationwide hep B vaccine rollout had had a tremendous impact, averting an estimated 4.3 million deaths from hep B–related causes among children born between 1992 and 2009. In the China-Gavi Program areas, the researchers estimated, based on their modeled projections, that the program pre-

vented 520,000 chronic hep B infections and 93,200 related deaths.

Given the vaccine's high efficacy rate in controlled trials (95 percent) and the frequency and high quality of China's national survey–based coverage measures, the researchers' models likely provide a reasonable approximation of real program impact. However, the results must be interpreted carefully. The evaluation design relied on existing estimates of the relationship between vaccination and downstream health effects: a 2006 sero-study provided strong evidence of the vaccine's health impact.[43] Nevertheless, attributing direct health impact to the program with certainty would require representative sero-surveys to detect infections plus long-term follow-up to establish whether hep B–attributable health consequences decrease over time. In the future, it will be important to monitor data sources such as cancer registries to understand the long-term impact of the vaccination program.

expertise from both within and outside China.[53] The program office's location within the National Immunization Program ensured Chinese ownership. It also facilitated communication with decision makers, integrated the program into other hep B activities, and assured timely implementation.[54] The structure of the Chinese health system itself was an enabling factor: detailed implementation guidance flowed smoothly from the program office to lower administrative levels.[55] This guidance created a sense of discipline and uniformity around program activities and strengthened hep B–related public health awareness.[56]

An innovative procurement strategy also helped increase the program's cost-effectiveness and stimulate broader regulatory change. Unlike prior Gavi-supported programs, the China-Gavi Program aimed to procure hep B vaccines and syringes from local suppliers. Gavi partners initially resisted these locally produced vaccines because they were not prequalified by the WHO, potentially setting an unwelcome precedent. However, the Chinese government overcame objections by working closely with the WHO to strengthen its regulatory framework, enabling its locally sourced vaccines to prequalify for United Nations procurement. This effective collaboration ultimately improved regulation for all vaccines in China.

The program's impact was facilitated by the government of China's 2005 decision, announced by Premier Jiabao Wen, to finance all costs of routine immunization nationally, including immunization for hep B. The policy shift was prompted by findings from a policy review on vaccine financing published in the aftermath of the severe acute respiratory syndrome (SARS) outbreak.[57] It shined a light on the inequitable financing of preventive services and highlighted that China was the only country in the region charging for routine childhood immunization services.[58]

Meanwhile, other factors outside the program enhanced its coverage and impact. For example, hospital deliveries rose from 58 percent of all births in 2002 to 93 percent in 2009, due in part to an incentive program that encouraged institutional delivery.[59] Bringing more newborns into health facilities, combined with the China-Gavi Program's efforts to ensure that timely birth dose coverage in all hospitals exceeded 95 percent, led to the dramatic overall increase in the coverage rates of newborns across China.[60]

Implications for Global Health

Policymakers recognize that people generally underinvest in preventive care. Because such underinvestment is often more pronounced among the poor, many policymakers have concluded that public funding of immunization is the most equitable way to finance essential immunization.[61] Yet China, with a population of 1.3 billion, only recently waived fees for key preventive care measures such as hep B vaccination. The engagement of Gavi and partner organizations helped catalyze this policy change, which reduced the hep B threat and increased health equity.

The China-Gavi experience illustrates how a relatively short-term program can catalyze large-scale change and national commitment. In 2004, the government of China supported just 27 percent of total hep B immunization costs.[62] The central government now absorbs the largest cost components of hep B prevention nationally: hep B vaccines, syringes, and provider fees. Training, supervision, and monitoring are all integrated into the routine immunization program.

China has since graduated from Gavi support. The country's booming economy means that per capita GDP now far exceeds the Gavi eligibility threshold of US$1,500. But the China-Gavi Program experience nevertheless yields lessons for Gavi and national governments on overcoming inequity in vaccine access. In middle-income countries such as China, using money and support to stimulate policy change can have national health impacts. The program also sheds light on how global health funders like Gavi can leverage their comparative advantages to achieve massive impact in middle-income countries. Gavi support—by providing a modest amount of resources for activities—stimulated policy changes on fees and the regulation of domestic manufacturing. These lessons may aid the rollout of other "new generation" vaccines for diseases such as pneumococcal disease in countries that will also soon graduate from Gavi support. Other aspects of the operational model, such as comanagement of the program by domestic and international coordinators, could also prove relevant elsewhere.[63]

Still, challenges remain. Rates of liver cancer are expected to dramatically decline as immunized Chinese children age, yet the vaccine will not help the estimated 93 million men and women already living with chronic hep B—and as of 2015, the government offered neither hep B screening nor treatment programs nationwide.[64] The timely birth dose remains difficult to deliver in some rural areas where home births are common.[65] In addition, hep B vaccine coverage remains low among adults, in large part due to remaining health user fees and travel costs.[66]

As a model for public health prevention, the China-Gavi Program offers relevant operational lessons on how to tackle inequity by building bridges between underserved people and lifesaving technologies. To reach the poorest, health advocates hope the program's experience will inspire China's EPI managers and senior health leaders to adopt and integrate a broader set of WHO-recommended vaccines into routine immunization programs, such as vaccines that protect against rotavirus, *Haemophilus influenzae* type B, and pneumococcal disease—vaccines that are licensed and widely used in China but are available only to those who can afford them.

REFERENCES

Chee, Grace, Zheng Xie, and Sharon Nakhimovsky. 2012. *Evaluation of GAVI–Government of China Hepatitis B Vaccination Program.* Bethesda, MD: Abt Associates. http://www.gavi.org/results/evaluations/evaluation-of-the-gavi-government-of-china-hepatitis-b-vaccination-programme/.

England, Sarah, Miloud Kaddar, Ashok Nigam, and Matilde Pinto. 2001. *Practice and Policies on User Fees for Immunization in Developing Countries.* Geneva: Department of Vaccines and Biologicals, World Health Organization. http://apps.who.int/iris/bitstream/10665/66712/1/WHO_V-B_01.07_eng.pdf.

Fan, Jin-Hu, Jian-Bing Wang, Yong Biang, Wang Xiang, Hao Liang, Wen-Qiang Wei, and Paolo Boffetta. 2013. "Attributable Causes of Liver Cancer Mortality and Incidence in China." *Asian Pacific Journal of Cancer Prevention* 14 (12): 7251–56. doi:10.7314/APJCP.2013.14.12.7251.

Fuqiang, Cui. 2013. "Scaling Up Hepatitis B Vaccination with the Support of GAVI in China: Lessons Learned for Introduction of New Vaccines and for the Future of Hepatitis B Control." PhD diss., Faculty of Science, University of Basel. http://edoc.unibas.ch/29237/.

Gavi. 2014. "Mission Indicators." In *GAVI Alliance 2013 Progress Report.* Geneva: Gavi. http://gaviprogressreport.org/2013/mission-indicators/.

———. 2016. "History of Gavi." Accessed February 9. http://www.gavialliance.org/about/mission/history/.

Hadler, Stephen C., Cui Fuqiang, Francisco Averhoff, Thomas Taylor, Wang Fuzhen, Li Li, Liang Xiaofeng, and Yang Weizhong. 2013. "The Impact of Hepatitis B Vaccine in

REFERENCES, *continued*

China and in the China GAVI Project." *Vaccine* 31 (Suppl 9): J66–72.

Hutton, David W., Samuel K. So, and Margaret L. Brandeau. 2010. "Cost-Effectiveness of Nationwide Hepatitis B Catch-Up Vaccination among Children and Adolescents in China." *Hepatology* 51 (2): 405–14. doi:10.1002/hep.23310.

Kane, M.A., S.C. Hadler, L. Lee, C.N. Shapiro, F. Cui, X. Wang, and R. Kumar. 2013. "The Inception, Achievements, and Implications of the China GAVI Alliance Project on Hepatitis B Immunization." *Vaccine* 31 (Suppl 9): J15–20.

Liang, Xiaofeng, Shengli Bi, Weizhong Yang, Longde Wang, Gang Cui, Fuqiang Cui, Yong Zhang, et al. 2009. "Epidemiological Setosurvey of Hepatitis B in China: Declining HBV Prevalence Due to Hepatitis B Vaccination." *Vaccine* 31: J21–J28.

Liang, X., F. Cui, S. Hadler, X. Wang, H. Luo, Y. Chen, M. Kane, C. Shapiro, W. Yang, and Y. Wang. 2013. "Origins, Design and Implementation of the China GAVI Project." *Vaccine* 31 (Suppl 9): J8–14. doi:10.1016/j.vaccine.2012.12.019.

Mirelman, Andrew, Amanda Glassman, and Miriam Temin. 2016. *Estimating the Avertable Disease Burden and Cost-Effectiveness in* Millions Saved *Third Edition.* CGD Working Paper. Washington, DC: Center for Global Development.

Ndumbe, P. 1996. "Childhood Vaccination: Achievements and Challenges." *Africa Health* 18 (6): 18–19.

PATH. "Using Auto-Disable Syringes." n.d. Accessed February 8, 2016. http://www.path.org/publications/files/SafeInjPDF-Module5.pdf.

Simonsen, L., A. Kane, J. Lloyd, M. Zaffran, and M. Kane. 1999. "Unsafe Injections in the Developing World and Transmission of Bloodborne Pathogens: A Review." *Bulletin of the World Health Organization* 77 (10): 789–800.

Smith, Richard D. 2006. "Responding to Global Infectious Disease Outbreaks: Lessons from SARS on the Role of Risk Perception, Communication and Management." *Social Science and Medicine* 63 (12): 3113–23. doi:10.1016/j.socscimed.2006.08.004.

Song, Guang-jun, Bo Feng, Hui-ying Rao, and Lai Wei. 2013. "Etiological Features of Cirrhosis Inpatients in Beijing, China." *Chinese Medical Journal* 126 (13): 2430–34.

WHO (World Health Organization). 2010. "Hepatitis B Vaccines: WHO Position Paper—Recommendations." *Vaccine* 28 (3): 589–90. doi:10.1016/j.vaccine.2009.10.110.

———. 2015a. "Emergencies Preparedness, Response: Hepatitis B." Accessed June 22. http://www.who.int/csr/disease/hepatitis/whocdscsrlyo20022/en/index3.html?

———. 2015b. "Hepatitis B." Fact Sheet 204. Updated July. http://www.who.int/mediacentre/factsheets/fs204/en/.

WHO China. 2003. *Public Health Options for China: Using the Lessons Learned from SARS.* Beijing: WHO China.

WHO, UNICEF (United Nation's Children Fund), Global Alliance for Vaccines and Immunization, Japan International Cooperation Agency, and US Centers for Disease Control and Prevention. 2005. *2004 International Review of the Expanded Programme on Immunizations (EPI) in China.* Beijing: Beijing Reizhe Publishing House.

WHO, UNICEF, and World Bank. 2009. *State of the World's Vaccines and Immunization.* 3rd ed. Geneva: WHO. http://www.unicef.org/media/files/SOWVI_full_report_english_LR1.pdf.

Zhou, Yuqing, Wang Huaqing, Jinshan Zheng, Xu Zhu, Wei Xia, and David B. Hipgrave. 2009. "Coverage of and Influences on Timely Administration of Hepatitis B Vaccines Birth Dose in Remote Rural Areas of the People's Republic of China." *American Journal of Tropical Medicine and Hygiene* 81 (5): 869–74. doi:10.4269/ajtmh.2009.09-0238.

Zhu, D., J. Wang, and K.R. Wangen. 2014. "Hepatitis B Vaccination Coverage Rates among Adults in Rural China: Are Economic Barriers Relevant?" *Vaccine* 32 (49): 6705–10. doi:10.1016/j.vaccine.2013.06.095.

ENDNOTES

1. WHO (2015b).
2. Fan et al. (2013); Song et al. (2013).
3. WHO (2015b).
4. WHO (2015a).
5. Kane et al. (2013).
6. WHO (2015b).
7. The other two doses are typically given at one month and six months of age.
8. WHO (2010).
9. Ndumbe (1996).
10. WHO, UNICEF, and World Bank (2009); Gavi (2015).
11. Gavi (2015).
12. Gavi (2015).
13. Gavi (2015).
14. Gavi (2015).
15. Initially called the Global Alliance for Vaccines and Immunization.
16. Gavi (2014).
17. Stephano Malvolti, personal communication with the author, August 14, 2014.
18. Kane et al. (2013).
19. Kane et al. (2013).
20. Zhou et al. (2009).
21. Chee, Xie, and Nakhimovsky (2012).
22. Kane et al. (2013).

ENDNOTES, *continued*

23. Fuqiang (2013).
24. Fuqiang (2013); Kane et al. (2013).
25. England et al. (2001).
26. Kane et al. (2013); Zhou et al. (2009).
27. Kane et al. (2013).
28. Kane et al. (2013).
29. At the time of Gavi's initiation, an estimated 12 billion injections per year occurred, of which 40–60 percent were considered unsafe (Simonsen et al. 1999). For more about the importance of using auto-disable syringes, see PATH (n.d.).
30. Stephano Malvolti, personal communication with the author, August 14, 2014.
31. Other program design elements that differ from typical Gavi arrangements include (1) engagement of an international program manager, (2) cofunding from the grant recipient country from the outset, and (3) program oversight by an organizational advisory committee.
32. Chee, Xie, and Nakhimovsky (2012).
33. Chee, Xie, and Nakhimovsky (2012).
34. Liang et al. (2013).
35. Liang et al. (2013).
36. Liang et al. (2013).
37. Hadler et al. (2013).
38. Hadler et al. (2013).
39. Kane et al. (2013).
40. Chee, Xie, and Nakhimovsky (2012).
41. Kane et al. (2013).
42. 2013.
43. Liang et al. (2009).
44. Liang et al. (2013).
45. Chee, Xie, and Nakhimovsky (2012); Kane et al. (2013).
46. Liang et al. (2013).
47. Hadler et al. (2013).
48. The estimation of the averted disease burden in DALYs used an assessment of program impact (Hadler et al. 2013) and estimates of the distribution of hepatocellular carcinoma, cirrhosis, and fulminant infection and associated DALY parameters such as disability weights and disease duration. Total program costs were derived from the same impact evaluation (Hadler et al. 2013). See Mirelman, Glassman, and Temin (2016).
49. Hutton, So, and Brandeau (2010).
50. Kane et al. (2013).
51. Chee, Xie, and Nakhimovsky (2012).
52. Liang Xiaofeng and Cui Fuqiang, personal communication with the author, October 27–30, 2014; Stephen Hadler, personal communication with the author, October–December 2014.
53. Chee, Xie, and Nakhimovsky (2012).
54. Chee, Xie, and Nakhimovsky (2012).
55. Chee, Xie, and Nakhimovsky (2012).
56. Chee, Xie, and Nakhimovsky (2012).
57. Kane et al. (2013); WHO et al. (2005); WHO China (2003). An outbreak of SARS, a viral respiratory disease, in southern China from November 2002 to July 2003 caused more than 8,000 infections and 775 deaths in 37 countries (Smith 2006). Although SARS placed an unexpected strain on Chinese health administration staff and delayed China-Gavi Program implementation, over time the outbreak provided some benefit to the hep B vaccine rollout. SARS helped elevate the position of health on the national agenda and stimulated increased public funding for health activities.
58. Kane et al. (2013); Lisa Lee, personal communication with the author, October 27–29, 2014.
59. Kane et al. (2013).
60. Stephen Hadler, personal communication with the author, October–December 2014.
61. England et al. (2001).
62. Chee, Xie, and Nakhimovsky (2012).
63. Kane et al. (2013).
64. Kane et al. (2013).
65. Kane et al. (2013).
66. Zhu, Wang, and Wangen (2014).

CASE 4

One Mosquito at a Time
Zambia's National Malaria Control Program

The Case at a Glance

HEALTH GOAL: To prevent and control malaria.

STRATEGY: Comprehensive national program to prevent and control malaria using insecticide-treated nets, indoor residual spraying, rapid diagnostic tests, and combination therapy drugs.

HEALTH IMPACT: Parasitemia dropped from 22 percent to 15 percent and incidence of severe anemia decreased from 14 percent in 2006 to 9 percent in 2012 in children under five. Under-five mortality dropped from 168 per 1,000 in 2006 to 109 per 1,000 in 2012. Saved 33,000 children's lives from 2001 to 2010.

WHY IT WORKED: Committed leadership. Multisectorial partnerships with significant private-sector involvement. Multifaceted, comprehensive program. Strong monitoring and evaluation.

FINANCING: Program budget was US$60 million in 2008. Cost-effectiveness ratio: US$13.50 per disability-adjusted life year averted from 2001 to 2010.

SCALE: National.

In South America, Southeast Asia, and sub-Saharan Africa, a tiny mosquito can harbor an enormous health risk. Its bite might seem harmless, but if it carries one of five *Plasmodium* protozoa, the parasites that cause malaria, paralyzing fatigue and headaches may soon strike. As with a terrible case of the flu, an infected individual's muscles and joints will ache while chills run through the body; vomiting or diarrhea may follow, especially in children. Without prompt treatment, those symptoms are likely to intensify, leading to neurologic, metabolic, and respiratory problems, and sometimes even death.

After the failed eradication campaigns of the 1960s and 1970s, the global malaria response floundered for decades. Yet since the turn of the 21st century, malaria control has experienced a renaissance commensurate with the enormous burden it represents in so many countries. Malaria control has attracted major aid commitments; since the 1990s, total international investments for malaria have exceeded those addressing all other health areas except for HIV/AIDS and maternal, newborn, and child health. Those big bucks complemented

high-level political and institutional commitment, including the launch of Roll Back Malaria in 1998, inclusion in the Millennium Development Goals in 2000, and the founding of the Global Fund to Fight AIDS, Tuberculosis and Malaria (Global Fund) in 2002.

Zambia's malaria program has been one of the most successful within this global movement. In 2000, Zambia implemented a formal, coordinated National Malaria Control Program (NMCP). The ambitious program included efforts to eradicate mosquitoes that carry the malaria parasite through measures such as distributing insecticide-treated nets (the Zambian government was among the first to distribute free bed nets at scale), conducting indoor residual spraying (treatment of indoor surfaces with insecticide), and introducing rapid diagnostic tests and combination drug therapies. It also implemented education and behavioral change communication strategies and embraced coordination with nongovernmental organizations (NGOs).

Today, significantly fewer Zambian children harbor the malaria parasite or die from the disease as compared with the 1990s. But the country is not completely immune

This case was originally authored by Lauren Post (initial draft by Yuna Sakuma).

to outbreaks. In fact, a major resurgence of malaria in 2009 and 2010 put the government's program to the test. Zambia rose to the occasion, effectively detecting, addressing, and ultimately overcoming the new resurgence of the deadly disease.

The Toll of Malaria

Malaria is caused by the bite of an infected female mosquito of the *Anopheles* genus, which transmits the *Plasmodium* parasite along with an itchy welt. Most high-income and several low- and middle-income countries with temperate climates have managed to eliminate malaria, while the remaining endemic areas are disproportionately poor and vulnerable.[1] More than half of all malaria deaths in 2000 were concentrated among the poorest 20 percent of people—the highest association with poverty of any disease of global public health importance.[2]

Children are particularly vulnerable. It is said that somewhere in the world, malaria kills a child every 30 seconds.[3] In 2000, this meant that worldwide, malaria accounted for 8 percent of infant mortality.[4] In sub-Saharan Africa, the immense malaria burden led to the deaths of an estimated 800,000 children under five in that year alone.

In 2000, Zambia, a low-income country in southern Africa, saw 3.3 million confirmed or presumed malaria cases among its population of about 10 million.[5] Malaria claimed more than 17,000 Zambian lives that year, mostly young children; it was the leading cause of childhood death.[6] Beyond its health impact, malaria also impeded Zambia's economic development. Frequent malaria illness and death among Zambians working in the country's copper mines—a major contributor to the Zambian economy—led to high rates of absenteeism, on-site injuries, and the costly need to replace staff.[7] This suppressed productivity and hamstrung the industry, slowing the country's economic growth.[8]

Putting an Idea in Motion: Zambia Goes All In with Proven Approaches

By 1990, malaria control in Zambia had hit a wall. Zambians recognized malaria as a killer disease, but few took measures to prevent it. The mining industry had shut down its indoor residual spraying efforts, previously the mainstay of the country's malaria control effort. Falling copper prices and rising oil prices had made spraying unaffordable for the mining companies.[9]

Treatment programs were also patchy. An erratic supply of medicines meant that rural areas frequently experienced stockouts. Even when drugs were available, they might not work: researchers in the Ministry of Health's malaria unit had started to notice a concerning resistance to chloroquine, the first-line antimalarial medication. Problems were not isolated to Zambia; most other countries where malaria was endemic faced similar challenges.

In the 1990s, stubborn malaria epidemics like Zambia's finally inspired global momentum for action. In 1998, Dr. Gro Harlem Brundtland, incoming director general of the World Health Organization (WHO), announced her intent to make "rolling back malaria" one of her top priorities.[10] Other international leaders heeded her call, and the Roll Back Malaria Partnership was launched later that year by the WHO, the United Nations Children's Fund (UNICEF), the United Nations Development Programme, and the World Bank. In 2000, 44 high-level country delegations gathered in Abuja, Nigeria, for the African Summit on Roll Back Malaria. The resultant Abuja Declaration reinvigorated the political will to pursue malaria control and created a benchmark to hold governments accountable.

That same year, a new report described a threefold jump in malaria incidence in Zambia since 1976, motivating the government to sign the Abuja Declaration. With its signature, the government committed to reaching 60 percent coverage of the population with malaria prevention and treatment measures by 2005. To do so, the government established a new National Malaria Control Center (NMCC) and laid the foundation for a reinvigorated malaria control program.

To roll out proven interventions in Zambia, the NMCC joined forces with churches, mission hospitals, NGOs, and service groups such as the Red Cross Society.[11] Zambia's mining and agriculture companies agreed to take action to complement and strengthen the government program. The Mopani and Konkola copper-mining companies and Zambia Sugar, with a combined total of 30,000 employees, distributed insecticide-treated nets, conducted indoor residual spraying, and offered testing at their company clinics.

The program's early success inspired donor support, which helped the government scale up efforts and implement its strategic plans. In 2003, the United States Agency for International Development (USAID) and the Global Fund made their first investments in the country program. They were joined in 2005 by the World Bank and the Malaria Control and Evaluation Partnership in Africa (MACEPA, a PATH program funded by the Bill & Melinda Gates Foundation), and in 2007 by the President's Malaria Initiative, a five-year, US$1.2 billion African initiative launched by US president George W. Bush.

The Malaria Plan in Action

The national strategy laid out four proven interventions to fight malaria (see Box 1): insecticide-treated nets (ITNs), indoor residual spraying (IRS), rapid diagnostic tests (RDTs), and combination therapy drugs. For all four components of the program, effective delivery proved essential to achieving impact at scale.

Bed net distribution became a core plank in the ministry's strategy. Health workers were sent door to door in at-risk communities to deliver free ITNs in time to beat the peak malaria transmission season, while clinics supplemented mass campaigns with routine ITN distribution to pregnant women and young children. MACEPA tested centralized versus district-level systems for distributing ITNs and found that distribution directly to districts was more practical and less costly.[12] Thus, ITNs went out at the district level, enabling streamlined and widespread coverage in previously underserved areas.

Staff delivered up to 20 times as many ITNs than in earlier years, reaching a high of nearly three million in 2012.[13] By this time, nearly two-thirds of Zambian households had at least one ITN.[14] However, net ownership is no guarantee of remaining malaria-free; the nets are only effective when used properly. Malaria surveys show that the number of nets distributed or owned does not necessarily correlate to the number of women and children who sleep under them.[15] In Zambia, community volunteers, including many members of the Anglican church, were entrusted with ensuring proper net installation and use. The government also participated. In Mongu, the capital of Western Province, one government official even threatened to confiscate any bed nets that were used as fishing nets or wedding dresses.[16]

IRS was another weapon in the fight against mosquitoes. Between 2008 and 2010, IRS protected at least five million Zambians each year.[17] IRS initially targeted densely populated urban areas and was later expanded to half of all districts nationwide.[18] The mining industry restarted IRS in 2000 along with renewed bed net distribution.

Zambian health officials next turned their attention to diagnosis, testing, and treatment. The NMCC and district health management teams distributed more than two million RDTs annually between 2008 and 2010, enabling health centers to diagnose suspected cases without charging for the tests. In rural areas, community health workers were taught to use the tests and dispense appropriate drugs, helping prevent misdiagnosis of other fevers and misuse of malaria medicine.

To counteract emerging drug resistance to older malaria medications, Zambia was among the first countries to introduce artemisinin-based combination therapies, first cautiously and then nationwide by 2005.[19] Meanwhile, prenatal clinics delivered intermittent preventive treatment in pregnancy, reaching 70 percent of pregnant women in prenatal care by 2010.[20]

Box 1. Components of Zambia's Malaria Prevention and Treatment Strategy

Insecticide-treated net (ITN): A mesh cloth, usually designed to cover a bed and create a physical barrier from mosquitoes. It further protects by killing mosquitoes on contact with the material. Since 2007, all ITNs distributed in Zambia have been long-lasting insecticidal nets, with insecticide in or around the fibers of the mesh.

Indoor residual spraying (IRS): A process of spraying long-acting chemical insecticides on the walls and roofs of homes. When a mosquito lands on any sprayed surface, it dies. IRS loses its effectiveness within a year, so the spraying is typically done annually before peak malaria season.

Rapid diagnostic tests (RDTs): Test cards that can determine the presence of the malaria parasite in a small sample of blood in about 20 minutes.

Combination therapy drugs: Resistance to malaria monotherapies such as chloroquine led the WHO to recommend combination therapies such as artemisinin-based combination therapies (ACTs) and intermittent preventive treatment in pregnancy (IPTp) as first-line treatments. ACT is the recommended treatment for *P. falciparum* malaria, the most common type of malaria in Africa. IPTp is an antimalarial combination drug for malaria prevention administered specifically to pregnant women during prenatal visits.

However, persistent supply chain problems led to frequent shortages and stockouts, posing a major barrier to RDT and drug distribution. To address this problem, the Ministry of Health, with support from the US government and the World Bank, designed and piloted two new supply chain systems in 2009. First, the project team tried placing a commodity planner at the district level to oversee district-level orders. It also tried instructing health facilities to submit orders directly to the central pharmacy. An impact assessment found that the second model was more cost-effective and efficient at relieving district-level bottlenecks. After one year, the second model dramatically reduced the stockout rate, from 48 percent to 6 percent for adult treatments and from 43 percent to 12 percent for pediatric treatments, thus significantly increasing the availability lifesaving drugs.[21]

Complementing its prevention and treatment activities, the government also mounted a public education campaign. To ensure that rural Zambians did not miss out on critical information, the government recruited health workers, church volunteers, and radio stations to promote behavior change. Community leaders learned to disseminate key messages, such as the importance of proper bed net use and what to do with a feverish child. They also learned how to dispel common myths, for example, the idea that malaria infection confers future immunity (it does not), or that malaria can be treated without drugs (it cannot).

A sophisticated malaria tracking system enabled the government to monitor progress and adjust its strategy as needed. In 2006, Zambia became the first country to conduct a Malaria Indicator Survey (MIS), a tool developed by Roll Back Malaria with support from USAID through its Demographic and Health Surveys Program.[22] To compile information for the biannual MIS, trained survey administrators blanketed the country, including remote rural areas. Dressed in orange T-shirts and traveling by bike, truck, and occasionally oxcart, the workers went door to door to survey households, to test and treat families, and to record their findings.[23] Collection of reliable data was challenging—access to transportation was a constant struggle and data were self-reported—but in spite of difficulties, Zambia's four biannual MIS surveys have provided valuable information to guide resource allocation.

In 2009 and 2010, the MIS revealed an alarming trend: rates of malaria and severe anemia had surged in Eastern, Luapula, and Northern provinces. The upswing was partially attributable to supply chain problems resulting from a drop in funding.[24] Procurement and implementation support was delayed in these areas, and ITNs had failed to show up where needed.[25] When the resurgence came to light, the Ministry of Health took action. By 2011, health officials had reestablished donor funding to fill the financial gap, enabling Zambia to distribute the needed ITNs in affected areas.

The Payoff: Fewer Bites, Healthier Children

Routine monitoring and evaluation show that Zambia's efforts have paid off, and malaria-specific health indicators have improved. Between 2006 and 2012, the share of children under five with malaria parasites in their blood dropped from 22 percent to 15 percent. At the same time, the share of children under five with severe anemia[26]—another metric because malaria parasites destroy red blood cells—decreased from 14 percent to 9 percent.[27] Most important, by 2008 the number of malaria deaths reported by health facilities had plunged by 66 percent compared with the number reported in 2000.[28]

Because malaria takes such a heavy toll on young children, successful malaria control would be expected to translate into better child survival. Indeed, expansion of the NMCP coincided with substantial reductions in child mortality, from 168 per 1,000 in 2001 to 109 per 1,000 in 2010.[29] The correlation between the two is compelling, although not conclusive (see Box 2).

Why don't we know for sure? Although the malaria community accepts all-cause child mortality as a robust measure, child mortality is a notoriously difficult metric.[30] Accurate statistics rely on birth and death registration, but underregistration is common in low-income countries. In such settings, infant and child mortality rates are typically estimated on the basis of survey and census data. Yet this approach is also problematic; such surveys are infrequent and rely on self-reporting.[31] Further, there are methodological difficulties in measuring cause-specific infant and child mortality rates. The causes of mortality are multifactorial—a child's death can result from numerous genetic and environmental factors—and it is difficult to tease out the precise cause of death.[32]

Even though it is not possible to attribute Zambia's shrinking all-cause child mortality to malaria control, modeling tools can help estimate the attributable impact. Prominent among these is a modeling software called the Lives Saved Tool (LiST).[33] Developed at Johns Hopkins University, LiST is used to estimate the number of lives saved among children under five according to the estimated impact of specific interventions. According to LiST,

Box 2. Strength of the Evidence

All-cause child mortality (ACCM) is a metric commonly used in malaria control programs because it accounts for deaths that are both directly and indirectly attributable to malaria, including via anemia and low birth weight.[35] It allows researchers to establish a correlation between ITN rollout and under-five mortality. But given that ACCM is an all-encompassing estimate that responds to various changes to the health system, it is difficult to attribute changes in health to an individual intervention.

Zambia's ACCM was likely influenced by other changes under way during the malaria program's scale-up. In 2004, funds started flowing from the President's Emergency Plan for AIDS Relief (PEPFAR) for HIV prevention, treatment, and care. Other child health interventions such as the pentavalent vaccine, the promotion of exclusive breast-feeding during a child's first six months of life, and tuberculosis interventions were also introduced.[36] The reduction in malaria may have decreased morbidity and mortality rates for other diseases and vice versa, but it is not possible to establish this with precision.[37]

The evidence does not enable a definitive statement on the impact of malaria control interventions on Zambian children's health. This is a common problem in the malaria world: specific interventions are proved efficacious in study circumstances, but national programs do not undergo experimental impact evaluations to show that interventions are effective at a large scale and are therefore a worthwhile investment relative to the resources required. Few studies of national malaria programs are randomized or designed with a counterfactual that would enable the attribution of a change in health status to a particular intervention. One reason is that some people consider it unethical to withhold, for the purposes of evaluation, interventions that are likely to be lifesaving. In Zambia, there have been trials with a control arm, but sample sizes were small, making it difficult to extrapolate results nationally.[38] The sum result is that it is impossible to know whether, for example, child immunizations were the driver of a decrease in child mortality in Zambia or whether the driver was the malaria program.

Some studies have attempted to isolate the impact of ITNs in other settings. A 2014 World Bank paper[39] used a decomposition method (a method that isolates the "explained" portion of a mortality reduction) to analyze the drivers of child mortality reduction in Kenya. Using Demographic and Health Survey (DHS) data, the authors showed that increased ITN ownership in malaria-endemic areas from 2003 to 2008 was responsible for as much as 58 percent of the total decline in the infant mortality rate and 39 percent of the postneonatal mortality decline. The study used DHS data to estimate the impact at a national level. It did not cover the details of ITN delivery, which leaves readers guessing as to exactly what made Kenya's antimalaria effort a success. Combining a similar study design with Zambia's relatively well-documented program could help better illuminate the specific contribution of ITNs to the decline in ACCM.

malaria control interventions saved the lives of 33,000 Zambian children under five between 2001 and 2010.[34]

Some of the strongest evidence of success comes from the efforts of mining and agriculture companies to serve rural communities that otherwise would lack access to lifesaving interventions. In their company clinics, Mopani Copper Mines, Konkola Copper Mines, and Zambia Sugar decreased recorded malaria cases by an astounding 94 percent.[40] Likewise, Dunavant Cotton saw a 45 percent reduction in the burden of malaria within the provinces where it distributed ITNs.[41]

Gains at What Price?

The Zambian government's funding for health is trending in the right direction: the government increased its health budget from US$270 million in 2007 to US$380 million in 2009, when it accounted for nearly 12 percent of the total budget.[42] The budget does not break down the amount spent on malaria and other specific diseases.[43]

The NMCC strategic plans define the cost of the malaria control program. In 2008, for example, the NMCC budgeted US$60 million for Zambia's national malaria program, which included external funding and US$25 million from the Ministry of Health. A little more than half of the total amount budgeted was allocated to ITNs; 15 percent was allocated to IRS, 9 percent to treatment, 5 percent to RDTs, and the remainder to other program costs.[44]

Between 2003 and 2010, external donor funding for Zambia's NMCP totaled nearly US$200 million—more than 60 percent of the program's total malaria financing over that time period. This sum included support for the costs of nets, insecticides, diagnostics, and antimalarial medications.

Zambia's private sector also contributed directly to malaria control. According to one study, Dunavant Cotton's malaria control campaign cost approximately US$5 per net, or US$0.21 per malaria case averted.[45] Using a conservative fatality rate of 1 death per 1,000 cases, the study estimates that the program cost US$210 per malaria death averted, making it highly cost-effective in terms of WHO guidelines. Even better, the study found that malaria control programs run by the Mopani and Konkola copper-mining companies and Zambia Sugar were actually cost saving, resulting in a 76 percent decrease in malaria-related spending at their company clinics— roughly two dollars saved for every dollar invested.[46]

Analysis conducted for *Millions Saved* assessed cases and deaths averted among children under five in Zambia between 2001 and 2010 (see Figure 1). The researchers estimated the cost-effectiveness ratio to be about US$13.50 for each disability-adjusted life year averted.[47]

The Keys to Lasting Success

Earlier malaria control strategies in Zambia, as in other countries, focused on killing mosquitoes using a single approach, such as IRS, with limited success.[48] Zambia's new strategy was multifaceted and comprehensive,

including a blend of proven interventions. It stressed both prevention and treatment, and included a monitoring and evaluation system that enabled data-driven decision making. Thus far, all signs point to its enduring success; even when faced with challenges, Zambia's consistent and coordinated efforts have helped the country overcome barriers and roll back malaria.

From the start, a committed government drove the program. A senior Ministry of Health official attributed the success to strong internal leadership, beginning with ministry staff and the ministerial task force, who were swift to initiate central and district-level action such as expanded grants to districts and the elimination of taxes on malaria control tools.[49] In a public show of support, President Rupia Banda donned malaria control T-shirts when appearing in public, had his own house sprayed, and made a high-profile request to accelerate bed net distribution.[50]

Broader health sector changes also helped, such as adapting national policies to WHO-recommended medications and removing taxes and tariffs on malaria commodities. The overall health budget increased in 2000, and in that same year health financing was decentralized so that districts had greater control over a larger pool of resources. The elimination of health user fees for primary care in most rural areas in 2006 helped expand access to the most vulnerable residents.[51]

Although the Zambian government led the charge against malaria, the strategy could not have succeeded without its diverse partners. Roll Back Malaria staff provided essential assistance to Zambia's NMCC in drafting the National Malaria Strategic Plan, which over time attracted funds from several donors, in particular the US President's Malaria Initiative and the Global Fund. Partners such as MACEPA and the World Bank also helped the government experiment with different approaches to delivering nets, diagnostic tests, and antimalarial drugs. This preparation ensured that the NMCC rolled out its program in the most effective, efficient, and cost-effective manner. And on the ground, community participation—from private

Figure 1. Lives of Children under Five Saved by Malaria Prevention in Zambia, 2001–2010

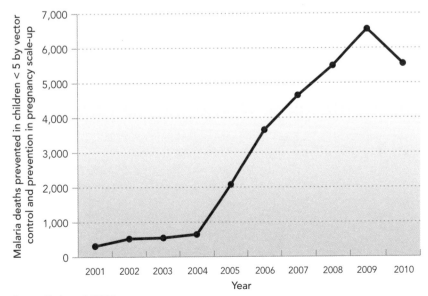

Source: Eisele et al. (2012).

businesses to NGOs and community health workers—complemented government efforts and proved critical to the program's overall success, particularly in rural areas.

Finally, Zambia's program emphasized monitoring and evaluation from the start, which helped health officials uncover problems and attract donor funding. Tracking mechanisms were in place early to ensure collection of the "right" data, such as whether households used ITNs correctly and consistently to prevent malaria infection. Furthermore, strong malaria monitoring and evaluation has led to positive spillovers for the country's overall health data system. In 2009, training workshops on data collection, analysis, and verification, supported by MACEPA, the World Bank, and the NMCC, yielded accurate, comprehensive malaria statistics.[52] Since then, the Ministry of Health has continued to facilitate similar workshops, strengthening local capacity for health data collection and analysis across a wider range of health indicators.

Implications for Global Health

International donors have dedicated significant resources to preventing and treating malaria: globally, funding reached US$2.1 billion in 2013.[53] Several African governments have also increased their resources to fight diseases such as malaria, although only South Africa and Rwanda have achieved the Abuja Declaration target of earmarking 15 percent of the government budget for the health sector.[54]

Increased funding has driven global gains. According to the WHO World Malaria Report for 2014, the number of malaria cases is down dramatically: 45 million fewer people were infected than in 2000.[55] Yet 128 million malaria cases in 2013 show clearly that the battle against the *Plasmodium* parasite is not over. And the resurgence of malaria in several districts of Zambia offers a sobering reminder of how fragile malaria gains can be. Even countries that have effectively eliminated malaria—including countries as diverse as Egypt and Georgia[56]—must actively guard against resurgence.

The experience of Zambia, one of the first African countries to scale up malaria control, yields important lessons on the delivery of a multifaceted, comprehensive national malaria program. For example, one important early step was the establishment of a coordination system between the central and lower levels of governments and between the government and donor organizations.

Zambia's experience also shows how, under the right circumstances, malaria control can go hand in hand with broader efforts to strengthen a country's health system by means of intensified surveillance, solid supply chains, and clear clinical guidelines for the treatment of common maladies. Still, there are valid concerns that a vertical program like malaria control that targets a specific health condition can crowd out or divert funds from primary healthcare delivery and other routine services. For example, one study found that Zambia's gains in malaria control interventions coincided with weaker routine polio immunization in some districts.[57]

Zimbabwe, which borders Zambia, may reap the benefits of lessons learned from its neighbor across the Zambezi River. In 2013, Zimbabwe and Zambia entered into a cross-border malaria initiative to coordinate malaria control interventions.[58] Both countries hope that synchronized efforts and consolidated policies—from rollout to measurement—will accelerate their efforts to eliminate malaria.

Zambia continues to work toward its ultimate goal of malaria elimination and is well on its way, having surpassed its 2000 Abuja Declaration commitment to halve malaria mortality. Zambians' proactive fight against malaria provides grounds for optimism. The country's success shows that with leadership, tools, support, and partners, even low-income countries can successfully take on the malaria menace.

REFERENCES

Against Malaria Foundation. "About Malaria." 2015. Accessed October 9. http://www.againstmalaria.com/faq_malaria.aspx.

Alarcon, Diana. 2007. "The Challenges of Measuring Child Mortality When Birth Registration Is Incomplete." Paper presented at the Global Forum on Gender Statistics, Rome. http://www.academia.edu/1554703/The_Challenges_of_measuring_child_mortality_when_birth_registration_is_incomplete.

Ashraf, Nava, Günther Fink, and David Weil. 2010. *Evaluating the Effects of Large Scale Health Interventions in Developing Countries: The Zambian Malaria Initiative.* Working Paper 16069. Cambridge, MA: National Bureau of Economic Research. http://www.nber.org/papers/w16069.pdf.

Barat, Lawrence M. 2006. "Four Malaria Success Stories: How Malaria Burden Was Successfully Reduced in Brazil, Eritrea, India, and Vietnam." *American Journal of Tropical Medicine and Hygiene* 74 (1): 12–16.

Carasso, Barbara S., Mylene Lagarde, Caesar Cheelo, Collins Chansa, and Natasha Palmer. 2012. "Health Worker Perspectives on User Fee Removal in Zambia." *Human Resources for Health* 10 (1): 40. doi:10.1186/1478-4491-10-40.

Chizema-Kawesha, E., J.M. Miller, R.W. Steketee, V.M. Mukonka, C. Mukuka, A.D. Mohamed, S.K. Miti, and C.C. Campbell. 2010. "Scaling Up Malaria Control in Zambia: Progress and Impact 2005–2008." *American Journal of Tropical Medicine and Hygiene* 83 (3): 480–88. doi:10.4269/ajtmh.2010.10-0035.

Cohen, Justin M., David L. Smith, Chris Cotter, Abigail Ward, Gavin Yamey, Oliver J. Sabot, and Bruno Moonen. 2012. "Malaria Resurgence: A Systematic Review and Assessment of Its Causes." *Malaria Journal* 11 (1): 122. doi:10.1186/1475-2875-11-122.

Colson, Katherine Ellicott, Laura Dwyer-Lindgren, Tom Achoki, Nancy Fullman, Matthew Schneider, Peter Mulenga, Peter Hangoma, Marie Ng, Felix Masiye, and Emmanuela Gakidou. 2015. "Benchmarking Health System Performance across Districts in Zambia: A Systematic Analysis of Levels and Trends in Key Maternal and Child Health Interventions from 1990 to 2010." *BMC Medicine* 13 (1). doi:10.1186/s12916-015-0308-5.

Conteh, L., E. Sicuri, F. Manzi, G. Hutton, B. Obonyo, F. Ediosi, P. Biao, et al. 2010. "The Cost-Effectiveness of Intermittent Preventive Treatment for Malaria in Infants in Sub-Saharan Africa." *PLoS One* 5 (6): e10313. doi:10.1371/journal.pone.0010313.

Demombynes, G., and S.K. Trommlerova. 2010. *What Has Driven the Decline of Infant Mortality in Kenya?* Policy Research Working Paper WPS 60572010. Washington, DC: World Bank.

Eisele, Thomas P., David A. Larsen, Neff Walker, Richard E. Cibulskis, Joshua O. Yukich, Charlotte M. Zikusooka, and Richard W. Steketee. 2012. "Estimates of Child Deaths Prevented from Malaria Prevention Scale-Up in Africa 2001–2010." *Malaria Journal* 11 (1): 93. doi:10.1186/1475-2875-11-93.

Friends of the Global Fight Against AIDS, Tuberculosis and Malaria. n.d. *Innovation for Greater Impact: Exploring Resources for Domestic Health Funding in Africa.* Washington, DC: Friends of the Global Fight Against AIDS, Tuberculosis and Malaria.

Gerson, Michael. 2012. "It Takes More Than a Village to Fight Malaria in Zambia." *Washington Post*, April 5. http://www.washingtonpost.com/opinions/it-takes-more-than-a-village-to-fight-malaria-in-zambia/2012/04/05/gIQA7AwMyS_story.html.

Glassman, Amanda, and Yuna Sakuma. 2013. "How Many Bed Nets Equal a Life Saved? Why Results Matter for Value for Money." *Global Health Policy Blog,* Center for Global Development, September 27. use http://www.cgdev.org/blog/how-many-bed-nets-equal-life-saved-%E2%80%93-why-results-matter-value-money .

Guillot, Michael, and David R. Gwatkin. 1999. *The Burden of Disease among the Global Poor: Current Situation, Future Trends, and Implications for Strategy.* Washington, DC: World Bank. http://www-wds.worldbank.org/external/default/WDSContentServer/WDSP/IB/2004/09/16/000090341_20040916152915/Rendered/PDF/291820Burden0of0disease.pdf.

IHME (Institute for Health Metrics and Evaluation). 2015. GBD Compare. Accessed October 29. http://vizhub.healthdata.org/gbd-compare.

Kawesha, Elizabeth Chizema. 2013. "What Will It Take for Zambia to Eliminate Malaria?" Bill & Melinda Gates Foundation blog, May 16. http://www.impatientoptimists.org/Posts/2013/05/What-Will-it-Take-for-Zambia-to-Eliminate-Malaria.

Ministry of Health. 2012. Zambia National Malaria Indicator Survey 2012. Lusaka, Zambia: Government of the Republic of Zambia.

Mirelman, Andrew, Amanda Glassman, and Miriam Temin. 2016. *Estimating the Avertable Disease Burden and Cost-Effectiveness in* Millions Saved *Third Edition.* CGD Working Paper. Washington, DC: Center for Global Development.

NMCP (National Malaria Control Program). 2015. "Scaling Up Malaria Control in Zambia: Using Results to Inform Actions." Lusaka, Zambia: Ministry of Health. http://www.path.org/files/ZambiaFactSheet.pdf.

Oloo, James A. 2005. "Child Mortality in Developing Countries: Challenges and Policy Options." *Eastern Africa Social Science Research Review* 21 (2).

REFERENCES, *continued*

Packard, Randall M. 2010. *The Making of a Tropical Disease: A Short History of Malaria.* Baltimore, MD: Johns Hopkins University Press.

Ricci, Francesco. 2012. "Social Implications of Malaria and Their Relationships with Poverty." *Mediterranean Journal of Hematology and Infectious Diseases* 4 (1). doi:10.4084/MJHID.2012.048.

Roll Back Malaria. 2011a. *A Decade of Partnership and Results.* Progress and Impact Series 7. Geneva: Roll Back Malaria. http://www.rollbackmalaria.org/microsites/ProgressImpactSeries/docs/report8-en.pdf.

———. 2011b. *Focus on Zambia.* Progress and Impact Series 2. Geneva: Roll Back Malaria. http://www.rollbackmalaria.org/microsites/ProgressImpactSeries/docs/report7-en.pdf.

———. n.d. "Strengthening Systems for Distributing Insecticide-Treated Mosquito Nets in Zambia." http://www.rollbackmalaria.org/files/files/toolbox/docs/rbmtoolbox/tool_RBMIlinDistrToolkit1.pdf.

Rowe, Alexander K., Samantha Rowe, Robert W. Snow, Eline L. Korenromp, Joanna R.M. Armstrong Schellenberg, Claudia Stein, Bernard L. Nahlen, Jennifer Bryce, Robert E. Black, and Richard W. Steketee. 2006. "The Burden of Malaria Mortality among African Children in the Year 2000." *International Journal of Epidemiology* 35 (3): 691–704. doi:10.1093/ije/dyl027.

Sedlmayr, Richard, Günther Fink, John M. Miller, Duncan Earle, and Richard W. Steketee. 2013. "Health Impact and Cost-Effectiveness of a Private Sector Bed Net Distribution: Experimental Evidence from Zambia." *Malaria Journal* 12 (1): 102. doi:10.1186/1475-2875-12-102.

Shiner, Cindy. 2013. "Zambia: Tracking a Lethal Foe." *AllAfrica,* January 10. http://allafrica.com/stories/201301101309.html.

Steketee, R.W., N. Sipilanyambe, J. Chimumbwa, J.J. Banda, A. Mohamed, J. Miller, S. Basu, S.K. Miti, and C.C. Campbell. 2008. "National Malaria Control and Scaling Up for Impact: The Zambia Experience through 2006." *American Journal of Tropical Medicine and Hygiene* 79 (1): 45–52.

UNDP (United Nations Development Programme). 2013. "UNDP Supports Cross Border Initiative to Roll Back Malaria Along the Zambezi River." News release, May 25. http://www.zm.undp.org/content/zambia/en/home/presscenter/pressreleases/2013/05/25/undp-supports-cross-border-initiative-to-roll-back-malaria-along-the-zambezi-river.html.

———. 2015. "Defeating Malaria, One of Zambia's Biggest Killers." Accessed November 11. http://www.zm.undp.org/content/zambia/en/home/ourwork/povertyreduction/successstories/defeating-malaria--one-of-zambias-biggest-killers-.html.

USAID (United States Agency for International Development), HHS (Department of Health and Human Services), CDC (Centers for Disease Control and Prevention), and US State Department. 2015. *President's Malaria Initiative: Zambia Malaria Operational Plan FY 2014.* Washington, DC: USAID. http://www.pmi.gov/docs/default-source/default-document-library/malaria-operational-plans/fy14/zambia_mop_fy14.pdf?sfvrsn=8.

White, Michael T., Lesong Conteh, Ricahrd Cibulskis, and Azra C. Ghani. 2011. "Costs and Cost-Effectiveness of Malaria Control Interventions: A Systematic Review." *Malaria Journal* 10: 337. doi:10.1186/1475-2875-10-337.

WHO (World Health Organization). 2009. "Malaria Deaths Decline by 66% in Zambia." News release, April 23. http://www.who.int/mediacentre/news/releases/2009/malaria_deaths_zambia_20090423/en/.

———. 2013a. "Malaria: Prevention of Reintroduction." May 7. http://www.who.int/malaria/areas/elimination/prevention_of_reintroduction/en/.

———. 2013b. *World Malaria Report 2013.* Geneva: WHO. http://www.who.int/malaria/publications/world_malaria_report_2013/en/.

———. 2014a. "Scale-Up in Effective Malaria Control Dramatically Reduces Deaths." News release, December 9. http://www.who.int/mediacentre/news/releases/2014/malaria-control/en/.

———. 2014b. *World Malaria Report 2014.* Geneva: WHO. http://www.who.int/malaria/publications/world_malaria_report_2014/report/en/.

World Bank. 2013. The Challenge of Ensuring Adequate Stocks of Essential Drugs in Rural Health Clinics. *From Evidence to Policy 76881.* Washington, DC: World Bank. http://www-wds.worldbank.org/external/default/WDSContentServer/WDSP/IB/2013/04/23/000356161_20130423144017/Rendered/PDF/768810BRI0Apri-0Box0377287B00PUBLIC0.pdf.

Young, M. 2000. *Report on Malaria Consultancy: Support to the Zambia National Roll Back Malaria Campaign.* Geneva: United Nations Children's Fund. http://www.unicef.org/evaldatabase/index_31217.html.

ENDNOTES

1. WHO (2013b).
2. Ricci (2012); Guillot and Gwatkin (1999).
3. Against Malaria Foundation (2015).
4. IHME (2015).
5. WHO (2013b, Annex 6D).
6. IHME (2015).
7. Kawesha (2013).
8. Kawesha (2013).

ENDNOTES, *continued*

9. Packard (2010, 213).
10. Roll Back Malaria (2011a).
11. Roll Back Malaria (2011b).
12. Roll Back Malaria (n.d.).
13. USAID et al. (2015).
14. UNDP (2015).
15. NMCP (2015); Glassman and Sakuma (2013).
16. Gerson (2012).
17. Roll Back Malaria (2011b).
18. Ashraf, Fink, and Weil (2010).
19. Ashraf, Fink, and Weil (2010).
20. Roll Back Malaria (2011b).
21. World Bank (2013).
22. NMCP (2015).
23. Shiner (2013).
24. Cohen et al. (2012).
25. Roll Back Malaria (2011b).
26. Hemoglobin less than 8g/dL.
27. Rowe et al. (2006); USAID et al. (2015); Ministry of Health (2012).
28. WHO (2009).
29. Roll Back Malaria (2011b); Chizema-Kawesha et al. (2010).
30. The malaria community uses all-cause child mortality as an outcome instead of malaria-specific mortality because it views this measure as robust. A child death is a memorable event, and most use the same standardized estimation procedure to track it.
31. Alarcon (2007).
32. Oloo (2005).
33. LiST is used to estimate the number of lives saved among children under five according to the estimated efficacy of the various malaria prevention interventions.
34. Roll Back Malaria (2011b).
35. Young (2000).

36. IHME (2015).
37. Ashraf, Fink, and Weil (2010).
38. Sedlmayr et al. (2013).
39. Demombynes and Trommlerova (2010).
40. Roll Back Malaria (2011b).
41. Sedlmayr et al. (2013).
42. Roll Back Malaria (2011b, 26).
43. Roll Back Malaria (2011b).
44. Ashraf, Fink, and Weil (2010).
45. Chizema-Kawesha et al. (2010).
46. Chizema-Kawesha et al. (2010).
47. The estimation of DALYs averted is based on deaths and cases averted for all newborns in Zambia. Averted deaths were from the Roll Back Malaria program in Zambia (Eisele et al. 2012) for scale-up of ITNs, intermittent preventive treatment in pregnancy (IPTp), and ITN during pregnancy. Cases averted used an application of the case-fatality ratio (Conteh et al. 2010). The costs per person protected by ITNs and IPTp were from a 2011 systematic review of malaria control measures (White et al. 2011). See Mirelman, Glassman, and Temin (2016).
48. Barat (2006).
49. Steketee et al. (2008).
50. Roll Back Malaria (2011b).
51. Carasso et al. (2012).
52. Ashraf, Fink, and Weil (2010).
53. WHO (2014b).
54. Friends of the Global Fight Against AIDS, Tuberculosis and Malaria (n.d.).
55. WHO (2014a).
56. WHO (2013a).
57. Colson et al. (2015).
58. UNDP (2013).

A Solid Foundation for Child Health

Mexico's Piso Firme Program

The Case at a Glance

HEALTH GOAL: To improve living standards and health, especially for mothers and children, among vulnerable groups living in high-density, low-income neighborhoods.

STRATEGY: Government program to replace dirt floors with cement in marginalized households using publicly provided materials and community labor.

HEALTH IMPACT: Nearly 20 percent fewer parasites, nearly 30 percent less diarrhea, 20 percent less anemia, and improved cognition in children under six. Levels of depression and perceived stress reduced by 12.5 percent and 10.5 percent, respectively, in their mothers. 408 lives saved and 40,748 disability-adjusted life years averted from 2007 to 2013.

WHY IT WORKED: Simple theory of change and highly visible benefit, which facilitated widespread outreach. High-level government commitment and complementary social programs. State and federal funding. Robust evaluation and culture of learning.

FINANCING: Coahuila State's program budget was US$5.5 million (US$162 per household). The federal government spent US$1.27 billion from 2007 to 2012 (US$468 per household), in 2010 dollars.

SCALE: Coahuila State installed 34,000 cement floors (2000–2005). The federal government installed 2.36 million cement floors (2007–2013).

All children have diarrhea from time to time, but children who live in houses with dirt floors have it often. When young children crawl and play on dirt floors, they are likely to ingest fecal material, exposing them to the harmful worms and parasites that thrive in excrement.[1] These pathogens can cause persistent diarrhea, among many other ailments. Not only is this unpleasant, but it also robs children of the nutrients that their growing young bodies need and slows their development, leading to wasting, anemia, and cognitive delays.[2] At its worst, diarrhea depletes the water and salt reserves that everyone needs to survive. Worldwide, diarrhea kills around 750,000 children every year.[3]

One simple measure to combat diarrhea was called a "no-brainer" by one global health expert: replace dirt floors in poor households with concrete. In 2006, an evaluation of the Piso Firme ("Solid Floor") program in the Mexican state of Coahuila provided irrefutable evidence that flooring improvements offered health and wellness benefits, particularly for young children and for women.[4] Living on new floors felt more comfortable and temperate than living on dirt floors. Mothers also liked that they were easier to clean; the new floors actually made them measurably happier.

Piso Firme proved so successful that President Felipe Calderon made a national commitment to eliminate dirt floors in target areas by 2012. Coverage of *pisos firmes* is not yet universal, but the Mexican government is quickly approaching its goal, eliminating an important pathway for diarrhea-causing pathogens that can kill children.[5]

The Toll of Dirt Flooring

Housing is a recognized social determinant of health. Both urban and rural areas have poor housing stock that exposes residents to various types of health risks. Key housing-related health risks include respiratory and car-

This case was originally authored by Miriam Temin.

diovascular diseases from indoor air pollution, communicable disease, injury, and threats to mental health. Urbanization intensifies this close relationship between housing and health.[6] With rapid urbanization, an ever-growing number of children are spending their formative years in makeshift housing on city peripheries, with governments struggling to catch up and provide adequate housing. The World Health Organization has reported that nearly 40 percent of urban growth worldwide is in unhealthy slum-type housing.[7] It is in such areas of Mexico that Piso Firme has had its greatest impact.

Dirt floors pose specific risks because they soak up fecal material that leaks or is tracked in by people and animals—a common occurrence in dense urban areas with underdeveloped sewage systems and limited sanitary facilities. Dirt floors are hard to clean and can harbor hookworm, sand fleas, and other worms and protozoans.[8] In Mexico, dirt floors are associated with an increased burden of intestinal parasites, even when compared with households whose residents are just as poor but have solid flooring, and controlling for other risk factors. Findings from elsewhere in Latin America tell a similar story.[9]

Infestations of worms and parasites pose immediate and long-term risks to children's health and development. Parasitic infestations bring diarrhea and micronutrient malnutrition, which in turn lead to anemia, protein-energy malnutrition, and swelling of the liver and spleen. Worms and parasites affect children's cognitive development, with knock-on effects for their future productivity.[10] As of 2015 there are still no cost-effective drugs for mass prevention or treatment of parasitic protozoan infections. (Deworming drugs have been developed and are in wide use. See chapter 6 in this volume.)[11]

Worldwide, children have seen significant health gains over the past two decades. In 2010, two million fewer children under five died than in 2000, and the reduction in diarrhea was among the top three reasons for this decline.[12] Consistent with the global trend, Mexican children are healthier than their parents were a generation ago. In the years leading up to the Millennium Development Goal deadline of 2015, Mexico was on track to meet the under-five mortality target: the mortality rate dropped from 20.4 deaths per 1,000 births in 2004 to 16.8 in 2010.[13]

But that is still not good enough. Worldwide, preventable diarrhea kills thousands of children every day—750,000 in 2010. It is the second leading cause of under-five mortality after the neonatal period.[14] And in Mexico, progress on child health is not equitably distributed, and serious health disparities persist. For example,

infant mortality rates are significantly higher in states in the south and southeast than those in the north. In addition, children are more likely to have a fever or diarrhea if they belong to an indigenous ethnic group, if they were born to mothers with a low education level, or if they live in rural areas—and these children are also less likely to receive proper medical treatment.[15] Urban children have a health advantage despite the housing-related health risks in dense informal settlements.

Putting an Idea in Motion: Mexico Moves from Concept to Concrete

In 2000, Enrique Martínez y Martínez was the Revolutionary Institutional Party candidate for governor in the northern state of Coahuila. When his campaign team told him of the many people who were living on dirt floors, he made a promise to the residents of his state to eliminate dirt floors statewide if he became governor.[16] Once elected, Martínez y Martínez launched his signature cement floor installation program, dubbed "Piso Firme," which provided more than 34,000 homes with much-needed cement flooring upgrades by 2005.[17]

The success in Coahuila, coupled with the governor's strong influence at the federal level, piqued national interest in the program and prompted the federal government to make large-scale cement floor installation a national strategic goal.[18] A number of social programs were already under way to combat poverty and marginalization: Mexico's pioneering social protection program, Progresa, later renamed Oportunidades, was the first large-scale conditional cash transfer program of its kind.[19] Simultaneously the government launched Seguro Popular ("Popular Insurance"), a public health insurance program for people living in poverty, a major step on the road to universal health coverage for all Mexicans. Smaller social programs complemented the objectives of Piso Firme, including national deworming activities and programs to improve rural and urban living conditions. Thus, Mexico's federal government was receptive to expanding Piso Firme.

Piso Firme in Action

Piso Firme's simplicity made it an attractive program. A caravan of cement trucks rolled up to eligible communities and delivered US$150 worth of cement to each participating household, enough to cover about 540 square feet with a five-inch-thick slab. Beneficiaries also received installation instructions, and family and community members provided the labor. The entire process of mixing and pouring the cement could be completed in just one day.

Piso Firme targeted disadvantaged families in marginalized communities. In Coahuila, program staff determined eligibility by knocking on doors, looking for homes with dirt floors, and offering those homeowners new floors—an offer that nearly all of them accepted.[20] Later, the national program used information from the census to identify beneficiary communities based on their degree of "socioeconomic marginalization."[21] Individuals within targeted communities were eligible if they could prove that they were living on a dirt floor and qualified as low income.

Piso Firme kicked off in Coahuila in 2000. By late 2003, it began its expansion throughout the country via several state and federal poverty-reduction programs.[22] By 2005, cement floors had been installed in approximately 300,000 homes. The scale-up of Piso Firme accelerated dramatically from 2007 to 2012, when the total number of cement floors installed reached an impressive 2.7 million (see Figure 1). By 2012, only 4.2 million people (3.6 percent of the population) were still living on dirt floors, down from 8 million (7.3 percent) in 2008.[23]

Despite the immense scale of the cement-floor installation, there still are houses with dirt floors, and these houses are not equitably distributed across Mexico.[24] Particularly concerning, nearly half of homes in predominantly indigenous areas and more than half in "very highly marginalized" areas have not yet received flooring upgrades.[25]

The Payoff: Less Diarrhea, Happier Moms

Piso Firme was clearly an operational success in Coahuila, immediately improving the living environment for tens of thousands of residents. Yet Governor Martínez y Martínez and the federal Secretariat for Social Development (Secretaría de Desarrollo Social, or SEDESOL) were not satisfied with an anecdotal demonstration of the program's success. They wanted to convincingly demonstrate the program's health impact—especially on children—via an independent impact evaluation, which the state of Coahuila and SEDESOL jointly funded. They brought on board academic and World Bank researchers, including the impact evaluation powerhouse Paul Gertler of the University of California, Berkeley, who had been one of the early evaluators of the federal government's Progresa program.

Figure 1. Thousands of Cement Floors Installed by Year, Mexico, 2007–2012

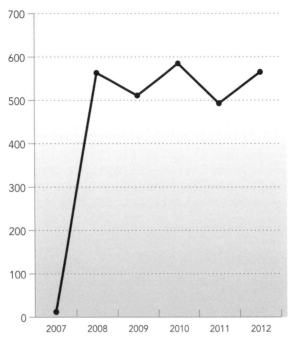

Source: CONEVAL (2014).

The impact evaluation yielded impressive findings.[26] Two to four years after their families had been offered an improved floor, children under six had nearly 20 percent fewer parasites, a 13 percent lower prevalence of diarrhea, and 20 percent less anemia than children in a matched control community. Less anemia meant better cognitive development: children in the treatment area scored 9 percent higher on the widely used vocabulary test, Test de Vocabulario en Imagenes Peabody ("Picture Peabody Language Development Test"), than children in the control community, whose families did not benefit from the offer of a concrete floor.[27]

Women also benefited from the flooring upgrades, highlighting the important relationship between mothers' and children's health. In the intervention community, the program reduced mothers' levels of depression and perceived stress by 12.5 percent and 10.5 percent, respectively, compared with the control group. The floors were also associated with mothers' increased satisfaction with the quality of their housing (15 percent higher than controls) and overall quality of life (19 percent higher).

The impact evaluation was designed to isolate the impact of Piso Firme from other changes in the neighborhood, the immediate living environment, and other potentially confounding factors (see Box 1). This enabled researchers to link the health effect specifically to the role of the cement floors in interrupting parasitic infection, demonstrating that the program had measureable positive impacts well beyond the broader benefits conferred by the economic growth occurring in Mexico at the time.

The Mexican government, using a broad approach to poverty measurement, also reported that the floor upgrades actually reduced poverty.[28] The government uses a multidimensional index to measure poverty that combines people's income level with their degree of social deprivation. The index includes people's level of education, social security, health services, access to food,

and quality of dwelling. The quality-of-dwelling metric gauged how solid people's homes were and included, unsurprisingly, the construction material of the floor. This approach reflected the government's strong commitment to cement-floor installation and enabled it to establish the link between flooring upgrades and poverty reduction.

By significantly improving the quality of dwellings across the country, especially in poor and extremely poor rural municipalities—the main target of the flooring upgrades—the scale-up of Piso Firme reduced multidimensional poverty in Mexico. According to calculations by the National Council for the Evaluation of Social Policy (CONEVAL), 9.7 percent of Mexicans would have lived in extreme poverty in the absence of govern-

Box 1. Strength of the Evidence

Measuring the health impact of housing upgrades is methodologically difficult; confounding factors and ethical challenges abound. The Piso Firme evaluation stands out for its robust design, which makes it an important contribution to the slim evidence base on the impact of housing on health in middle-income settings.

The phased rollout of the program created a natural experiment, making it possible to compare Piso Firme beneficiaries with otherwise similar households that had not received the benefit. The evaluators focused their investigation on the La Laguna metropolitan area, an urban agglomeration spanning the border between Coahuila and Durango states. The neighborhoods on either side of the border were socioeconomically and culturally similar, with one important difference: Coahuila was the first state to implement the Piso Firme benefit, starting in year 2000, whereas Durango State still had not done so by that time. Evaluators sampled treated households on the Coahuila side and then used census data from 2000, before program implementation, to identify geographical areas within the Durango neighborhoods that could serve as controls, carefully matching them to treatment areas in Coahuila.[31]

Surveying a randomly selected sample within each group, the researchers were then able to credibly isolate the effects of Piso Firme. They found important health and welfare gains in program areas based on an "intent-to-treat" analysis of the program's effect. The intent-to-treat approach is robust because almost no one turned down a concrete floor when it was offered to them by the program. By including questions about overall housing improvements and the

perceived value of homes with or without concrete floors, the researchers were also able to rule out the possibility that health gains were due to an income effect (for example, because beneficiaries had additional income via the US$150 in-kind transfer to devote to other health-improving activities). Finally, they exploited the difference in prevalence of concrete flooring across treatment and nontreatment areas to estimate the impact of having a concrete floor on health outcomes. The researchers ultimately found that a higher percentage of concrete flooring in a sample of homes is associated with significant reductions in anemia, diarrhea, and parasite prevalence, whether the floors were installed through Piso Firme or otherwise.

It is important to note limitations related to the Coahuila study design. The authors took steps to ensure comparability across the treatment and control groups; nonetheless, because this is a quasi-experimental study that did not benefit from randomization to treatment, it is possible that residual confounding remained. A replication study is currently under way to shed additional light on the results.[32]

The Mexico results are consistent with compelling evidence from elsewhere on the benefits of solid flooring. Un Techo Para Mi Pais ("A Roof for My Country"), a regional Latin American organization that provides low-cost houses to extremely poor slum dwellers, includes cement flooring in some of its houses. A randomized study of the housing's impact found that the houses improved the occupants' sense of well-being and happiness. And in El Salvador, children in houses with cement floors had less diarrhea than those in the control group.[33]

ment-sponsored cement floors; the floors reduced that percentage to 8.9 percent in 2012.[29]

The researchers who carried out the impact evaluation pointed out the specific characteristics of the children who benefited from Piso Firme in Coahuila. They lived in low-income urban households that were poor, but not very poor. They had adequate nutrition and access to a safe water supply, and they received regular deworming treatment. It is likely that similar children would receive comparable benefits from a flooring upgrade. However, the evaluators caution against generalizing too broadly; where the setting and population differ, the same impact cannot be assured. For example, in rural areas without a safe water supply, children are more likely to contact parasites in a variety of places, which might reduce the benefits of living on a concrete floor.

Questions remain. For example, the health impact of the Coahuila program may have been different depending on which room in the house received the upgrade—covering a kitchen floor may pay bigger health dividends than bedroom upgrades. Similarly, the impact may have varied depending on how much of a household flooring material was changed: an upgrade from all dirt to all concrete floors may offer greater benefits than covering the one remaining dirt floor in a partially upgraded home. Thus it is possible that poorer households benefited more from Piso Firme, given that they were more likely to have all dirt floors prior to the program. A second-generation evaluation replication study is exploring these questions; its findings will yield further insights from Mexico's experience.[30]

Gains at What Price?

Mexican government support for Piso Firme came from state and federal budgets. In Coahuila State, the total program cost US$5.5 million from 2000 to 2005, or US$162 per household. The cost grew significantly under the national expansion: MXN16.3 billion (US$1.2 billion) from the federal budget for the years 2007 to 2013—an average of US$460 per household (2007 dollars).[34] This difference can be explained in part by the significant increase in transport costs for the national rollout: in Coahuila, the cement was transported in an urban setting, whereas the national effort required trucking cement to more remote areas.[35]

In Coahuila, researchers found that Piso Firme was cost-effective for cognitive development in particular.[36]

They measured a 9 percent boost in children's scores on the Picture Peabody Language Development Test after they received a cement floor. This compares favorably with the 12 percent increase that Oportunidades yielded with a unit cost of between US$210 and US$750 per household.

To assess the cost-effectiveness of Piso Firme, the total number of diarrhea and anemia cases it averted among the population eligible for a flooring upgrade was modeled for *Millions Saved*. From these two health outcomes, the estimate yielded a mortality impact of 408 averted deaths (all from diarrhea) in the scale-up period (2007 to 2013), which converts to 40,748 disability-adjusted life years (DALYs) averted. An estimate of the cost-effectiveness ratio was not calculated because it was not possible to estimate the full health effects of the program.[37]

The Keys to Lasting Success

Mexico stands out for its top-notch evaluation system, which has helped the government improve the design of its social programs across the board. It is a legal requirement that all public social programs undergo annual external evaluations, an effort that is led by CONEVAL.[38] The government has taken a lead in demonstrating how constructive independent evaluations can influence social policy.[39] All evaluation results must be made public, and this transparency helps media and civil society organizations hold the government accountable on its promise to deliver social benefits.[40]

This system enabled the national Piso Firme program to rest on a strong foundation: the association between cement flooring and child health gains that had been established by the impact evaluation. The simplicity of the intervention and evidence of its impact made it easy for planners to describe a theory of change that could be widely understood and widely communicated. The evaluation results emerged around the time that Piso Firme was being scaled up, providing a valuable asset for its supporters. The program's innovative nature plus its rigorous impact evaluation attracted considerable international attention.

Within Mexico, the ability to quantify the health impact of the simple in-kind transfer—the "no-brainer" aspect of the intervention—attracted government funding and sustained political commitment that facilitated scale-up. The leadership of Governor Martínez y Martínez in the first large-scale program and his sway at the national level, paired with the government's general commitment to social issues and poverty reduction, generated the right environment for widespread expansion. In 2008, Piso Firme received a boost in support and funding when it became part of the federal government's human development strategy, Vivir Mejor ("Living Better"). While no longer a discrete program with its own budget, the provision of cement floors is now managed through a number of federal programs aimed at improving living conditions in rural and urban areas.[41] Several states also offer concrete flooring materials as part of their own social development programs.

Cement floor installation provides an excellent opportunity for the government to make its commitment to poverty reduction tangible. The government has capitalized on this, providing placards to homes with upgraded floors reading, "En mi hogar el piso es firme" ("In my home, the floor is solid"), accompanied by a Vivir Mejor logo.[42] These images appear in promotional materials and social media—even President Felipe Calderón tweeted about Piso Firme's success.[43]

Implications for Global Health

As population growth concentrates in urban areas, policymakers face pressure to confront the health effects of low-quality housing. The success of Piso Firme illustrates the potential of a narrowly defined, well-targeted housing program. Replacing dirt floors with cement ones is likely to improve the health of urban children who already have adequate nutrition and access to a safe water supply—circumstances that leave dirt floors as one of the last routes of parasite transmission. Closing the flooring pathway has relevance for child health, maternal well-being, and urban housing, while also contributing to the burgeoning evidence base on the social determinants of health.

Installing cement floors is not the most effective way to reduce diarrhea in all settings. Basic water, sanitation, and hygiene improvements, among other strategies, may be higher priorities for diarrhea prevention in disease-endemic regions.[44] And the cost of Piso Firme may be unaffordable for some governments, even as it proves realistic in middle-income settings such as Mexico.

The long-term gains of investments in young children's health have been firmly established, but the other aspect of the Piso Firme story is more surprising: the impact of child health and housing on mothers. Worldwide, women carry the bulk of responsibility for maintaining the family living environment and providing child care, and it is typically their job to fix domestic problems when they arise.[45] Childhood illness and low-quality housing take a toll on women's mental health and overall well-being; the Piso Firme evaluation results confirmed that improvements in child health and housing can also improve mothers' well-being.

Reports of Piso Firme's impact have had an influence beyond Mexico's borders—similar programs elsewhere often feature the Mexican evaluation results in their promotional materials. Habitat for Humanity has built more than 500,000 houses in 80 countries, often including cement floors in new houses or housing upgrades. Habitat Nicaragua runs a similar program, which includes a campaign to upgrade floors called Un Piso para Jugar ("A Floor to Play On").[46] Project Ethiopia is a grassroots effort started by two Americans to advance development "one village at a time" in Ethiopia. A donation of US$400 pays for a concrete floor for a household; US$1,200 provides a floor for a room in a school.[47]

Replacing dirt floors with cement floors seems like a simple and obvious measure, but prior to the launch of Piso Firme, no low- or middle-income country had taken action on this measure at scale. Piso Firme has been a big win for Mexico, one with implications for other middle-income countries with growing slum communities that have begun investing in improving living conditions and housing stock for the poor.[48] Mexico's experience shows that simple interventions are worthwhile, especially when they are subjected to an impact evaluation and results are published in peer-reviewed journals. Mexico's program provided lessons in targeting, equity, and operational improvements to improve public health. Piso Firme is a valuable contribution to the evidence base on how cement floors and other targeted housing improvements can improve health and well-being for slum-dwelling children and the women who care for them.

REFERENCES

Arroyo, Ernesto Cordero. 2009. *Mejoramiento de la Vivienda Rural: Impacto de la Instalación de Piso Firme y Estufas Ecológicas en las Condiciones de Vida de los Hogares*. Mexico City: Procuraduria Agraria. http://www.pa.gob.mx/publica/rev_40/notas/ernesto%20cordero%20arroyo.pdf.

Basurto, Maria Pia, Ramiro Burga, Jose Luis Flor Toro, and Cesar Huaroto. 2013. *Replication Plan Study: "Housing, Health and Happiness."* Washington, DC: International Initiative for Impact Evaluation (3ie). http://www.3ieimpact.org/media/filer_public/2014/01/13/basurto_revised_replication_plan.pdf.

Calderon, Felipe. 2012. Twitter post, Nov. 24, 12:35 p.m. https://twitter.com/felipecalderon/status/272438397841317888.

Cattaneo, Matias D., Sebastian Galiani, Paul J. Gertler, Sebastian Martinez, and Rocio Titiunik. 2009. "Housing, Health, and Happiness." *American Economic Journal: Economic Policy* 1 (1): 75–105. doi:10.1257/pol.1.1.75.

Center for Sustainable Development. 2015. "Household Concrete Floors as a Health Measure in Sustainable Development." Accessed November 19. http://www.csd-i.org/installing-concrete-floors.

Chávez, Axel. 2013. "Fracosó el Programa 'Piso Firme' de Sedesol." *Milenio*, June 9. http://www.milenio.com/hidalgo/Fracaso-programa-Piso-Firme-Sedesol_0_148785597.html.

Collins, George, Thomas McLeod, Njilah Isaac Konfor, Clarisse B. Lamnyam, Leo Ngarka, and Nfor Leo Njamnshi. 2009. "Tungiasis: A Neglected Health Problem in Rural Cameroon." *International Journal of Collaborative Research on Internal Medicine and Public Health* 1 (1): 2–10.

CONEVAL (National Council for the Evaluation of Social Policy). 2010. "Cambios en el Índice Absoluto de Marginación por Entidad Federativa." In *Informe de la Evaluación Específica de Desempeño 2012–2013*. Mexico City: CONEVAL. http://www.conapo.gob.mx/work/models/CONAPO/Resource/1755/1/images/02Capitulo.pdf.

———. 2014. *Impact of Cement Floors on Poverty in Mexico 2008–2012*. Mexico City: CONEVAL.

Engle, Patrice L., Maureen M. Black, Jere R. Behrman, Meena Cabral de Mello, Paul J. Gertler, Lydia Kapiriri, Reynaldo Martorell, and Mary Eming Young. 2007. "Strategies to Avoid the Loss of Developmental Potential in More than 200 Million Children in the Developing World." *Lancet* 369 (9557): 229–42. doi:10.1016/S0140-6736(07)60112-3.

Galiani, Sebastian, Paul Gertler, Ryan Cooper, Sebastian Martinex, Adam Ross, and Raimundo Undurraga. 2013. Shelter from the Storm: Upgrading Housing Infrastructure in Latin American Slums. Working Paper 19322. Cambridge, MA: National Bureau of Economic Research.

Gamboa, M.I., J.A. Basualdo, L. Kozubsky, E. Costas, E. Cueto Rua, and H.B. Lahitte. 1998. "Prevalence of Intestinal Parasitosis within Three Population Groups in La Plata, Argentina." *European Journal of Epidemiology* 14: 55–61.

Hábitat para la Humanidad Nicaragua. 2015. "Un Piso para Jugar." Accessed October 13. http://www.habitatnicaragua.org/proyectos/fondo-anual/un-piso-para-jugar/.

Harhay, Michael O., John Horton, and Piero L. Olliaro. 2010. "Epidemiology and Control of Human Gastrointestinal Parasites in Children." *Expert Review of Anti-infective Therapy* 8 (2): 219–34. doi:10.1586/eri.09.119.

Hesham, M.S., A.B. Edariah, and M. Norhayati. 2004. "Intestinal Parasitic Infections and Micronutrient Deficiency: A Review." *Medical Journal of Malaysia* 59 (2): 284–93.

Hotez, Peter. 2008. "Hookworm and Poverty." *Annals of the New York Academy of Sciences* 1136 (1): 38–44. doi:10.1196/annals.1425.000.

INEGI (Instituto Nacional de Estadística y Geografía). 2013. *The Millennium Development Goals in Mexico: Progress Report 2013*. Aguascalientes, Mexico: INEGI. http://200.23.8.225/odm/Doctos/ResInfMex2013_ing.pdf.

———. 2015. *Módulo de Condiciones Socioeconómicas (MCS)*. Accessed November 4. http://www.inegi.org.mx/est/contenidos/proyectos/encuestas/hogares/modulos/mcs/.

Jacobsen, Kathryn H., Priscila S. Ribeiro, Bradley K. Quist, and Bruce V. Rydbeck. 2007. "Prevalence of Intestinal Parasites in Young Quichua Children in the Highlands of Rural Ecuador." *Journal of Health, Population and Nutrition* 25 (4): 399–405.

Joseph, J. Keith, Junior Bazile, Justin Mutter, Sonya Shin, Andrew Ruddle, Louise Ivers, Evan Lyon, and Paul Farmer. 2006. "Tungiasis in Rural Haiti: A Community-Based Response." *Transactions of the Royal Society of Tropical Medicine and Hygiene* 100 (10): 970–74. doi:10.1016/j.trstmh.2005.11.006.

Kassebaum, Nicholas J., Amelia Bertozzi-Villa, Megan S. Coggeshall, Katya A. Shackelford, Caitlyn Steiner, Kyle R. Heuton, Diego Gonzalez-Medina, and Ryan Barber. 2014. "Global, Regional, and National Levels and Causes of Maternal Mortality during 1990–2013: A Systematic Analysis for the Global Burden of Disease Study 2013." *Lancet* 384 (9947): 980–1004. doi:10.1016/S0140-6736(14)60696-6.

Lamberti, M., C.L. Fischer Walker, and R.E. Black. 2012. "Systematic Review of Diarrhea Duration and Severity in Children and Adults in Low- and Middle-Income Countries." *BMC Public Health* 12: 276. doi:10.1186/1471-2458-12-276.

Langer, Ana, Afaf Meleis, Felicia M. Knaul, Rifat Atun, Meltem Aran, Héctor Arreola-Ornelas, Zulfiqar A. Bhutta, et al. 2015. "Women and Health: The Key for Sustainable Development." *Lancet* 386 (9999): 1165–1210. doi:10.1016/S0140-6736(15)60497-4.

Levine, Ruth. 2004. "Improving the Health of the Poor in Mexico." In *Millions Saved: Proven Successes in Global*

REFERENCES, *continued*

Health, 2nd ed. Washington, DC: Center for Global Development.

Liu, Li, Hope L. Johnson, Simon Cousens, Jamie Perin, Susana Scott, Joy E. Lawn, Igor Rudan, et al. 2012. "Global, Regional, and National Causes of Child Mortality: An Updated Systematic Analysis for 2010 with Time Trends since 2000." *Lancet* 379 (9832): 2151–61. doi:10.1016/S0140-6736(12)60560-1.

Lopez, A.S., J.M. Bendik, J.Y. Alliance, J.M. Roberts, A.J. da Silva, I.N.S. Moura, M.J. Arrowood, M.L. Eberhard, and B.L. Herwaldt. 2003. "Epidemiology of *Cyclospora cayetanensis* and Other Intestinal Parasites in a Community in Haiti." *Journal of Clinical Microbiology* 41 (5): 2047–54. doi:10.1128/JCM.41.5.2047-2054.2003.

Mirelman, Andrew, Amanda Glassman, and Miriam Temin. 2016. Estimating the *Avertable Disease Burden and Cost-Effectiveness in* Millions Saved *Third Edition.* CGD Working Paper. Washington, DC: Center for Global Development.

Morales-Espinoza, E.M., H.J. Sánchez-Pérez, M.M. García-Gil, G. Vargas-Morales, J.D. Méndez-Sánchez, and M. Pérez-Ramírez. 2003. "Intestinal Parasites in Children, in Highly Deprived Areas in the Border Region of Chiapas, Mexico." *Salud Pública de México* 45 (5): 379–88.

Pick, Susan. 2011. "Mexico's Struggle to 'Vivir Mejor.'" *OUPblog,* February 15. http://blog.oup.com/2011/02/live-better/.

Project Ethiopia. 2015. "Projects." Accessed November 4. http://projectethiopia.com/projects.

Salomon, Joshua A., Theo Vos, Daniel R. Hogan, Michael Gagnon, Mohsen Naghavi, Ali Mokdad, Nazma Begum, et al. 2012. "Common Values in Assessing Health Outcomes from Disease and Injury: Disability Weights Measurement Study for the Global Burden of Disease Study 2010." *Lancet* 380 (9859): 2129–43. doi:10.1016/S0140-6736(12)61680-8.

Stevens, Gretchen, Rodrigo H. Dias, Kevin J.A. Thomas, Juan A. Rivera, Natalie Carvalho, Simón Barquera, Kenneth Hill, and Majid Ezzati. 2008. "Characterizing the Epidemiological Transition in Mexico: National and Subnational Burden of Diseases, Injuries, and Risk Factors." *PLoS Medicine* 5 (6): e125. doi:10.1371/journal.pmed.0050125.

Székely, Miguel. 2011. *Toward Results-Based Social Policy Design and Implementation.* Working Paper 249. Washington, DC: Center for Global Development.

Teruel, Graciela. 2013. "Mexico's Monitoring and Evaluation System." PowerPoint presentation. http://www.3ieimpact.org/media/filer_public/2013/10/25/mexicos_monitoring__evaluation_system.pdf.

Thomson, H., M. Petticrew, and D. Morrison. 2001. "Health Effects of Housing Improvement: Systematic Review of Intervention Studies." *BMJ* 323 (7306): 187–90. doi:10.1136/bmj.323.7306.187.

Ugbomoiko, Uade Samuel, Liana Ariza, Ifeanyi Emmanuel Ofoezie, and Jörg Heukelbach. 2007. "Risk Factors for Tungiasis in Nigeria: Identification of Targets for Effective Intervention." *PLoS Neglected Tropical Diseases* 1 (3): e87. doi:10.1371/journal.pntd.0000087.

United Nations. 2015. "Children under Five Mortality Rate per 1,000 Live Births." *Millennium Development Goals Indicators.* Accessed October 13. http://mdgs.un.org/unsd/mdg/SeriesDetail.aspx?srid=561.

Velasquez, F.R., H. Garcia-Lozano, E. Rodriguez, Y. Cervantes, A. Gomez, M. Melo, L. Anaya, et al. 2004. "Diarrhea Morbidity and Mortality in Mexican Children: Impact of Rotavirus Disease." *Pediatric Infectious Disease Journal* 23 (10 Suppl): S149–55.

WHO (World Health Organization). 2010. *International Workshop on Housing, Health and Climate Change: Developing Guidance for Health Protection in the Built Environment—Mitigation and Adaptation Reponses.* Meeting Report. Geneva: WHO.

———. 2013. "Diarrhoeal Disease." Fact Sheet 330. Updated April. http://www.who.int/mediacentre/factsheets/fs330/en/.

WHO and UN-Habitat (United Nations Human Settlements Programme). 2010. *Hidden Cities: Unmasking and Overcoming Health Inequities in Urban Settings.* Kobe, Japan: WHO and UN-HABITAT.

WHO Commission on Social Determinants of Health. 2008. *Closing the Gap in a Generation: Health Equity through Action on the Social Determinants of Health. Commission on Social Determinants of Health Final Report.* Geneva: WHO.

ENDNOTES

1. Ugbomoiko et al. (2007).
2. Hesham, Edariah, and Norhayati (2004).
3. WHO (2013).
4. Cattaneo et al. (2009).
5. CONEVAL (2014).
6. Thomson, Petticrew, and Morrison (2001); WHO Commission on Social Determinants of Health (2008).
7. WHO (2010).
8. Hotez (2008); Collins et al. (2009).
9. Morales-Espinoza et al. (2003); Jacobsen et al. (2007); Lopez et al. (2003); Gamboa et al. (1998).
10. Engle et al. (2007).
11. Harhay, Horton, and Olliaro (2010).
12. Liu et al. (2012).
13. United Nations (2015); INEGI (2013).
14. Liu et al. (2012).
15. Stevens et al. (2008).
16. The government programs Microregiones and Comision Nacional para el Desarrollo de los Pueblos Indigenas included similar interventions prior to 2000. Flooring components of these programs were relatively small and

ENDNOTES, *continued*

targeted rural areas with a high density of indigenous populations. Microregiones covered selected communities in six municipalities in Coahuila and nine municipalities in Durango in 2003 (see Cattaneo et al. 2009, 4).

17. Cattaneo et al. (2009).

18. Cattaneo et al. (2009).

19. A conditional cash transfer program offers a set amount of money to beneficiaries on a predictable schedule when they adhere to established conditions, which are often related to family members' attendance at school and participation in health programs (Levine 2004).

20. Cattaneo et al. (2009).

21. CONEVAL (2010).

22. By 2005, state-level Piso Firme programs were established in Chihuahua (http://municipios.chihuahua.gob.mx) and Guanajuato (http://www.leon.gob.mx), and the Piso Firme subcomponent of the Programa para Desarrollo Local Microregiones (Microregion Program for Local Development) was expanded (http://www.sedesol.gob.mx).

23. CONEVAL estimates are based on information from the Microregiones Unit of SEDESOL and MCS-ENIGH 2008, 2010, and 2012 (INEGI 2015).

24. Chávez (2013).

25. Arroyo (2009).

26. Cattaneo et al. (2009).

27. The researchers used an "intent-to-treat" approach for their analysis, as described in Box 1. The same researchers constructed an alternate model to estimate the effect of a complete replacement of dirt floors by cement floors, which they estimated would lead to a 78 percent reduction in parasitic infestations, a 49 percent reduction in diarrhea, an 81 percent reduction in anemia, and a 36–96 percent improvement in cognitive development among young children. Worms were controlled separately through the national albendazole distribution program.

28. CONEVAL (2014).

29. CONEVAL (2014).

30. Basurto et al. (2013).

31. Cattaneo et al. (2009).

32. Basurto et al. (2013).

33. Galiani et al. (2013).

34. CONEVAL (2014).

35. Luis Gerardo Mejia Sanchez, personal communication with the author, June 19, 2014.

36. Cattaneo et al. (2009).

37. The estimates of program size were calculated from the eligible population. DALYs averted were derived from diarrhea and anemia cases averted and distribution of severity (Velasquez 2004; Lamberti 2012); disability weights (Salomon et al. 2012; Kassebaum et al. 2014); and program efficacy (Cattaneo et al. 2009). The reported large reduction in prevalence of parasites, 19.6 percent, was excluded. Costs were examined, but the estimation of cost-effectiveness in terms of cost per DALY averted was not appropriate and not reported. See Mirelman, Glassman, and Temin (2016).

38. Székely (2011); Teruel (2013).

39. Székely (2011).

40. Pick (2011).

41. Programa para el Desarrollo de Zonas Prioritarias (PDZP), Vivienda Digna, and Vivienda Rural. Vivienda Digna and Vivienda Rural are part of FONHAPO, the former urban focused and the latter rural focused.

42. Pick (2011).

43. Calderon (2012). Piso Firme's visibility has invited some criticism. For example, concerns have been raised that Piso Firme's top-down delivery may override home owners' own priorities for home improvement, such as improving roofing or upgrading sanitation facilities. Irregularities have been reported, from corruption or simulated rigged bids and illegal charges to poor work and delays that are related to elections (see Chávez 2013 ["SEDESOL's 'Piso Firme' Program Failed"]).

44. Joseph et al. (2006); Ugbomoiko et al. (2007); Center for Sustainable Development (2015).

45. Langer et al. (2015).

46. Hábitat para la Humanidad Nicaragua (2015).

47. For more information, see Project Ethiopia (2015).

48. WHO and UN-Habitat (2010).

CASE 6

A Fresh Start for a Bright Future
Kenya's School-Based Deworming Program

The Case at a Glance

HEALTH GOAL: To eliminate parasitic worms as a public health problem.

STRATEGY: Nongovernmental organization intervention, later scaled up to a nationwide government program, providing mass deworming treatment to Kenyan schoolchildren.

HEALTH IMPACT: Reduced prevalence of any soil-transmitted helminth infection by 83 percent and prevalence of two schistosomiasis varieties by 58 percent and 67 percent among Kenyan schoolchildren in four high-burden provinces between 2012 and 2014.

WHY IT WORKED: Multisectoral effort leveraging existing school infrastructure to facilitate delivery of medication. International resources and technical assistance that complemented domestic political commitment and leadership. Extensive monitoring and accountability infrastructure.

FINANCING: Cost about US$0.56 per treated student per year. Cost-effectiveness ratio: US$47.20 per disability-adjusted life year averted.

SCALE: 6.4 million children (2013–2014 school year).

Proper childhood nutrition lays the foundation for children to learn, thrive, and grow into healthy adults. Yet worldwide, close to 900 million children are at risk of infection with soil-transmitted worms or helminths, with many at dual risk for schistosomiasis too.[1] For infected children, getting proper nutrition is a daily fight against the intestinal parasites that feed on their blood and other tissues, suppressing their appetites and preventing their bodies from absorbing enough nutrients.

In the Busia region of western Kenya, where more than 90 percent of schoolchildren were infected with soil-transmitted helminths, *Schistosoma* worms, or both in 1998, researchers were eager to test whether a worm-free childhood could provide the foundation for lifelong health, wellness, and learning.[2] The results of their randomized evaluation, first released in 2001, were inspiring: school-based deworming treatment kick-started a virtuous cycle of lower worm loads, growth, and increased school attendance. Convinced by the intervention's success, the Kenyan government, with support from donors, later adopted annual deworming as national policy, giving approximately six million Kenyan schoolchildren a

better chance to thrive every year. If the results of the Busia evaluation hold steady across Kenya's parasitic worm–endemic regions, the ripple effects from this intervention could have massive implications for Kenya's future human and economic development.

The evidence of success in the Kenyan setting has inspired a global response, including mass deworming programs in other countries, including India, the country with the highest worm burden globally. However, the global evidence on mass deworming is mixed; some studies indicate that the impact depends in part on intestinal worm prevalence, and later studies have yielded varied findings, underlining the need for caution in applying the results of specific trials to different contexts.

The Toll of Soil-Transmitted Helminths and Schistosomiasis

Two types of intestinal worms—soil-transmitted helminths (STHs) and the schistosome worms that cause schistosomiasis—thrive in areas where sanitary condi-

This case was originally authored by Rachel Silverman.

tions are poor and access to healthcare is limited or altogether lacking. Together, they affect nearly a quarter of the world's population, with the burden particularly acute in children and widely spread across Latin America, Asia, and Africa.[3]

STHs include several species of worms—most commonly roundworms, whipworms, and hookworms—that lodge within victims' intestinal tracts. Once there, they feast on their host's tissue and lay thousands of eggs each day, which are subsequently expelled via feces. Children acquire STH infection when contaminated soil reaches their mouths while they are playing outdoors, drinking from a contaminated water source, or eating unwashed fresh produce. Many mild STH infections are asymptomatic, but severe infections can occur when a child is reinfected with the same parasite multiple times, thereby increasing the child's "worm load" and the severity of symptoms.[4]

Schistosomiasis is of a different etiology but is often grouped with STH infections because of a complementary treatment strategy and the frequency of dual infection. Schistosomiasis is caused by tiny schistosome worms that invade a host's veins along the intestinal and urinary tracts. Schistosome eggs provoke an immune reaction when they become trapped in human tissue, causing chronic inflammation and pain. Infected children expel eggs when they defecate; eggs subsequently make their way to nearby water sources, where they hatch and thrive within freshwater snails. The parasitic cycle is completed when children bathe in contaminated waters, giving schistosome larvae the opportunity to penetrate their skin.[5]

Intestinal worms rarely kill their hosts, but they can dramatically affect their lives. The vast majority of the disease burden they cause results in developmental delays and decreased quality of life. Severe STH infections can suppress children's appetites, prevent proper nutrient absorption, and chip away at their iron and protein reserves, leading to anemia, vitamin A deficiency, stunting, and diarrhea. Potential complications of schistosomiasis include ulcers, kidney failure, genital lesions, and stunted growth.[6] At the time the Busia intervention began, a Global Burden of Diseases, Injuries, and Risk Factors study suggested that STH and schistosome infections resulted in more than 7.7 million disability-adjusted life years (DALYs) annually, including over 4.5 million DALYs among schoolchildren ages 5 to 14.[7]

Kenyan children were particularly hard hit. In 2008, a national fecal survey revealed intestinal parasites in 57 percent of Kenyan schoolchildren (five million children), including a whopping 70 percent of all 13- and 14-year-olds. With infections primarily caused by contaminated soil or water, STH infection and schistosomiasis thrived among the 40 percent of rural Kenyans without access to piped water or sanitation facilities.[8] The burden has historically been concentrated along the coast and the Lake Victoria basin. These two regions have dense agricultural populations, favorable climates for parasite survival, high poverty rates, and in the Lake Victoria basin, a heavy reliance on contaminated water for bathing and washing clothes or food.[9]

In the southern Busia region, abutting Lake Victoria, a worm-filled childhood was the norm. As of 1998, 92 percent of children were infected with at least one intestinal parasite, and 37 percent suffered from moderate or severe infection.[10] By robbing these children of needed health and nutrition during a key phase of their intellectual and physical development, intestinal worms stunted their growth and adult life prospects, trapping them in a cycle of poverty.

Putting an Idea in Motion: Deworming Expands from Study to Scale-Up

For years, medical professionals and economists had theorized that mass deworming could unlock untapped health and educational potential for hundreds of millions of children worldwide. Yet their conviction was not matched by solid evidence: as of 2000, the combined findings of all studies suggested that deworming had only a modest impact on children's physical growth and an inconclusive effect on their cognitive performance.[11]

In western Kenya, two leading development economists, Edward Miguel of the University of California, Berkeley, and Michael Kremer of Harvard University, wanted to take a closer look. Previous studies, they contended, had important limitations: they suffered from small sample sizes, failed to measure all relevant outcomes, and did not account for the benefits of reduced parasite transmission even for untreated schoolchildren. As a result, those previous studies might have missed a causal relationship between mass deworming and improved life prospects.[12]

In partnership with a Dutch NGO, the Internationaal Christelijk Steunfonds Africa (ICS), and the Busia District Ministry of Health, Miguel and Kremer found an ideal opportunity to test their hypothesis. Rolled out over three years, ICS's Primary School Deworming Project (PSDP) targeted children in 75 primary schools in southern Busia with anti-STH and antischistosome treatment.[13] Although the program was not the first of its kind, nor the first such program to undergo a randomized evaluation, it did have one distinctive characteristic: Miguel and Kremer convinced ICS to randomize the timing of treatment introduction by school (a cluster-randomized study design). This allowed them to establish causality between the intervention and its outcomes, and to more fully account for the side benefits of treatment on untreated classmates and friends.[14] In southern Busia, the extremely high burden of intestinal worms meant that if mass deworming worked, almost all children there would see improvements in their quality of life and development.

In 2001, three years after the initial rollout, the duo released a working paper detailing the program's exciting results: despite incomplete uptake, primarily because some children were absent on treatment day, children in the deworming treatment group had improved growth and fewer school absences.[15]

The paper was widely circulated within academia, earning citations in renowned economic and global development reports.[16] With assistance from the World Bank, the researchers translated this academic exposure into meetings with key Kenyan stakeholders. Both the government and donors were impressed with the paper's findings and seized the opportunity to incorporate school-based deworming into the new national school health policy, which was under development during the same time period. By 2006, the World Bank had joined the Kenyan government and several other donors in funding the massive Kenyan Education Sector Support Program, which included money earmarked for school-based deworming at a national scale.[17]

Even with money set aside, operationalization of the deworming initiative was slow. The Ministry of Education was severely understaffed (just four people worked exclusively on school health for the entire country), hamstrung by a budget freeze, and distracted by everyday crises. It had scarce time to plan and coordinate the many cross-sectoral details of implementation that such a program would require.[18]

In 2007, events outside Kenya's borders helped school-based deworming regain its prior momentum. Kremer was a member of the World Economic Forum of Young Global Leaders, a body that met regularly to address global issues. At that year's meeting, he and MIT economist Esther Duflo successfully nominated school-based deworming as a component of the Young Global

Leaders education platform.[19] The publicity generated by the meeting helped Kremer and Duflo's fledgling Deworm the World Initiative raise its first seed money, allowing them to hire and second a staff member for the Kenyan Ministry of Education.[20]

Reinvigorated by the extra set of hands and increased attention, preparations moved along. Feed the Children donated 300 million deworming pills to Deworm the World for use in Kenya and elsewhere. This allowed the government to keep costs low and sidestep bureaucratic procurement procedures.[21] The government used a nationwide fecal survey and mapping exercise to identify high-burden areas and guide the design of the intervention.[22] In 2009, school-based deworming went live at scale.

But after just one round, mass deworming came to a halt when new revelations of corruption hit the Ministry of Education. Donors fled the education sector en masse and suspended the Kenyan Education Sector Support Program, which had served as the source of financing for the deworming program. The government and donors alike wanted the deworming program to continue, but neither was willing to channel the funds through the corruption-tainted Ministry of Education.[23]

Deworm the World stepped up to the plate to provide technical assistance and become the program's "fiscal agent," handling financial management and taking the lead on fundraising. With generous donations from the Children's Investment Fund Foundation (CIFF) and the END Fund, school-based deworming resumed in 2012.

National Deworming in Action

Deworming requires just one dose of a deworming drug per child per year, but delivering that one dose necessitated a sophisticated program. Kenya's national deworming program was a wide-ranging vertical and horizontal collaboration entailing the participation of officials across ministries and disciplines at every level of government. Within the Kenyan government, a strong partnership between the Ministry of Health and the Ministry of Education was essential for program success. The Ministry of Health provided technical guidance, while the Ministry of Education lent its infrastructure and huge cadre of teachers to administer the school-based treatment.[24]

The program was run at the national level by a steering committee that set overall policy and a management committee that managed day-to-day operations. From there, supplies, training, and guidelines flowed down through the different layers of regional and local government and ultimately to primary schools. Program insiders call this the "cascade" process, and it is the foundation for mass deworming implementation.[25]

It works like this: Representatives of the national program first meet with education and health directors at the county level. Then, as part of ongoing implementation, "master trainers" from the county governments visit subcounties and wards to calculate the quantity of deworming drugs needed and instruct local ministry officials in training teachers to carry out the program and administer the drug. Once up to speed, those officials train teachers on their role in the program. Finally, trained teachers and community health extension workers help educate community members about the upcoming deworming treatment that their children will undergo.[26]

With all the preparations in place, schools are ready for the annual "deworming day." When children ages 2 to 14 arrive at their local primary school, teachers distribute deworming tablets and watch each child swallow a tablet of albendazole for STHs. In high-schistosomiasis-prevalence areas, children also receive an appropriate dose of praziquante for schistosomes. Ministry of Health and Ministry of Education officials are on hand to supervise and manage any adverse effects—which are extremely rare—through an extensive protocol. Nonenrolled children who live nearby are also encouraged to visit the school on deworming day to participate in the program.[27]

Teachers track the number of children dewormed on forms designed for this purpose. School-level data flow up in what program leaders call the "reverse cascade": monitoring forms are collected in schools; data are compiled by local authorities; and the results make their way up through subcounty and county officials and, finally, to the national office. In addition, the program contracts the Kenya Medical Research Institute to administer twice-yearly stool- and urine-based prevalence surveys in four high-burden regions. The combined feedback from this surveillance enables program leaders to closely monitor progress toward coverage targets and to tweak program design.[28]

The Payoff: Worm-Free Childhoods

Encouraging results from the Busia trial provided a strong basis for national scale-up. Researchers' analysis of the data showed that one year after the intervention, children who received deworming treatment were 44 percent less likely to have a moderate or severe worm infection than before.[29] As a result, they were significantly taller, were less likely to report general ill health or being sick in the past week, and were less likely to miss school than they would have been without treatment. What's more, benefits accrued not only to those treated with deworming drugs but also to their untreated peers because fewer parasites were transmitted.

Ten years after their initial study, researchers conducted a long-term follow-up study on the effects of the deworming program. In the first two groups of schools to receive treatment—that is, schools receiving two to three additional years of free deworming relative to the control group—former students had substantially better labor market outcomes, higher incomes, and better self-reported health. Among female former students, miscarriages were reduced by more than two-thirds.[30] These results suggested that early access to free deworming had a lifelong impact on schoolchildren's health and quality of life.

Another study found that the mass deworming campaign had major knock-on effects for the students' younger siblings—babies at the time of the program who were too young to be dewormed and had never received deworming treatment directly. A decade later, those schoolchildren enjoyed gains in cognitive performance "comparable to between 0.5 and 0.8 years of schooling" when compared with similar children whose communities had never received deworming.[40]

Since the Busia program, Deworm the World and the government of Kenya have tried to replicate these benefits nationwide. The national scale-up represents a significant operational success in a country that struggles with limited educational and health system capacity. By 2014, the program was administering anti-STH medication to 6.4 million children and antischistosome treatment to 890,000 children each year.[41]

The long-term impact of Kenya's national program is not yet known, but early results are encouraging. In 2008, fecal surveys turned up a national STH prevalence of 57 percent in Kenyan schoolchildren.[42] By late 2014, four high-burden provinces had seen dramatic reductions in infection, with STH prevalence falling to just 6 percent. Between 2012 and 2014, those same high-burden regions also saw prevalence of the two different schistosomiasis varieties drop by 58 percent (to 0.6 percent prevalence) and 67 percent (to 7.6 percent prevalence), respectively, representing major health gains for Kenyan children.[43]

Gains at What Price?

The launch of Kenya's deworming program was made possible by financial support from the World Bank and other donors to the Kenyan Education Sector Support Program. Later financial support was provided by the END Fund and CIFF via Deworm the World, serving as fiscal agent and technical support partner. Drugs are donated by pharmaceutical companies through the World Health Organization global drug donation program. In Kenya, school-based deworming costs just US$0.56 per child, and the per-child cost is even lower in other countries.[44]

Deworming appears to be and is widely recognized as a highly cost-effective intervention, although estimates from different sources vary substantially depending on the underlying parameters.[45] An analysis of Kenya's national school-based deworming program conducted for *Millions Saved* yielded a cost-effectiveness ratio of US$47.20 per DALY averted.[46] The estimate indicates that if everyone in need received treatment, the intervention would be highly cost-effective. Importantly, this calculation does not capture the nonhealth benefits, mainly increased school attendance. Any cost-effectiveness estimate will vary depending on the underlying prevalence and intensity of the parasite and the local cost of deworming, which can be as low as US$0.09 per child, the cost in Bihar, India.[47]

There is considerable debate regarding the actual cost per DALY averted by school-based deworming—and even whether DALYs are an appropriate metric by which to judge its benefits. Because the Busia treatment generated schooling and economic gains, plus knock-on gains among children who never received deworming treatment, some question the accuracy of limiting the deworming benefits to a measure of health status such as a DALY. Ongoing uncertainty about the short- and long-term health benefits of deworming (see Box 1), and the appropriate disability weights for STH and schistosomiasis infection, further compound the measurement challenge.[48]

Box 1. Strength of the Evidence

Miguel and Kremer's pilot evaluation and two follow-up papers published 10 years later exploited one experiment—the randomized rollout of mass deworming treatment in Busia—to evaluate a broad range of short- and long-term health and welfare outcomes.[31] As cluster-randomized studies that accounted for treatment externalities, these papers, even though in a single district, represent strong evidence of the effects of deworming on school attendance and health outcomes. In 2015, however, a pair of studies that attempted to replicate and then reanalyze the 2004 study results raised questions about some of its core findings.[32] The subsequent debate about research methods—dubbed "worm wars" by some in the field—was ongoing at the time of writing.

Some skepticism has also arisen about the generalizability of Miguel and Kremer's 2004 results to other countries and regions, particularly the impact on school attendance and physical growth.[33] In 2012, a Cochrane systematic review on the impact of deworming concluded that so far the evidence that mass deworming improved weight gain, hemoglobin levels, cognitive outcomes, or school attendance was limited or mixed, although it did attribute some benefits to targeted deworming programs paired with a screening component.[34] The review noted that the initial Busia study program was conducted almost 15 years ago, during a period when the overall STH and schistosomiasis burden was extremely high (and rising) due to abnormal El Niño–related weather conditions.[35] An updated 2015 Cochrane review concluded, similarly, that treating infected children may help with weight gain but the evidence of the benefits of mass deworming for children's growth, health, and cognition remains unconvincing.[36] A cluster-randomized controlled trial from India, published in 2013, failed to find a relationship between mass STH treatment and improved weight gain or mortality; it did not evaluate cognitive outcomes.[37]

However, some economists and deworming advocates dispute important methodological choices made by the Cochrane authors, alleging that their review presents an "incomplete and misleading summary of the evidence" base, noting two follow-up studies that link the initial deworming project to long-term cognitive and productivity gains.[38] Critics also cite more recent results from a study in Uganda that associated exposure to deworming programs with cognitive improvements, although the study did not identify significant improvements in weight gain following statistical adjustment for clustering.[39] It will be important to continue tracking the results of other studies to shed light on the relevance of the Busia results in other settings and to inform the ongoing debate on the benefits of deworming.

The Keys to Lasting Success

The 2011 corruption scandal in the Ministry of Education could have heralded the end of an otherwise effective program. Deworm the World's assumption of fiscal control—though unavoidable given the circumstances—was a step away from full government control of the program. Even so, the program's international donors worked hard to ensure continued leadership from the Ministries of Health and Education, while continuing to offer their support to those agencies. Ongoing coordination between the partners was ensured by their representation in the national steering and management committees.[49]

In addition, the national deworming effort benefited from forward-thinking donors that were willing to make multiyear funding commitments. Both CIFF and the END Fund committed five-year grants to the program starting in 2012, allowing Deworm the World and "all partners [to] focus on the long game, rather than having to demonstrate quick and potentially superficial wins to obtain more funding on an annual grant cycle."[50] These longer-term commitments made it possible to shift scarce human resources away from fundraising and toward implementation, and gave program leaders the flexibility to make real-time adjustments in the delivery strategy to achieve their coverage goals.[51]

Reliance on donors does, however, make the program vulnerable once this funding expires. The sustainability of the deworming effort may be in question as Kenya, a growing middle-income country, faces funding battles for other disease priorities in its transition toward a larger government budget and increased public spending.

Achieving national scale required savvy program design. To reach millions of children, the government had to walk a fine line. On the one hand, the quest for scale demanded decentralized implementation across hundreds of local authorities; on the other, government officials and donors needed national accountability for the impact of their investments. The program tackled this challenge through a two-way hierarchical structure, the cascade and reverse cascade processes. These mechanisms gave districts the needed flexibility to adapt the program to local contexts, but also the standards and structure to ensure program efficacy and children's safety across a large and diverse country. In addition, the inclusion, beginning in 2013, of deworming metrics in the job performance contract of the minister of health and education ensured that the success of the deworming program would be taken seriously as a core responsibility.[52]

Implications for Global Health

The premise behind mass deworming has always been intuitively appealing. In highly endemic areas like Busia, parasitic intestinal worms were thought to rob children of scarce nutrients while suppressing their appetites and preventing normal digestion, leaving them malnourished, prone to disease, and unable to concentrate in school. But until 2001, no researcher had drawn a clear causal link between mass deworming and short-term benefits, particularly school attendance. Miguel and Kremer's evaluation was a game changer, providing clear evidence to corroborate the simple theory and laying the groundwork to build a global deworming movement.

After helping launch Deworm the World in 2007, Kremer became its founding president. Kremer's program, now called the Deworm the World Initiative (under the umbrella of the nonprofit Evidence Action since 2013), helped deworm a total of 37 million children in 2013 and 2014 through programs in Kenya and India.[53] Mass deworming campaigns are recommended by the World Health Organization and have been endorsed as a priority policy by the Copenhagen Consensus, an international collaboration of global experts aiming to identify solutions to the world's most pressing social problems.[54]

Despite the global momentum, including new funding commitments from CIFF and the Bill & Melinda Gates Foundation, among others, questions about the overall evidence base have made some donors wary about devoting their limited health resources to mass deworming campaigns.[55] The continuing debate also underlines the need to situate evaluation results, particularly those from a single trial or in a specific setting, within the totality of the evidence base, to understand baseline levels of endemicity, and to exercise caution when acting on evidence from a single study or generalizing the results to different epidemiological and cultural contexts.

Many governments have decided that mass school-based deworming is a solid investment. In India, the government of Bihar state began large-scale implementation of mass school-based deworming in 2011, with notable operational success. In Bihar, the deworming program is primarily government funded and managed, with the Deworm the World Initiative providing technical assistance and relatively modest "catalytic funds" to get the ball rolling. By 2015, the initiative had expanded its work in India to another two states.[56] The Indian government also implemented the first round of a national program with the initiative's technical support, targeting an astounding 140 million children at risk for worm infection.[57] The Deworm the World Initiative is widely cited by "good giving" organizations such as GiveWell and Giving What We Can as a highly effective and cost-effective charity.[58]

In sum, Kenya's deworming experience shows that pairing decentralized delivery with measures to promote national accountability can work. It also illustrates that public health interventions can impact more than health, reinforcing the need to look at synergistic gains in education, productivity, and growth when calculating cost-effectiveness estimates. Health gains can quantifiably improve other important social outcomes. In Kenya, deworming's wide-ranging benefits changed the lives of millions of children for the better.

REFERENCES

Alderman, Harold, Joseph Konde-Lule, Isaac Sebuliba, Donald Bundy, and Andrew Hall. 2006. "Effect on Weight Gain of Routinely Giving Albendazole to Preschool Children during Child Health Days in Uganda: Cluster Randomised Controlled Trial." *BMJ* 333 (7559): 122. doi:10.1136/bmj.38877.393530.7C.

Ashraf, Nava, Neil Buddy Shah, and Rachel Gordon. 2010. *Deworming Kenya: Translating Research into Actions (A)*. Harvard Business School Case 910-001. Cambridge, MA: Harvard Business School.

Awasthi, Shally, Richard Peto, Simon Read, Susan M. Richards, Vinod Pande, Donald Bundy, and DEVTA (Deworming and Enhanced Vitamin A) team. 2013. "Population Deworming Every 6 Months with Albendazole in 1 Million Pre-school Children in North India: DEVTA, a Cluster-Randomised Trial." *Lancet* 381 (9876): 1478–86. doi:10.1016/S0140-6736(12)62126-6.

Baird, Sarah, Joan Homory, Michael Kremer, and Edward Miguel. 2011. "Worms at Work: Long-Run Impacts of Child Health Gains." Working Paper, Harvard University, Cambridge, MA.

Berger, Alexander. 2011. "Errors in DCP2 Cost-Effectiveness Estimate for Deworming." GiveWell blog, September 29. http://blog.givewell.org/2011/09/29/errors-in-dcp2-cost-effectiveness-estimate-for-deworming/.

———. 2012. "New Cochrane Review of the Effectiveness of Deworming." GiveWell blog, July 13. http://blog.givewell.org/2012/07/13/new-cochrane-review-of-the-effectiveness-of-deworming/.

Bill & Melinda Gates Foundation. 2014. "Global Partners Are Taking the 'Neglect' out of 'Neglected Tropical Diseases.'" News release, April 2. http://www.gatesfoundation.org/Media-Center/Press-Releases/2014/04/Global-Partners-Are-Taking-the-Neglect-out-of-Neglected-Tropical-Diseases.

Copenhagen Consensus Center. 2015. "Outcome: The Expert Panel Findings." Accessed October 13. http://www.copenhagenconsensus.com/copenhagen-consensus-iii/outcome.

Council of Economic Advisers. 2003. *Annual Report of the Council of Economic Advisers*. Washington, DC: United States Government Printing Office. http://www.presidency.ucsb.edu/economic_reports/2003.pdf.

Croke, Kevin. 2014. "The Long Run Effects of Early Childhood Deworming on Literacy and Numeracy: Evidence from Uganda." Working paper, Harvard School of Public Health, Boston. http://scholar.harvard.edu/files/kcroke/files/ug_lr_deworming_071714.pdf.

Davey, Calum, Alexander M. Aiken, Richard J. Hayes, and James R. Hargreaves. 2015. "Re-analysis of Health and Educational Impacts of a School-based Deworming Programme in Western Kenya: A Statistical Replication of a Cluster Quasi-randomized Stepped-Wedge Trial." *International Journal of Epidemiology* 44 (5): 1581–92. doi:10.1093/ije/dyv128.

Dickson, R., S. Awasthi, C. Demellweek, and P. Williamson. 2000. "Anthelmintic Drugs for Treating Worms in Children: Effects on Growth and Cognitive Performance." *Cochrane Database of Systematic Reviews* 2000 (2). Article CD000371. http://onlinelibrary.wiley.com/doi/10.1002/14651858.CD000371/abstract.

Duflo, Annie, Alissa Fishbane, Rachel Glennerster, Michael Kremer, Temina Madon, and Edward Miguel. 2012. "Cochrane's Incomplete and Misleading Summary of the Evidence on Deworming." Innovations for Poverty Action blog, July 20. http://www.poverty-action.org/blog/cochrane%25E2%2580%2599s-incomplete-and-misleading-summary-evidence-deworming.

Evidence Action. 2015a. "Deworm the World Initiative." Accessed July 8. http://www.evidenceaction.org/#deworm-the-world.

———. 2015b. "Impact Report: Our First 24 Months." Accessed October 13. http://www.evidenceaction.org/impact-first-report/.

———. 2015c. "World's Largest Deworming Program in India to Start With Support from Evidence Action." Evidence Action blog, February 9. http://www.evidenceaction.org/blog-full/largest-deworming-program-in-india-to-start-with-support-from-evidence-action.

GiveWell. 2011. "Combination Deworming (Mass Drug Administration Targeting Both Schistosomiasis and Soil-Transmitted Helminths)." http://www.givewell.org/international/technical/programs/deworming/2011-report.

REFERENCES, *continued*

———. 2015. "Top Charities." Accessed July 8. http://www. givewell.org/charities/top-charities.

Giving What We Can. 2015. "Top Charities." Accessed July 8. http://www.givingwhatwecan.org/top-charities.

Government of Kenya. 2014. *Performance Contract between the Government of Kenya and the Cabinet Secretary Ministry of Health for the Period July 2013 to June 2014.* Nairobi, Kenya: Government of Kenya. http://www. devolutionplanning.go.ke/wp-content/uploads/2014/08/MINISTRY-OF-HEALTH.pdf.

Harrison, Jessica. 2015. "School for Scaling." *Stanford Social Innovation Review,* April. http://www.ssireview.org/articles/entry/school_for_scaling.

Hotez, Peter J., Donald A.P. Bundy, Kathleen Beegle, Simon Brooker, Lesley Drake, Nilanthi de Silva, Antonio Montresor, et al. 2006. "Helmith Infections: Soil-Transmitted Helminth Infections and Schistosomiasis." In *Disease Control Priorities in Developing Countries,* 2nd ed. Washington, DC: World Bank.

Kabaka, Stewart, and Christine Wanza Kisia. 2011. "National Deworming Program: Kenya's Experience." Background paper prepared for the World Conference on Social Determinants of Health, Rio de Janeiro, Brazil, October 19–21.

Miguel, Edward, and Michael Kremer. 2004. "Worms: Identifying Impacts on Education and Health in the Presence of Treatment Externalities." *Econometrica* 72 (1): 159–217.

Ministry of Education, Science and Technology. 2014. *Kenya National School-Based Deworming Programme: Year 2 Report.* Nairobi, Kenya: Ministry of Education, Science and Technology.

Mirelman, Andrew, Amanda Glassman, and Miriam Temin. 2016. *Estimating the Avertable Disease Burden and Cost-Effectiveness in* Millions Saved *Third Edition.* CGD Working Paper. Washington, DC: Center for Global Development.

Mwandawiro, Charles S., Birgit Nikolay, Jimmy H. Kihara, Owen Ozier, Dunstan A. Mukoko, Mariam T. Mwanje, Anna Hakobyan, Rachel L. Pullan, Simon J. Brooker, and Sammy M. Njenga. 2013. "Monitoring and Evaluating the Impact of National School-Based Deworming in Kenya: Study Design and Baseline Results." *Parasites and Vectors* 6 (1): 198. doi:10.1186/1756-3305-6-198.

Ozier, Owen W. 2014. *Exploiting Externalities to Estimate the Long-Term Effects of Early Childhood Deworming.* Policy Research Working Paper 7052. Washington, DC: World Bank.

Taylor-Robinson, David C., Nicola Maayan, Karla Soares-Weiser, Sarah Donegan, and Paul Garner. 2015. "Deworming Drugs for Soil-Transmitted Intestinal Worms in Children: Effects on Nutritional Indicators, Haemoglobin, and School Perfor-

mance." In *Cochrane Database of Systematic Reviews* 2015 (7). Article CD000371. http://onlinelibrary.wiley.com/doi/10.1002/14651858.CD000371.pub6/abstract.

Ted, Miguel, and Michael Kremer. 1999. "The Educational Impact of De-worming in Kenya." Working paper, Harvard University, Cambridge, MA. http://www.cid.harvard.edu/archive/events/cidneudc/papers/worm_sep.pdf.

WHO (World Health Organization). 2013. *Improved School-Based Deworming Coverage through Intersectoral Coordination: The Kenya Experience.* Brazzaville, Republic of the Congo: WHO Regional Office for Africa.

———. 2014. "Number of Children (Pre-SAC and SAC) Requiring Preventive Chemotherapy for Soil-Transmitted Helminthiases, 2013." http://apps.who.int/neglected_diseases/ntddata/sth/sth.html.

———. 2015a. "Schistosomiasis: A Major Public Health Problem." Accessed July 8. http://www.who.int/schistosomiasis/en/.

———. 2015b. "Soil-Transmitted Helminth Infections." Fact Sheet 366. Updated May. http://www.who.int/mediacentre/factsheets/fs366/en/.

Williams, Katherine. 2015. "How Do We Calculate the Cost of Deworming." Evidence Action blog, January 16. http://www.evidenceaction.org/blog-full/how-do-we-calculate-the-cost-of-deworming.

World Bank. 2006. *World Development Report 2006: Equity and Development.* Washington, DC: World Bank.

ENDNOTES

1. WHO (2014).
2. Miguel and Kremer (2004).
3. WHO (2015b).
4. WHO (2015b).
5. WHO (2015a).
6. Hotez et al. (2006).
7. WHO (2014).
8. WHO (2013).
9. Kabaka and Kisia (2011).
10. Miguel and Kremer (2004).
11. Dickson et al. (2000).
12. Miguel and Kremer (2004).
13. Per World Health Organization recommendations, schistosomiasis treatment was provided only in schools with greater than 30 percent schistosomiasis prevalence (see Miguel and Kremer 2004).
14. Miguel and Kremer (2004).
15. Miguel and Kremer (2004).
16. See, for example, Council of Economic Advisers (2003) and World Bank (2006).
17. Ashraf, Shah, and Gordon (2010).
18. Ashraf, Shah, and Gordon (2010).

ENDNOTES, *continued*

19. Ashraf, Shah, and Gordon (2010).
20. Michael Kremer, personal communication with the author, September 26, 2014.
21. Ashraf, Shah, and Gordon (2010).
22. Kabaka and Kisia (2011).
23. Jessica Harrison, personal communication with the author, September 19, 2014.
24. Harrison (2015).
25. Ministry of Education, Science and Technology (2014).
26. Ministry of Education, Science and Technology (2014).
27. Ministry of Education, Science and Technology (2014).
28. Ministry of Education, Science and Technology (2014).
29. Davey et al. (2015).
30. Baird et al. (2011).
31. Miguel and Kremer (2004); Ozier (2014); Baird et al. (2011).
32. Davey et al. (2015).
33. Duflo et al. (2012); Berger (2012).
34. Taylor-Robinson et al. (2015).
35. Berger (2012).
36. Taylor-Robinson et al. (2015).
37. Awasthi et al. (2013).
38. Duflo et al. (2012).
39. Croke (2014); Alderman et al. (2006).
40. Ozier (2014).
41. Ministry of Education, Science and Technology (2014).
42. WHO (2013).
43. Ministry of Education, Science and Technology (2014).
44. Based on figures used by the Deworm the World Initiative (see Williams 2015). Because of its small scale and inbuilt evaluation costs, the initial Busia program cost considerably more, at a total of US$1.46 per treated student (see Ted and Kremer 1999).
45. Berger (2011).
46. The estimation of DALYs averted was based on the estimated population aged 5–16 years, baseline year prevalence estimates (see Mwandawiro et al. 2013), and World Health Organization (WHO) weighting recommendations for disability from worms and schistosomiasis, yielding a DALY estimate consistent with WHO Global Health Estimates. Costs were derived from GiveWell (2011). See Mirelman, Glassman, and Temin (2016).
47. Williams (2015).
48. GiveWell (2011).
49. Harrison (2015).
50. Harrison (2015, 59).
51. Harrison (2015).
52. Government of Kenya (2014).
53. Evidence Action (2015b).
54. Copenhagen Consensus Center (2015).
55. Bill & Melinda Gates Foundation (2014).
56. Evidence Action (2015a).
57. Evidence Action (2015c).
58. See, for example, GiveWell (2015) and Giving What We Can (2015).

CASE 7

An Outbreak Halted in Its Tracks
Eliminating Polio in Haiti

The Case at a Glance

HEALTH GOAL: To eliminate circulating polioviruses and eradicate all poliovirus strains.

STRATEGY: School- and community-based polio vaccination for children under age 10 via National Immunization Days and house-to-house campaigns.

HEALTH IMPACT: Outbreak stopped. Last case of paralytic polio in Haiti in 2001.

WHY IT WORKED: Swift action after first case of paralytic polio was identified. Coordination between Haiti, the Dominican Republic, and international donors. Improved surveillance and monitoring.

FINANCING: US$4.82 million.

SCALE: More than 90 percent of 2.5 million Haitian children under age 10.

Polio is a highly infectious virus whose best-known lasting effect is paralysis, often of the legs and lower body. The virus attacks the motor neurons of the spinal cord and brain stem. A person who contracts paralytic polio will feel tired, stiff, and in pain; will have trouble breathing; and may experience muscle spasms. More acute muscle pain, loss of reflexes, and sudden paralysis can follow. These symptoms may be temporary or cause permanent disability, requiring a person to use a wheelchair or crutches, or in the most severe cases, may end in death. There is no cure for polio, and in many affected countries there are few supportive therapies to treat its symptoms and prevent further health complications.

When an individual is confirmed to be suffering from paralytic polio, he or she is seen as the "tip of an epidemic iceberg."[1] Without proper vaccine coverage and surveillance, one case of polio can escalate quickly into an epidemic. Ridding the world of polio is an ongoing struggle. Some countries have seen polio return after being designated polio-free for many years.

This was the case in 2000 in Haiti, when a two-year-old girl in Haiti's Northwest Department contracted paralytic polio from a circulating vaccine-derived strain of the virus. Largely due to poor sanitation, limited vaccine cov-

erage, and weak surveillance, the outbreak caused 20 more cases across Hispaniola, a Caribbean island shared by Haiti and the Dominican Republic, over the next year.[2]

Haiti's broader political and health system challenges added to the perilous mix of risks that opened the door to polio.[3] Ongoing political instability is one reason Haiti was, and remains, the poorest country in the western hemisphere—in 2001, 55 percent of the population lived on less than US$1 per day.[4] This level of extreme poverty was a lasting effect of the traumas of the 1990s, when Haitians faced serious violations of their human rights, poverty, malnutrition, and unstable institutions as the country struggled to establish democracy and the rule of law.

The outbreak might have been worse. Despite the adverse political environment and the government's small contribution to the health sector—only 1–2 percent of the gross domestic product—the Ministry of Public Health and Population and international agencies such as the Pan American Health Organization (PAHO) and the US Centers for Disease Control and Prevention (CDC) quickly invoked aggressive control measures and cut off circulation of the virus when polio broke out.[5] Although vaccination coverage rates fluctuated between

This case was originally authored by Lauren Post.

2001 and 2013, immunization against polio has largely been sustained.[6] Haiti managed to stave off yet another polio outbreak after an earthquake in 2010, when some feared the disease might reemerge alongside a tragic cholera outbreak.[7]

Around the globe, polio is nearing elimination. In August 2015, the entire continent of Africa marked one year without a case of wild polio. But countries remain at risk of outbreaks for an extended period after the apparent elimination of the disease, especially where surveillance systems are weak. Haiti's experience in combating a resurgent outbreak of polio serves as a cautionary and inspiring story of how an extremely poor country with limited human resources can do basic public health right.

The Toll of Poliomyelitis

Commonly known as polio, poliomyelitis is caused by polioviruses, which can emerge in a "wild" or natural form or, in some cases, as a result of a mutation of the live version of the virus that is used in the oral polio vaccine. Although the majority of people who contract polio do not exhibit symptoms, others experience flu-like signs, including fever, sore throat, nausea, or headache.[8] And in the least common yet most extreme scenario, polio invades the central nervous system, affecting the brain and spinal cord and causing paralysis.

The disease is commonly spread by an infected person's feces; the insidious virus can spread both before and after symptoms appear.[9] Ninety percent of infected people don't exhibit symptoms, but they still have the ability to infect others. Even worse, the virus remains viable outside the body for up to two months, surviving in water, food, feces, and even clothing, where it can easily infect others through contact. Young children with low resistance to the virus, especially in places with poor sanitation, are at particularly high risk for infection.

Polio can be prevented with a vaccine, which comes in two forms, an injection and an oral vaccine. The injected polio vaccine (IPV) is made from a version of the poliovirus that has been deactivated; it provides immunity after four shots and is the standard in high-income countries.[10] The oral polio vaccine (OPV), developed by Dr. Albert Sabin, is made from a weakened but still active strain of the poliovirus and requires at least three doses for immunity.[11] OPV is cheaper than IPV, but OPV provides intestinal immunity and was the vaccine of choice in the Americas to eradicate wild poliovirus. Like other vaccines, both IPV and OPV work by activating an immune response in the body so that the body builds up antibodies to protect itself from the virus.

Thanks to these vaccines, the world has seen a dramatic reduction in polio cases from an estimated 350,000 cases in 1988 to an all-time low of just about 100 cases in 2015.[12] Most of the 126 countries where polio was formerly endemic had succeeded in eliminating polio by 2001.[13]

Ironically, however, this success has come with a specific risk: the widely used OPV can cause polio, threatening communities that have low immunity and poor vaccine coverage. This occurs because the active form of the virus in OPV can replicate in the intestines, be excreted when people defecate, and spread around a community. Although this can be beneficial because the excreted virus can help others build up their immune responses to the virus (known as passive or herd immunity), it can also be dangerous, posing the risk of creating a type of polio known as circulating vaccine-derived poliovirus (cVDPV). This type of virus can circulate for longer than a year and can mutate into a form that acts like a wild virus, easily transmitting to people who are not immune and potentially paralyzing them.[14]

In Latin America in the 1970s, there were an estimated 15,000 paralysis cases and 1,750 deaths from polio every year. Following the successful eradication of polio in the United States, PAHO began a polio eradication campaign in the 1970s in Latin America and the Caribbean. In 1977, countries in the region added OPV to PAHO's Expanded Program on Immunization (EPI) schedule to combat wild poliovirus.

The plan for eliminating wild poliovirus across North, Central, and South America had been realized under the leadership of Dr. Ciro de Quadros, director of the immunization program at PAHO. De Quadros found his inspiration in the successful control programs in Brazil and Cuba, which, in 1963, was the first country in the region to successfully eradicate wild poliovirus.[15] De Quadros enlisted the help of Rotary International, the United States Agency for International Development (USAID), the United Nations Children's Fund (UNICEF), the Inter-American Development Bank, and the Canadian Public Health Association to launch widespread OPV immunization campaigns. The campaigns and robust country surveillance systems proved successful, and polio's spread was curtailed.[16] The last case of paralytic polio was documented in Peru in 1991.[17] After maintaining zero polio cases for three years, the World Health Organization (WHO)–designated

Region of the Americas was officially certified polio-free in 1994. The region thought it had seen the end of polio.

Putting an Idea in Motion: Haiti's Surveillance System Sounds the Alarm

Haiti's health system was on particularly shaky ground following a violent coup d'état in 1991. President Jean-Bertrand Aristide, the first democratically elected president in Haiti, was overthrown and forced into exile, and the military proceeded to violate citizens' human rights. The turmoil led donor countries and multilateral agencies to suspend their support and technical aid to the Haitian Ministry of Public Health and Population's programs.[18]

Haiti's weak health system degraded further under these conditions. Extremely low polio vaccine coverage, alongside poor sanitation conditions, continued to plague the country throughout the 1990s.[19] Shortly after the region was deemed polio-free, the Haitian government suspended concentrated mass immunizations that took place on National Immunization Days.[20] These OPV immunization campaigns were a tried-and-true strategy for fighting the virus, but interest in and financing for them had faded in Haiti after the wild poliovirus had been wiped out.[21] The result was devastating: the share of children under one year old receiving at least three doses of OPV stagnated at 30–50 percent during the 1990s.[22] Haiti's staggering debt obligations also contributed to health system weaknesses; domestic funding for basic sanitation and public health interventions was simply cut.[23]

A lack of investment in water quality measures and sanitation also created conditions conducive to a polio outbreak. The political climate contributed to these conditions; corrupt officials and violence against ordinary citizens got in the way of much-needed rural water and sanitation improvement projects over several decades. This was particularly troubling because vaccine-derived poliovirus can live in water and be transmitted via feces.[24]

Despite these challenges, there was one piece of good news: Haiti's epidemiological surveillance system (ESS) had remained more or less intact. This was thanks in large part to the Haitian Children's Institute (Institut Haitien de l'Enfance), a private group that conducts national health surveys.

In Haiti, the last case of paralytic polio had been documented by the ESS in 1989.[25] However, in the summer of 2000, a two-year-old girl in the country's Northwest Department experienced acute flaccid paralysis (AFP), a

sudden onset of paralysis, and the case was reported by the ESS. A follow-up investigation by Haiti's Ministry of Public Health and Population, PAHO's Caribbean Epidemiology Center, and the CDC confirmed the worst fears: polio was back.[26] Shortly after that, another case of AFP was confirmed as poliomyelitis across the border in the Dominican Republic.

It was the ESS routine surveillance system that detected the initial new case in 2000. Per ESS requirements, the case was investigated as suspected poliomyelitis. A stool sample was sent to a laboratory within the region—PAHO's poliovirus laboratory at the Caribbean Epidemiology Center—and the poliovirus was isolated.[27] The isolate was then sent to the CDC poliovirus laboratory for further investigation and confirmation of the findings.[28]

Following the CDC's confirmation, Haitian health officials learned they were dealing with a poliovirus that was derived from the vaccine, one that was biologically similar to the wild poliovirus. In other words, a vaccine-derived virus had developed the ability to behave like its naturally occurring cousin, causing paralysis and rapid person-to-person transmission.[29] It seemed likely that the virus had already infected thousands more who may have been contagious but had not exhibited symptoms. It was not long before several more cases of paralytic polio were confirmed on Hispaniola; by early 2001, 8 cases had been confirmed in Haiti and 14 in the Dominican Republic.[30]

The lab analysis traced the source of this particular strain to an OPV dose given to a child in a community with low vaccine coverage in late 1998 or early 1999.[31] Epidemiologists concluded that the outbreak first began among nonimmune children in Haiti and spread to the Dominican Republic a few months later via contaminated food or an infected person.[32]

The confirmed cases were all in children ages 2 to 12 who were either entirely or partially unvaccinated and mostly living in areas with partial OPV coverage.[33] In the Northwest Department, the site of the first case, vaccination coverage was only 40 percent as of 2001.[34]

Polio Vaccination in Action

PAHO and the CDC jumped in to help Haiti stop polio in its tracks. The two agencies sent 16 epidemiologists to conduct an active search for AFP cases in both countries.[35] They reached out to religious leaders, teachers, day care center directors, mothers, and traditional healers to locate unreported cases of AFP.[36]

Meanwhile, the government of Haiti put aggressive control measures back in place. Initial action included vaccination near the site where paralytic polio had been detected, plus vaccination nationwide at fixed posts such as at health facilities. In early 2001, the Ministry of Public Health and Population, with the technical help of PAHO, conducted two rounds of vaccination. But inadequate planning, logistical problems, and heavy rains undermined the government's early control activities, and immunization reached barely 40 percent of the 1.2 million Haitian children under the age of five.[37] By mid-2001, Haiti was in trouble—the government and its partners had not managed to immunize enough of the population to guarantee protection.

This prompted the minister of health, Dr. Jean Claude Voltaire, to launch a new strategy that was even more ambitious: nationwide school-based vaccination of all children under 10 followed by two rounds of house-to-house OPV vaccination of all remaining eligible children. By this point the international response had also intensified. PAHO, UNICEF, the World Bank, the Canadian government, and USAID provided technical and financial support to the Health and Education Ministries for the new strategy. The intensified efforts led to two national immunization campaigns in the spring and fall of 2001.

Sensitive and timely reporting of AFP had proved to be critical for controlling polio. The ESS was key in the detection of and response to the outbreak, yet the surveillance system had weak links. At the time of the outbreak, more than half of the paralysis notification sites had not been completing their weekly reports, and not one AFP case reported over the previous five years had stool specimens collected and tested.[38] To improve surveillance, more than 100 local healthcare workers were trained to conduct active case searches during their community-based activities.[39] PAHO also continued to send epidemiologists to reinforce surveillance activities, and the Ministry of Public Health and Population even offered a reward of US$100 to anyone who reported a laboratory-confirmed case.[40]

The government of Haiti coordinated its efforts with the government of the Dominican Republic, sharing information across the border. By late 2001, coordination had turned into collaboration. Senior health officials from the two countries' ministries of public health met at the main border area to devise a plan for ensuring that all children passing through the official border crossings were vaccinated at one of the specially placed vaccine posts on either side.[41]

The measles vaccine program in both countries had been put on hold when paralytic polio arose. However, children needed protection from both deadly epidemics, and experts determined that a joint polio and measles campaign would be both efficient and effective. By mid-2001, the first ladies of both countries were working with health ministers, government authorities, nongovernmental organizations, and international agencies to inaugurate a combined measles-polio campaign.[42] Both vaccines were administered when the third national OPV immunization campaign took place the following year.

The success of the immunization campaigns and surveillance activities were hard won, as Haiti's Ministry of Public Health and Population had to overcome significant logistical problems. Gaining access to Haiti's poorest, most vulnerable areas was a particular challenge. Most of the country's roads were in terrible condition, and half of the country's health centers lacked adequate cold-chain equipment such as refrigerators to keep OPV viable. Some vaccine vials spoiled or broke, and some vaccination activities had to be rescheduled.[43]

The Payoff: Polio Eliminated, Again

Haiti's immunization campaigns effectively controlled the polio outbreak by blanketing the country with protection. The Expanded Program on Immunization (EPI) in the Americas reported that 2.4 million OPV doses were administered to children during the first National Immunization Day and house-to-house mop-up, reaching 88 percent of children under age 10.[44] The second campaign did even better, reaching 93 percent of the target population.[45] Local monitoring reports from healthcare workers on polio vaccine coverage and suspected AFP cases were used to validate the administrative data reported by the EPI. This confirmed approximately 90 percent immunization coverage, and mop-up activities bumped that percentage even higher.[46]

At a meeting in August 2001, one year after the first confirmed case of paralytic polio, George A.O. Alleyne, the director of PAHO, called Haiti's polio campaign a "success story."[47] In fact, a case of paralytic polio that had been diagnosed on April 26, 2001, in a two-year-old in Port-au-Prince turned out to be the last documented case in Haiti.[48] The Dominican Republic also put a stop to the circulating vaccine-derived virus. A case there in January 2001 was later confirmed as the last.[49]

No new cases of paralytic polio were reported after the immunization campaigns, confirming their success. It is generally recognized that routine immunization prevents and stops polio outbreaks; without it, immunization coverage drops, levels of immunity decline, and wild or vaccine-derived poliovirus can find fertile ground. Still, it remains unclear which aspects of Haiti's efforts were the most effective and efficient, and how big an impact the campaigns had (see Box 1).

Gains at What Price?

Stopping the vaccine-derived paralytic poliovirus outbreak cost Haiti and its partners a total of US$4.82 million, according to the EPI.[50] Of that, Haiti's Ministry of Public Health and Population, despite its limited budget, managed to contribute 20 percent—about 2 percent of its total public health expenditure in 2001—to the effort.[51] Partners contributed the rest: the Canadian International Development Agency, PAHO, the World Bank, the WHO, Rotary International, UNICEF, and USAID.[52] UNICEF's role was of particular importance, as the organization paid for the vaccines and for cold chain equipment to keep vaccines viable when transported and stored.

Modeling the cost-effectiveness of combating an outbreak like polio is inherently difficult given the significant uncertainty around how and where an outbreak will spread. Quantifying costs due to a "societal reaction" such as anxiety or violence is also difficult.[53] Furthermore, given the lack of an attributable estimate of health impact, it is a challenge to estimate the cost-effectiveness of the polio eradication efforts in Haiti. However, it is clear that a large value is placed on the eradication of polio through the mobilization of the government and international partners. Haiti and external donors demonstrated this by the large sums they have invested in eliminating polio.

Notwithstanding methodological challenges, cost-benefit analyses of global polio eradication have been undertaken because eradication will have numerous long-term social benefits and is generally perceived as a global public good.[54] The Global Polio Eradication Initiative (GPEI) estimates that eradicating polio at the global level will cost US$5.5 billion from 2013 to 2018.[55] That's a lofty estimate—but failing to achieve global eradication would likely cost much more in terms of longer-term treatment

Box 1. Strength of the Evidence

Haiti's efforts to control the polio outbreak appear to be a success: the country has not seen a case since 2001. However, only an impact evaluation could demonstrate that the country controlled the outbreak using the most effective tactics.

Another challenge in attributing impact to Haiti's ramped-up activities is confirming the actual coverage—the reported immunization data are based on the number of doses administered and the estimated target population, which can be inaccurate. In fact, in some cases the coverage rate was reported to exceed 100 percent because data were simply divided by the estimated target population, which was based on out-of-date census data. For instance, in mid-2001, it was reported that 2.4 million doses of OPV had been administered to an estimated 2.26 million children. This method of assessing coverage depends heavily on strong local record keeping to feed vital statistics systems and accurate population estimates, both of which are challenging in low-resource countries like Haiti.

costs. Eradicating polio by 2018 would result in massive savings, with some estimates showing a savings of US$40 billion to US$50 billion by 2035, and most of those savings would be in the world's poorest countries.[56]

The Keys to Lasting Success

Haiti's polio success can be attributed to several factors: a quick response from the government and international agencies, the government's commitment to controlling polio, sustained and then improved surveillance, and effective coordination with the neighboring government of the Dominican Republic and other partners.

Although the immunization program and surveillance system failed to provide an early warning of the circulating vaccine-derived polio outbreak in Hispaniola, Haiti stepped up to the plate and deployed its vaccination program and screening capabilities after a case was discovered. Notably, the more rigorous activities Haiti undertook following the disappointment of the initial attempt followed international good practice—the model for polio control that had proved the importance of vaccine coverage and sensitive surveillance decades earlier. In the

1970s and 1980s, the success of polio eradication programs was based mainly on three strategies: National Immunization Days, house-to-house mop-up campaigns in the vicinity of every new outbreak and in areas that were hard to reach, and surveillance using a system that included analysis and diagnosis in virology labs.[57] These lessons from history proved hard to ignore.

Although Haiti's finances were in dire straits, its renewed political commitment to eliminating polio was commendable. The Ministry of Public Health and Population's funding of one-fifth of the polio control program demonstrated that the government was serious about cutting off the polio epidemic quickly. The most visible sign of government commitment was health minister Voltaire's and first lady Mildred Trouillot Aristide's leadership on the combined polio-measles campaign.

Haiti's Ministry of Public Health and Population could not have halted the outbreak on its own. Bilateral and multilateral aid agencies and foreign governments mounted a robust and sustained response to the need to detect cases of paralytic polio. Their financial support and technical expertise were indispensable. Coordination and cooperation between the governments of Haiti and the Dominican Republic led to meetings to ensure that the two countries' efforts were in sync, especially at the border, which proved to be essential.

The underlying causes of Haiti's polio outbreak—a weak health system and struggling sanitation efforts—still persist. Thus, Haitians must remain vigilant to ensure that another epidemic of the vaccine-derived virus does not occur. National reform of the water and sanitation sector was not voted into law until 2009, and the devastating earthquake of 2010 derailed long-term infrastructure plans in favor of pressing humanitarian needs.[58] Efforts to reduce the risk of another outbreak rely on the government's ability not only to ensure polio vaccination coverage but also to build up capacity for water and sanitation improvements and hygiene education to ensure that a vaccine-derived poliovirus does not spread from feces to water or food (see also chapters 20 and 22 on sanitation programs in Indonesia and Peru, respectively).

Implications for Global Health

The GPEI, launched in 1988, has led the way toward an astounding 99 percent reduction in polio incidence worldwide. Still, wild and vaccine-derived polioviruses remain threats in a few strongholds, notably in the populous and complex nations of Pakistan and Afghanistan.

Polio's ability to cross borders underscores the urgency of closing the gaps in immunity and bringing an end to polio. Whereas the outbreak on Hispaniola was restricted to two countries that share one island, the circulation of wild and vaccine-derived polioviruses in Nigeria spread to 20 countries across Africa, the Middle East, and Southeast Asia between 2003 and 2008 (see Box 2).[59] But polio elimination programs face budget shortfalls, and it has become increasingly difficult to maintain high levels of vaccine coverage in countries that have been certified polio-free.[60] Some governments are asking why so much money is needed for such a small number of cases,[61] and "donor fatigue" remains a threat to polio funding.[62]

Furthermore, there is some debate about the best strategies for polio control. Some claim that polio vaccination campaigns now deliver fewer returns than they did when the burden of disease was higher, and that those resources may be better spent, for example, on water and sanitation infrastructure.[63] However, national immunization days remain a proven tool. Take more recent polio breakouts in India and Nigeria, where canceling some or all routine national immunization days resulted in a jump in polio cases and likely set both countries back millions of dollars. And when India brought back national immunization days several years later, the polio epidemic subsided. Time and again countries have seen this trend reoccur, fostering a widespread acceptance of routine national immunization days as a critical tactic to curb the spread of the poliovirus.

To achieve global eradication, the leaders of the GPEI— the WHO, Rotary International, the CDC, UNICEF, and the Bill & Melinda Gates Foundation—and affected-country governments need to agree upon an endgame strategy. This will inevitably require the elimination of the oral vaccine to prevent a vaccine-derived polio outbreak.

There are two potential strategies for eliminating the use of OPV. The first is a transition from OPV to IPV. However, there are questions about the efficacy of IPV in preventing poliovirus circulation in the highest-risk settings: IPV provides less protection than OPV to unimmunized people because IPV does not create herd immunity.[64] IPV is also more expensive, which could be a challenge in low- and middle-income countries if the vaccine costs are not incorporated into current vaccination programs.[65] Still, IPV would reduce the risk of having to pay to respond to a vaccine-derived outbreak caused by OPV.[66] The second strategy is a carefully coordinated termination of OPV without replacing it with IPV. However, this could cause new outbreaks of vaccine-derived virus if not coordinated on a global scale.[67]

An alternative option is to continue to rely on OPV to keep the disease under tight control. Yet as the case of Haiti demonstrates, using OPV indefinitely could be lethal if not coupled with sensitive surveillance, maintenance of vaccine stockpiles, and investments in eradicating polio's underlying causes such as contaminated water and poor sanitation. Most health economists and advocacy groups argue that a carefully planned strategy for worldwide cessation of OPV use should be implemented.[68] Some have also argued that there is an ethical imperative to eradicate polio when the world has the means to do so, and that it would cost less to eradicate the virus than to control it.[69]

Although the GPEI deadline for eradicating polio has been pushed from 2000 to 2007 to 2018, achieving this goal is still feasible. The essential ingredients—broad population immunity and sensitive surveillance systems—are almost within reach. Some even say the world has never been closer to eradication, despite the number of polio cases in Pakistan and Afghanistan.[70] The resurgence of polio in Haiti remains a prime example of what can happen if a country scales back its vaccine campaigns.

The need for rapid responses to health emergencies is only increasing. As the Ebola outbreak of 2014 confirmed, without international preparedness and vigilance, a small disease outbreak can quickly spin out of control, with massive health and economic implications throughout a region. Haiti's experience shows that regional crises can be prevented with smart partnerships among neighboring governments and international health and aid agencies. Having the WHO, CDC, PAHO, UNICEF, and others at the ready was essential to preventing paralytic polio from spreading further on the island of Hispaniola and beyond.

But a focus on eradicating polioviruses via vaccines is not enough. The continued neglect of water and sanitation improvements remains troubling; Haiti's cholera outbreak in 2010 shows that Haitians remain highly vulnerable to waterborne health threats. Without effective investments in water and sanitation, public health authorities must remain doubly vigilant. And international partners should consider the merits of investing in significant water and sanitation improvements in the near term, rather than continuously having to respond to emergency funding requests for vaccination programs over the long term.

Box 2. Achieving Polio-Free Status in Nigeria[71]

Nigeria, despite nearly 30 years of polio eradication efforts, experienced 801 cases of wild poliovirus in 2008—the most of any country that year.[72] Challenges to eliminating polio abounded: geographic diversity, poor infrastructure, tensions between the Muslim north and the Christian south, and a lingering mistrust of biomedicine.

But new leadership of Nigeria's National Primary Health Care Development Agency in 2008 revived the country's commitment to managing polio. Based on learnings from Nigeria's previous polio strategies, the Ministry of Health undertook an ambitious new campaign targeting 160 million people in 36 states. The campaign was funded by the WHO, Rotary International, the CDC, UNICEF, and the Bill & Melinda Gates Foundation.

To improve accountability, the Ministry of Health established an Emergency Operations Center (EOC) to oversee the campaign and to ensure that all key international and national players—especially state governments—were doing their job to improve vaccination coverage. The campaign strategy also included working with traditional leaders to gain community buy-in, increasing the number and efficiency of community vaccinators, and implementing geographic information system technology to identify vaccine coverage shortcomings.

The efforts proved successful: the last case of wild poliovirus occurred in 2014, and the WHO announced that Nigeria was polio-free in September 2015. Between 2014 and 2018, the campaign is expected to avert between 30,000 and 35,000 deaths and save US$4 billion.[73] The mechanisms created by the campaign, such as the EOC, also helped halt an incursion of Ebola in 2015.

Nigeria's experience offers lessons for countries still fighting polio: develop a context-specific strategy; improve accountability; establish community trust; and implement frequent, independent monitoring.

REFERENCES

Alleyne, George A.O. 2001. "Health in Haiti." *Revista Panamerica de Salud Publica / Pan American Journal of Public Health* 10 (3): 149–51. http://www.scielosp.org/scielo.php?pid=S1020-49892001000900001&script=sci_arttext.

Alsan, Marcella M., Michael Westerhaus, Michael Herce, Koji Nakashima, and Paul E. Farmer. 2011. "Poverty, Global Health and Infectious Disease: Lessons from Haiti and Rwanda." *Infectious Disease Clinics of North America* 25 (3): 611–22. doi:10.1016/j.idc.2011.05.004.

Aylward, Bruce, and Tadataka Yamada. 2011. "The Polio Endgame." *New England Journal of Medicine* 364 (24): 2273–75. doi:10.1056/NEJMp1104329.

CDC (Centers for Disease Control and Prevention). 1994. "International Notes Certification of Poliomyelitis Eradication: The Americas, 1994." *Morbidity and Mortality Weekly Report*, October 7.

———. 2001. "Public Health Dispatch: Outbreak of Poliomyelitis: Dominican Republic and Haiti, 2000–2001." *Morbidity and Mortality Weekly Report*, October 5.

———. 2014. "Global Health—Polio: What Is Polio?" Last updated October 15. http://www.cdc.gov/polio/about/.

de Quadros, Ciro, and Monica Brana. 2001a. "Haiti's Polio Campaign: A Success Story." *EPI Newsletter*, August.

———. 2001b. "Update: OPV-Derived Poliomyelitis Outbreak in the Dominican Republic and Haiti." *EPI Newsletter*, February.

———. 2001c. "Update: Vaccine Derived Polio Outbreak in Hispaniola." *EPI Newsletter*, June.

———. 2002. "Haiti and the Dominican Republic Join Efforts to Control Polio and Measles on the Island of Hispaniola." *EPI Newsletter*, June.

Elias, Chris. 2014. "Economic Case for Eradicating Polio: Gates Foundation." *CNBC*, January 22. http://www.cnbc.com/2014/01/22/economic-case-for-eradicating-polio-gates-foundation.html.

Fast, Shannon M., Marta C. González, and Natasha Markuzon. 2015. "Cost-Effective Control of Infectious Disease Outbreaks Accounting for Societal Reaction." *PLoS ONE* 10 (8). doi:10.1371/journal.pone.0136059.

Gelting, Richard, Katherine Bliss, Molly Patrick, Gabriella Lockhart, and Thomas Handzel. 2013. "Water, Sanitation and Hygiene in Haiti: Past, Present, and Future." *American Journal of Tropical Medicine and Hygiene* 89 (4): 655–70.

Global Polio Eradication Initiative. 2013. *Economic Case for Eradicating Polio*. Geneva: Global Polio Eradication Initiative. http://www.polioeradication.org/portals/0/document/resources/strategywork/economiccase.pdf.

———. 2014. *Global Polio Eradication Initiative Financial Resource Requirements, 2013–2018*. Geneva: World Health Organization. http://www.polioeradication.org/Portals/0/Document/Financing/FRR_EN_A4.pdf.

———. 2015. "Fact File: Polio Eradication and Endgame Strategic Plan 2013–2018." Accessed September 22. http://www.polioeradication.org/Resourcelibrary/Strategyandwork.aspx.

———. 2016a. "Oral Polio Vaccine (OPV)." Accessed February 14. http://www.polioeradication.org/Polioandprevention/Thevaccines/Oralpoliovaccine(OPV).aspx.

———. 2016b. "Polio This Week as of 10 February 2016." Accessed February 22. http://www.polioeradication.org/Dataandmonitoring/Poliothisweek.aspx.

Immunization Action Coalition. 2015. "Ask the Experts: Diseases and Vaccines—Polio." Last reviewed February 25. http://www.immunize.org/askexperts/experts_pol.asp.

Jack, Andrew. 2005. "Donor Fatigue Puts Brake on Drive to Eradicate Polio." *Financial Times*, April 12. http://www.ft.com/intl/cms/s/1/f2ececca-ab87-11d9-893c-00000e2511c8.html?siteedition=uk#axzz3mPcK7nD8.

Kaufmann, Judith R., and Harley Feldbaum. 2009. "Diplomacy and the Polio Immunization Boycott in Northern Nigeria." *Health Affairs* 28 (4): 1091–1101. doi:10.1377/hlthaff.28.4.1091.

Kew, Olen, Victoria Morris-Glasgow, Mauricio Landaverde, Cara Burns, Jing Shaw, Zacarıas Garib, Jean André, et al. 2002. "Outbreak of Poliomyelitis in Hispaniola Associated with Circulating Type 1 Vaccine-Derived Poliovirus." *Science* 296 (5566): 356–59. doi:10.1126/science.1068284.

Kew, Olen M., Peter F. Wright, Vadim I. Agol, Francis Delpreyroux, Hiroyuki Shimizu, Neal Nathanson, and Mark Pallansch. 2004. "Circulating Vaccine-Derived Polioviruses: Current State of Knowledge." *Bulletin of the World Health Organization* 82 (1): 16–23.

Levine, Ruth. 2004. "Eliminating Polio in Latin America and the Caribbean." In *Millions Saved: Proven Successes in Global Health*, 39–46. Washington, DC: Center for Global Development.

Modlin, John F. 2010. "The Bumpy Road to Polio Eradication." *New England Journal of Medicine* 362 (25): 2346–49. doi:10.1056/NEJMp1005405.

Nathanson, Neal, and Paul Fine. 2002. "Poliomyelitis Eradication: A Dangerous Endgame." *Science* 296 (5566): 269–70. doi:10.1126/science.1071207.

Nathanson, Neal, and Olen M. Kew. 2010. "From Emergence to Eradication: The Epidemiology of Poliomyelitis Deconstructed." *American Journal of Epidemiology* 172 (11): 1213–29. doi:10.1093/aje/kwq320.

PAHO (Pan American Health Organization). 1994. "Epidemiological Surveillance in Haiti: Experiences and Outlook." *Epidemiological Bulletin*, Summer.

———. 2001. "Costa Rica Embarks on Accelerated Rubella and Congenital Rubella Syndrome Program." *EPI Newsletter: Expanded Program on Immunization in the*

REFERENCES, *continued*

Americas, February. http://www1.paho.org/english/ad/fch/im/sne2301.pdf?ua=1.

———. 2007. "Haiti." In *Health in the Americas, 2007.* Vol. 2, 412–29. Washington, DC: PAHO. http://www1.paho.org/hia/archivosvol2/paisesing/Haiti%20English.pdf.

PAHO and WHO (World Health Organization). 2012. "Haiti." In *Health in the Americas, 2012,* Country Volume, 395–407. Washington, DC: PAHO. http://www.paho.org/saludenlasamericas/index.php?option=com_docman&task=doc_view&gid=134&Itemid=.

———. 2015. "Haiti: Immunization Coverage, 1995–2014." Country Profile. Last updated December 7. http://www.paho.org/hq/index.php?option=com_docman&task=doc_download&Itemid=270&gid=4175&lang=en.

Premji, Aly, Pagie W. Scholar, Azfar Hossain, Lisa Wanda, Jamal Edwards, Kunal Potnis, Laura Winn, et al. 2016. *The Next Country to Be Polio-Free: A Case Study of Nigeria's Challenges, Successes, and Lessons Learned for the Global Quest to Eradicate Polio.* CGD Policy Paper. Washington, DC: Center for Global Development.

Renne, E. P. 2012. "Polio in Nigeria." *History Compass* 10 (7): 496–511. doi:10.1111/j.1478-0542.2012.00859.x.

Rey, Michel, and Marc P. Gerard. 2008. "The Global Eradication of Poliomyelitis: Progress and Problems." *Comparative Immunology Microbiology and Infectious Diseases* 31 (2–3): 317–25. doi:10.1016/j.cimid.2007.07.013.

Rosenstein, Scott, and Emily Hoch. 2011. "Concerns of Polio in Haiti." *Foreign Policy,* January 25. http://foreignpolicy.com/2011/01/25/concerns-of-polio-in-haiti/.

Thompson, Kimberly M., Radboud J. Duintjer Tebbens, Mark Pallansch, Olen M. Kew, Roland W. Sutter, R. Bruce Aylward, Margaret Watkins, et al. 2008. "The Risks, Costs, and Benefits of Possible Future Global Policies for Managing Polioviruses." *American Journal of Public Health* 98 (7): 1322–30. doi:10.2105/AJPH.2007.122192.

Venczel, Linda, James Dobbins, Jean André, Fernando Laender, Hector Izurieta, Patrick Delorme, and Henri-Claude Voltaire. 2003. "Measles Eradication in the Americas: Experience in Haiti." *Journal of Infectious Disease* 187 (Suppl 1): S127–32. doi:10.1086/368029.

WHO (World Health Organization). 1997. *Field Guide: For Supplementary Activities Aimed at Achieving Polio Eradication, 1995 Revision.* Geneva: WHO. http://www.who.int/immunization/monitoring_surveillance/resources/Field_guide_polio_96.pdf.

———. 2014. "Poliomyelitis." Fact Sheet 114. Updated October. http://www.who.int/mediacentre/factsheets/fs114/en/.

———. 2016. Global Health Expenditure Database: NHA Indicators. Accessed February 11. http://apps.who.int/nha/database/ViewData/Indicators/en.

Wilson, James. 2014. "The Ethics of Disease Eradication." *Vaccine* 32 (52): 7179–83. doi:10.1016/j.vaccine.2014.10.009.

ENDNOTES

1. Nathanson and Kew (2010).
2. Modlin (2010).
3. Rey and Gerard (2008).
4. PAHO (2007).
5. WHO (2014).
6. PAHO and WHO (2012, 2015).
7. Rosenstein and Hoch (2011).
8. CDC (2014).
9. CDC (2014).
10. Immunization Action Coalition (2015).
11. Global Polio Eradication Initiative (2016a).
12. Global Polio Eradication Initiative (2016b); WHO (2014).
13. Rey and Gerard (2008).
14. Modlin (2010).
15. Nathanson and Kew (2010).
16. WHO (2014); CDC (1994).
17. WHO (2014).
18. PAHO (1994).
19. de Quadros and Brana (2002).
20. Kew et al. (2002).
21. de Quadros and Brana (2001a); de Quadros and Brana (2002).
22. PAHO (2001).
23. Haiti has had a long history of debt obligations to foreign governments, including France and the United States, and multilateral institutions, such as the Inter-American Development Bank. Haiti's debt began in 1804, when it gained independence and France demanded reparations. Since then, Haiti has paid back the reparations but has incurred additional debt through loans from other countries and international financial institutions. A large portion of this debt was incurred during periods of dictatorship (e.g., during the Duvalier family's rule from 1957 to 1986) (Alsan et al. 2011).
24. Gelting et al. (2013).
25. Kew et al. (2002).
26. Kew et al. (2002); de Quadros and Brana (2001b).
27. de Quadros and Brana (2001a).
28. de Quadros and Brana (2001a).
29. CDC (2001).
30. de Quadros and Brana (2002).
31. Kew et al. (2002).
32. Kew et al. (2004).
33. CDC (2001); Nathanson and Fine (2002).
34. de Quadros and Brana (2001a).
35. de Quadros and Brana (2001a).
36. WHO (1997).
37. de Quadros and Brana (2001b).

ENDNOTES, *continued*

38. de Quadros and Brana (2001a).
39. de Quadros and Brana (2001c).
40. de Quadros and Brana (2001c).
41. de Quadros and Brana (2002).
42. de Quadros and Brana (2002).
43. Venczel et al. (2003).
44. Venczel et al. (2003).
45. Venczel et al. (2003).
46. de Quadros and Brana (2001c).
47. Alleyne (2001).
48. de Quadros and Brana (2001b).
49. de Quadros and Brana (2001b).
50. de Quadros and Brana (2001c).
51. Calculations were based on WHO National Health Accounts indicators (see WHO 2016). Total health expenditure was US$198 million in 2001; public health expenditure was US$51.48 million (26 percent of total health expenditure).
52. de Quadros and Brana (2001c).
53. Fast, González, and Markuzon (2015).
54. Wilson (2014).
55. Elias (2014); Global Polio Eradication Initiative (2014).
56. Elias (2014).
57. Levine (2004).
58. Gelting et al. (2013).
59. Kaufmann and Feldbaum (2009).
60. Kew et al. (2004).
61. Jack (2005).
62. Rey and Gerard (2008).
63. Rey and Gerard (2008).
64. Modlin (2010).
65. Nathanson and Kew (2010); Aylward and Yamada (2011).
66. Thompson et al. (2008).
67. Nathanson and Kew (2010).
68. Kew et al. (2002).
69. Nathanson and Kew (2010).
70. Jon Andrus, personal communication with the author, July 16, 2015; Global Polio Eradication Initiative (2016b).
71. Premji et al. (2016).
72. Renne (2006).
73. Global Polio Eradication Initiative (2013).

Learning from Disappointment
The Integrated Management of Childhood Illness in Bangladesh

The Case at a Glance

HEALTH GOAL: To reduce under-five deaths from diarrhea, pneumonia, malaria, measles, and malnutrition.

STRATEGY: Integrated approach to train health workers, strengthen public-sector health facilities, and improve family and community practices.

HEALTH IMPACT: Increased exclusive breast-feeding. Reduced stunting. No significant reduction in under-five mortality.

WHY IT DIDN'T WORK: A national decline in child mortality that may have overtaken the program's impact. A mismatch between interventions and epidemiology. A focus on the public sector instead of the private sector, where many sought care. Inadequate supervision. Rapid secular gains in health. Persistence of unhealthy family practices.

FINANCING: US$2.4 million in Matlab, Bangladesh, from 1999 to 2008.

SCALE: Local, scaled up to national.

Bangladesh has made its mark on the global development landscape. In the finance arena, it is known as the birthplace of the microcredit movement. And in the sphere of global health, it is known for the development of oral rehydration therapy, a simple diarrhea treatment that has saved millions of lives around the world.[1] Demographers and health researchers also know Bangladesh as the home of the International Centre for Diarrhoeal Disease Research, Bangladesh (ICDDR,B). Based in Matlab subdistrict, ICDDR,B has produced groundbreaking public health research using its population surveillance site, the longest-running site of its kind in the world and a source of critical demographic insights over many decades.

In the mid-1990s, Matlab offered a perfect testing ground for a new approach to saving children's lives: the Integrated Management of Childhood Illness (IMCI). Up to that time, child health programs typically delivered every intervention separately, each with its own dedicated budget, personnel, infrastructure, and supplies. This was called the vertical approach. But child health experts at the World Health Organization (WHO) and United Nations Children's Fund (UNICEF) theorized that they could increase the efficiency and effectiveness of child

health programs with an integrated approach that touched many bases at once instead of siloing interventions. To test their theory, these two global health giants developed IMCI, an approach that integrates training health workers, strengthening health systems and service delivery, and improving family and community practices. They hoped this new approach would dramatically reduce the major causes of under-five mortality and undernutrition, and at a lower cost than the conventional practice.

The early IMCI experience in Bangladesh looked promising, yielding measurably improved quality of care and health-seeking behavior for sick children.[2] But when IMCI was rigorously evaluated in Matlab, the grand vision did not deliver for child survival: it improved intermediary measures but failed to accelerate reductions in child mortality above and beyond the ongoing national trend. Many factors played a role in the disappointing results, including a mismatch between the interventions provided and the main causes of childhood illness in the area, a focus on the public sector when most sought care from private providers, and the persistence of unhealthy family practices. The significant child health gains in Bangladesh also limited the ability of the impact evaluation to measure a mortality effect. The integrated deliv-

This case was originally authored by Miriam Temin.

ery of proven interventions to treat sick children has merit; the main lesson of Bangladesh's experience is that IMCI implementation requires systems improvement and community interventions to achieve impact at scale.

The Toll of Childhood Illness

Worldwide, the sheer number of child deaths dropped during the 1990s, but even so, nearly 11 million children under five died each year. Just five preventable health conditions—diarrhea, pneumonia and other acute respiratory infections, malaria, measles, and malnutrition—accounted for around 70 percent of all mortality in young children.[3]

Like many other countries, Bangladesh saw massive gains in child survival in the 1990s. Between 1993 and 2000, under-five mortality fell from 133 to 94 per 1,000 children, an average annual decrease of 5.3 percent.[4] Despite the generally positive trend, pneumonia, diarrhea, malnutrition, serious infections, and injuries still killed far too many young Bangladeshi children.[5] In Matlab, the under-five mortality rate looked slightly better than the national average: approximately 89 per 1,000 live births in 2000.[6]

These preventable child deaths reflected the abysmal quality of diagnosis and referral nationwide. Around the time IMCI was introduced in Matlab, a small study found that first-level providers correctly diagnosed the illness of only one in five children, and a mere half of the very sick children who needed a referral to a physician received one.[7] Young Bangladeshis also faced the threat of unhealthy infant feeding practices, unhealthy traditions of care for sick children at home, and limited availability of drugs to treat the main killer diseases.[8]

In Matlab, most sick children received their healthcare from private providers. A study conducted in 2000 found that caregivers brought more than 40 percent of sick children to private village practitioners or allopathic drug sellers, providers who frequently lacked medical training.[9]

Putting an Idea in Motion: Matlab Moves from Silos to Systems

IMCI was grounded on the fact that children often suffer from more than one infection at a time.[10] A mother might bring her toddler to a drugstore because his diarrhea has lasted for days and he shows signs of dehydration, and she might leave the shop with a treatment in hand, satisfied that she has something to stem his illness. But she might not know that many common childhood ailments present the same symptoms, complicating their diagnosis. Neither she nor the medicine seller might know that her child's listlessness is caused not by his diarrhea but by a respiratory infection that could become acute and land him in the hospital.

In the years before IMCI, vertical approaches had dominated the field of child health. Some observers feared that these approaches fueled misdiagnoses and inefficiency. Staff of the WHO's Department of Child and Adolescent Health and Development believed that by integrating vertical approaches into a single cohesive program, countries could improve the diagnosis of life-threatening illness and speed up referrals, leading to better treatment and health outcomes. The WHO, along with UNICEF and other technical partners, developed IMCI for countries where infant mortality was high, which they defined as 40 or more deaths per 1,000 live births.[11]

In 1997, a multicountry evaluation (MCE) was launched to test the impact and cost-effectiveness of IMCI (with support from the Bill & Melinda Gates Foundation, the United States Agency for International Development [USAID], and others over its life span). In 1998, Bangladesh joined Brazil, Peru, Uganda, and Tanzania as an MCE site. At that time, the Bangladeshi government had already incorporated IMCI into its child health policies but had yet to begin implementation.[12] Under pressure from ICDDR,B and the WHO, the government finally put IMCI into action.[13]

In consultation with the Ministry of Health and Family Welfare, ICDDR,B and the WHO selected Matlab as a good place to test how the integrated introduction of proven child health interventions worked in a real-world setting. Matlab offered compelling advantages: baseline cause-specific mortality data and ICDDR,B's presence. As an evidence-producing institution managed as an international organization, ICDDR,B offered strong technical capacity and local staff to conduct the work. The project team randomized IMCI introduction to facilitate a rigorous evaluation with ICDDR,B as the anchor; Bangladesh was the first of the countries in the MCE to do this.

IMCI in Action

IMCI is an approach to the delivery of a set of interventions, not a set of specific interventions. It recommends activities to promote three broad objectives (see Figure 1), called the three pillars of IMCI:

1. Improve health worker skills

2. Improve public-sector health systems

3. Improve family and community practices

The idea driving IMCI is that the effectiveness of a package of child health interventions—each one proven effective on its own in smaller-scale efficacy studies—will be greater than the sum of the parts. At its start, IMCI targeted children from one week to five years old who were at risk for pneumonia, diarrhea, malaria, measles, or undernutrition.

Within each objective, IMCI's architects instructed national health planners to nail down context-specific plans based on local epidemiology, health systems, and cultural considerations, all supported by materials from the WHO and UNICEF that could be customized to the context. A priority was to improve case management by health workers. Case management is the coordination of children's care across a continuum of different types of providers and services using the most effective and cost-effective interventions available. For example, IMCI training materials instructed health workers on topics such as symptom-based diagnosis and treatment, and on counseling caretakers on home-based care, including administering medication to sick children, the importance of follow-up visits to facilities, and proper nutrition and breast-feeding. IMCI also prioritized making available a reliable supply of drugs such as antibiotics and antimalarials so health workers could treat common childhood illnesses.[14]

To move IMCI from theory to practice in Bangladesh, the government and the evaluation team had to adapt the broad objectives and materials to the context of Matlab's public healthcare system. ICDDR,B provided baseline data on child health, which were quickly supplemented by results from other formative studies. The IMCI implementers used this evidence to zero in on the most pressing healthcare challenges: referral completion and family behavior related to care seeking, home-based care, and infant feeding and nutritional practices.[15]

Initially, the IMCI team prioritized health worker training in Matlab. Village-level practitioners from the private sector completed two-day training courses on the correct case management of sick children, covering appropriate treatment and referrals for severe illness. To reinforce the training materials, the village practitioners were given referral guidelines and registration tools to take home with them.

The IMCI team strengthened facilities—the second IMCI pillar—by boosting the drug supply in intervention clinics and recruiting additional staff to fill vacant posts.

Figure 1. Integrated Management of Childhood Illness (IMCI) Strategy: Planning and Management Activities

Improving health worker skills

- Develop/adapt case management guidelines and standards
- Train public health providers
- Define roles for nongovernmental/private providers
- Improve and maintain health worker performance
- Use training to orient health workers to problem solving in the community

Improving the health system to deliver IMCI

- Improve availability of drugs and supplies
- Improve service quality and organization at health facilities
- Improve referral pathways and services
- Identify/develop methods for sustainable finance and ensure equity of access
- Link IMCI and health information systems

Improving family and community practices

- Support/strengthen community organization and participation
- Promote appropriate family response to childhood illness
- Contribute to prevention and promote child health and nutrition actions
- Create an enabling, safe, and supportive environment

Source: WHO and UNICEF (1999).

The third IMCI pillar, improving community and family practices, focused on five key elements of care: essential newborn care by families at home, the feeding and nutrition of infants and young children, early childhood development, drowning prevention, and family care practices for sick children. Activities under this pillar aimed to move IMCI away from its tight focus on clinical care and included case management of sick children by health workers in the community (known as community case management), training of informal health providers, counseling, and community mobilization and participation.[16] The program mobilized imams to educate their congregations during Friday sermons and reinforced those lessons through community-based theater.

Unfortunately, the third pillar took longer to get off the ground, and IMCI remained heavily focused on what occurred within healthcare facilities. Few of the activities to improve family and community practices had been rolled out during the study period of the Matlab evaluation.

As early results of monitoring emerged, the IMCI team adjusted its staffing and treatment policies.[17] For example, to accelerate the implementation of the third pillar, the government recruited a new cadre of salaried village health workers for community case management and household counseling. These workers received training, drugs, supervision, and monitoring to manage nonsevere cases of pneumonia and diarrhea in the children's homes and refer children with severe illness to clinics. Later, ongoing problems with referrals prompted another significant change: new guidelines allowed first-level providers to treat severe pneumonia directly, leaving referrals for children with serious danger signs.

Seeing that it was possible to implement IMCI in Matlab and two other subdistricts, the government started to scale up IMCI in earnest in 2003.[18] Eventually the Ministry of Health and Family Welfare merged its diarrhea and acute respiratory infection programs into a single IMCI program. IMCI has since become part of the undergraduate medical curriculum and has been integrated into nursing and medical assistant training schools.[19]

The Payoff: No Difference for Under-Five Mortality

Over six years, a cluster-randomized trial assessed IMCI's impact in first-level government health facilities and their respective catchment areas—a rigorous effectiveness trial of public health delivery in a real-world setting.[20] The trial was a collaboration between the government, ICDDR,B, and the WHO, with UNICEF as an active partner.[21] Given the evaluation's careful design and implementation, coupled with the high caliber of its researchers, most experts in the field accept its findings as highly credible (see Box 1).

Key family practices, care seeking, and quality of care all significantly improved under IMCI. Caregivers took sick children to a health worker more often, and providers delivered more effective healthcare than the standard that children received elsewhere.[22] Mothers started following healthier feeding practices and more frequently offering their babies exclusive breast-feeding for the first six months of their lives, and fewer children suffered from stunting.[23] While these trends were not unique to the IMCI catchment areas, progress there occurred at a far faster rate than in other parts of the country, indicating that the approach had an effect.

Nearly all inputs, outputs, and outcomes that could be expected to save children's lives improved as a result of IMCI—yet despite IMCI's positive effect on important risk factors, it did not significantly reduce child deaths compared with the study's control areas within the time frame of the evaluation.

The implications of this sobering conclusion are blunted, however, when they are considered within the broader context of trends that were already under way. On a national scale, child deaths were declining in Bangladesh, and the under-five mortality rate was dropping more quickly than evaluators had anticipated. USAID's Demographic and Health Survey for 2007 reported that under-five mortality dropped by 7 percent each year between 1999 and 2004.[24] As a result, Bangladesh was one of only six countries that had cut child mortality in half or better since 1990, from 151 deaths per 1,000 children in 1990 to 65 per 1,000 in 2007. The overall positive trends in child mortality may have muted IMCI's impact.

At What Price?

In the Matlab study, implementing IMCI was not expensive, costing about US$2.4 million over the decade from 1999 to 2008, including evaluation costs.[26] At a national level, IMCI is now included in the government's primary healthcare operation plan and budget, and global partners, primarily UNICEF, directly support different IMCI activities.

Box 1. Strength of the Evidence

With support from the WHO, the Bill & Melinda Gates Foundation, USAID, and others, an interdisciplinary group developed an overarching methodology for the multicountry evaluation (MCE) of the Integrated Management of Childhood Illness (IMCI) approach. The MCE aimed to generate results that could be reasonably compared across the countries; in practice, however, each country adapted the methodology to fit local circumstances.

In Bangladesh, the evaluation exploited Matlab's data-rich environment to obtain accurate measures of baseline health and demographics. Researchers were able to cluster randomize the IMCI rollout in order to estimate an attributable impact. They selected 20 first-level government health facilities and their catchment areas (covering around 350,000 people in total) as the randomization clusters; clusters were then paired and randomly assigned to either IMCI or the usual services. Researchers used household and health facility surveys to measure changes in intermediate outputs and outcomes, especially nutrition and mortality.[25]

The randomized approach, designed by independent experts, enabled the program to attribute health impacts specifically to IMCI. Yet even the best-laid plans sometimes encounter unforeseen complications. In this case, external to IMCI, Bangladesh stunned the global health world with fast mortality declines in treatment and control areas alike. The development was great for Bangladeshi children, but bad for statistical power: as fewer children died in Matlab, under-five deaths became a rarer event, requiring a larger sample size to be detected.

As a result, the researchers were not able to determine whether IMCI in fact had no effect on the mortality rate or whether they simply lacked sufficient statistical power to identify small effect sizes. For example, the point estimate for the diarrhea-specific mortality rate in the treatment areas was less than half the point estimate measured in the control areas, but the difference was not enough to be considered significant by the researchers' prespecified criteria. Furthermore, there was likely contamination of the study sample that could have reduced the measured differences when people from treatment and control areas came together for social or commercial reasons and talked about their activities.

The WHO expected that IMCI, once correctly implemented, would cost significantly less than the current care, and its donors did not perceive the approach as expensive.[27] In Bangladesh in particular, a health economics investigation in the late 1990s found that national IMCI implementation could save the country more than US$4 million each year.[28]

In the mid-1990s, an early estimate of the likely cost-effectiveness of IMCI found that "implementation of the integrated cluster of treatments, including hospital services, would cost between [US]$30 and [US]$100 per DALY [disability-adjusted life year]" averted, deeming it a worthwhile investment at the time.[29] However, the original estimates of cost-effectiveness came out well before implementation challenges were documented, and the estimates proved to be overly optimistic. Without a documented effect on child mortality in Matlab specifically, it is difficult to determine whether IMCI was cost-effective.

Why IMCI Fell Short in Matlab

The null result in Matlab disappointed policymakers, especially given that the MCE researchers considered the

Bangladesh initiative to be the "best-possible implementation of IMCI."[30] Why did the measured reduction in risk factors fail to save lives in the study area above and beyond the secular trend? A number of factors may have limited IMCI's impact, ranging from changes in the broader environment to basic IMCI design, human resource constraints, and local family practices.

During the time frame of the IMCI evaluation in the first few years of this century, Bangladesh was changing. Rapid economic growth, increasingly educated mothers, and expanding access to electricity, water, sanitation, and mobile phones contributed to the swift decline in child mortality. Children further benefited from growing coverage of other health sector interventions: vitamin A supplementation, childhood immunization, family planning, a national nutrition program, and others.[31] The children in Matlab, in particular, were protected by the full range of essential childhood immunizations and greater-than-average use of oral rehydration therapy for diarrhea.[32]

These were not mere contextual factors for the IMCI researchers; they had serious implications for their study design and their result. When baseline data analysis revealed lower-than-expected child mortality, researchers realized that their study might be "underpowered"—in other words, the smaller number of child deaths made it harder to prevent enough of them to achieve statistical significance, given the sample size.

Other factors also contributed. For instance, the IMCI approach targeted children with a certain epidemiological profile in countries with high infant mortality rates. The WHO recognized that one size did not fit all—by the late 1990s, the organization was emphasizing country adaptation and training droves of IMCI "adaptation consultants."[33] But Bangladesh's experience, combined with evaluation results from other IMCI countries, suggests that more tailored IMCI implementation guidance might have helped.[34]

IMCI's original design did not necessarily offer a good fit for Bangladesh's evolving epidemiological profile. In Matlab, for example, acute respiratory infection, mostly pneumonia, killed more young children than diarrhea. But the evaluation found that IMCI had a greater effect on diarrhea than on pneumonia, and this limited its overall effect on mortality.[35] Antibiotic resistance, the result of widespread use of antibiotics by village doctors and drugstores, also played a role. IMCI promoted the use of co-trimoxazole to treat pneumonia, but in Bangladesh that drug was less effective than a different antibiotic used in non-IMCI areas.[36] Despite concerns about the case mix and antibiotic regimen, IMCI stayed close to its original design; after all, the evaluation aimed to assess whether IMCI as first conceived would work when implemented in the Matlab context.[37]

Originally, the IMCI guidelines did not cover the health issues of babies in their first week of life, which is a particularly risky period for newborns that was not well understood at the time that IMCI was developed. For example, initially IMCI did not deal with special care for low-birth-weight babies and early initiation of exclusive breast-feeding, which are critical to newborn health and survival. In 2009, health planners adapted IMCI guidelines to cover newborn care.[38] But more than three-quarters of all babies in Bangladesh still were born at home, far from IMCI-strengthened health facilities and trained health workers. Despite the new guidelines, having an impact on newborn infant care remained a challenge in light of IMCI's largely facility-based application.[39]

The efforts focused on improving community and family practices aimed to overcome demand-side hurdles related to the everyday household and community factors that prevented families from seeking quality care for sick children, but this component did not come to life in time to boost the evaluation results. In addition to frequent home delivery, parents often declined to visit health workers when referred because of the cost or the referral center's inaccessibility, or because parents failed to recognize the severity of their child's illness.[40] Even after IMCI recruited village health workers, families continued to frequent unqualified village doctors.[41]

Despite the provision of training under IMCI, human resource limitations continued to constrain healthcare delivery in Bangladesh. In the public sector, there was no system for supervision, monitoring, and health system support below the district level.[42] More generally, IMCI focused on government providers and facilities and largely ignored the private sector, yet this is where most Bangladeshis sought healthcare.[43]

The MCE also assessed IMCI implementation in Peru, Brazil, Uganda, and Tanzania. Researchers controlled for changing circumstances but could randomize only in Matlab, and other possible confounders were not rigorously addressed in the other analyses. Thus the strength of the conclusions from other MCE countries was limited compared with that from Bangladesh.

Four of the five MCE countries struggled to maintain quality under the national rollout.[44] In Uganda, for example, IMCI training improved health worker performance, but overall service quality remained low. Evaluators concluded that training was not enough. Maximizing health workers' performance requires policies that are supportive, consistent, and clearly communicated, along with supervision and high-quality training.[45]

Evaluators also studied the effects of the first two IMCI components in rural Tanzania, where the results looked more promising. In IMCI districts, case management improved and children under five were 13 percent less likely to die, but because IMCI implementation was not randomized, it was not possible to fully control for the influence of contextual factors.[46]

Implications for Global Health

The Matlab evaluation found that the implementation of IMCI in this setting improved some outcomes, but not enough to prevent child mortality beyond the existing national trend. Children in Matlab were healthier than children in many other countries where IMCI has been implemented, which could limit the generalizability of the impact evaluation results. Nevertheless, the findings of the evaluation team on the effects of the Matlab experience are consistent with results from other MCE countries. The evaluation results have pushed IMCI staff to recognize both the potential and the limitations of the approach, and the need to address the issues that generated the most deaths, to enhance health systems, and to bring about community-based behavior change.[47]

IMCI's architects may not have appreciated the complexity of implementing a multifaceted, horizontal approach in Bangladesh and beyond.[48] IMCI's sustained success relies upon a strong health system, but it offered few ways to strengthen weak health systems.[49] MCE experts agree that the approach underestimated the importance of health-system factors, noting that "solutions to larger problems in political commitment, human resources, financing, . . . program management, and decentralization are essential underpinnings of successful efforts to reduce child mortality."[50]

By the end of 2003, 108 less-developed countries had begun early implementation or expansion of IMCI's first two pillars. IMCI's training tools proved particularly popular; many IMCI countries started with efforts to train health workers and did not go beyond this.[51] Nonetheless, human resource problems were common; across a wide range of IMCI countries, an insufficient number of IMCI-trained staff and inconsistent monitoring continued to hinder treatment and quality. Supervisory systems have also proved hard to sustain, even in Tanzania, the earliest IMCI adopter.[52]

The challenge goes well beyond influencing the performance of health systems. IMCI attached high hopes to the impact of significant household and community involvement, but it has been difficult to find ways to influence health behaviors in the community.[53] The global health world now recognizes the essential role of the community in healthcare, but the evidence base on these community-based interventions is nascent and requires more attention, as do efforts to better understand barriers to access.[54]

Global funding for IMCI has waned in favor of more vertical child health programs in recent years, leaving many ministries of health with a commitment to IMCI but no funds for its rollout.[55] IMCI advocates charge that funding for the integrated approach is tenuous because vertical programs view it as a threat. But despite the mixed evaluation results, the MCE team still considers case management to be the "gold standard" approach for countries that implement IMCI, although it cautions that implementation must be flexible enough to adapt to local epidemiology and employ proven, cost-effective approaches to manage individual children's illnesses. They also recommend giving more attention to the most vulnerable mothers and children, which calls for flexible approaches to reach new babies at home.[56]

In theory, IMCI had all the components necessary to change behavior and reduce child mortality; however, many of them did not have a track record of real-world success on these indicators. The evaluation of the implementation of IMCI in Matlab illustrates the difficulty of implementing complicated interventions—the complexity of the approach, with its three components, was something that might have worked under controlled conditions but was difficult to put into practice where limited healthcare infrastructure and human resources were the norm.

It would be a mistake to conclude that the evaluation in Matlab means that primary healthcare provision with IMCI cannot affect child mortality. The lack of measurable mortality impact does not preclude the modification of the IMCI approach and its use in populations that could benefit from it. The results from Matlab and other sites suggest the need to evaluate the impact of the different IMCI components and to modify the program to facilitate delivery and boost effectiveness as part of a systems approach. And through careful tailoring to a country's epidemiology, giving healthcare providers enough skills training to influence their practices, and improving quality and other key determinants, IMCI may have the potential to reduce child mortality at scale.

REFERENCES

Ahmed, Haitham M., Marc Mitchell, and Bethany Hedt. 2010. "National Implementation of Integrated Management of Childhood Illness (IMCI): Policy Constraints and Strategies." *Health Policy* 96 (2): 128–33. doi:10.1016/j.healthpol.2010.01.013.

Ahmed, Syed Masud, Housne Ara Begum, and Kaosar Afsana. 2007. *Maternal, Neonatal and Child Health Programmes in Bangladesh*. Research Monograph Series 32. Dhaka, Bangladesh: BRAC.

Arifeen, S.E., J. Bryce, E. Gouws, A.H. Baqui, R.E. Black, D.M.E. Hoque, E.K. Chowdhury, et al. 2005. "Quality of Care for Under-Fives in First-Level Health Facilities in One District of Bangladesh." *Bulletin of the World Health Organization* 83 (4): 260–67.

Arifeen, Shams E., D.M. Emdadul Hoque, Tasnima Akter, Muntasirur Rahman, Mohammad Enamul Hoque, Khadija Begum, Enayet K. Chowdhury, et al. 2009. "Effect of the Integrated Management of Childhood Illness Strategy on Childhood Mortality and Nutrition in a Rural Area in Bangladesh: A Cluster Randomised Trial." *Lancet* 374 (9687): 393–403. doi:10.1016/S0140-6736(09)60828-X.

Bryce, J. 2005. "Programmatic Pathways to Child Survival: Results of a Multi-Country Evaluation of Integrated Management of Childhood Illness." *Health Policy and Planning* 20 (90001): i5–17. doi:10.1093/heapol/czi055.

Bryce, Jennifer, Cesar G. Victora, Jean-Pierre Habicht, J. Patrick Vaughan, and Robert E. Black. 2004. "The Multi-Country Evaluation of the Integrated Management of Childhood Illness Strategy: Lessons for the Evaluation of Public Health Interventions." *American Journal of Public Health*: 94 (3): 406–15. doi:10.2105/AJPH.94.3.406.

Chowdhury, Enayet K., Shams El Arifeen, Muntasirur Rahman, D.M. Emdadul Hoque, M. Altaf Hossain, Khadija Begum, Ashraf Siddik, et al. 2008. "Care at First-Level Facilities for Children with Severe Pneumonia in Bangladesh: A Cohort Study." *Lancet* 372 (9641): 822–30. doi:10.1016/S0140-6736(08)61166-6.

Duke, Trevor. 2009. "Child Survival and IMCI: In Need of Sustained Global Support." *Lancet* 374 (9687): 361–62. doi:10.1016/S0140-6736(09)61396-9.

El Arifeen, Shams. 2008. "Child Health and Mortality." *Journal of Health, Population, and Nutrition* 26 (3): 273–79.

El Arifeen, Shams, Tasnima Akhter, Hafizur Rahman Chowdhury, Kazi Mizanur Rahman, Enayet Karim Chowdhury, and N. Alam. 2005. "Causes of Death in Children Under Five Years of Age." Dhaka, Bangladesh: National Institute of Population Research and Training.

El Arifeen, S., L.S. Blum, D.M. Hoque, E.K. Chowdhury, R. Khan, R.E. Black, C.G. Victora, and J. Bryce. 2004. "Integrated Management of Childhood Illness (IMCI) in Bangladesh: Early Findings from a Cluster-Randomised Study." *Lancet* 364 (9445): 1595–1602.

Gwatkin, Davidson R. 2004. "Integrating the Management of Childhood Illness." *Lancet* 364 (9445): 1557–58. doi:10.1016/S0140-6736(04)17324-8.

Harding, April, Henrik Axelson, and Flavia Bustreo. 2010. "Child Health and the Missing Link: Working with the Private Sector for Better Results." Draft document for discussion. http://www.who.int/pmnch/topics/child/child_missinglink.pdf.

ICDDR,B (International Centre for Diarrhoeal Disease Research, Bangladesh). 2003. *Health and Demographic Surveillance System Matlab. Vol. 90, Registration of Health and Demographic Events 2001*. Dhaka, Bangladesh: ICDDR,B. http://www.icddrb.org/publications/cat_view/52-publications/10049-hdss-annual-reports?start=10.

———. 2008. "Promoting Case Management for Severe Pneumonia in Children: How We May Do It Differently and Better." http://www.icddrb.org/media-centre/news?id=376&task=view.

Khan, M.M., K.K. Saha, and S. Ahmed. 2002. "Adopting Integrated Management of Childhood Illness Module at Local Level in Bangladesh: Implications for Recurrent Costs." *Journal of Health, Population, and Nutrition* 20 (1): 42–50.

NIPORT (National Institute of Population Research and Training), Mitra and Associates, and Macro International. 2009. *Bangladesh Demographic and Health Survey 2007*. Dhaka, Bangladesh, and Calverton, MD: NIPORT. http://dhsprogram.com/pubs/pdf/FR207/FR207[April-10-2009].pdf.

Nosites, Emily, Rob Hackleman, Kristoffer L.M. Weum, Jullian Pintye, Lisa Manhart, and Stephen Hawes. 2012. "Bangladesh Zinc Case Study." Working paper, University of Washington Global Health Start Program, Seattle.

Pariyo, George W., Eleanor Gouws, Jennifer Bryce, Gilbert Burnham, and Uganda IMCI Impact Study Team. 2005. "Improving Facility-Based Care for Sick Children in Uganda: Training Is Not Enough." *Health Policy and Planning* 20 (Suppl 1): i58–68. doi:10.1093/heapol/czi051.

Rehydration Project. 2014. "Oral Rehydration Therapy: 25 Years of Saving Lives." Last updated April 21. http://rehydrate.org/ors/25years-saving-lives.htm.

Schellenberg, Joanna R.M. Armstrong, Taghreed Adam, Hassan Mshinda, Honorati Masanja, Gregory Kabadi, Oscar Mukasa, Theopista John, et al. 2004. "Effectiveness and Cost of Facility-Based Integrated Management of Childhood Illness (IMCI) in Tanzania." *Lancet* 364 (9445): 1583–94. doi:10.1016/S0140-6736(04)17311-X.

Streatfield, P.K., S.E. Arifeen, and A. Al-Sabir. 2011. *Bangladesh Maternal Mortality and Health Care Survey 2010: Summary of Key Findings and Implications*. Dhaka, Bangladesh: National Institute of Population Research and Training.

REFERENCES, *continued*

Tulloch, J. 1999. "Integrated Approach to Child Health in Developing Countries." *Lancet* 354 (Suppl 2): 16–20.

UNICEF (United Nations Children's Fund). 2009. *National Report Bangladesh: Global Study on Child Poverty and Disparities.* Dhaka, Bangladesh: UNICEF.

———. 2010. *Child Survival in Bangladesh.* Dhaka, Bangladesh: UNICEF. http://www.unicef.org/bangladesh/Child_Surviva_in_Bangladesh.pdf.

———. 2012. *IMCI Newsletter: Performance Report for January to December 2010.* Issue 3. Dhaka, Bangladesh: Directorate General of Health Services. http://www.dghs.gov.bd/licts_file/images/IMCI/imci_issue_3_march_2012.pdf.

WHO (World Health Organization). 2015. "Maternal, Newborn, Child and Adolescent Health: Integrated Management of Childhood Illness (IMCI)." Accessed December 15. http://www.who.int/maternal_child_adolescent/topics/child/imci/en/.

WHO and UNICEF. 1999. *IMCI Information: Planning National Implementation of IMCI.* Geneva: World Health Organization. http://apps.who.int/iris/bitstream/10665/65002/3/WHO_CHS_CAH_98.1C_eng.pdf.

World Bank. 1993. *World Development Report 1993: Investing in Health.* Oxford, UK: Oxford University Press.

ENDNOTES

1. Rehydration Project (2014).
2. El Arifeen et al. (2004).
3. Tulloch (1999).
4. El Arifeen 2008).
5. El Arifeen et al. (2005).
6. ICDDR,B (2003).
7. El Arifeen et al. (2005).
8. Arifeen et al. (2005).
9. Arifeen et al. (2009); Harding, Axelson, and Bustreo (2010).
10. Arifeen et al. (2005).
11. Bryce (2005).
12. Nosites et al. (2012).
13. Shams El Arifeen, personal communication with the author, December 19, 2014.
14. Bryce (2005).
15. Arifeen et al. (2005); Bryce (2005).
16. UNICEF (2009).
17. Duke (2009).
18. Shams El Arifeen, personal communication with the author, December 19, 2014.
19. UNICEF (2012).
20. Duke (2009).
21. Chowdhury et al. (2008).
22. Arifeen et al. (2005).
23. Arifeen et al. (2009).
24. NIPORT, Mitra and Associates, and Macro International (2009).
25. Arifeen et al. (2009).
26. Sk. Masum Billah, personal communication with the author, August 4, 2015.
27. WHO (2015); Schellenberg et al. (2004).
28. Khan, Saha, and Ahmed (2002).
29. World Bank (1993, 114).
30. Bryce (2004, 413).
31. Ahmed, Begum, and Afsana (2007).
32. Alejandro Cravioto, personal communication with Amanda Glassman, October 30, 2015.
33. Bryce (2005).
34. Bryce (2005).
35. Arifeen et al. (2009).
36. Arifeen et al. (2009).
37. Shams El Arifeen, personal communication with the author, December 19, 2014.
38. UNICEF (2010).
39. Streatfield, Arifeen, and Al-Sabir (2011).
40. ICDDR,B (2008).
41. Arifeen et al. (2009).
42. UNICEF (2010); Shams El Arifeen, personal communication with the author, December 19, 2014.
43. Harding, Axelson, and Bustreo (2010); El Arifeen et al. (2005).
44. Bryce (2005).
45. Pariyo et al. (2005).
46. Schellenberg et al. (2004).
47. Shams El Arifeen, personal communication with the author, December 19, 2014.
48. Gwatkin (2004).
49. Arifeen et al. (2005).
50. Bryce (2005, i5).
51. Ahmed, Mitchell, and Hedt (2010).
52. Schellenberg et al. (2004).
53. Gwatkin (2004).
54. Duke (2009).
55. Duke (2009).
56. Bryce (2005); Shams El Arifeen, personal communication with the author, December 19, 2014.

PART II

Expanding Access to Health Services

In Thailand, the government defined a health benefits plan, enrolled previously uninsured citizens, and paid clinical teams to find and provide care to eligible citizens. In Argentina, incentives encouraged provincial and local health sector staff to enroll uninsured mothers and children in a new subsidy scheme and provide them with key services. In Brazil, the federal government established a standardized package of primary healthcare services, transferring funds to municipalities based on the number of people covered and the risk profiles of their respective populations. And in Rwanda, the government paid providers an extra bonus based on the quantity and quality of care they provided.

Within these programs, greater use led to better health; governments drove impact by defining the "right" services and beneficiary populations and by providing quality care. But increased access and utilization of health services does not automatically translate into health gains. Elsewhere in the world, many universal coverage and insurance schemes have increased utilization without demonstrably improving health—as experience illustrates in the United States, China, and Vietnam.[1] One case profiled in this section, Gujarat State's subsidy for private-sector deliveries, resulted in disappointment: infant and maternal deaths did not decline, although the program did result in more deliveries in health facilities instead of at home.

The outcome in Gujarat highlights the importance of accurately diagnosing and addressing the obstacles to accessing care, such as availability and quality. As these cases show, policymakers must provide both to citizens to improve their health.

REFERENCES

Davis, Karen, Kristof Stremikis, David Squires, and Cathy Schoen. 2014. *Mirror, Mirror on the Wall, 2014 Update: How the U.S. Health Care System Compares Internationally*. New York: Commonwealth Fund. http://www.commonwealthfund.org/publications/fund-reports/2014/jun/mirror-mirror.

Economist. 2014. "Health Care in Vietnam: Limping Along," September 20. http://www.economist.com/news/asia/21618894-ordinary-folk-are-sick-and-tired-their-public-hospitals-limping-along.

Qi, Liyan, and Lauri Burkitt. 2015. "Falling through the Cracks of China's Health-Care System." *Wall Street Journal*, January 4. http://www.wsj.com/articles/falling-through-the-cracks-of-chinas-health-care-system-1420420231.

NOTE

1. Davis et al. (2014); Qi and Burkitt (2015); *Economist* (2014).

Health Access for All
Thailand's Universal Coverage Scheme

The Case at a Glance

HEALTH GOAL: To provide all citizens with quality healthcare on an equitable basis, according to need, regardless of socioeconomic status.

STRATEGY: Government-initiated and government-managed insurance program to provide free access to an affordable, comprehensive health benefits package including outpatient, inpatient, preventive, and emergency care.

HEALTH IMPACT: Increased healthcare utilization. Decreased infant mortality. Decreased likelihood of people reporting too sick to work. Decreased proportion of households facing financial hardship from health expenditures.

WHY IT WORKED: Effective strengthening of the healthcare system. Separation of purchasing and provision responsibilities between two agencies. "Capitation" payment system. Long-term, dedicated leadership.

FINANCING: US$35 (BHT1,200) per person in 2002. US$80 (BHT2,700) per person in 2011.

SCALE: 48 million members (2011).

A Thai man afflicted with a respiratory infection might miss work for a week, or maybe longer. Visiting a doctor would enable a quick return to work, but this man is his household's main breadwinner, and the out-of-pocket payment could compromise his ability to buy food and clothing for his family. Faced with this unappealing choice, many Thais would elect to forgo healthcare, leading to missed work and reduced productivity. But too many absences could cost a person his or her job, reinforcing the vicious cycle between poor health and poverty. Such were the unappealing choices for many Thais before the introduction of universal health coverage.

Achieving universal access to healthcare has been a goal of most high-income countries since the postwar era. Recently, the introduction of universal health coverage, a system whereby all people can obtain health services without suffering financial hardship, has gained momentum in low- and middle-income countries. Advocates and researchers alike highlight the enormous potential of universal health coverage to promote both health and human rights.[1]

As global momentum built, Thailand took its first steps toward creating such a system. In 2001, the Thai government executed one of the most ambitious healthcare reforms ever undertaken in a developing country: the Universal Coverage Scheme (UCS).[2] Aiming to provide universal access to essential healthcare and reduce catastrophic health spending caused by out-of-pocket payments, Thailand's UCS provided health insurance coverage to 18 million people in less than a year.[3] As a result, Thais were less likely to be too sick to work. Even better, fewer babies in poorer provinces died.[4] Thailand showed that middle-income countries can achieve universal health coverage with evidence-based, inclusive, and transparent policies, making it a role model for other countries in pursuit of coverage for all.

The Toll of Being Uninsured

Worldwide, many health systems fail to protect families from the financial risk of paying for healthcare. In more than 35 countries, out-of-pocket payments accounted for more than half of total health spending in 2012.[5] Faced with the urgent need to help a dangerously sick child, spouse, or parent, people do what they need to do

This case was originally authored by Yuna Sakuma.

to get help. For families living in poverty, help may be beyond their means. In many settings, more than one in four people are forced to borrow money or sell their belongings to pay for healthcare.[6] Illness can thus prompt a financial catastrophe, defined as healthcare payments equal to at least 40 percent of a household's nonfood consumption.

Health insurance can protect people from spending a large proportion of their household income on healthcare so that they avoid the impoverishing effects of paying out of pocket for care. Evidence from 40 low- and middle-income countries confirms that in countries with greater health insurance coverage, people are less likely to sell off their possessions or borrow money to buy healthcare.[7]

Beyond financial protection, insurance coverage can improve health status where the health system is functional. This works in two ways. First, health insurance improves access to care by reducing the cost barrier. Second, lower out-of-pocket payments keep people from falling into poverty due to spending on healthcare. By protecting household finances, health insurance reduces the risk that children will be exposed to the conditions of extreme poverty and associated diseases—including pneumonia and infection, both important causes of infant mortality.[8]

In Thailand before the UCS, almost one in four people were uninsured.[9] Others were covered by insurance that offered only partial protection. The result: more than 17,000 Thai children under five died in 2000 (18.9 per 1,000 live births), two-thirds from easily preventable infectious diseases,[10] and out-of-pocket health spending tipped one in five of the poorest Thai households below the national poverty line.[11]

Putting an Idea in Motion: A Political Promise Becomes Real-World Policy

In Thailand, the introduction of the UCS followed a long string of efforts to improve equity in health. In 1975, the government had made free health services available to people living in poverty. Recognizing the problem of the lack of health centers in rural areas, the government froze new investments in urban hospitals between 1982 and 1986. It reallocated those resources to rural district hospitals and health centers, trained and employed doctors and community health workers, and recruited and trained village volunteers to strengthen primary care.

Despite progress, about 25 percent of Thai people were still without insurance in 2001. Coverage was inequitably distributed, and medical indicators reflected this imbalance. Where large proportions were enrolled in the Medical Welfare Scheme—a healthcare scheme that covered people living in poverty, the elderly, children, veterans, monks, and priests—rates of infant mortality were higher than in other areas.[12] This association between coverage by the Medical Welfare Scheme and poorer health outcomes confirmed that where poverty was greater, there were more infant deaths. The 1997 Asian financial crisis exacerbated the effects of inequitable health coverage, weakening the Thai economy along with its health system. Unemployment, the proportion of people living below the poverty line, and costs of drugs and medical supplies all increased, even as the Ministry of Public Health saw its budget slashed.[13]

In 1999, Thai reformers and public-health experts had produced convincing reports that deemed universal health coverage financially and programmatically feasible.[18] But previous efforts to introduce a universal scheme, led by reformers in the Ministry of Public Health, had stalled.[19] Dr. Sanguan Nitayaramphong, who would later oversee the UCS rollout, had worked tirelessly to persuade politicians and the public to embrace universal health coverage, but so far his ideas had not taken hold.[20]

Reformers saw a window of opportunity to push forward a radical change in how Thais accessed healthcare in the lead-up to the 2001 elections.[21] The populist Thai Rak Thai party, led by Thaksin Shinawatra (who would become the prime minister), made universal health coverage a major element of its platform. The party became the heart of the movement for universal coverage, alongside government activists and civil society advocates. In its campaign, Thai Rak Thai promised that the proposed new scheme would protect Thais without insurance coverage. Its slogan was "30 baht treats all diseases." (Thirty baht is about US$0.70.)

Civil society also played a crucial role. Jon Ungphakorn, a senator in the Thai parliament and a social activist, built a coalition of 11 local nongovernmental organizations to support the "30 baht" scheme. The group led a campaign to advocate for equality in coverage and improved financial protection. Civil society held five seats on the parliamentary commission to review drafts of the UCS legislation, giving these representatives genuine influence over policy design.[22]

Thai Rak Thai's landslide win in the national election in January 2001 finally opened the path for change.[23] The government proceeded with rapid implementation of its universal coverage scheme, despite the recommendation of World Bank and World Health Organization senior advisors to pursue a gradual introduction.[24] Although Thai leaders were cautious—particularly with budget execution—they believed a quick rollout would build confidence in their leadership.[25]

The government's initial plan was to merge resources from the four existing health coverage schemes—the Medical Welfare Scheme (MWS), Health Card Scheme (HCS), Social Security Scheme (SSS), and Civil Servants Medical Benefits Scheme (CSMBS) (see Box 1)—into a single cohesive program. Their aim was to prevent overlap and inequity, but they met resistance from the departments responsible for each individual program, especially the civil servants and trade unionists who benefited from the two employment-based schemes, the SSS and the CSMBS.[26] Not wanting to lose momentum, the government compromised, pooling the resources of a subset rather than the entirety of the existing schemes (MWS and HCS, schemes for the poor and near-poor). The compromise allowed for passage of the National Health Security Act in 2002, and the UCS was ready to take flight.[27]

Box 1. Healthcare Insurance Schemes

Medical Welfare Scheme (MWS): Free medical services at public health facilities for the poor (monthly earnings less than BHT1,000 [US$30]), the elderly, children, veterans, monks, and priests; funded through general tax revenues.[14]

Health Card Scheme (HCS): Publicly subsidized voluntary health insurance for the near-poor population, with an up-front cost of BHT500 (US$15) per household per year.[15]

Social Security Scheme (SSS): Compulsory for private-company employees and temporary public employees; funded by equal-share contributions from employers, employees, and the government.[16]

Civil Servants Medical Benefits Scheme (CSMBS): Insurance for civil servants and public employees and their families; funded through general tax revenues.[17]

The Universal Coverage Scheme in Action

The UCS rollout was swift. Starting with six provinces in mid-2001, the scheme was extended to nearly all of Thailand's 75 provinces by the end of the year. Bangkok's districts were covered by mid-2002.[28] As the UCS reached an additional 18 million people by combining existing pools from the MWS and the HCS, the group of uninsured Thais shrank dramatically. All citizens were eligible for the UCS—existing CSMBS and SSS members as well as the uninsured and previous MWS and HCS members. By 2011, the UCS was covering 48 million members and their families, leaving less than 2 percent of the Thai population without health insurance coverage.[29]

One of the scheme's central administrative features was that the provider and the purchaser of health services were two discrete entities. The Ministry of Public Health was responsible for providing health services, and a new independent entity, the National Health Security Office (NHSO), managed and operated the UCS. The reason for creating this structure was so that the NHSO, as a purchaser, could enforce better provider accountability.

To enroll in the system, people registered with a contracting unit, usually a district healthcare provider network, and received a gold card. The card entitled enrollees to free care at health centers in their home district and contracted hospitals, plus referrals to provincial or tertiary-care hospitals in urban areas.[30] Health volunteers and other providers helped identify potential beneficiaries through their work in communities, supplemented by mass media campaigns to drum up interest.[31]

The UCS gave its members access to a comprehensive benefits package. In the program's initial design, the existing health insurance schemes determined which benefits the plan offered. The UCS covered outpatient and inpatient care; accident and emergency services; dental and other high-cost care; and diagnostics, special investigations, medicines, and medical supplies. It also stressed disease prevention through clinic-based preventive and health-promotion services at health centers. Using a systematic process that considers factors such as equity and ethics in addition to cost-effectiveness, over time the government has added more expensive services to the UCS benefits package—one reason the per-person budget has grown.

The UCS was primarily financed by general income taxes, so it was proportionately more heavily funded by the rich than the poor.[32] Initially, users paid a co-payment of BHT30 (about US$0.70) per visit.[33] However, collection of the co-payments ultimately cost more than the revenue they generated. Following a military coup in 2006, eliminating the co-payment also helped the incoming public health minister show his party's dedication to the UCS.[34]

The Payoff: Greater Access, Better Health

In the decade after its launch, the UCS increased access to healthcare—particularly among babies and women aged 20 to 30 years—and its members have gotten healthier. There are credible signs that the UCS contributed to this progress (see Box 2). When the financial barriers to health services were lowered, previously uninsured Thais sought more healthcare. Those with the lowest incomes increased their use of health services the most, while the poorest women of reproductive age and their infants saw the largest gains.[35] Indeed, the association between poverty and infant mortality disappeared, suggesting that the UCS succeeded in erasing the equity gap in infant health.[36]

One year after the UCS launched, people were less likely to report that illness had prevented them from going to work than before—an improvement that researchers also attributed to the UCS. The effect was far larger for workers older than 65.[40] By keeping Thailand's aging workers healthy, it is conceivable that the UCS improved labor productivity.

In addition to improving health, studies also found that the UCS reduced financial risk; after its launch, health expenditures impoverished fewer Thais than before. Some households still fell below the poverty line owing to spending on medicine and healthcare, but the proportion of them shrank—from 2.7 percent in 2000 to less than 0.5 percent in 2009.[41] Although causation is difficult to establish, the reduction in healthcare-related poverty was stronger in households with one or more UCS members, suggesting that the UCS played a role in the trend.

Gains at What Price?

The government's overall expenditure on health increased from BHT84.5 billion (US$2.6 billion) in 2001 to BHT116.3 billion (US$3.6 billion) in 2002, and continued to increase steadily to BHT247.7 billion (US$7.6 billion) by 2008.[42] The UCS is entirely funded by the government of Thailand, mostly through revenue from general taxes.

Box 2. Strength of the Evidence

Researchers have long wondered whether increasing health coverage actually improves health. Many studies have been unable to isolate the effects of universal health coverage or insurance schemes from other unobservable factors. By definition, establishing a true counterfactual is a challenge for any "universal" approach in the absence of a randomized rollout.

Thailand's UCS rollout was not randomized; nonetheless, several research teams have undertaken robust analyses of its impact. Ten years after the scheme's launch, one such group used time-series analysis of survey data to assess the program's impact on healthcare utilization, health, and financial risk protection.[37] The findings suggested a positive impact, although the researchers could not produce definitive conclusions. To assess changes in financial protection, the researchers also used a model to assess impact. This modeling exercise used a hypothetical counterfactual to suggest that the UCS reduced the number of households that were impoverished by healthcare expenditures. The observational evaluation has important limitations, as it could not eliminate all sources of potential bias, such as economic growth.

However, two other studies have corroborated these findings, demonstrating a relationship between UCS implementation and specific health gains. The first, by Gruber, Hendren, and Townsend,[38] compared changes over time in utilization and infant mortality among poor UCS beneficiaries and among wealthier Thais who already had access to insurance through formal-sector employment. Even after ruling out a set of other explanations, such as changes in vital statistics reporting and changing economic conditions, the analysis strongly suggests that the UCS helped reduce infant mortality. The second study, by Wagstaff and Manachotphong,[39] found a proxy for health within the Thai Labor Force Survey: self-reported illness that prevented people from going to work. They used the stepwise rollout of the UCS to link that metric with the total time that the UCS was available in the respondents' province of residence. They found that longer exposure to the UCS was associated with less risk of missing work due to illness.

The UCS budget, determined by the number of beneficiaries multiplied by a standard per-person rate, also increased in absolute and per capita terms. In 2002 the government allocated roughly BHT1,200 (US$35) per beneficiary, and it increased this to about BHT2,700 (US$80) by 2012.[43] Meanwhile, government expenditure on other schemes, such as the SSS, remained flat. Thailand has achieved near universal coverage at slightly lower cost to the government relative to the country's gross domestic product than other upper-middle-income countries such as Colombia and South Africa.[44]

The Keys to Lasting Success

A stable and dedicated leadership sustained the UCS. The Thai Rak Thai party integrated the scheme into its 2001 election promises, and the leaders who had pushed for reforms continued in leadership positions after the election. Nitayaramphong, secretary-general of the National Health Security Office, worked hard to get politicians and citizens to accept the UCS. His successor in 2008 was his longtime deputy, Dr. Winai Sawasdivorn, and he maintained that momentum.[45] Tangible benefits made the Thai Rak Thai party popular and sustained its power, which allowed it to nurture and strengthen the program.[46]

Thai reformers were quick to learn from international experience, existing Thai health coverage schemes, and the initial stages of the UCS rollout. For example, the implementation of the SSS informed the decision to separate healthcare purchasing from healthcare provision. Under the UCS, a capitation system, which provided funding per person, replaced fee-for-service payments; this helped contain costs by shifting utilization away from more expensive services, toward primary care and prevention. The UCS invested in information technology systems to reduce administrative costs, and it centralized the procurement of medicines and devices, using the sheer size of UCS coverage as leverage to negotiate for lower prices. The UCS architects' ability to craft a strategy based on past experiences ultimately improved the scheme's efficiency.

Prior to the UCS rollout, the Thai government took measures to improve the capacity of the health system to meet increased demand under the UCS.[47] By building up rural health services, for example, the government increased the availability of healthcare for more than half of the population. The UCS also gave hospital budgets a boost. Their BHT1,200 (US$35) and up per-patient budgets greatly exceeded the roughly BHT250 (US$8) reimbursements that MWS members had previously received.[48] More money meant that public facilities could provide more and better health services.

Another important factor in the program's success was the country's judicious approach to determining which health services and technologies would receive UCS coverage. These decisions are made through an evidence-based, systematic process conducted by the Health Intervention and Technology Assessment Program (HITAP), an autonomous public arm of the Ministry of Public Health. HITAP was created in response to the large increase in public health spending after the implementation of the UCS. Its function is to consider cost-effectiveness, budget impact, equity, ethics, and supply-side capacity for scale-up to determine the scope of UCS benefits. Over time, through the HITAP-led process, the UCS has expanded its benefits package to include interventions such as dialysis to treat kidney failure and antiretroviral therapy to treat AIDS.[49]

This coverage scheme has been justly praised, but it has some critics. Some charge that, despite increased budgets, UCS-contracted hospitals provide a lower quality of care than those available to CSMBS and SSS enrollees, and there are differences in the availability of treatment and length of stay. At the time of writing, the government is taking steps to address these concerns and improve the equity of hospital care.[50]

Implications for Global Health

Many countries have pursued quality healthcare for all.[51] Some have found success, such as Colombia, South Korea, and Turkey; others, such as the Philippines, have seen universal health coverage reforms stall out.[52] In comparison, Thailand's UCS rolled out so rapidly that some labeled it a "big bang" reform.[53] But this big bang was preceded by years of study, development, and preparation that helped ensure the reform's ultimate success. Thailand showed that a lower-middle-income country can achieve universal health coverage under the right circumstances. Sustained political commitment, sound public financing and oversight policies, and civil society engagement all helped make it possible.

Thailand is a leader in the use of evidence to inform health policy decision making. HITAP is one of the very few agencies in low- or middle-income countries to systematically assess whether health technologies will be eligible for coverage.[54] Decisions on health coverage—who gets what coverage and at what level—are reached through an open and evidence-based process. To make policy development more participatory, a diverse panel of health professionals, academics, patient groups, and civil society organizations oversees the prioritization of health interventions. The process is attractive due to its built-in accountability and ability to contain costs, and the Thai government is working to share its experience with others.

There are many ways to finance universal health coverage. Thailand's experience adds to a growing body of evidence that health-financing systems do not have to rely on fees from health-system users. The majority of Thais receive health coverage without fees, their benefits financed by tax revenues. (Some Thais—private-company employees and temporary public employees—contribute directly to universal health coverage.)[55]

The growing UCS budget casts some doubt on its sustainability. To address this concern, a group of researchers have suggested that the UCS devote more of its budget to preventive and health-promotion services, which currently account for a little less than 20 percent of the budget.[56] They also recommend that health planners continue to carefully analyze new and available interventions based on cost-effectiveness evidence and thus their implications for the budget, and also that planners make their priority setting explicit.[57] Other countries will watch carefully to see how Thailand tackles the sustainability challenge.

Expanding health coverage can improve health by increasing access (removing some of the barriers to health services) and by providing financial protection (reducing the risks associated with impoverishment from out-of-pocket medical costs).[58] Experience shows time and again that free healthcare alone does not guarantee better health without other complementary elements. By providing free and also cost-effective services while at the same time strengthening its health system, Thailand managed to keep workers healthy and save young lives. While challenges remain, Thailand's UCS is working. It can provide a model and inspiration for other countries on the path to universal health coverage.

REFERENCES

Australian Department of Foreign Affairs and Trade. 2015. "Australia's Aid Program." Accessed July 8. http://dfat.gov.au/aid/Pages/australias-aid-program.aspx.

Averill, Ceri, and Anna Marriott. 2013. Universal Health Coverage: Why Health Insurance Schemes Are Leaving the Poor Behind. Oxford, UK: Oxfam International.

Diaz, Yadira, Eduardo Andres Alfonso, and Ursula Giedion. 2013. The Impact of Universal Coverage Schemes in the Developing World: A Review of the Existing Evidence. Working Paper 75326. Washington, DC: World Bank. http://documents.worldbank.org/curated/en/2013/01/17291221/impact-universal-coverage-schemes-developing-world-review-existing-evidence.

Glassman, Amanda, and Kalipso Chalkidou. 2012. Priority-Setting in Health: Building Institutions for Smarter Public Spending. A Report of the Center for Global Development's Priority-Setting Institutions for Global Health Working Group. Washington, DC: Center for Global Development. http://www.cgdev.org/publication/priority-setting-health-building-institutions-smarter-public-spending.

Gruber, Jonathan, Nathaniel Hendren, and Robert M. Townsend. 2013. "Access to Health Care among Thailand's Poor Reduces Infant Mortality." Consortium on Financial Systems and Poverty, June 6. http://www.cfsp.org/news/access-health-care-among-thailands-poor-reduces-infant-mortality#.U-tojvldVHU.

———. 2014. "The Great Equalizer: Health Care Access and Infant Mortality in Thailand." American Economic Journal: Applied Economics 6 (1): 91–107. doi:10.1257/app.6.1.91.

Hanvoravongchai, Piya. 2013. Health Financing Reform in Thailand: Toward Universal Coverage under Fiscal Constraints. Working Paper 75000. Washington, DC: World Bank.

HISRO (Health Insurance System Research Office). 2012. Thailand's Universal Coverage Scheme: Achievements and Challenges. An Independent Assessment of the First 10 Years (2001–2010). Nonthaburi, Thailand: HISRO. http://www.hsri.or.th/sites/default/files/THailand%20UCS%20achievement%20and%20challenges_0.pdf.

Hughes, D., and S. Leethongdee. 2007. "Universal Coverage in the Land of Smiles: Lessons from Thailand's 30 Baht Health Reforms." Health Affairs 26 (4): 999–1008. doi:10.1377/hlthaff.26.4.999.

IHME (Institute for Health Metrics and Evaluation). 2015. "Compared Annualized Rates of Decline in Each MDG from 1999–2002." Accessed October 20. http://vizhub.healthdata.org/mdg/.

REFERENCES, *continued*

Joint Learning Network for Universal Health Coverage. 2015. "Thailand: Universal Coverage Scheme." Accessed October 20. http://programs.jointlearningnetwork.org/content/universal-coverage-scheme.

Kruk, M.E., E. Goldmann, and S. Galea. 2009. "Borrowing and Selling to Pay for Health Care in Low- and Middle-Income Countries." *Health Affairs* 28 (4): 1056–66. doi:10.1377/hlthaff.28.4.1056.

Limwattananon, Supon. 2007. "Catastrophic and Poverty Impacts of Health Payments: Results from National Household Surveys in Thailand." *Bulletin of the World Health Organization* 85 (8): 600–6. doi:10.2471/BLT.06.033720.

Limwattananon, S., V. Vongmongkol, P. Prakongsai, W. Patcharanarumol, K. Hanson, V. Tangcharoensathien, and A. Mills. 2011. *The Equity Impact of Universal Coverage: Health Care Finance, Catastrophic Health Expenditure, Utilization and Government Subsidies in Thailand.* London: Consortium for Research on Equitable Health Systems. http://r4d.dfid.gov.uk/Output/188980.

Marten, Robert. 2014. "7 Things You Should Know about Universal Health Coverage." *Investing in Health* (blog), World Bank, April 28. http://blogs.worldbank.org/health/7-things-you-should-know-about-universal-health-coverage.

Nitayarumphong, Sanguan. 2006. *Struggling along the Path to Universal Health Care for All.* Nonthabury, Thailand: National Health Security Office.

Pannarunothai, Supasit, Samrit Srithamrongsawat, Manit Kongpan, and Patchanee Thumvanna. 2000. "Financing Reforms for the Thai Health Card Scheme." *Health Policy and Planning* 15 (3): 303–11.

Rosenquist, Rebecka, Olga Golichenko, Tim Roosen, and Julia Ravenscroft. 2013. "A Critical Player: The Role of Civil Society in Achieving Universal Health Coverage." *Global Health Governance* 6 (2).

Sen, Amartya, and Thomas W. Lamont. 2015. "Universal Health Care: The Affordable Dream." *Harvard Public Health Review* 4 (April). http://harvardpublichealthreview.org/universal-health-care-the-affordable-dream/.

Tangcharoensathien, Viroj, Siriwan Pitayarangsarit, Walaiporn Patcharanarumol, Phusit Prakongsai, Hathaichanok Sumalee, Jiraboon Tosanguan, and Anne Mills. 2013. "Promoting Universal Financial Protection: How the Thai Universal Coverage Scheme Was Designed to Ensure Equity." *Health Research Policy and Systems* 11 (1): 25. doi:10.1186/1478-4505-11-25.

Towse, A. 2004. "Learning from Thailand's Health Reforms." *BMJ* 328 (7431): 103–5. doi:10.1136/bmj.328.7431.103.

UNICEF (United Nations Children's Fund). 2015. "UNICEF Statistics: Number of Deaths of Children under Five." Accessed October 20. http://www.data.unicef.org/child-mortality/under-five.html.

Wagstaff, Adam, and Wanwiphang Manachotphong. 2012. *The Health Effects of Universal Health Care: Evidence from Thailand.* Policy Research Working Paper 6119. Washington, DC: World Bank.

WHO (World Health Organization). 2014. "Thailand's Health Ambitions Pay Off." *Bulletin of the World Health Organization* 92 (7): 472–73. doi:10.2471/BLT.14.030714.

———. 2016. Global Health Expenditure Database: NHA Indicators. Accessed February 8. http://apps.who.int/nha/database/ViewData/Indicators/en.

Wibukoikorasert, S., and S. Thaiprayoon. 2008. "Thailand: Good Practice in Expanding Health Coverage—Lessons from the Thai Health Care Reforms." In *Good Practices in Health Financing: Lessons from Reforms in Low- and Middle-Income Countries,* edited by Pablo E. Gottret, George Schieber, and Hugh Waters. Washington, DC: World Bank.

World Bank. 2015a. "World Bank Group Releases 22-Country Study of Universal Health Coverage." News release, February 14. http://www.worldbank.org/en/news/press-release/2013/02/14/World-Bank-Group-releases-22-country-study-of-universal-health-coverage.

———. 2015b. *World Development Indicators.* Accessed October 20. http://data.worldbank.org/data-catalog/world-development-indicators.

ENDNOTES

1. Marten (2014).
2. Gruber, Hendren, and Townsend (2013, 2014).
3. Wibukoikorasert and Thaiprayoon (2008).
4. Gruber, Hendren, and Townsend (2013).
5. WHO (2016).
6. Kruk, Goldmann, and Galea (2009).
7. Kruk, Goldmann, and Galea (2009).
8. Sen and Lamont (2015).
9. HISRO (2012); Wibukoikorasert and Thaiprayoon (2008).
10. UNICEF (2015); IHME (2015).
11. Limwattananon (2007).
12. Gruber, Hendren, and Townsend (2014).
13. Australian Department of Foreign Affairs and Trade (2015).
14. Wibulpolprasert and Thaiprayoon (2008).
15. Pannarunothai et al. (2000).
16. Wibulpolprasert and Thaiprayoon (2008).
17. Wibulpolprasert and Thaiprayoon (2008).
18. HISRO (2012).
19. Wibulpolprasert and Thaiprayoon (2008).
20. WHO (2014); Nitayarumphong (2006).
21. WHO (2014); Hughes and Leethongdee (2007).
22. Rosenquist et al. 2013; HISRO (2012).
23. Hughes and Leethongdee (2007); Wibulpolprasert and Thaiprayoon (2008); HISRO (2012).
24. Hughes and Leethongdee (2007); WHO (2014).

ENDNOTES, *continued*

25. WHO (2014).
26. Towse (2004).
27. HISRO (2012).
28. Gruber, Hendren, and Townsend (2013); Wagstaff and Manachotphong (2012).
29. Hanvoravongchai (2013).
30. Towse (2004).
31. Joint Learning Network for Universal Health Coverage (2015).
32. Limwattananon et al. (2011).
33. Joint Learning Network for Universal Health Coverage (2015).
34. Tangcharoensathien et al. (2013).
35. Gruber, Hendren, and Townsend (2013); HISRO (2012).
36. Gruber, Hendren, and Townsend (2014).
37. HISRO (2012).
38. 2014.
39. 2012.
40. Wagstaff and Manachotphong (2012).
41. HISRO (2012).
42. HISRO (2012); using the April 2015 exchange rate, US$1 = BHT32.57.
43. HISRO (2012).
44. World Bank (2015a); WHO (2016).
45. Tangcharoensathien et al. (2013).
46. Tangcharoensathien et al. (2013).
47. WHO (2014).
48. Gruber, Hendren, and Townsend (2014).
49. HISRO (2012).
50. Hughes and Leethongdee (2007).
51. World Bank (2015b).
52. Hughes and Leethongdee (2007).
53. Hughes and Leethongdee (2007).
54. Glassman and Chalkidou (2012).
55. Averill and Marriott (2013).
56. Yot Teerawattananon, personal communication with the author, January 15, 2015.
57. Yot Teerawattananon, personal communication with the author, January 15, 2015.
58. Diaz, Alfonso, and Giedion (2013).

Paying for Provincial Performance in Health
Argentina's Plan Nacer

The Case at a Glance

HEALTH GOAL: To improve birth outcomes of babies born into poverty by expanding health coverage and improving service delivery.

STRATEGY: Government program to provide health coverage to poor pregnant women and children, with payment linked to improved health outcomes.

HEALTH IMPACT: Reduced in-hospital neonatal mortality: 74 percent for Plan Nacer beneficiaries, 22 percent for all Plan Nacer clinic users. 72,800 disability-adjusted life years (DALYs) averted and 733 lives saved from 2005 to 2008.

WHY IT WORKED: Consistent commitment by national and provincial governments. Provision of performance incentives across all levels of the health system. Targeting of the uninsured for priority maternal and child health service benefits. Development and enforcement of systems for regular audits, feedback, and evaluation to support a culture of learning, flexibility, and accountability. Empowerment of providers to control new funds and innovate.

FINANCING: Estimated cost-effectiveness ratio: US$814 per DALY averted.

SCALE: Two million pregnant women, infants, and children under six, and 7,254 health facilities (late 2012).

In the aftermath of the economic crisis in Argentina in 2001, poverty deepened nationwide. Argentines saw their per capita income cut in half, while unemployment soared to 25 percent.[1] Facing higher prices, millions of families struggled to put food on the table, and inadequate nutrition left many pregnant women and children at risk. Images of stunted, malnourished children shocked Argentines, as a World Health Organization official stated that 20 percent of Argentina's children suffered from malnutrition. International news media reported the sad irony: "Economic crisis sharpens poverty in world's fourth biggest food-exporting country."[2]

The economic crisis quickly evolved into an acute health crisis. Many pregnant women could not access health services; families could provide neither healthcare nor adequate nutrition for their children. Widespread unemployment left large swaths of the population without health insurance, increasing the demand for underfinanced public healthcare. This caused a dramatic shift in how people sought healthcare through the three tracks of Argentina's healthcare system: away from private health-

care and into social insurance for workers (funded by umbrella organizations for workers' unions, called *obras sociales*) and public healthcare. Provincial governments, responsible for delivering health services within their jurisdictions, could not keep up.[3] Maternal and child health had been improving; now these gains slowed, and then ultimately reversed.

To address the dire situation of mothers and infants, in 2004 the Argentine government began a new health initiative: Plan Nacer, literally "Birth Plan." Following the lead of other countries in the region, such as Honduras (see chapter 17 in this volume), Plan Nacer expanded health coverage to uninsured pregnant women and children.[4] But the program went further: it also used financial incentives to motivate provinces and healthcare providers to enroll participants and discernibly improve their use of key health services. Using a sophisticated design, Plan Nacer significantly improved birth outcomes and reduced neonatal mortality. A decade after the program's rollout, Argentina boasted some of the region's best ratings on standard health indicators.

This case was original authored by Miriam Temin.

The Toll of the Economic Crisis

Argentina's economic crisis, which started in 2001 and lasted three years, pushed roughly half of all households below the poverty line.[5] As poverty rose, overall population health deteriorated. The crisis jeopardized the health of those living in poverty by limiting their food intake and degrading their nutritional status. But for pregnant women, insufficient and unhealthy diets were especially dangerous because they also impacted their unborn babies, who were more likely than others to suffer from low birth weight, medically defined as less than 2,500 grams (5 pounds 8 ounces).[6] Low birth weight is a bad omen for infants' future development and a factor in nearly all newborn deaths worldwide.[7]

Beyond the heightened risk of neonatal death—death less than four weeks after birth—a baby's size at birth plays an important role in its ability to thrive. Low birth weight is associated with persistent health problems, poor cognitive development, low school achievement, and reduced lifetime earnings.[8] It occurs most frequently among babies born into poverty. In Argentina, this meant that many people born during the financial crisis would suffer from lifelong disadvantages.[9]

As low birth weight became more common in Argentina, access to quality healthcare grew more difficult, further threatening newborn health. By 2003, the infant mortality rate was 16.5 per 1,000 live births, more than double that of neighboring Chile.[10] According to experts, up to 6 in 10 newborn deaths could have been avoided with prenatal checkups, appropriate care during labor and delivery, and early diagnosis and treatment.[11] Thus, the nationwide trend was a preventable catastrophe, making each death even more of a tragedy.

The financial crisis had left half the population and 65 percent of children without health insurance, and basic services such as those for pregnant women and children had become unavailable to many uninsured families. While wealthier families could afford private insurance or received coverage from their employers, the poor and unemployed streamed toward the already struggling public system.

Putting an Idea in Motion:
Argentina Crafts a Better Plan for Births

In Argentina, the national constitution had guaranteed universal health coverage since 1994. Everyone in the country, with or without insurance, could seek healthcare through the public health system. The public health system had also been decentralized, reflecting the government's federal structure: the provincial governments, not the national government, held primary responsibility for providing healthcare. A majority of national public health financing flowed through provincial governments, and each of Argentina's 23 provinces plus the autonomous city of Buenos Aires had its own ministry of health.[12]

When the country began to emerge from the economic crisis, healthcare provided through the *obras sociales* and private services was unaffordable or unavailable to the large number of Argentines without insurance or work—a group that had ballooned due to high unemployment.[13] For the unemployed, the constitutional guarantee of health coverage could be met only by public health services. For pregnant women in poverty, there was no choice but to turn to public health facilities for the free prenatal care they offered.

But policymakers worried that the public health sector was already stretched too thin.[14] Public services had been chronically underfunded. Even worse, they failed to get the most health out of the available resources, and their inefficiency had proved hard to address.[15] Health funds traditionally flowed from national to provincial to local budgets with no strings attached, leaving the national Ministry of Health with little leverage to improve efficiency, accountability, or the impact of provincial health spending on health outcomes.[16]

Argentine health authorities noted the link between the weak public health services and women's deteriorating health status.[17] It was clear that improving the efficiency of public health spending and the health of uninsured women and children had become urgent public priorities.[18] National and provincial public health leaders agreed that significant changes were needed to improve coordination between the levels of government, identify the populations eligible for public-sector coverage, and assess whether the new approach was working by measuring the system's performance.

Donors also perceived the need for change. Results-based financing (RBF) was beginning to generate excitement elsewhere. In Argentina, the World Bank saw an opportunity to improve accountability between the different levels of the health system by incorporating RBF into the budget-transfer mechanism.[19]

Thus the government and World Bank joined forces to design Plan Nacer, first introduced in a new Federal

Health Plan for 2004–2007 and financed with the help of a World Bank loan.[20] The program was initially launched in nine northern provinces, home to Argentina's highest maternal and child mortality rates. Then, starting in 2007, the program gradually expanded across Argentina, achieving national coverage by 2012.[21]

Plan Nacer in Action

Plan Nacer enhanced the existing health system by providing incentives to provincial governments, which they passed on to healthcare providers.[22] Plan Nacer had five components:[23]

1. Legally binding agreements between national and provincial health ministries
2. Enrollment of health providers
3. Enrollment of the target population
4. Increased funding for delivery of priority services
5. Record keeping, reporting, audits, and evaluation

The first phase of the program laid a firm foundation upon which Plan Nacer could build. At the national level, the Ministry of Health determined the health targets the provinces were expected to achieve across 10 performance indicators, including health outcomes (for example, birth weight), service delivery (such as vaccinations), and equity (including training staff to care for indigenous populations). Plan Nacer staff recognized that an influx of new users could overwhelm existing health services, so during the initial phase facilities received start-up funds to help them buy new equipment and train extra staff.[24] Finally, Plan Nacer staff established contractual relationships between central and provincial health ministries and between provincial health ministries and public providers.

Public health providers' enrollment in Plan Nacer signaled their agreement to provide beneficiaries with the array of maternal and child health services covered under Plan Nacer. These had been specified by the federal government and focused on preventive care. Participating providers further agreed to track all service delivery and provide regular reports to provincial authorities. They also agreed to regular external audits, with the threat of penalties for inaccurate reporting.[25] By the end of 2008, Plan Nacer had contracted almost 2,000 public health providers—57 percent of the total[26]—and by the end of 2012, 7,254 health facilities were participating.[27]

Participating providers and provincial health staff worked to enroll eligible people: pregnant women and their newborns (until 45 days postpartum) and children under the age of six who did not have health insurance.[28] Enrollment was purely voluntary, but financial incentives helped motivate providers to bring participants on board. Once enrolled, the beneficiary women, babies, and young children enjoyed free access to the menu of Plan Nacer health services.[29] By the end of 2008, the program had enrolled 82 percent of the eligible population in priority provinces,[30] and by the end of 2012, two million pregnant women and children were enrolled.[31]

The central government paid for Plan Nacer through an RBF model. The national Ministry of Health allocated a per capita value of about US$5 to the program; this was the amount the ministry estimated it would take to fill the gap between the status quo and top-notch health-service provision. The specific amount of the transfers from the central government to the provinces varied, reflecting the provinces' differing performance in enrolling beneficiaries, delivering Plan Nacer services, and improving patients' health status.

Each month, the central government transferred 60 percent of the per capita value to provinces based on the number of beneficiaries enrolled; the more people a province enrolled, the more funding it received to pass on to health facilities.[32] Provinces were then eligible to receive the remaining 40 percent of the per capita value in payments spaced four months apart. The exact amount that they received depended on their performance in achieving health goals, measured using the 10 indicators. Provinces then redeployed their Plan Nacer resources to compensate contracted health providers for providing services to beneficiaries—these funds served as a performance incentive.

By giving public providers incentives to achieve health outcomes, provincial health staff encouraged them to deliver effective services. And thanks to additional Plan Nacer financing, hospitals and clinics could afford to improve service delivery. Staying within broad central guidelines, providers had flexibility to determine the best use of "surplus" Plan Nacer funds that remained after covering the costs of service delivery. Facilities typically spent the extra money on staff salaries, supplies, and facility maintenance.[33]

To track the satisfaction of the beneficiaries and the quality of the Plan Nacer services they received, a series of five user surveys were conducted in the initial nine northern provinces.[34] By the fifth survey, more than 80 percent of respondents reported that they held positive views of the program.

The Payoff: Babies Survive Their Infancy

Plan Nacer used a novel design based on RBF principles. Given the rapid growth of RBF in the region and the innovative nature of Argentina's model, the World Bank made impact evaluation a condition for its loan.[35] Plan Nacer was expanded incrementally, which made it possible to learn along the way, recognize lessons, and use them to improve aspects of program design. The evaluation, a collaboration between the World Bank and the Argentine Ministry of Health, covered the years 2005 to 2008 in seven of nine original Plan Nacer provinces.[36] The program's evaluation stands out because it is the first robust impact evaluation of an RBF program in Latin America.

In the evaluated provinces, birth outcomes improved and neonatal mortality decreased. Researchers convincingly demonstrated that Plan Nacer benefited every newborn in participating health facilities, and that it was even better for babies born to mothers enrolled in the plan (see Box 1).[37]

In large hospitals, Plan Nacer reduced enrolled babies' risk of neonatal death by an astonishing 74 percent. Even nonbeneficiaries saw impressive gains; babies born in participating facilities were 22 percent less likely to die during the neonatal period, whether or not they and their mothers were enrolled in the plan.[38] More and better prenatal care explained the plan's mortality effect: the incentives worked by bringing more pregnant women in for services and by improving the quality of care they received. The evaluators determined this by analyzing changes in the number of prenatal care visits, the probability of receiving a tetanus vaccine, and rates for cesarean sections. For example, women enrolled in Plan Nacer were 20 percent less likely to need a risky C-section than nonbeneficiaries—a result of the plan's efforts to

identify and solve problems early on, well before delivery. All these findings are particularly interesting in light of earlier studies that found mixed impact of prenatal care on neonatal outcomes.[39]

The evaluators attributed a little more than half of Plan Nacer's neonatal mortality effect to reductions in low birth weight (Figure 1). They calculated that beneficiaries were 19 percent less likely to have low-birth-weight babies, which made newborns more resilient.[40] Better case management of at-risk mothers explained this major accomplishment. And when babies did arrive underweight despite providers' best efforts, better postnatal care helped them survive into childhood.

Aggregating these results across the seven provinces, Plan Nacer averted an estimated 733 neonatal deaths, 1,071 low-birth-weight babies, and 72,800 total disability-adjusted life years (DALYs) between 2005 and 2008.

Gains at What Price?

Plan Nacer accomplished a great deal without costing much. On average, funding for the incentives totaled less

Figure 1. Average Birth Weight over Time

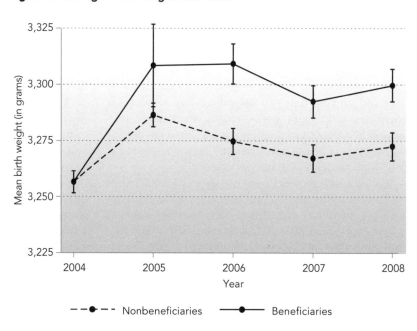

Source: Gertler, Giovagnoli, and Martinez (2014).
Note: The figure plots mean birth weight by year and beneficiary status. The individual is defined as a beneficiary if she was enrolled in Plan Nacer when she gave birth and if the clinic she visited during pregnancy was incorporated into Plan Nacer.

Box 1. Strength of the Evidence

The evaluation component of Plan Nacer was designed to analyze the separate effects of the program on healthcare facilities—hospitals and clinics—and on healthcare users.[41] The evaluation used data from 2004 to 2008 in seven of the nine provinces that implemented Plan Nacer's first phase. One province was excluded because of the plan's rapid introduction; a second was left out because of incomplete birth records. Unlike many impact evaluations that rely on expensive one-off household surveys, Plan Nacer evaluators used large administrative data sets, including birth certificate records from public maternity hospitals and other facility utilization data, which allowed them to analyze the impact of the program on events that were serious but relatively infrequent: low birth weight and neonatal mortality. As a result, the evaluation's sample covered a large number of events: birth outcomes for 282,000 pregnant women. This made the evaluation results more representative and credible.

The evaluation design exploited the phasing in of the plan over time to compare women and health facilities that were enrolled in the plan early with those that enrolled later. Researchers conducted two analyses to determine the impact of the program on all users of participating clinics and on Plan Nacer beneficiaries in participating clinics: intent-to-treat and treatment-on-the-treated. They com-

pared the treatment group with a similar group of individuals who were not beneficiaries of Plan Nacer and assessed the impact of the program in both groups before and after it was implemented as a way to control for confounding factors.

A counterfactual situation would be the most convincing way to show a causal relationship between Plan Nacer and the change in birth outcomes, but the widespread coverage of the plan made it impossible to establish a genuine counterfactual. Researchers used a number of econometric methods to present a strong case, but they noted that the evaluation results should be considered along with important limitations. They identified no differences in terms of birth outcome trends between clinics that enrolled early as compared with those that enrolled late, but one cannot fully discount the possibility that underlying differences could have led to biased results. Information on the quality in and actual use of health facilities was limited, and there was no analysis of outcomes in the postnatal period. Finally, the external validity of results was limited because neonatal mortality data described only a subset of the population (45 percent of births across 40 hospitals), although evaluators noted that the data were comparable to those of the region overall.

than 1 percent of total public spending on health at the provincial level. For instance, the program spent just US$39 million, a small portion of Argentina's roughly US$4 billion in total public spending on health in 2008, the final year of the impact evaluation.[42] Of course, Plan Nacer's budget covered only the costs of the incentives; the funding model worked because it was an add-on to the routine financing for the rest of the healthcare system in the provinces, including providers' salaries.

In Plan Nacer's first phase, from 2005 to 2008, the central government transferred a total of US$107 million to the first nine provinces. This was supplemented by a loan of US$136 million from the World Bank, and provincial governments later took on more than 30 percent of the total costs.[43] By cofinancing Plan Nacer along the way, the provincial governments gained autonomy and flexibility, which they then passed on to facilities.[44]

The program's evaluators concluded that Plan Nacer was highly cost-effective in the Argentine context, with an estimated cost per DALY of US$814, well under the gross domestic product per capita of US$6,075.

The Keys to Lasting Success

Argentina's new way of delivering and distributing health services paid off: the sophisticated system succeeded in expanding coverage, improving quality, fostering the delivery of appropriate healthcare, and ultimately improving health. Extending the use of incentives across all levels of the health system, empowering providers to control the use of new funds, and creating a culture of accountability were keys to Plan Nacer's success.

High-level public health officials contributed to Plan Nacer's design from the beginning, with the formation of a strong political and technical team at the national Ministry of Health—a distinctive group of strategic thinkers who could interact with a range of partners and stay abreast of the changing context. The team members also had the courage to challenge the status quo and identify emerging opportunities, allowing them to fine-tune management tools and performance goals as the program evolved.[45] Plan Nacer established a cooperative way of working that included shared leadership.

Martin Sabignoso was named as Plan Nacer's national coordinator and head of the Ministry of Health team. Initially trained as a lawyer, he ably led the program over multiple years and through ministerial changes at both the national and provincial levels, as well as through its nationwide expansion. His team cites his enthusiasm and charisma as making a difference in program management. The central management unit maintained a supervisory and steering role to ensure that the program achieved its goals and drove better performance.

Plan Nacer worked well within Argentina's health system, leveraging the central government's influence over a decentralized system to shape the plan's implementation and management. Plan Nacer staff carefully balanced financial flows across the system, using a relatively modest pot of health funds to encourage efficient use of the far larger provincial health budgets.[46] By combining incentives for both enrollment and services, Plan Nacer staff ensured an appropriate balance of effort—for example, preventing a situation in which providers might enroll beneficiaries without providing services.

By devolving management and decision making to provincial and lower levels, the program increased autonomy, empowered providers, and nurtured creativity. Often, the decision about how to use extra Plan Nacer resources was made on the basis of group consensus.[47] In one facility, creative providers passed an incentive on to users: at Christmas, a health center in La Pampa (a central province) bought bicycles using Plan Nacer funds for all those children whose vaccines and checkups were up to date.[48]

Plan Nacer's implementers attributed the program's success to the measurement, feedback, and learning that emerged over the course of the program, creating a culture of accountability. The intensive process of auditing and verifying clinic records made it possible to check the validity of payments, while the penalties that providers faced for improper recording and billing of services succeeded in improving records and data quality.[49] Program leaders also made a commitment to ongoing learning from the auditing process. Audits enabled staff to review progress; for example, early assessments turned up problems with contracting providers and reaching enrollment targets.[50] In response to evidence that emerged along the way, staff added new performance and health impact indicators, increased targets, and developed formulas for differentiating incentive payments according to the complexity of achieving each goal.[51]

Plan Nacer also promoted social accountability.[52] To educate enrollees on program benefits, some facilities posted menus of covered services. Staff also linked patient satisfaction as expressed on user opinion surveys to service providers' incentive payments. These activities reportedly empowered beneficiaries to demand expanded services and better quality. In addition, a Plan Nacer website publicized the performance of each province and the amount of funds disbursed.[53]

Finally, postcrisis trends such as improving macroeconomic conditions and improved political and institutional stability coincided with the rollout of the plan and contributed to its smooth implementation.[54] Through political changes, consistent government commitment helped Plan Nacer succeed. Following the reelection of President Cristina Fernández de Kirchner in 2011, the health ministers in 13 of the 24 provinces were replaced. However, all provincial Plan Nacer coordinators kept their jobs, suggesting that even the new health ministers understood Plan Nacer's value and popularity.

The Implications for Global Health

With Plan Nacer, Argentina became the first low- or middle-income country to use incentives to simultaneously expand health coverage and improve birth outcomes, and it documented its experience with a solid impact evaluation. Thanks to the evaluation and the wide dissemination of its results, Argentina's experience is inspiring other countries to pay for results rather than inputs. Panama, the Dominican Republic, and Guatemala are using payment arrangements modeled on Plan Nacer's, and Argentines have shared their insights with health planners in Egypt, South Africa, Turkey, and Ukraine, among other countries.[55]

Argentina started with a stronger economy and a more advanced health system than many other countries, and so the funding gap was relatively small. Still, Plan Nacer was not expensive to implement, and it is considered highly cost-effective. This suggests that aspects of the approach can be implemented even in health systems with fewer resources. Perhaps the most important resource is leadership by a team of individuals who understand and respond to the institutional dynamics within the health system and collaborate with their counterparts at different levels to effectively drive change. An RBF model also needs a reliable system for collecting and communicating data. Here, too, other countries can learn from Argentina's dedicated audit and verification systems, which allowed Plan Nacer to improve over time.

As an agreement between federal and provincial ministries, Plan Nacer differs from the standard pay-for-performance approach practiced elsewhere, such as in Rwanda (see chapter 12 of this volume). Nevertheless, it includes pay-for-performance elements that can inform critical design decisions for RBF programs, such as the size and source of the budget, its financing structure, and the size of incentive payments. It also highlights the importance of investing in facilities before launch, to help them cope with the increased demand that is sure to follow. Policymakers must also carefully consider which services to cover; one risk is that incentives can discourage health workers from providing nonincentivized services.[56]

Lessons from Plan Nacer can be instructive for health ministries that are taking on RBF and working toward universal health coverage. And Argentina itself is still working to make sure that Plan Nacer covers all people in need. It is still a challenge to reach the poorest and those living in the most remote areas, and some vulnerable groups remain underserved because they are unaware of their entitlement to health benefits.[57] As of 2009, 2 million of the nearly 15 million Argentines who lacked health insurance were eligible for Plan Nacer.[58] Even though some providers sent mobile teams to seek out pregnant women and children in isolated areas, some critics charged that the program was underinvested in outreach to hard-to-reach groups.[59]

To extend its reach, Plan Nacer has grown to include additional populations. In 2012, with the support of the World Bank, the government started a new program, Programa Sumar ("Additional Program"), to expand health coverage to children ages 6 to 19 and women ages 20 to 64. In mid-2015, the new program expanded again to cover uninsured men 20 to 64 years old. Building on the same RBF principles as Plan Nacer, the new program had reached 16 million children under age 10, adolescents, pregnant women, and adult women and men as of July 2015.[60] Continuing to expand access by paying for results will be integral to further improving efficiency, equity, and the health of all Argentines.[61]

REFERENCES

Abramovich, Victor, Laura Pautassi, and Victoria Furio. 2008. "Judicial Activism in the Argentine Health System: Recent Trends." *Health and Human Rights* 10 (2): 53–65.

Almond, Douglas, Kenneth Y. Chay, and David S. Lee. 2005. "The Costs of Low Birth Weight." *Quarterly Journal of Economics* 120 (3): 1031–83. doi:10.1093/qje/120.3.1031.

Almond, Douglas, and Janet Currie. 2011. "Killing Me Softly: The Fetal Origins Hypothesis." *Journal of Economic Perspectives* 25 (3): 153–72. doi:10.1257/jep.25.3.153.

Baldock, Hannah. 2002. "Child Hunger Deaths Shock Argentina." *Guardian*, November 24. http://www.theguardian.com/world/2002/nov/25/famine.argentina.

Behrman, Jere R., and Mark R. Rosenzweig. 2004. "Returns to Birthweight." *Review of Economics and Statistics* 86 (2): 586–601. doi:10.1162/003465304323031139.

Black, Sandra E., Paul J. Devereux, and Kjell G. Salvanes. 2007. "From the Cradle to the Labor Market? The Effect of Birth Weight on Adult Outcomes." *Quarterly Journal of Economics* 122 (1): 409–39.

Cavagnero, Eleonora, Guy Carrin, Ke Xu, and Ana Mylena Aguilar-Rivera. 2006. *Health Financing in Argentina: An Empirical Study of Health Care Expenditure and Utilization.* Working Paper 8. Mexico City: Fundación Mexicana para la Salud.

Cortez, Rafael. 2009. *Argentina—Provincial Maternal and Child Health Insurance: A Results-Based Financing Project at Work.* Washington, DC: World Bank. https://openknowledge.worldbank.org/handle/10986/10218.

Cortez, Rafael, and Daniela Romero. 2013. *Argentina Increasing Utilization of Health Care Services among the Uninsured Populations: The Plan Nacer Program.* UNICO Studies Series 74956. Washington, DC: World Bank.

Cortez, Rafael, Daniela Romero, Vanina Camporeale, and Luis Perez. 2012. *Results-Based Financing for Health in Argentina: The Plan Nacer Program.* Washington, DC: World Bank. http://www-wds.worldbank.org/external/default/WDSContentServer/WDSP/IB/2013/04/29/000445729_20130429160310/Rendered/PDF/716480WP0box-370forHealthinArgentina.pdf.

Currie, Janet. 2011. *Inequality at Birth: Some Causes and Consequences.* Working Paper 16798. Cambridge, MA: National Bureau of Economic Research.

Economist. 2002. "Argentina's Collapse: A Decline without Parallel," February 28. http://www.economist.com/node/1010911.

Eichler, Rena, and Amanda Glassman. 2008. "Health Systems Strengthening via Performance-Based Aid." Brookings Global Economy and Development, Global Health Financing Initiative Working Paper 3. Washington, DC:

REFERENCES, *continued*

Brookings Institution. http://www.brookings.edu/~/media/research/files/papers/2008/9/global%20health%20glassman/09_global_health_glassman.pdf.

Gasparini, Leonardo C., and Mónica Panadeiros. 2004. *Argentina: Assessing Changes in Targeting Health and Nutrition Policies.* HNP Discussion Paper 30471, Reaching the Poor Program Paper 1. Washington, DC: World Bank. http://www-wds.worldbank.org/external/default/WDSContentServer/WDSP/IB/2004/11/18/000090341_20041118090341/Rendered/PDF/304710RPP1ARGAssessingChanges.pdf.

Gertler, Paul, Paula Giovagnoli, and Sebastian Martinez. 2014. *Rewarding Provider Performance to Enable a Healthy Start to Life.* Policy Research Working Paper 6884. Washington, DC: World Bank. http://documents.worldbank.org/curated/en/2014/05/19546892/rewarding-provider-performance-enable-healthy-start-life-evidence-argentinas-plan-nacer.

Giedion, Ursula, Ricardo A. Bitran, and Ignez Tristao, eds. 2014. *Health Benefit Plans in Latin America: A Regional Comparison.* Washington, DC: Inter-American Development Bank. https://publications.iadb.org/bitstream/handle/11319/6484/Health-Benefit-Plans.pdf?sequence=1.

Glassman, Amanda. 2013. "How Many Bed Nets Equal a Life Saved? Why Results Matter for Value for Money." *Global Health Policy Blog,* Center for Global Development, September 27. http://www.cgdev.org/blog/how-many-bed-nets-equal-life-saved-%E2%80%93-why-results-matter-value-money.

Krauss, Clifford. 2001. "Argentina's Provinces Struggle to Stay Afloat." *New York Times,* November 18. http://www.nytimes.com/2001/11/18/international/americas/18ARGE.html.

Ministry of Health. 2015. "Reporte de Gestion Sumar." PowerPoint presentation. Accessed November 8. http://www.msal.gob.ar/sumar/images/stories/pdf/07-RG-JUL-2015.pdf.

Musgrove, Philip. 2011. *Financial and Other Rewards for Good Performance or Results: A Guided Tour of Concepts and Terms and a Short Glossary.* Washington, DC: World Bank. https://www.rbfhealth.org/sites/rbf/files/RBFglossarylongrevised_0.pdf.

Perazzo, Alfredo, and Erik Josephson. 2014. *Verification of Performance in Results-Based Financing Programs: The Case of Plan Nacer in Argentina.* Discussion Paper 95083. Washington, DC: International Bank for Reconstruction and Development / World Bank. https://openknowledge.worldbank.org/bitstream/handle/10986/21712/950830W-P0Box390ntina0Final00PUBLIC0.pdf?sequence=1.

Sabignoso, Martin. 2014. "Avanzando hacia la cobertura universal y efectiva en salud." PowerPoint presentation. April, Argentina: Buenos Aires. http://diplomaturaredes.

blogs.hospitalelcruce.org/files/2015/05/Presentaci%C3%B3n-Programa-SUMAR-Seminario-Diplomatura-en-Redes-de-Salud.-Viernes-10-de-abril.pdf.

Villar, J., H. Ba'aqeel, G. Piaggio, P. Lumbiganon, J. Miguel Belizán, U. Farnot, Y. Al-Mazrou, et al. 2001. "WHO Antenatal Care Randomised Trial for the Evaluation of a New Model of Routine Antenatal Care." *Lancet* 357 (9268): 1551–64.

World Bank. 2015. "Mortality Rate, Infant (per 1,000 Live Births)." Data. Accessed August 7. http://data.worldbank.org/indicator/SP.DYN.IMRT.IN.

ENDNOTES

1. *Economist* (2002).
2. Baldock (2002).
3. Krauss (2001); Abramovich, Pautassi, and Furio (2008).
4. Giedion, Bitran, and Tristao (2014).
5. Cortez et al. (2012, 2).
6. Currie (2011).
7. Gertler, Giovagnoli, and Martinez (2014); Behrman and Rosenzweig (2004); Almond, Chay, and Lee (2005).
8. Behrman and Rosenzweig (2004); Almond, Chay, and Lee (2005); Black, Devereux, and Salvanes (2007).
9. Almond and Currie (2011).
10. Perazzo and Josephson (2014); World Bank (2015).
11. Giedion, Bitran, and Tristao (2014).
12. Giedion, Bitran, and Tristao (2014).
13. Cavagnero et al. (2006).
14. Cortez et al. (2012).
15. Cortez et al. (2012).
16. Glassman (2013).
17. Gasparini and Panadeiros (2004).
18. Cortez et al. (2012).
19. Cortez et al. (2012).
20. Eichler and Glassman (2008).
21. Gertler, Giovagnoli, and Martinez (2014).
22. Martin Sabignoso, personal communication with the author, August 29, 2014; Cortez et al. (2012).
23. Cortez et al. (2012).
24. Cortez et al. (2012).
25. Cortez et al. (2012).
26. Musgrove (2011).
27. Martin Sabignoso, personal communication with the author, August 29, 2014.
28. Cortez et al. (2012).
29. Priority services cover healthcare promotion; delivery; preventative and diagnostic visits for pregnant women, mothers, and children; laboratory services; and imaging (Giedion, Bitran, and Tristao 2014).
30. Musgrove (2011).
31. Martin Sabignoso, personal communication with the author, August 29, 2014.

ENDNOTES, *continued*

32. Cortez et al. (2012).
33. Gertler, Giovagnoli, and Martinez (2014).
34. Cortez et al. (2012).
35. Martin Sabignoso, personal communication with the author, August 29, 2014.
36. Cortez et al. (2012).
37. Gertler, Giovagnoli, and Martinez (2014).
38. Gertler, Giovagnoli, and Martinez (2014).
39. Villar et al. (2001).
40. Gertler, Giovagnoli, and Martinez (2014).
41. This account is based on Cortez and Romero (2013, 6).
42. Cortez et al. (2012).
43. The World Bank later provided an additional US$300 million for the expansion to the remaining provinces (Cortez 2009).
44. Gertler, Giovagnoli, and Martinez (2014).
45. Cortez et al. (2012).
46. Cortez et al. (2012).
47. Sabignoso (2014).
48. Sabignoso (2014, 23).
49. Gertler, Giovagnoli, and Martinez (2014); Cortez et al. (2012).
50. Cortez and Romero (2013).
51. Cortez et al. (2012).
52. Cortez et al. (2012).
53. Eichler and Glassman (2008).
54. Cortez et al. (2012).
55. Cortez et al. (2012).
56. Cortez et al. (2012).
57. Cortez et al. (2012).
58. Gertler, Giovagnoli, and Martinez (2014).
59. Cortez et al. (2012, 24).
60. Ministry of Health (2015).
61. Cortez et al. (2012).

Tackling Disease at Its Roots
Brazil's Programa Saúde da Família

The Case at a Glance

HEALTH GOAL: To promote health, prevent disease, and decrease hospitalizations from conditions that can be prevented or treated in the community.

STRATEGY: National public health program to deliver primary care and preventive health services at the community level.

HEALTH IMPACT: Decrease in death and hospitalization rates from cardiovascular disease. Accelerated decline in infant mortality. An estimated 450,000 lives saved from 1996 to 2012.

WHY IT WORKED: Government commitment at federal, state, and municipal levels. Decentralization of decision-making authority to lower levels. Community engagement and commitment to empowering communities. Existence of other social programs to amplify impact. Use of multiskilled professional teams.

FINANCING: BRL2.4 billion (US$30 billion) in 2008, accounting for 8 percent of the total government health budget.

SCALE: 116 million people, around 57 percent of Brazil's population (mid-2014).

At sunrise in Minas Gerais, a poor state in southeastern Brazil, a middle-aged woman struggles for breath while trudging uphill to her job on a coffee plantation. Her family is poor and her husband smokes, drinks heavily, and suffers from diabetes. Her children have begun flirting with alcohol use, and worse. The household diet is unhealthy because nutritious foods are too expensive. Her head pounds; she thinks her swollen legs reflect her fatigue. But her symptoms signal a much more serious medical condition: the onset of congestive heart failure.

Around the world, people in low- and middle-income countries are changing their lifestyles, and this changes their health profiles. People are living longer as disease patterns have shifted away from infectious killers and maternal health risks toward chronic ailments. This transition poses daunting new challenges to governments with weak health systems and limited healthcare coverage. Although sound strategies exist for preventing and managing chronic diseases at the community level, consensus is lacking on how to turn these strategies into broad action in low- and middle-income countries.

Brazil, an emerging global economic leader, has made progress in this area. In 1994, Brazil's government began building what has become the largest comprehensive, community-based primary healthcare program in the world: the Programa Saúde da Família (PSF) ("Family Health Program"). Since then, the PSF has made remarkable strides in reducing deaths and illness from cardiovascular disease, while also contributing to major improvements in infant survival.[1]

The authors of an article in the *British Medical Journal* described the PSF as "probably the most impressive example worldwide of a rapidly scaled up, cost-effective, comprehensive primary care system."[2] The Brazilian public health program certainly offers important insights for other nations, but it still has room for improvement, as inequities in access to care persist. And uncertainties about its funding cast a shadow over its future.

The Toll of Chronic Disease

Low- and middle-income countries face a tricky balancing act: they must manage a decreasing yet still significant incidence of infectious disease and maternal health threats while also grappling with a surge in noncommuni-

This case was originally authored by Alix Beith, with contributions from Frederico Guanais de Aguiar.

cable diseases (NCDs), which have doubled or tripled in recent decades.[3] Among NCDs, cardiovascular disease is the biggest story: it is the top killer across the globe. Worldwide, the number of deaths from heart disease and stroke are expected to swell from roughly 17 million in 2008 to 23 million by 2030. The vast majority of those deaths occur in low- and middle-income countries.

Brazil mirrors this global trend. Since the 1960s, Brazil has undergone major demographic, epidemiological, and nutritional changes. Even though malaria, tuberculosis, and AIDS still take a considerable toll, and neglected tropical diseases such as Chagas disease, dengue, and schistosomiasis linger, NCDs are now responsible for nearly three-quarters of all deaths in Brazil, and 31 percent of the total deaths are from cardiovascular causes alone.[4]

In Brazil, as in most other nations, substantive shifts in diet, physical activity, and other behaviors have elevated the cardiovascular threat. It is generally acknowledged that preventing heart disease and stroke requires changing individual lifestyles and creating environments that promote health. Primary healthcare services can address cardiovascular disease risk factors such as high blood pressure and high blood glucose levels. Health programs can educate, encourage, or even offer financial incentives for stopping smoking, eating right, and engaging in regular physical activity. Yet geography, low socioeconomic status, and a raft of other conditions impede efforts to prevent and detect cardiovascular disease around the world.

In Brazil, public health services were once scarce or even nonexistent in disadvantaged areas, yet many had to rely on them. In the early 1990s, only about 60 percent of the national population could access the higher-quality private health services—those who paid social security taxes and those who could afford to pay out of pocket.[5] Reflecting these inequities in access to care, life expectancy in Brazil's wealthier southern regions was, on average, eight years greater than in its poorer northeast regions.[6]

Putting an Idea in Motion: A New Constitution Guarantees Free Healthcare for All

In Brazil, dramatic political and social change had set the stage for health-sector reform. In 1985, emerging from two decades of military rule, the country embarked on a "redemocratization" process. Civic organizations pushed for a free public health system for all. In 1988 a new federal constitution recognized health and equitable access to health services as universal human rights; as such, they are the responsibility of the state.

Two years later, a new health system was born: the national Sistema Único de Saúde (SUS) ("Unified Health System"). The SUS featured shared financing between different levels of the government, decentralization, participation by both the private sector and communities, and other reforms.[7] Government health planners phased in the SUS gradually, shifting its emphasis over time from tertiary (specialized) medical care to disease prevention and health promotion. Slowly but surely, the SUS gave more and more residents in rural areas and smaller municipalities access to free health services that they had previously lacked.

The PSF was the government's main program for the delivery of primary healthcare under the SUS. And it was called "the linchpin for the successes of the Unified Health System."[8] The PSF began in 1994 as a relatively small pilot program in the northeastern state of Ceara that provided free healthcare to one million people under the direction of local municipalities. Partly inspired by the Cuban healthcare model and built on principles of fairness and solidarity, the PSF aimed to deliver disease prevention, health promotion, and treatment and referral services at the community level through a network of multidisciplinary primary-healthcare teams. The pilot family health program quickly became the main strategy for Brazil's entire national health system, which took the same decentralized approach. The program expanded rapidly from 1998 to 2007 as it pursued its mission to equalize access to primary care services throughout the country.[9]

The PSF in Action

From the start, the PSF encouraged health workers to focus on "whole-person care."[10] Public healthcare teams were instructed to get to know people in their coverage areas and provide them with appropriate holistic services, free of charge. This community-level team approach aimed to build trust with area residents and increase their willingness to approach the health system for help.

Each primary-care team included a doctor, a nurse, a nurse assistant, a social worker, and four to six community health workers; some municipalities also chose to add dental professionals. The health units covered geographic areas of approximately 3,500 residents each, with the doctor and nurses delivering most medical treatment at a health facility. Meanwhile, the community health workers conducted health promotion and education activities, brought preventive care to mothers and children, and provided medical care for minor injuries and illnesses. Each health worker covered as many as 120 families and tried to visit every household at least once a month.[11] Thus, the community health workers formed a crucial link between the health teams and the residents.

By keeping tabs on the local population, healthcare workers could track pregnancies and target pre- and post-natal guidance. They knew which new babies needed vaccinations, and they could quickly treat acute conditions or make referrals for prompt care. More recently, with the new emphasis on the prevention and treatment of heart disease and diabetes, the teams have started working to identify, monitor, and manage individuals with early onset of chronic conditions and to promote lifestyle changes that stave off such ailments in the first place.[12]

The PSF continued to see rapid expansion. By mid-2014, the public health program was providing comprehensive primary-care services in 95 percent of Brazil's municipalities. More than 37,300 healthcare teams and 261,600 community health workers covered around 60 percent of the national population.[13]

To further expand access, São Paulo and some other municipalities have contracted private medical groups associated with large hospitals to manage and provide services in PSF clinics. However, this measure has stirred up controversy; to some Brazilians, involving the private sector runs counter to the fundamental ideology of a "health system for all."[14]

The Payoff: Stronger Hearts, Fewer Hospital Visits

The PSF has undoubtedly improved the health of Brazilians, a conclusion supported by a growing body of evidence (see Box 1).[15] But precisely quantifying the program's impact is challenging because of the changing political and societal landscape in which it has operated.

Research has linked the PSF with decreases in the number of heart disease and stroke deaths, as well as a plunge in hospitalizations for these conditions. The longer the program's services have been operating in a given locale, the stronger the associated benefits.[16] The PSF is also associated with fewer hospitalizations for other conditions that can be easily treated within the community. For example, in 2002, 126,000 fewer people wound up hospitalized for respiratory problems than in 1999.[17]

The PSF has also loosened the grip of other threats to health. Nationally, immunization and prenatal-care coverage have soared to near universal levels.[18] Even better, the program is credited with accelerating the decline in infant mortality. In municipalities that had decentralized public administration and expanded PSF services, infant mortality rates dropped by around 25 percent more than in municipalities that had not decentralized and have not implemented the PSF.[19] The apparent lesson: ceding management authority to lower levels of government can amplify a health program's benefits.

Overall, a conservative estimate suggests that the PSF saved almost 450,000 lives between 1996 and 2012.[20] Poorer Brazilians have reaped the greatest benefits, as the program has made tremendous progress in closing the health equity gap—the result of establishing healthcare units in previously underserved areas.[21] The PSF now covers 72 percent of the population in the poor northeast but only 36 percent of those in the wealthier southeast.[22]

However, the PSF did not dramatically change the national financial risk associated with health problems. According to the World Health Organization, out-of-pocket spending on health has decreased only slightly in Brazil since the early years of this century. Consumers' out-of-pocket spending on health was still 30 percent of the overall health expenditure in 2013, compared with 35 percent in 2003.[23] Although this figure compares favorably with the figures for some of Brazil's neighbors, it still suggests that many poor residents continue to lack financial protection when catastrophic health shocks hit—requiring secondary and tertiary healthcare that the PSF does not provide.

Gains at What Price?

In 2008, about 8 percent of the government's overall health budget of BRL2.4 billion (US$30 billion) went to the PSF, some of which the federal government transferred to municipalities to provide PSF health services. Municipalities typically receive around US$15 from the federal health budget per person enrolled. The precise allocation is determined by an increasingly complex formula. Among other factors, the formula takes account of the proportion of a municipality's population covered by the PSF; its population density, income per capita, and poverty rate; and the proportion of the residents who have supplemental private health insurance coverage.[30]

Box 1. Strength of the Evidence

The Programa Saúde da Família (PSF) began a period of social and economic transformation in Brazil. This makes it difficult to disentangle the impact of the program from many other changes at that time that may have influenced health outcomes, including life expectancy, maternal death, and infant mortality.

Nonetheless, several studies have sought to assess the PSF's health benefits. Many of these controlled for potentially confounding factors such as socioeconomic status, education, access to water, government health expenditure, and hospital beds per capita. According to three such studies—by Macinko and others;[24] Aquino, de Oliveira, and Barreto;[25] and Guanais[26]—Brazilian states and/or municipalities where a higher proportion of residents enrolled in the PSF saw faster declines in infant mortality rates.

In 2009, health planners developed an additional metric to assess performance: a set of medical conditions unlikely to require hospitalization if prevented or accurately managed at the community level. By measuring avoidable hospitalizations, the investigators were able to gauge the program's preventive health impact.[27] Using this list, Brazilian authorities convincingly documented the PSF's benefits in averting hospitalizations from heart disease and stroke.

In a study of more than 1,600 Brazilian municipalities, researchers tracked changes in death rates from cardiovascular disease over time.[28] Their analysis identified a strong "dose-response" relationship between the proportion of the population covered by PSF and cardiovascular deaths. This investigation surveyed a sample of municipalities with high-quality data, which makes the findings for those areas reliable; however, the results are not necessarily generalizable beyond the cities in the study.

Because the researchers for this study used so-called ecological data that were collected at a population level, their results come with an additional caveat. The findings may suffer from the "ecological fallacy"—the erroneous suggestion that an association observed at the aggregate level (e.g., between aggregate PSF coverage and heart disease in a municipality) implies an association at the individual level (e.g., a person with PSF coverage might expect to see a reduction in his or her risk of dying from a heart attack, which is not actually a valid assumption).[29] This ecological fallacy thus limits researchers' ability to extrapolate program results to individuals and to understand the specific pathways of the PSF's overall impact.

The typical annual cost for one PSF team was about US$154,000 in 2010, or US$44 per capita, and only about one-third of the total cost is covered by the federal transfer.[31] The appropriate balance of federal and municipal funding for the PSF is a topic of debate. Most municipalities foot more than 50 percent of the operating bill themselves, and most states also offer financing. There is scope to increase the states' contribution as more than half of Brazil's 26 states fail to meet the 12 percent of their total budgets that they are federally mandated to spend on health. Municipalities do better: some municipalities exceed the federal target of 15 percent and devote more than 30 percent of their budgets to health.[32]

To explore the cost-effectiveness of the PSF, researchers calculated that a municipality of 100,000 inhabitants with program coverage of 40 percent would be expected to spend between US$1.3 million and US$2 million on the PSF annually. In such a municipality, the PSF would save an estimated 57 lives after five years and 150 lives after eight years of PSF operation.[33] This is considered highly cost-effective in the Brazilian context.

Yet funding for the PSF is fragile. Although federal funding for health has increased in absolute terms over the past decade, adjustment for inflation shows that the real purchasing power of the funding is declining.[34]

The Keys to Lasting Success

The PSF succeeded in increasing the demand for healthcare in Brazil, but meeting that demand posed a challenge. In the program's early years, people from rural areas flocked to cities in search of health services, not realizing that those same services could be accessed closer to home via the PSF teams. That issue faded with time as rural families gained confidence in their local services. A second challenge was that despite the program's expansion and the creation of new healthcare facilities, emergency-room crowding persisted because few medical professionals could provide specialized care to people near their homes. In response, the government started rolling out community-based specialized and emergency clinics in 2008.[35] In urban areas, they also aggregated several PSF teams in the same health facility, enabling them to offer more specialized services such as ultrasounds.[36]

Competitive salaries for doctors in rural and underserved areas have also helped to some degree, although the economic incentive has not been sufficient to attract enough of them. Municipal-level health staff have introduced innovative measures, such as awarding doctors points on their medical residency exams for prior PSF clinical experience, and collective hiring of doctors by municipalities using pooled resources that are shared between different teams.[37] In 2013 the government of President Dilma Rousseff began recruiting doctors from Cuba to address Brazil's shortage, especially in rural, poorly served areas, through a program called Meis Medicos ("More Doctors").[38]

Despite these and other challenges, contextual factors helped foster success. Devolving authority to government structures below the federal level seems to have amplified the PSF's impact on infant mortality. The decentralization empowered municipalities, giving them responsibility for PSF staff hiring and firing. It also gave municipalities control over when and where to open new PSF facilities.

As of yet there is no consensus on the "right" balance between centralized and decentralized management of the PSF program, in particular the degree to which municipalities should cofinance the PSF. The program is primarily understood to be a municipal responsibility, although in recent years the federal government has attempted to increase funding to poorer municipalities in an effort to equalize spending levels. So far the additional assistance has been marginal at best.[39]

The government's social programs also may have helped. In 2003, a new administration led by President Luiz Inácio Lula da Silva merged the country's multiple conditional cash transfer programs into one, called Bolsa Família, literally "Family Purse." The merged program provides households with payments of up to US$83 per month, conditional on their health and education practices. Bolsa Família implementation was rapid—13 million families were enrolled by 2010—and as of 2015 it is the largest conditional cash transfer program in the world. A study highlighted an important synergy between Bolsa Família and the PSF: as Bolsa Família coverage increased, the association between PSF coverage and reduced post-neonatal mortality grew stronger.[40] In this case, supply-side incentives (additional funding and health staff) and demand-side incentives (cash for complying with the health and other conditions) working in tandem seemed to have had a greater impact than each separately.

Community engagement is strong. Every municipality and state has a health council that meets regularly to set PSF priorities, analyze policies, and assess health outcomes. In some communities, residents are actively involved in the local health council. Their engagement gives PSF end users considerable influence over budget allocation decisions, supervision of accounts, and approval of management reports.[41]

Despite gains under PSF, the fight for health equity continues. Access to health services still correlates with income level. For example, in 2008, more than 80 percent of women 25 years or older in the highest income bracket had a mammogram, compared with less than 30 percent of their peers in the lowest income bracket.[42] Other questions linger—for example, what scope of services should the PSF offer? Should the program expand to cover additional conditions such as mental health that might be most effectively managed within the community? And how well will the system work as it confronts the consequences of the large-scale outbreak of the Zika virus?

Implications for Global Health

Brazil's PSF experience offers lessons on how to effectively and equitably prevent, identify, and manage chronic conditions within communities. Increased access to high-quality primary healthcare relieved some of the strain on tertiary care and prevented unnecessary hospitalizations for these conditions. These gains are particularly relevant to large countries like Brazil, with strong central governments and smaller subnational governments. Countries like India, Nigeria, and South Africa might usefully adapt some elements of the PSF experience. Yet even a relatively strong health system cannot make a country immune to vulnerabilities, such as infectious disease outbreaks.

The role of community health workers proved central to the success of the program, and also to the collection of data that confirmed its success. Worldwide, evidence of the health impact of community-based workers has been limited despite the growing number of low- and middle-income countries that rely on this cadre. Studies of the PSF confirmed that community health workers made a salient contribution to observed health gains and the PSF's community-based provision of free comprehensive healthcare close to home improved health equity.

Community health workers also collected population-based data to feed into disease surveillance, a major contribution to PSF monitoring that offered a marked improvement over facility-based data.

A clear lesson from Brazil's experience is that strong political commitment does not guarantee population-wide consensus about the appropriate role for a universal scheme. The SUS covers everyone, but approximately one-quarter of Brazilians still opt to purchase supplemental coverage from the private insurance market. Some people argue that the PSF should focus its limited resources on the poor and let middle-class and wealthier Brazilians purchase private insurance and healthcare, as many already do. Other people find it hard to square such

a scenario with the philosophy of universal coverage, and argue that more federal funding is needed to improve the PSF. It is encouraging that additional funding for primary care may be coming through an emerging federal government results-based financing scheme, which would link a larger pot of health funding with better health worker performance.[43]

Will the PSF and the broader healthcare system continue to sustain progress in countering heart disease and improving health equity? There is no consensus about the future of the PSF. Nevertheless, the Brazilian experience shows that scaled-up community-level primary healthcare can improve the early detection and management of cardiovascular disease and other pressing health challenges.

REFERENCES

Alfradique, Maria Elmira, Palmira de Fátima Bonolo, Inês Dourado, Maria Fernanda Lima-Costa, James Macinko, Claunara Schilling Mendonça, Veneza Berenice Oliveira, et al. 2009. "Ambulatory Care Sensitive Hospitalizations: Elaboration of Brazilian List as a Tool for Measuring Health System Performance (Project ICSAP-Brazil)." *Cadernos de Saúde Pública* 25 (6): 1337–49.

Aquino, Rosana, Nelson F. de Oliveira, and Mauricio L. Barreto. 2009. "Impact of the Family Health Program on Infant Mortality in Brazilian Municipalities." *American Journal of Public Health* 99 (1): 87–93. doi:10.2105/AJPH.2007.127480.

Bevins, Vincent. "Brazil's President Imports Cuban Doctors to Ease Shortage." 2014. *Los Angeles Times*. January 6. http://www.latimes.com/world/la-fg-ff-brazil-doctors-20140106-story.html.

Departamento de Atenção Básica. 2015. "Histórico de Cobertura da Saúde da Família." Accessed November 3. http://dab.saude.gov.br/portaldab/historico_cobertura_sf.php.

Dugan, B., W. Hsiao, M. Roberts, M. Sinclair, and J. Noronha. 2013. *Brazil's National Health System*. Boston: Harvard School of Public Health and Harvard Kennedy School. http://www.ministerialleadershipinhealth.org/wp-content/uploads/sites/19/2013/07/Brazils-National-Health-System-Reform.pdf.

Guanais, Frederico C. 2010. "Health Equity in Brazil." *BMJ* 341: c6542. doi:10.1136/bmj.c6542.

———. 2013. "The Combined Effects of the Expansion of Primary Health Care and Conditional Cash Transfers on Infant Mortality in Brazil, 1998–2010." *American Journal of Public Health* 103 (11): 2000–6. doi:10.2105/AJPH.2013.301452.

Guanais, F.C., and J. Macinko. 2009a. "The Health Effects of Decentralizing Primary Care in Brazil." *Health Affairs* 28 (4): 1127–35. doi:10.1377/hlthaff.28.4.1127.

———. 2009b. "Primary Care and Avoidable Hospitalizations: Evidence from Brazil." *Journal of Ambulatory Care Management* 32 (2): 115–22. doi:10.1097/JAC.0b013e31819942e51.

Harris, Matthew, and Andy Haines. 2010. "Brazil's Family Health Programme: A Cost Effective Success That Higher Income Countries Could Learn From." *British Medical Journal* 341 (7784): 1171.

Johnson, Christopher, Jane Noyes, Andy Haines, Kathrin Thomas, Chris Stockport, Antonio Neves Ribas, and Matthew Harris. 2013. "Learning from the Brazilian Community Health Worker Model in North Wales." *Globalization and Health* 9 (1): 25. doi:10.1186/1744-8603-9-25.

Jurberg, Claudia. 2008. "Flawed but Fair: Brazil's Health System Reaches Out to the Poor." *Bulletin of the World Health Organization* 86 (4): 241–320.

Kepp, Michael. 2008. "Cracks Appear in Brazil's Primary Health-Care Programme." *Lancet* 372 (9642): 877. doi:10.1016/S0140-6736(08)61379-3.

Macinko, James, Ines Dourado, Rosana Aquino, Palmira de Fatima Bonolo, Maria Fernanda Lima-Costa, Maria Guadalupe Medina, Eduardo Mota, Veneza de Oliveira, and Maria Turci. 2010. "Major Expansion of Primary Care in Brazil Linked to Decline in Unnecessary Hospitalization." *Health Affairs* 29 (12): 2149–60. doi:10.1377/hlthaff.2010.0251.

Macinko, James, Maria de Fátima Marinho de Souza, Frederico C. Guanais, and Celso Cardoso da Silva Simões. 2007. "Going to Scale with Community-Based Primary

REFERENCES, *continued*

Care: An Analysis of the Family Health Program and Infant Mortality in Brazil, 1999–2004." *Social Science and Medicine* 65 (10): 2070–80. doi:10.1016/j.socscimed.2007.06.028.

Mendes, Áquilas, and Rosa Maria Marques. 2014. "O Financiamento da Atenção Básica e da Estratégia Saúde da Família no Sistema Único de Saúde." *Saúde em Debate* 38 (103). doi:10.5935/0103-1104.20140079.

Paim, Jairnilson, Claudia Travassos, Celia Almeida, Ligia Bahia, and James Macinko. 2011. "The Brazilian Health System: History, Advances, and Challenges." *Lancet* 377 (9779): 1778–97. doi:10.1016/S0140-6736(11)60054-8.

Pinto, Hêider Aurélio, Allan Nuno Alves de Sousa, Alcindo Antônio Ferla, Hêider Aurélio Pinto, Allan Nuno Alves de Sousa, and Alcindo Antônio Ferla. 2014. "O Programa Nacional de Melhoria do Acesso e da Qualidade da Atenção Básica: Várias Faces de Uma Política Inovadora." *Saúde em Debate* 38 (SPE): 358–72. doi:10.5935/0103-1104.2014S027.

Rasella, D., M.O. Harhay, M.L. Pamponet, R. Aquino, and M.L. Barreto. 2014. "Impact of Primary Health Care on Mortality from Heart and Cerebrovascular Diseases in Brazil: A Nationwide Analysis of Longitudinal Data." *BMJ* 349: g4014. doi:10.1136/bmj.g4014.

Rocha, Romero, and Rodrigo R. Soares. 2010. "Evaluating the Impact of Community-Based Health Interventions: Evidence from Brazil's Family Health Program." *Health Economics* 19 (Suppl 1): 126–58. doi:10.1002/hec.1607.

Rothman, Kenneth J., Sander Greenland, and Timothy L. Lash, eds. 2008. *Modern Epidemiology.* Philadelphia: Lippincott Williams & Wilkins.

Vieira, Roberta da Silva, and Luciana Mendes Santos Servo. 2013. *Estimativas de Custos dos Recursos Humanos em Atenção Básica: Equipes de Saúde da Família (ESF) e Equipes de Saúde Bucal (ESB).* Nota Técnica 16. Brasilia, Brazil: Instituto de Pesquisa Econômica Aplicada.

WHO (World Health Organization). 2010. "Brazil's March towards Universal Coverage." *Bulletin of the World Health Organization* 88 (9): 641–716.

———. 2014. "Brazil." Noncommunicable Diseases (NCD) Country Profiles. http://www.who.int/nmh/countries/bra_en.pdf?ua=1.

———. 2015. Global Health Expenditure Database. Accessed October 20. http://apps.who.int/nha/database/Select/Indicators/en.

ENDNOTES

1. Rasella et al. (2014).
2. Harris and Haines (2010).
3. NCDs have tripled in some places where accidents contribute significantly.
4. Dugan et al. (2013); Macinko et al. (2010); WHO (2014).
5. Kepp (2008).
6. Dugan et al. (2013).
7. Macinko et al. (2010).
8. Harris and Haines (2010).
9. Rocha and Soares (2010).
10. Macinko et al. (2010).
11. Johnson et al. (2013).
12. Macinko et al. (2010).
13. Departamento de Atenção Básica (2015).
14. Federico Guanais, personal communication with the author, July–September 2014.
15. Macinko et al. 2007; Aquino, de Oliveira, and Barreto (2009).
16. Rasella et al. (2014).
17. Guanais and Macinko (2009a).
18. Dugan et al. (2013).
19. Infants between the ages of 28 and 364 days were included in this analysis (Guanais and Macinko 2009a).
20. Federico Guanais, personal communication with the author, July–September 2014.
21. Jurberg (2008).
22. Guanais (2010).
23. WHO (2015).
24. 2007.
25. 2009.
26. 2013.
27. Alfradique et al. (2009).
28. Rasella et al. (2014).
29. Rothman et al. (2008).
30. Kepp (2008); Mendes and Marques (2014).
31. Vieira and Servo (2013); Rocha and Soares (2010).
32. WHO (2010).
33. Rocha and Soares (2010).
34. Paim et al. (2011).
35. Guanais (2013).
36. Federico Guanais, personal communication with the author, 2014.
37. Federico Guanais, personal communication with the author, 2014.
38. Bevins (2015).
39. For a description of this scheme, the National Program for Access and Quality Improvement in Primary Care, see Pinto et al. (2014).
40. Guanais (2013).
41. WHO (2010).
42. Guanais (2010).
43. Pinto et al. (2014).

CASE 12

Motivating Health Workers, Motivating Better Health
Rwanda's Pay-for-Performance Scheme for Health Services

The Case at a Glance

HEALTH GOAL: To improve maternal, infant, and child survival.

STRATEGY: Incentive payments to healthcare providers to motivate better quantity and quality of health services.

HEALTH IMPACT: Dramatically increased the proportion of hospital births and the number of preventive visits for children under five. Improved weight gain in infants and reduced stunting in young children.

WHY IT WORKED: Rigorous impact evaluation that proved scalability. Program design that responded to underlying causes of low worker productivity. Focus on both quantity and quality of care. Independent verification of provider reporting to ensure robust results and deter abuse.

FINANCING: US$0.30 per person per year.

SCALE: National.

Around the world, smart, compassionate, and motivated young people find themselves drawn to healthcare professions. Across wealthy and poor countries alike, a career as a doctor, nurse, midwife, pharmacist, or technician promises far more than a paycheck. Rwanda is no exception: in a 2010 study, 76 percent of health workers there "agreed that saving lives is more important to them than having a high salary."[1]

Despite the good intentions of health workers, youthful idealism and enthusiasm can eventually give way to disappointment and cynicism. Health workers too often arrive at understaffed and poorly managed facilities, where their colleagues receive neither rewards for outstanding performance nor sanctions for sloppiness. When no one appears to value or validate their hard work, their own intrinsic motivation may erode. A culture of mediocrity can arise in its place, and patients' health and safety can fall through the cracks.[2]

By the late 1990s, the government of Rwanda was eager to get back on track and address a deadly combination of health sector deficiencies and the aftereffects of the horrific 1994 genocide, which extinguished more than one-tenth of its population. For the post-genocide Ministry of Health, the lagging morale and lackluster performance

of its health professionals was a priority concern. Its solution: a new set of financial incentives intended to reward providers not on the basis of their rank or seniority but for the work they did that actually improved health. By 2008, the pay-for-performance scheme went nationwide, demonstrating that a financial incentive scheme, when implemented with rigorous verification of performance, can improve population health even in a low-resource setting. Yet a decade later, these gains might be threatened by an increasingly restrictive human rights environment and involvement in regional conflicts, which have, at points, prompted some donors to suspend or withdraw support to the Rwandan government.[3]

The Toll of Unmotivated Health Workers

To Rwandan children who are sick, nurses and doctors may seem like miracle workers, equipped with the skills and knowledge to return them to health. But those same health workers are also men and women with their own lives, challenges, and aspirations—and when their work environments deteriorate, their performance can deteriorate as well.

This case was originally authored by Rachel Silverman.

113

In low-income countries like Rwanda, governments often fail to fairly compensate health workers for their work, either because they cannot afford it or because they fail to grant them high budgetary priority. In many countries, deficiencies in management and human resource systems might also impede timely payments, with health workers at times going weeks or months without pay. The daily grind on the job can be similarly dispiriting, particularly when health workers lack the necessary supplies to fulfill their professional responsibilities and serve their patients' needs, or when male doctors condescend to, harass, or even abuse female health workers. Work in underresourced health sectors can become downright dangerous when the lack of protective equipment leaves health workers exposed to infectious airborne and blood-borne diseases. Many workers experience physical or psychological violence, including verbal abuse, threats, and assault from disgruntled patients or their families.[4]

Faced with poor pay and unpalatable working conditions, some health workers leave the country to work elsewhere or abandon the profession entirely. The World Health Organization reported in 2006 that 57 countries, including Rwanda and 35 others in sub-Saharan Africa, faced a critical shortage of doctors, nurses, and midwives, in part fueled by attrition of personnel, that threatened those countries' prospects of achieving their health goals.[5] Other demotivated health workers may stay in their jobs but frequently fail to show up for work. Health worker absenteeism, the percentage of health workers identified by spot checks as not working on a given day, was measured at 35 percent in Bangladesh and 37 percent in Uganda in 2006.[6]

Because health workers are essential to any health system, the repercussions of their inadequate performance are deeply felt by users of health services. In Uganda, supply shortages and lack of supervisor feedback were strongly associated with poor performance among community health workers.[7] In rural India, health workers were more likely to prescribe unnecessary or even harmful drugs than to follow the correct treatment protocol—and some have hypothesized that low provider motivation might at least partially explain the abysmal quality of care.[8] Around the world, fear of indifferent or disrespectful care from providers dissuades expectant mothers from seeking skilled birth attendance, putting them and their newborns at risk.[9]

In Rwanda, these problems were compounded by the devastation wrought by the 1994 genocide. In its after-math, the health sector's physical infrastructure was left degraded, with nearly all facilities destroyed. An astounding three-quarters of all health workers either fled or lost their lives during the conflict, creating an acute human resource crisis exacerbated by low motivation and poor performance among those remaining.[10]

In the face of deep damage to infrastructure and the health workforce, coupled with continued unrest and instability, the health of the Rwandan population deteriorated markedly. Between 1993 and 1995, infant mortality rose by 15 percent, while child mortality surged by 41 percent, from 179 to 253 per 1,000 live births. The subsequent years saw slow but steady gains in Rwandans' health. However, Rwanda's lost years had long-term knock-on effects. Important measures of child health, such as infant and under-five mortality rates, remained worse in 2000 than their pre-genocide levels a decade earlier.[11]

Putting an Idea in Motion: A New Approach Kick-Starts Rwanda's Devastated Health Sector

By 1995, Rwanda was a broken nation. Beginning in April 1994, neighbor had turned against neighbor to fuel a 100-day killing spree. At the end, an estimated 800,000 men, women, and children—more than 10 percent of Rwanda's total population—had been killed.[12] By July, military victory by President Paul Kagame's Rwandan Patriotic Front had booted the Hutu extremists from government and ended the genocide against the minority Tutsis. Over the next several years, however, continued instability prevented the fledgling government from providing all but the most basic services with the assistance of emergency relief organizations.[13]

As Rwanda's political climate stabilized in the late 1990s, national leaders and international humanitarian organizations turned to reconstructing the country's economy, institutions, and social fabric.[14] The shattered health sector presented a particularly daunting challenge. Facing the acute human resource shortage, international nongovernmental organizations (NGOs) began experimenting with ways to motivate health workers and produce better health outcomes under difficult circumstances at the provincial level. One idea in particular took hold: financial payments to reinvigorate health workers' motivation, which the NGOs hoped would boost health worker productivity and the quality of care.[15]

Starting in 2002, a Dutch NGO, the Catholic Organization for Relief and Development Aid (CORDAID), began "purchasing" health services in Cyangugu province by offering payments to all government and NGO facilities, as well as some private dispensaries, based on the quantity and quality of health services provided—an approach described as "pay for performance" (P4P).[16] At the same time, another Dutch organization, HealthNet International, initiated a similar scheme in Butare that was implemented by Rwandan government institutions.[17] Three years later, Belgian Technical Cooperation began a third local program in Kigali, Rwanda's capital city.[18]

Health workers in the initial P4P sites embraced the new approach, and early results gave policymakers grounds for optimism. An observational study found that, when compared with facilities in two other provinces with similar characteristics, Cyangugu and Butare health centers saw relatively large improvements in outpatient consultations, facility-based childbirth, and family planning coverage between 2001 and 2004. They also outperformed comparison facilities on a simple index of service quality.[19] Likewise, in Kigali, the introduction of the performance-based program coincided with rapid growth in the uptake of health services and major health improvements. For example, in less than one year, the proportion of hospital or facility deliveries among all births rose by 9 percentage points, to 30 percent, and the percentage of children participating in regular growth monitoring roughly doubled, ultimately reaching 94 percent.[20] Even though it was not possible to prove that these increases were the results of the P4P approach, the signs were extremely encouraging.

Despite the promising early returns, P4P was still a new and largely untested concept. But the Rwandan government had few qualms about undertaking bold experiments to achieve major gains in social welfare and economic development. In 2000, the Ministry of Finance and Economic Planning released its Vision 2020 document, which outlined its aspiration to "fundamentally transform Rwanda into a middle-income country by the year 2020," including in its aims a fourfold increase in gross domestic product per capita, a halving of infant mortality, and an 80 percent drop in maternal mortality.[21] The Ministry of Health saw in P4P an opportunity to accelerate health improvements and strengthen the health sector. And after seeing the apparent success of the preliminary pilots, the government was ready to take the plunge and expand the initiative nationwide.[22]

Some of Rwanda's development partners initially voiced concerns about the initiative. They believed it would be "too risky, too complex, and too hard to implement." However, Rwanda had a reputation as a trustworthy and competent "donor darling"—one with tight control over its population and against corruption. Thus, the government forged ahead despite donors' qualms, ultimately earning their support. Nonetheless, all parties found common ground on the need for proof that preliminary results from the pilot projects would hold at scale.[23]

To facilitate a rigorous impact evaluation, the World Bank reached out to University of California, Berkeley, economist Paul Gertler for help in leading the design of a staged P4P scale-up.[24] The first three programs had already covered 13 Rwandan districts. Gertler and his team split the remaining 17 districts into two groups. In the first group, P4P was introduced in mid-2006. In the second group, introduction was delayed until 2008; in the meantime, health facilities received lump-sum budget supplements equal to the average P4P payment in treatment districts.[25] By the close of 2008, research showed that P4P was running smoothly at facilities across the country.

The Pay-for-Performance Scheme in Action

Typically, health workers in low- and middle-income countries are paid a fixed salary according to their education, position, and seniority. In other words, the salary does not depend directly on the number of patients served or the quality of care provided. In contrast, P4P schemes tie at least part of providers' remuneration directly to various aspects of their job performance, such as the number of people seen or services provided, the quality and appropriateness of those services, and sometimes their patients' health outcomes.

In Rwanda, P4P incentive payments were tied to health centers' provision of 14 different services for maternal, child, and general health, ranging from US$0.09 for a first prenatal care visit to US$4.59 for a facility-based delivery or emergency obstetric referral.[26] Four of the indicators rewarded appropriate referral of complex cases to higher levels of care; for those, reimbursement occurred only if hospital documentation confirmed that the referral was medically necessary. In addition, the government incentivized the provision of a range of HIV and tuberculosis services with similar per-unit performance payments.

The incentive payments were calculated according to a formula based on the quantity and coverage of health services, and then adjusted according to the quality of service delivery.

Each month, facilities forwarded their service provision records to a district committee. The committee first calculated the total incentive payment for each service by multiplying the reimbursement rate for that service by the number of times that service was provided. Then the incentive payments for all 14 indicators were added together to determine the total "base" payment amount for the facility.[27] Once each quarter, auditors made surprise visits to each facility, checking for inconsistencies or misreporting. Generally, few discrepancies were found, although some clever "gaming" may have evaded detection.

To motivate health workers to deliver high-quality care, facilities' overall base incentive payment was adjusted based on the quality of care they provided. In other words, a facility would receive only a portion of its base incentive payment if it scored low on a quality metric. This quality check was performed each quarter by a local district hospital supervisor.[28]

Quality is notoriously difficult to measure objectively. For the purposes of this program, the quality was calculated using standardized tools such as a quality score that incorporated 13 dimensions of facility conditions and patient care. Each facility's monthly base incentive payment was multiplied by its most recent quality score, and the resulting product was disbursed as the final incentive payment.[29] Facilities received the incentive payments with no strings attached and were free to allocate those funds as they saw fit. Most of them used the funds to top up staff salaries, on average by 38 percent over preincentive levels.[30]

The scheme was not without its problems. Some Rwandan health workers reported that the program distorted their prioritization, requiring them to use scarce time to complete the administrative tasks (filling out forms) required to get paid at the expense of providing critical care to their patients.[31] Some health workers tried to game the system by filling out patient charts with services that had not been provided. Others refrained from dispensing specific drugs in an attempt to head off supply stockouts. (Stockouts were counted as part of the composite quality score; if they occurred, the facility would see an overall reduction in its P4P base payment.)[32]

The Payoff: Diligent Health Workers, Healthier Population

The Rwandan government wanted to know if its new approach was making a difference. With the World Bank offering the connections and financial backing, the government found Gertler and other prominent researchers eager to help find out. Together, they designed a randomized controlled trial to evaluate the program that enabled them to draw strong conclusions about the relationship between the P4P reform and health impact (see Box 1). The results were generally positive.

Health workers cranked up their effort under P4P. Health facility staff soon reported gains in personal motivation, a greater "spirit of entrepreneurship," improved camaraderie among team members, and more respectful and attentive patient interaction. Overall, "P4P [gave] them a feeling that their work [was] appreciated more."[33] Absenteeism dropped, efficiency rose, and health workers got creative in their attempts to draw underserved populations into the healthcare system, particularly for high-paying services like institutional deliveries.[34]

Despite the implementation problems noted above, the evaluation found that P4P brought impressive gains in utilization and quality of care. Compared with districts that received an equivalent increase in their budgets but did not implement the program in the initial phase, P4P districts saw a 14 percent increase in the proportion of all births taking place in a hospital, a 27 percent increase in preventive visits for children under age two, and an 8 percent increase in the proportion of mothers receiving a tetanus vaccine during a prenatal visit.[35] The quality of prenatal care, as measured using a standard composite score, also improved in the P4P districts.[36]

After only two years, P4P areas saw infant and child health gains. Infants under age one saw significant improvements in their weight for age, and children aged two to four years were also considerably less likely to be stunted, compared with those in the control districts. This showed that the P4P program was enough to reverse the ongoing effects of chronic malnutrition in young children.[37]

Rwanda's entire population experienced rapid health gains during the first decade of the present century. In the period between 2005 and 2010, which coincided with P4P scale-up, nationwide maternal mortality dropped by 36 percent, infant deaths by 35 percent, and child deaths by 40 percent.[38] P4P at scale was likely one of the factors making Rwandans healthier, but it was not the only one: other relevant changes include huge increases in overall

Box 1. Strength of the Evidence

Rwanda's P4P program has been rigorously evaluated by numerous research teams. Researchers have exploited multiple data sources with similar results, so their impact estimates are highly credible.

First, the program rollout was designed to enable an impact evaluation. Financial incentives were first introduced in a subset of randomly selected districts in 2006 (the treatment group), with the remaining districts phasing in P4P two years later (the control group). In the interim, facilities in the control districts received no-strings-attached quarterly payments equal to the average reward payments for treatment districts. This smart strategy allowed researchers to equalize resources across both groups and isolate the impact of incentives from the confounding effect of a budget increase. After two years, researchers found that P4P districts had seen important gains in service utilization and child nutrition above and beyond the changes seen in the control group.

Several years later, a second set of researchers used a different data set in an attempt to validate and expand upon the initial analysis. Sherry, Bauhoff, and Mohanan[40] looked at the results from two demographic and health surveys (DHSs) conducted in Rwanda preintervention in 2005 and postintervention in 2007–2008. Parts of their analysis confirmed previous findings on the impact of P4P, particularly gains in institutional deliveries and no change in childhood immunization; they also found significant gains in prenatal iron supplementation and urinalysis in treatment areas. However, they were unable to identify any associated health impact of P4P on the indicators covered by DHS data, such as breast-feeding, vision, anemia, and infectious disease in young children. Nonetheless, their successful replication of the first evaluation's headline findings instills high confidence in the overall strength of the evidence on the effectiveness of the program.

health spending by the government and donors, bed net distribution, and community health insurance schemes.[39] Consequently, it is impossible to quantify the specific amount the P4P program contributed with certainty.

Gains at What Price?

In just six years, per capita health spending swelled by almost 500 percent, from US$8 in 2002 to US$47 in 2008.[41]

Because all the gains from the program were compared with the performance of a control group of facilities with equal resources, the only additional costs from the P4P intervention resulted from its higher administrative and verification costs. These additional costs totaled approximately US$0.30 per person per year. Although this amount might appear small by US standards, it is significant in the Rwandan context, adding up to about 1.2 percent of combined donor and government spending.[42]

The Keys to Lasting Success

Rwanda's P4P program did not work in isolation. It coincided with several other important reforms that made health services more accessible for Rwandans and

strengthened the overall health sector. Starting in 2001, the government underwent a process of decentralization, and eventually authorities devolved most control over health spending to district staff and individual facilities with control over their own budgets and human resources. Facilities had sufficient space and flexibility to respond to the new incentive structure with meaningful management changes, for instance, by firing ineffective staff or increasing salaries and benefits for their best workers.[43]

Coverage of affordable community health insurance schemes (called *mutuelles*) expanded simultaneously, reaching 85 percent of Rwandan families by 2008 and enabling enrollees to access health services during moments of need with a modest co-pay.[44] Undergirding all these changes was massive growth in the overall resources for health that drew on a combination of strong donor support and a growing government contribution.

The Rwandan government spearheaded these changes. The postgenocide government was ambitious and data driven, with a zero-tolerance attitude toward fraud and corruption, although it also limited political freedom and had a problematic human rights record, particularly after 2012.[45] On top of the data verification efforts, it is possible that the government's hard-line attitude toward corruption dissuaded health facilities from manipulating or misreporting their results in a bid for additional incentive payments. Still, serious questions remain about the sustainability of P4P and Rwanda's health improvements more broadly, including whether the reported health improvements fully reflect reality. (The Rwandan government has been accused of manipulating other development statistics, though it adamantly denies such claims.)[46] Several donors have at times suspended at least part of their funding to the Rwandan government, and others may do so in the future.[47]

Implications for Global Health

When health facilities are faced with chronic deficiencies in supplies, infrastructure, staff support, and management—on top of low salaries—human resource crises can become the norm. But for policymakers confronting this seemingly intractable problem, the Rwandan P4P program offered a concrete, adaptable management tool. P4P enabled the government to boost the health impact of its existing health workforce while simultaneously improving morale and retention. It was among the first such programs to undergo rigorous evaluation in a low- or middle-income country, and its combination of feasibility and demonstrated success helped spark a global revolution in performance-based compensation for health workers.

In 2007, funding from Norway and the United Kingdom allowed the World Bank to launch the Health Results Innovation Trust Fund (HRITF), an initiative to support similar efforts worldwide. By the close of 2014, HRITF had helped P4P programs get off the ground in more than 30 countries across Asia, sub-Saharan Africa, and Latin America (including Argentina's Plan Nacer; see chapter 10 of this volume). The Global Fund to Fight AIDS, Tuberculosis and Malaria has also hopped on the P4P bandwagon, offering support to performance-based programs in Benin, for example.[48]

The global movement toward P4P programs has raised new questions about what they need to succeed—and as with most things, the devil is in the details. For example, what size should the payment be for each service? What is the best way to measure quality? How much independent verification of results is needed to deter misreporting and gaming of the system?[49] Will increased utilization of health services necessarily lead to better population health? And could well-intentioned but poorly designed incentives inadvertently harm patients?

For now, answers are few and far between, but these questions are spurring a generation of researchers at HRITF and elsewhere to figure out what works. One lesson is crystal clear: health workers are human beings with human needs. And if policymakers can align health workers' aspirations with the needs of their populations, health can improve.

REFERENCES

Bagonza, James, Simon P.S. Kibira, and Elizeus Rutebemberwa. 2014. "Performance of Community Health Workers Managing Malaria, Pneumonia and Diarrhoea under the Community Case Management Programme in Central Uganda: A Cross Sectional Study." *Malaria Journal* 13: 367. doi:10.1186/1475-2875-13-367.

Basinga, Paulin, Paul J. Gertler, Agnes Binagwaho, Agnes L.B. Soucat, Jennifer Sturdy, and Christel M.J. Vermeersch. 2011. "Effect on Maternal and Child Health Services in Rwanda of Payment to Primary Health-Care Providers for Performance." *Lancet* 377 (9775): 1421–28. doi:10.1016/S0140-6736(11)60177-3.

Bowser, Diana, and Kathleen Hill. 2010. *Exploring Evidence for Disrespect and Abuse in Facility-Based Childbirth: Report of a Landscape Analysis.* USAID TRAction project. Boston: Harvard School of Public Health.

Chaudhury, Nazmul, Jeffrey Hammer, Michael Kremer, Karthik Muralidharan, and F. Halsey Rogers. 2006. "Missing in Action: Teacher and Health Worker Absence in Developing Countries." *Journal of Economic Perspectives* 20 (1): 91–116.

Das, Jishnu, Alaka Holla, Veena Das, Manoj Mohanan, Diana Tabak, and Brian Chan. 2012. "In Urban and Rural India, a Standardized Patient Study Showed Low Levels of Provider Training and Huge Quality Gaps." *Health Affairs* 31 (12): 2274–2784.

di Martino, Vittorio. 2002. *Workplace Violence in the Health Sector: Country Case Studies: Brazil, Bulgaria, Lebanon, Portugal, South Africa, Thailand and an Additional Australian Study.* Synthesis Report. Geneva: ILO/ICN/WHO/PSI Joint Programme on Workplace Violence in the Health Sector. http://www.who.int/violence_injury_prevention/injury/en/WVsynthesisreport.pdf.

Doyle, Mark. 2015. "UK Stops £21m Aid Payment to Rwanda." *BBC News,* November 30. http://www.bbc.com/news/uk-politics-20553872.

Economist. 2012. "A Painful Dilemma: The Rwandan Government's Human-Rights Record Is So Bad That

REFERENCES, *continued*

Donors Should Start Withdrawing Aid," August 4. http://www.economist.com/node/21559943?zid=309&ah=80dcf288b8561b012f603b9fd9577f0e.

———. 2013. "The Pain of Suspension," January 12. http://www.economist.com/news/middle-east-and-africa/21569438-will-rwandas-widely-praised-development-plans-now-be-stymied-pain.

Germain, Nicolas. 2015. "Rwanda Accused of Manipulating Poverty Statistics." *France 24,* November 2. http://www.france24.com/en/20151102-rwanda-accused-manipulating-poverty-statistics.

Gertler, Paul, and Christel Vermeersch. 2012. *Using Performance Incentives to Improve Health Outcomes.* Policy Research Working Papers. Washington, DC: World Bank. http://elibrary.worldbank.org/doi/book/10.1596/1813-9450-6100.

———. 2013. *Using Performance Incentives to Improve Medical Care Productivity and Health Outcomes.* Berkeley: University of California, Berkeley. http://haas.berkeley.edu/faculty/papers/gertler_incentives.pdf.

Habineza, Christian. 2010. "Performance Based Financing—Rwanda Piloted Project in Ex-Cyangugu." Presentation, July 9. http://www.multicountrypbfnetwork.org/Rwanda_Presentation_PBF_exchange_visit.pdf.

HRITF (Health Results Innovation Trust Fund). 2016. "Benin." *RBF Health.* Accessed February 9. http://www.rbfhealth.org/rbfhealth/content/benin.

Human Rights Watch. 2015. "World Report 2015: Rwanda." Accessed October 28. https://www.hrw.org/world-report/2015/country-chapters/rwanda.

Kalk, Andreas, Friederike Amani Paul, and Eva Grabosch. 2010. "'Paying for Performance' in Rwanda: Does It Pay Off?" *Tropical Medicine and International Health* 15 (2): 182–90. doi:10.1111/j.1365-3156.2009.02430.x.

Morgan, Lindsay. 2010. "Signed, Sealed, Delivered? Evidence from Rwanda on the Impact of Results-Based Financing for Health." RBF Health Feature 54103. Washington, DC: World Bank. http://www-wds.worldbank.org/external/default/WDSContentServer/WDSP/IB/2010/04/20/000333037_20100420030817/Rendered/PDF/541030BRI0RBF-110Box345636B01PUBLIC1.pdf.

NISR (National Institute of Statistics of Rwanda). 2015. "NISR Refutes Wrong Allegations on Its Latest Poverty Report by France 24," November 3. http://statistics.gov.rw/press/press-release/nisr-refutes-wrong-allegations-its-latest-poverty-report-france-24

Overseas Development Institute. 2011. *Rwanda's Progress in Health: Leadership, Performance and Insurance.* London: ODI Publications. http://www.developmentprogress.org/sites/developmentprogress.org/files/resource_report/rwanda_report_-_master_0.pdf.

Republic of Rwanda. 2012. *Rwanda Vision 2020.* Kigali, Rwanda: Republic of Rwanda. http://www.minecofin.gov.rw/fileadmin/templates/documents/NDPR/Vision_2020_.pdf.

Rusa, Louis, and Gyuri Fritsche. 2007. "Rwanda: Performance-Based Financing in Health." In *Emerging Good Practice in Managing for Development Results Sourcebook,* 2nd ed. Washington, DC: World Bank.

Rusa, Louis, Miriam Schneidman, Gyuri Fritsche, and Laurent Musango. 2009. "Rwanda: Performance-Based Financing in the Public Sector." In *Performance Incentives for Global Health: Potential and Pitfalls.* Washington, DC: Center for Global Development. http://www.cgdev.org/publication/9781933286297-performance-incentives-global-health-potential-and-pitfalls.

Sekabaraga, C., A. Soucat, F. Diop, and G. Martin. 2011. "Innovative Financing for Health in Rwanda: A Report of Successful Reforms." In *Yes Africa Can: Success Stories from a Dynamic Continent,* edited by Punam Chuhan-Pole and Manka Angwafo. Washington, DC: World Bank.

Serneels, Pieter, and Tomas Lievens. 2008. *Institutions for Health Care Delivery: A Formal Exploration of What Matters to Health Workers—Evidence from Rwanda.* Working Paper CSAE WPS/2008-29. Oxford, UK: Centre for the Study of African Economies, University of Oxford. http://www.csae.ox.ac.uk/workingpapers/pdfs/2008-29text.pdf.

Sherry, Tisamarie B., Sebastian Bauhoff, and Manoj Mohanan. 2015. *Multitasking and Heterogeneous Treatment Effects in Pay-for-Performance in Health Care: Evidence from Rwanda.* SSRN Scholarly Paper ID 2170393. Rochester, NY: Social Science Research Network. http://papers.ssrn.com/abstract=2170393.

Soeters, Robert, Laurent Musango, and Bruno Meessen. 2005. *Comparison of Two Output Based Schemes in Butare and Cyangugu Provinces with Two Control Provinces in Rwanda.* The Hague, Antwerp, and Butare: Global Partnership on Output-Based Aid, World Bank, and Rwandan Ministry of Health.

United Human Rights Council. 2016. "Genocide in Rwanda." Accessed February 9. http://www.unitedhumanrights.org/genocide/genocide_in_rwanda.htm.

US Department of State. 2015. "Country Reports on Human Rights Practices for 2014." Accessed October 28. http://www.state.gov/j/drl/rls/hrrpt/humanrightsreport/index.htm.

US House Committee on Foreign Affairs. 2015. "Subcommittee Hearing: Developments in Rwanda." May 20. http://foreignaffairs.house.gov/hearing/subcommittee-hearing-developments-rwanda.

WHO (World Health Organization). 2006. *Working Together for Health: The World Health Report 2006.* Geneva: WHO.

REFERENCES, *continued*

World Bank. 2015a. Data. Accessed November 10. http://databank.worldbank.org/data/reports.aspx?-source=2&country=RWA&series=&period=.

————. 2015b. "Rwanda." Data. Accessed October 28. http://data.worldbank.org/country/rwanda.

————. 2015c. "Health Expenditure per Capita (Current US$)." Data. Accessed October 28. http://data.worldbank.org/indicator/SH.XPD.PCAP?page=2.

ENDNOTES

1. Kalk, Paul, and Grabosch (2010, 185).
2. Serneels and Lievens (2008); WHO (2006).
3. Human Rights Watch (2015); US Department of State (2015); US House Committee on Foreign Affairs (2015); *Economist* (2013); Doyle (2015).
4. di Martino (2002); WHO (2006).
5. WHO (2006).
6. Chaudhury et al. (2006).
7. Bagonza, Kibira, and Rutebemberwa (2014).
8. Das et al. (2012).
9. Bowser and Hill (2010).
10. Overseas Development Institute (2011).
11. World Bank (2015a).
12. United Human Rights Council (2015).
13. Overseas Development Institute (2011).
14. Overseas Development Institute (2011).
15. Habineza (2010).
16. Rusa and Fritsche (2007); Habineza (2010).
17. Rusa and Fritsche (2007).
18. Rusa et al. (2009).
19. Soeters, Musango, and Meessen (2005).
20. Rusa and Fritsche (2007).
21. Republic of Rwanda (2012).
22. Overseas Development Institute (2011).
23. Morgan (2010).
24. Morgan (2010).
25. Rusa and Fritsche (2007).
26. Basinga et al. (2011).
27. Basinga et al. (2011).
28. Basinga et al. (2011).
29. Basinga et al. (2011).
30. Basinga et al. (2011).
31. Kalk, Paul, and Grabosch (2010).
32. Kalk, Paul, and Grabosch (2010).
33. Kalk, Paul, and Grabosch (2010, 185).
34. Gertler and Vermeersch (2012); Basinga et all. (2011).
35. Gertler and Vermeersch (2012).
36. Basinga et al. (2011).
37. Gertler and Vermeersch (2013).
38. World Bank (2015b).
39. Kalk, Paul, and Grabosch (2010).
40. 2015.
41. World Bank (2015c).
42. Basinga et al. (2011).
43. Sekabaraga et al. (2011).
44. Sekabaraga et al. (2011).
45. *Economist* (2012); Morgan (2010); US House Committee on Foreign Affairs (2010).
46. Germain (2015); NISR (2015).
47. *Economist* (2013); Doyle (2015).
48. HRITF (2016).
49. Kalk, Paul, and Grabosch (2010).

CASE 13

Learning from Disappointment
Reducing the Cost of Institutional Delivery in Gujarat, India

The Case at a Glance

HEALTH GOAL: To reduce infant and maternal deaths by increasing institutional deliveries.

STRATEGY: Government payments through Chiranjeevi Yojana to private doctors to pay for normal or cesarean-section deliveries for below-poverty-level and tribal women.

HEALTH IMPACT: No evidence of a change in the probability of institutional delivery or birth-related complications in the general population between 2005 and 2010. No reduction in out-of-pocket expenditure for delivery.

WHY IT DIDN'T WORK: Poor targeting of program. Insufficient enrollment of doctors and women. Inadequate reimbursement level and persistent need for out-of-pocket expenditures. Insufficient evidence to inform better execution. Gaps in quality of care. Cultural barriers to hospital births.

FINANCING: US$32 million from 2006 to 2012.

SCALE: More than 800 participating hospitals in Gujarat (2012).

Most of the time, babies arrive without complications—at least 85 percent of all births occur without a serious problem.[1] But when complications do arise they can be fatal, threatening both mother and infant. Most maternal death occurs during labor, during delivery, or immediately after delivery.[2] The World Health Organization recommends that help be close by when a woman gives birth. Ideally, a woman should give birth in an equipped facility that can provide lifesaving emergency care at the moment it is needed.[3]

In Gujarat, a state in northwest India, the rate of loss of mothers and babies during childbirth was unacceptably high, in part because only 55 percent of births took place in a medical facility as of 2005. This was in sharp contrast to Kerala, in southwest India, where coverage of facility births had reached 99 percent.[4] In 2005, Gujarat's government designed and introduced a new scheme to improve birth outcomes: Chiranjeevi Yojana (CY), the "Eternal Life" scheme. It aimed to tackle the state's low rate of institutional delivery by removing one of the most important barriers for below-the-poverty-line (BPL) and tribal women: the cost of the service.

The scheme held great promise. CY was built on a strong foundation of international good practice, a vibrant private sector, and political commitment by the state's leadership. And many families benefited from CY: by 2012, the pool of roughly 800 enrolled obstetricians had delivered 800,000 babies in health facilities, including a third of all births to BPL and tribal women, the scheme's target population.[5]

Despite these impressive numbers, however, there is no evidence that CY reduced maternal or infant deaths.[6] This is partly explained by changes in the overall health landscape: rates of institutional delivery were already rapidly increasing, and indicators of maternal and infant health were on the rise. These underlying trends reduced the relative impact of CY's contribution. In addition, some of the features of CY's design turned out to be less valuable than its planners expected.[7] Even though improving maternal and infant health is a global health priority for which funding is at an all-time high, the CY experience serves as a cautionary tale for programs that seek to achieve this goal by increasing institutional delivery.[8]

This case was originally authored by Miriam Temin.

121

The Toll of Maternal and Infant Mortality

Worldwide, mothers and babies today are more likely to survive delivery than their forebears in decades past. In India, a lower-middle-income country, maternal and child health has improved significantly in recent years. Maternal mortality dropped from 212 deaths per 100,000 live births in 2007 to 178 in 2012. In the same period, annual infant mortality declined from 55 to 42 deaths per 1,000 live births.[9] But not surprisingly, these health gains have not been evenly distributed, and mortality rates vary significantly by socioeconomic status and by state.

Gujarat State in northwestern India is one of the five wealthiest states in the country.[10] Its 60 million residents benefit from an economy that is growing by nearly 10 percent per year.[11] Indians view the government of Gujarat as progressive when it comes to health, and its representatives have become national advocates for insurance coverage for the poor.[12]

This leadership paid off in statewide maternal and infant mortality statistics that looked better than the national averages. For example, from 2010 to 2012, 122 women died annually in childbirth per 100,000 live births in Gujarat, compared with 178 nationwide.[13] One reason for better maternal health was the rising number of institutional deliveries: the average proportion of women delivering in institutions more than doubled from 2001 to 2010, from 40.7 percent to 89.3 percent, a significant and durable shift away from home births.[14] CY contributed to these improving statistics. Yet despite the program, maternal health has improved at a slower pace in Gujarat than in India as a whole.[15]

Putting an Idea in Motion: Gujarat Smooths the Path to Institutional Delivery

Facility-based care during labor and delivery is a global recommendation. While there is no guarantee that all possible problems will be successfully dealt with in a hospital or clinic, facilities that provide maternity care are more likely than other places to have the trained staff, infrastructure, and protocols necessary to manage most complications.[16] Children delivered in a facility also benefit in secondary ways; for example, they are more likely than those born at home to receive their vaccinations and be breast-fed.[17]

In India, the National Rural Health Mission was the government's flagship program to widely increase access to healthcare, put in place in 2005.[18] Shifting all deliveries into institutions was a national objective under this program. India is one of two countries (Nigeria is the other) that account for a third of all maternal deaths in the world, making this an urgent priority.[19]

Despite the national objective, India's public healthcare system lacked the capacity to cope with all pregnant women.[20] Human resource distribution problems were common, and emergency obstetric care was sparse. For example, in Gujarat's rural areas, a mere seven or eight government obstetricians served a population of 32 million.[21] Women in Gujarat had a difficult time reaching government facilities, and if and when they arrived the quality of care was low. Private doctors, in contrast, were more readily available. Three-quarters of all the doctors in Gujarat worked in the private sector,[22] and 60 percent of all deliveries in Gujarat took place in private facilities by 2010.[23] The shift to private care also signaled women's widespread lack of trust in public facilities and their perception that private care was better.[24]

In India, healthcare is provided and funded at the state level. It was up to the most powerful politician in Gujarat, Chief Minister Narendra Modi, to fix problems with the health sector in his state. Modi made clear that his government was open to working with either public or private providers to do so—whichever could do a better job.

Modi wanted to make specific changes that would ensure the health of mothers and babies.[25] His government recognized that private providers were available to pregnant women where public providers were not. The state government designed a scheme that leveraged the vibrant private sector by incentivizing it to serve the subpopulations of women that had the highest risk of maternal mortality: poor and tribal women. The government aimed to do this by paying private providers to deliver babies for women who possessed a BPL or tribal designation. By 2005, the state government was ready to launch CY in five disadvantaged pilot districts with the support of civil society organizations and the German development organization Deutsche Gesellschaft für Internationale Zusammenarbeit (GIZ).[26] Following the reported success of the pilot, CY expanded statewide in 2007.

Chiranjeevi Yojana in Action

The design of the scheme was relatively straightforward: the government recruited private obstetricians, contracted them to deliver babies for tribal and BPL women, and paid them for the deliveries and associated costs. Community leaders, local obstetric and gynecological societies, and district health teams helped attract eligible doctors.[27] Doctors' enrollment criteria were clear: ownership of basic facilities; at least 15 beds; and access to blood, anesthesiologists, and emergency surgery.[28]

Obstetricians could claim reimbursement for eligible deliveries on a monthly basis. For every 100 deliveries, the District Programme Management Unit paid them a fixed amount. A leading nongovernmental organization, Society for Education Welfare and Action–Rural (SEWA Rural), calculated the payment based on average expenses for 100 routine and complicated deliveries;[29] the reimbursement rate was finalized following consultations with important stakeholders, for example obstetric and gynecological societies.[30] The reimbursement rate increased over the years, reaching INR380,000 for every 100 deliveries by 2013 (roughly US$69 per delivery in 2013).[31] The scheme covered only the costs of delivery, not prenatal or postnatal care. Part of the reimbursement amount was intended to go to the women for transport and food, plus a small incentive payment for their escorts.[32]

The government hoped that the program would attract BPL and tribal women—groups with higher rates of home deliveries and maternal complications than other women. The potential beneficiaries had to show proof of eligibility—a BPL or tribal card—to be treated by a CY doctor under the scheme.[33] Community health workers were charged with informing women of their eligibility.

The Payoff: No Difference for Maternal Health

After observing low uptake of CY, in 2009 the government commissioned an independent evaluation from the Collaboration for Health System Improvement and Impact Evaluation in India (COHESIVE-India). The evaluation's findings, since corroborated by other studies, came as a surprise: many women did shift from home births to institutional delivery over this period, but CY did not appear to accelerate the shift.[34] In other words, there was no evidence that the scheme significantly increased the likelihood of institutional delivery for women in the target group,[35] nor for women in the broader population.[36]

The increase in facility deliveries and the improving health of Gujarat's women and babies was great news; however, the evaluation indicated that CY had little to do with it. Consistent with the finding that CY did not significantly affect access to institutional delivery, the evaluation also failed to find a significant effect of the scheme on indicators of maternal and infant health in the general population (see Box 1). The researchers' analysis suggested that 54 percent of all women statewide had delivery complications after CY's launch—and the scheme did not reduce this probability.[37] It is worth noting that the analysis assessed outcomes for all pregnant women statewide, not the poorer women in the scheme's target population; with the evidence available, it is not possible to determine if this influenced the study's conclusions.

Notably, CY coincided with an increased rate of cesarean sections among BPL women, according to another study, although researchers could not conclusively confirm whether these were needed procedures.[38] CY was actually designed to disincentivize unnecessary cesarean sections through a standard per-delivery reimbursement rate—that is, doctors were paid the same amount per 100 deliveries whether or not they performed C-sections. This may have actually reduced the likelihood that doctors would perform a C-section on a CY woman even when medically necessary, and would instead refer the complicated cases elsewhere to avoid the medical risks and costs.[39]

CY's founders were convinced that lower financial barriers to facility-based delivery would improve outcomes for new mothers and their babies. The cost barrier was real: Indians' out-of-pocket payments for healthcare are among the highest in the world.[40] The average household expenditure for a normal private delivery in India is US$84, an impossible sum for many in CY's target population.[41] Unfortunately, out-of-pocket expenditures for delivery held steady over five years of CY implementation.[42] News articles shed light on one explanation: some participating doctors offered eligible women additional services beyond those covered by CY with no discernible benefits for health.[43] Studies have confirmed these reports, also finding that some doctors pocketed the portion of the CY payment intended for transport and food reimbursement.[44]

Box 1. Strength of the Evidence[45]

The government of Gujarat invited the Collaboration for Health System Improvement and Impact Evaluation in India (COHESIVE-India) to evaluate Chiranjeevi Yojana in 2009. Using the phased introduction—first in five northern districts and then in the remainder of the state—researchers conducted a retrospective study with the later districts serving as controls for the first wave.

Researchers used population-level data to account for bias in the self-selection of pregnant women into facility births. They also triangulated their results with analysis of district-level household and facility survey data. Their findings were consistent across the two different data sources: the program showed no significant impact on the probability of institutional delivery or on birth-related complications.

Their conclusions must be interpreted with a number of limitations. First, the initial five districts differed from the rest of the state in important ways—residents were more rural, poorer, and less literate—which may have influenced the results. Second, changes in maternal mortality impact are notoriously difficult to measure because maternal deaths are relatively infrequent, leading to statistical uncertainty around

the evaluation's study results. Third, the study relied on mothers' self-reported recollections about whether they experienced complications, which are often biased.[46] Finally, the evaluators compared their sample not only with the poorer women in the target group but also with the entire population of women in Gujarat. It is possible that this wide-lens view may have obscured an effect for the smaller subsample.

The COHESIVE-India evaluation is not the only word on this program; indeed, its findings contradict several previous studies of the same program. The different study designs explain at least some of these discrepancies and suggest that the COHESIVE-India results are likely to be more accurate than those found in earlier studies. Of particular note in previous studies is the use of before-and-after comparisons, which made it hard to distinguish CY's impact from other ongoing trends—most importantly, the already increasing rate of institutional delivery before program implementation. Yet another large evaluation, funded by the European Union, is ongoing, poised to yield further insights into CY's performance and impact.

At What Price?

Funding for CY came from central government coffers through the National Rural Health Mission.[47] At CY's inception in 2006, the government of Gujarat paid providers INR1,850 (US$40) for every delivery to beneficiaries, gradually increasing the reimbursement to INR3,800 (US$69) by mid-2013. In total, the state government paid out US$32 million to participating hospitals between 2006 and 2012.

CY's funding came via three different sources, which made it difficult to track. This may have accounted for underspending: as of early 2010, news reports alleged that 36 percent of the total project budget remained undisbursed.[48]

At the same time that the CY allocation grew, state funding for health also expanded. According to state government sources, the state budget allocated for health increased in both absolute and proportionate terms, from 3.1 percent to 4.2 percent of the total state budget between 2005 and 2010. This reflected a total state health budget of INR11.55 billion (US$266 million) in 2005 and INR29.88 billion (US$434 million) in 2010.[49]

Why Chiranjeevi Yojana Fell Short in Gujarat

CY was well conceived: it had a credible theory of change, leveraged a vibrant private sector, and benefited from high-level political commitment.[50] So what explains the limited impact? A number of issues appear to have constrained CY, including targeting, financing, coverage, and management. The quality of private maternity care and social determinants that make home births attractive also limited the program's impact. However, it is impossible to fully appreciate the role of these factors without more qualitative data, underscoring the need for more studies that use a range of methods.

The scheme financed delivery for an enormous number of women, but were they the right women? Evidence suggests no—that CY struggled to reach its target population.[51] Some of the women who shifted into CY were already using private healthcare, while other eligible women continued delivering at home. Part of the problem was identifying the right women. As is common in India, CY relied heavily on BPL cards to determine eligibility. In theory, households receive the cards when they score 20 or below on an index of multidimensional poverty.[52]

In practice, around 40 percent of eligible households in Gujarat do not have a BPL card, and around 40 percent of BPL card holders do not meet the official eligibility criteria.[53]

Another targeting challenge related to geographic coverage. The distribution of CY-enrolled doctors had a distinctly urban bias, and women in some rural areas were less aware of the scheme than women elsewhere.[54] This is disappointing because the scheme emphasized rural penetration—the health commissioner and director even conducted personal visits to convince rural doctors to join.[55] Yet CY uptake was higher in the more rural districts, suggesting some rural women found their way to participating urban doctors.[56]

The government planned that CY reimbursements would be sufficient to cover all delivery costs, from medical care to food to transportation. Yet despite several increases over the scheme's lifespan, doctors complained that the reimbursement level was too low to cover these expenses. This affected CY in several ways.

First, the reimbursement level influenced who joined: only 740 of the 2,000 private obstetricians in the state had signed up by 2006.[57] The scheme initially attracted younger doctors with new medical practices; these providers seized on CY as a way to build their client base.[58] And some doctors saw CY as a charitable undertaking rather than a true public-private partnership. Altruistic early adopters signed up,[59] but the lack of financial incentive likely deterred many doctors.

Second, the reimbursement level likely played a role in provider attrition. The number of participating obstetricians grew to 870 in 2008, but then fell to 660 by 2010, exacerbating CY's inadequate coverage.[60] As of 2011, 40 percent of subdistricts had no participating providers.[61] Some early adopters may have left as the demand for CY deliveries increased and their nonreimbursed expenses grew, eroding their bottom line.[62] Notably, most attrition came from large cities, where some doctors feared that a poorer client base would damage their reputations.[63] Rural doctors, who faced less competition and were less concerned about stigma associated with lower-status clients, may have been a better fit for the scheme. Some doctors who stuck with CY were those who would otherwise have had trouble attracting clients, perhaps because they provided low-quality care.

Third, the low reimbursement level made the scheme more of a subsidy for women than a ticket to free care. Women continued to face transportation costs, informal payments, and other expenses.[64] Some doctors—responding to insufficient reimbursement—passed on their costs to women, either by charging them for other services or by keeping the amount earmarked for them. A combination of these factors kept demand for CY low. Because families still had to pay for delivery, they may have decided that the benefit of receiving private maternity care from a participating doctor—potentially an unpopular one—failed to outweigh the cost.

Another challenge was that CY managers lacked solid evidence to inform their planning. While consultations with professional organizations, providers, and other stakeholders had preceded the launch, there was no comprehensive formative research on the barriers to institutional delivery or the quality of private maternity care to inform the design.[65] Insufficient monitoring remained a problem throughout, leaving unanswered questions about quality, referrals, and details of the deliveries.[66] Furthermore, the payments to doctors were based on self-reports, which were not checked or followed up.[67] Participating doctors had no incentive to report accurately and may have falsified records to claim a higher reimbursement.[68]

Implications for Global Health

CY was the first large-scale public-private partnership to increase institutional delivery in a low- or middle-income country, and it was widely viewed as a success, even receiving the *Wall Street Journal* Asian Innovations Award in 2006.[69] Based on the CY experience, the government of Gujarat launched other insurance schemes for the poor. Mukhyamantri Amrutum Yojana (MAY), for example, provides up to US$3,400 per family to treat critical illness in a government facility.[70] Yet research on CY has yielded contradictory results, highlighting the implications of study design and the paramount importance of experimental or quasi-experimental research, supplemented by qualitative inquiry.

CY shares features with other programs that provide vouchers and eliminate user fees, either for specific subgroups or entire populations (described elsewhere in *Millions Saved*). The removal of health user fees is an increasingly popular policy choice and an important step toward universal health coverage. CY's experience resonates elsewhere, for example, with India's Janani Suraksha Yojana (JSY) to promote institutional births—the largest conditional cash transfer program in the world and a central spoke in the National Rural Health Mission.

While JSY has increased uptake of public-sector deliveries, it too faces controversy about its health impact.[71]

Eliminating user fees, however, is not sufficient on its own to improve health outcomes; other barriers to accessing healthcare persist in health systems, communities, and households. Social determinants, for example, profoundly influence access to health services, warranting serious consideration in programs to equitably improve maternal health.[72] Gender inequality also shapes women's access to healthcare, and their low social position limits their control over their own health during pregnancy. Among one sample of CY beneficiaries, none of the women chose where they would give birth; rather, auxiliary nurses, midwives, husbands, and mothers-in-law made the decision on their behalf.[73] Empowering women is a clear priority, but the route to institutional delivery also must run past their families and trusted community health workers.

Other noncost barriers must be addressed as well, including the reasons that women in Gujarat continue to deliver at home: the convenience of home delivery, fear of health facilities, and the difficult trip to the hospital.[74] The powerful norms that influence maternity care decisions fell far outside of the scope of CY.

With the ascendance of former state secretary Modi to prime minister in 2013, elements of the CY design may show up elsewhere in India. Gujarat's experience reveals the importance of carefully considering many different components of program design, including financing, monitoring, entry criteria, and quality assurance, alongside the social determinants of health. And as India works to achieve health equity, lessons from CY, JSY, and other demand-side health financing approaches must inflect the next generation of financing programs to increase health equity.

REFERENCES

Acharya, Akash, and Paul McNamee. 2009. "Assessing Gujarat's 'Chiranjeevi' Scheme." *Economic and Political Weekly* 44 (48).

Berman, Peter, Rajeev Ahuja, and Laveesh Bhandari. 2010. "The Impoverishing Effect of Healthcare Payments in India: New Methodology and Findings." *Economic and Political Weekly* 45 (16): 65–71.

Bhat, Ramesh, Dileep V. Mavalankar, Prabal V. Singh, and Neelu Singh. 2009. "Maternal Healthcare Financing: Gujarat's Chiranjeevi Scheme and Its Beneficiaries." *Journal of Health, Population, and Nutrition* 27 (2): 249–58.

Bhat, R., B.B. Verma, and E. Reuben. 2001. "Hospital Efficiency: An Empirical Analysis of District Hospitals and Grant-in-Aid Hospitals in Gujarat." *Journal of Health Management* 3 (2): 167–97. doi:10.1177/0972063 40100300202.

Campbell, Oona M.R., and Wendy J. Graham. 2006. "Strategies for Reducing Maternal Mortality: Getting on with What Works." *Lancet* 368 (9543): 1284–99. doi:10.1016/S0140-6736(06)69381-1.

Center for Health Market Innovations. 2016. "Chiranjeevi Yojana (CY)." Accessed February 8. http://healthmarketinnovations.org/program/chiranjeevi-yojana-cy.

Chaturvedi, Sarika, Sourabh Upadhyay, and Ayesha De Costa. 2014. "Competence of Birth Attendants at Providing Emergency Obstetric Care under India's JSY Conditional Cash Transfer Program for Institutional Delivery: An Assessment Using Case Vignettes in Madhya Pradesh Province." *BMC Pregnancy and Childbirth* 14 (1): 174. doi:10.1186/1471-2393-14-174.

Dansereau, Emily, Santosh Kumar, and Christopher Murray. 2013. "Distance and Institutional Deliveries in Rural India." *Ideas for India*, April 19. http://www.ideasforindia.in/article.aspx?article_id=132#sthash.5JW3fXbj.dpuf.

De Costa, Ayesha, Kranti S. Vora, Kayleigh Ryan, Parvathy Sankara Raman, Michele Santacatterina, and Dileep Mavalankar. 2014. "The State-Led Large Scale Public Private Partnership 'Chiranjeevi Program' to Increase Access to Institutional Delivery among Poor Women in Gujarat, India: How Has It Done? What Can We Learn?" *PLoS ONE* 9 (5): e95704. doi:10.1371/journal.pone.0095704.

De Costa, Ayesha, Kranti Vora, Eric Schneider, and Dileep Mavalankar. 2015. "Gujarat's Chiranjeevi Yojana: A Difficult Assessment in Retrospect." *Bulletin of the World Health Organization* 93 (6): 436A–436B. doi:10.2471/BLT.14.137745.

Economist. 2011. "An Indian Summary," June 21. http://www.economist.com/content/indian-summary.

———. 2015. "The Gujarat Model," January 10. http://www.economist.com/news/finance-and-economics/21638147-how-modi-nomics-was-forged-one-indias-most-business-friendly-states.

Ganguly, Parthasarathi, Kate Jehan, Ayesha de Costa, Dileep Mavalankar, and Helen Smith. 2014. "Consideration of Private Sector Obstetricians on Participation in the State

REFERENCES, *continued*

Led 'Chiranjeevi Yojana' Scheme to Promote Institutional Delivery in Gujarat, India: A Qualitative Study." *BMC Pregnancy and Childbirth* 14: 352.

Government of Gujarat. 2008. Annual Administrative Report 2007–2008. Gandhinagar, India: Government of Gujarat. http://www.gujhealth.gov.in/images/pdf/aar07-08.pdf.

———. n.d. Chiranjeevi Yojana: An Innovative Partnership with the Private Sector Obstetricians to Provide Skilled Care at Birth to the Poor in Gujarat. Gandhinagar, India: Government of Gujarat. http://www.gujhealth.gov.in/images/pdf/chiranjeevi-yojana-details.pdf.

Hashmi, Sameer. 2014. "Can India's Economy Model Itself on Gujarat?" *BBC News*, May 5. http://www.bbc.com/news/business-27257790.

Hayden, Michael Edison. 2014. "Gujarat Experiments with Expansion of Public Health Insurance." *New York Times*, April 3. http://india.blogs.nytimes.com/2014/04/03/gujarat-experiments-with-expansion-of-public-health-insurance.

IBNLive.com. 2011. "Gujarat's Private-Public Partnership in Healthcare," July 27. http://www.ibnlive.com/videos/india/gujarats-pvt-public-partnership-in-healthcare-387323.html.

Indian Express. 2011. "Chiranjeevi Scheme Failed to Deliver: CAG Report," March 31. http://archive.indianexpress.com/news/chiranjeevi-scheme-failed-to-deliver-cag-report/769645/.

IHME (Institute for Health Metrics and Evaluation). 2014. *Financing Global Health 2013: Transition in an Age of Austerity.* Seattle, WA: IHME.

IIPS (International Institute for Population Sciences) and Macro International. 2008. *Kerala: National Family Health Survey (NFHS-3) 2005–06.* Mumbai, India: IIPS. http://rchiips.org/nfhs/NFHS-3%20Data/ke_state_report_for_website.pdf.

Konar, Hiralal, and Asit Baran Chakraborty. 2013. "Maternal Mortality: A FOGSI Study (Based on Institutional Data)." *Journal of Obstetrics and Gynaecology of India* 63 (2): 88–95. doi:10.1007/s13224-012-0258-1.

Kumar, Chandan, and Ravi Prakash. 2011. "Public-Private Dichotomy in Utilization of Health Care Services in India." *Consilience: The Journal of Sustainable Development* 5 (1): 25–52.

MATIND. 2015. "Chiranjeevi Yojana—'Eternal Life Program' in Gujrat." Accessed August 7. http://matind.eu/the-project/chiranjeevi-yojana-eternal-life-program-in-gujarat/.

MAQARI (Medical Advice, Quality, and Availability in Rural India) Team. 2011. *Mapping Medical Providers in Rural India: Four Key Trends.* CPR Policy Brief. New Delhi, India: Centre for Policy Research. http://cprindia.org/sites/default/files/policy-briefs/policy%20brief_1%20(1).pdf.

Mavalankar, Dileep, Amarjit Singh, Sureshchandra R. Patel, Ajesh Desai, and Prabal V. Singh. 2009. "Saving Mothers and Newborns through an Innovative Partnership with Private Sector Obstetricians: Chiranjeevi Scheme of Gujarat, India." *International Journal of Gynecology and Obstetrics* 107 (3): 271–76. doi:10.1016/j.ijgo.2009.09.008.

Mavalankar, Dileep V., Kyanti S. Vora, K.V. Ramani, Parvathy Raman, Bharati Sharma, and Mudita Upadhyaya. 2009. "Maternal Health in Gujarat, India: A Case Study." *Journal of Health, Population, and Nutrition* 27 (2): 235–48.

Ministry of Health and Family Welfare. 2006. *Bulletin on Rural Health Statistics in India 2006.* New Delhi, India: Ministry of Health and Family Welfare. http://www.mohfw.nic.in/index1.php?lang=1&level=5&sublinkid=3023&lid=2221.

Mohanan, Manoj, Sebastian Bauhoff, Gerard La Forgia, Kimberly Singer Babiarz, Kultar Singh, and Grant Miller. 2014. "Effect of Chiranjeevi Yojana on Institutional Deliveries and Neonatal and Maternal Outcomes in Gujarat, India: A Difference-in-Differences Analysis." *Bulletin of the World Health Organization* 92 (3): 187–94. doi:10.2471/BLT.13.124644.

Mohanty, S.K., and A. Srivastava. 2013. "Out-of-Pocket Expenditure on Institutional Delivery in India." *Health Policy and Planning* 28 (3): 247–62. doi:10.1093/heapol/czs057.

Natarjan, T. 2013. "Health Care Delivery in Gujarat." Chapter 4 in "Public Health Management: A Study of Reproductive and Child Health Management." Thesis, Maharaja Sayajirao University of Baroda. http://shodhganga.inflibnet.ac.in:8080/jspui/bitstream/10603/7509/11/11_chapter%204.pdf.

National Health Mission. 2013. "State Wise Information: Gujarat." New Delhi, India: Ministry of Health and Family Welfare. http://nrhm.gov.in/nrhm-in-state/state-wise-information/gujarat.html#health_profile.

Odiit, A., and B. Amuge. 2003. "Comparison of Vaccination Status of Children Born in Health Units and Those Born at Home." *East African Medical Journal* 80 (1).

Office of the Registrar General. 2011. "Maternal and Child Mortality and Total Fertility Rates: Sample Registration System (SRS)." Presentation, July 7. http://censusindia.gov.in/vital_statistics/SRS_Bulletins/MMR_release_070711.pdf.

———. 2013. "A Presentation on Maternal Mortality Levels (2010–12)." Presentation, December 20. http://www.censusindia.gov.in/vital_statistics/SRS_Bulletins/MMR_2010-12-Report_Pres_19.12.2013.ppt.

OPHI (Oxford Poverty and Human Development Initiative). 2010 Country Briefing: India. www.ophi.org.uk/wp-content/uploads/Country-Brief-India.pdf.

Raman, A. Venkat, and James Warner Björkman. 2015.

REFERENCES, *continued*

"Public/Private Partnership in Health Care Services in India." Accessed August 7. http://www.pppinharyana.gov.in/ppp/sector/health/report-healthcare.pdf.

Sachan, D. 2014. "New Government Gears Up for India's Health Challenges." *Lancet* 383 (9935): 2112.

Sanneving, Linda, Nadja Trygg, Deepak Saxena, Dileep Mavalankar, and Sarah Thomsen. 2013. "Inequity in India: The Case of Maternal and Reproductive Health." *Global Health Action* 6 (0). doi:10.3402/gha.v6i0.19145.

Sharma, Bharati, Giri Gayatri, Kyllike Christensson, K.V. Ramani, and Eva Johansson. 2013. "The Transition of Childbirth Practices among Tribal Women in Gujarat, India: A Grounded Theory Approach." *BMC International Health and Human Rights* 13:41.

Sidney, Kristi, Ayesha De Costa, Vishal Diwan, Dileep V. Mavalankar, Helen Smith, and the MATIND Study Team. 2012. "An Evaluation of Two Large Scale Demand Side Financing Programs for Maternal Health in India: The MATIND Study Protocol." *BMC Public Health* 12 (1): 699. doi:10.1186/1471-2458-12-699.

Singh, Amarjit, Dileep V. Mavalankar, Ramesh Bhat, Ajesh Desai, S.R. Patel, Prabal V. Singh, and Neelu Singh. 2009. "Providing Skilled Birth Attendants and Emergency Obstetric Care to the Poor through Partnership with Private Sector Obstetricians in Gujarat, India." *Bulletin of the World Health Organization* 87 (12): 960–64. doi:10.2471/BLT.08.060228.

Sloan, N.L., E. Amoaful, P. Arthur, B. Winikoff, and S. Adjei. 2001. "Validity of Women's Self-Reported Obstetric Complications in Rural Ghana." *Journal of Health, Population, and Nutrition* 19 (2): 45–51. http://www.ncbi.nlm.nih.gov/pubmed/11503346.

Statistics Times. 2015. "Indian States by GDP Growth 2015," August 19. http://statisticstimes.com/economy/gdp-growth-of-indian-states.php.

Times of India. 2011. "Government Scheme to Arrest Infant Mortality Fails to Deliver," March 31. http://timesofindia.indiatimes.com/city/ahmedabad/Govt-scheme-to-arrest-infant-mortality-fails-to-deliver/articleshow/7829660.cms?referral=PM.

UNFPA (United Nations Population Fund). 2015. "Midwifery." Accessed July 8. http://www.unfpa.org/midwifery.

WHO (World Health Organization), UNICEF (United Nations Children's Fund), UNFPA (United Nations Population Fund), and World Bank. 2012. *Trends in Maternal Mortality: 1990 to 2010: WHO, UNICEF, UNFPA, and the World Bank Estimates.* Geneva: WHO. http://www.who.int/reproductivehealth/publications/monitoring/9789241503631/en/.

ENDNOTES

1. UNFPA (2015).
2. Konar and Chakraborty (2013).
3. Campbell and Graham (2006).
4. IIPS and Macro International (2008).
5. Mohanan et al. (2014); De Costa et al. (2014).
6. Sachan (2014).
7. Some of the story was still being told at the time of writing. The ongoing EU-funded MATIND evaluation will yield important new insights: MATIND (2015).
8. IHME (2014).
9. Office of the Registrar General (2011).
10. Gujarat is described as the fourth or fifth wealthiest state, depending on the metric used (*Economist* 2011).
11. Hashmi (2014); *Economist* (2015); *Statistics Times* (2015).
12. Mavalankar, Vora, et al. (2009).
13. Office of the Registrar General (2013).
14. De Costa et al. (2014).
15. National Health Mission (2013).
16. Chaturvedi, Upadhyay, and De Costa (2014); UNFPA (2015).
17. Odiit and Amuge (2003).
18. Sharma et al. (2013).
19. WHO et al. (2012).
20. De Costa et al. (2014).
21. Singh et al. (2009); Ministry of Health and Family Welfare (2006).
22. Bhat, Verma, and Reuben (2001); MAQARI Team (2011); Kumar and Prakash (2011).
23. De Costa et al. (2014).
24. Kumar and Prakash (2011).
25. MATIND (2015).
26. Mavalankar, Vora, et al. (2009).
27. Bhat et al. (2009).
28. Mavalankar, Singh, et al. (2009).
29. Government of Gujarat (n.d.).
30. De Costa et al. (2014).
31. Bhat et al. (2009).
32. Singh et al. (2009).
33. Raman and Björkman (2015).
34. Mohanan et al. (2014).
35. De Costa et al. (2014).
36. Mohanty and Srivastava (2013).
37. Mohanan et al. (2014).
38. De Costa et al. (2014).
39. Ganguly et al. (2014).
40. Berman, Ahuja, and Bhandari (2010).
41. Mohanty and Srivastava (2013).
42. Mohanan et al. (2014).
43. Mohanty and Srivastava (2013).
44. Bhat et al. (2009); Indian Express (2011).
45. Mohanan et al. (2014); Sidney et al. (2012); De Costa et

REFERENCES, *continued*

al. (2015).

46. See, for example, Sloan et al. (2001).
47. Center for Health Market Innovations (2015).
48. *Times of India* (2011); *Indian Express* (2011).
49. Natarjan (2013).
50. Ayesha De Costa, personal communication with the author, June 14, 2014.
51. De Costa et al. (2014).
52. The multidimensional poverty index summarizes household status in relation to three dimensions (education, health, standards of living) and 10 indicators (years of schooling, school attendance, child mortality, nutrition, electricity, sanitation, water, floor, cooking fuel, and assets) (see OPHI 2010).
53. Mohanan et al. (2014).
54. IBNLive.com (2011).
55. Singh et al. (2009).
56. De Costa et al. (2014).
57. Government of Gujarat (2008); Ganguly et al. (2014).
58. Manoj Mohanan, personal communication with the author, May 13, 2015.
59. Acharya and McNamee (2009).
60. Ganguly et al. (2014).
61. De Costa et al. (2014).
62. Ayesha De Costa, personal communication with the author, June 14, 2014.
63. De Costa et al. (2014); Ganguly et al. (2014).
64. Bhat et al. (2009).
65. Manoj Mohanan, personal communication with the author, May 13, 2015; Raman and Björkman (2015).
66. De Costa et al. (2014); Singh et al. (2009).
67. Bhat et al. (2009).
68. *Indian Express* (2011); Bhat et al. (2009).
69. De Costa et al. (2014).
70. Hayden (2014).
71. De Costa et al. (2014).
72. Sanneving et al. (2013).
73. Bhat et al. (2009).
74. Sharma et al. (2013); Dansereau, Kumar, and Murray (2013).

PART III

Using Targeted Cash Transfers to Improve Health

This section profiles cash transfer programs that improved health and nutrition. Cash transfer programs—cash payments to people who meet specific criteria, generally the extremely poor—are among the best-evaluated interventions in the world. Most programs explicitly name better health and nutrition among their goals, but many are also motivated by objectives beyond health—often a broad social mandate to protect the most vulnerable. For example, Kenya began cash transfers to orphans and vulnerable children in response to the crippling AIDS epidemic, and South Africa's Child Support Grant aimed to narrow the country's deep racial and economic divides.

In cash transfer programs, recipients typically are given money to use as they see fit. The evidence shows that transfers are most often used in helpful ways, improving the broader social determinants of poor health. In Pakistan's Punjab province, for example, incentives to keep girls in school reduced adolescent pregnancies and delayed marriages, improving girls' health and also future prospects. Likewise, cash for poor parents in South Africa and caregivers in Kenya improved overall living conditions, which in turn advanced outcomes for child health and reduced risky adolescent behaviors.

The first edition of *Millions Saved* profiled Mexico's successful Progresa program (now called Oportunidades), one of the world's first and best-evaluated *conditional* cash transfer programs: eligible families had to fulfill certain preconditions to receive the benefit. This edition highlights both conditional cash transfers and their siblings, unconditional cash transfers—programs through which eligible families receive transfers with no strings attached. A few evaluations have directly compared the two; in some settings, those studies suggest that conditionality can boost the use of health services, but in others conditionality did not appear to make a positive difference.

The cash transfer programs described in this section are large in scale, with each program covering hundreds of thousands or millions of recipients. Low- and middle-income country governments are the main implementers, and many programs are fully within budget. External agencies, particularly multilateral and regional development banks and large international organizations such as the United Nations Children's Fund (UNICEF), have played an important role in advising governments on design and evaluation.

In general, cash transfer programs are inexpensive to run, making them feasible even in the poorest of settings. However, these multidimensional programs have many objectives beyond health impact; this complexity makes it difficult to fully analyze cost-effectiveness.

Cash transfer programs are not a magic bullet. In Honduras, a conditional cash transfer program failed to achieve the desired health impact despite the other benefits the program generated. This "learning from disappointment" example highlights the importance of good design: targeting the right incentives to the right people at the right time.

REFERENCE

Attanasio, Orazio P., Veruska Oppedisano, and Marcos Vera-Hernández. 2015. "Should Cash Transfers Be Conditional? Conditionality, Preventive Care, and Health Outcomes." *American Economic Journal: Applied Economics* 7 (2): 35–52. doi:10.1257/app.20130126.

CASE 14

Giving Vulnerable Children a Fair Shot
Kenya's Social Cash Transfer Program

The Case at a Glance

HEALTH GOAL: To promote the physical and mental welfare of orphans and vulnerable children.

STRATEGY: Government program providing regular social cash transfers to the primary caregivers of orphans and vulnerable children.

HEALTH IMPACT: Among girls: delayed sexual debut and reduced the likelihood of multiple sexual partners and early pregnancy. Among boys: improved mental health.

WHY IT WORKED: Effective targeting of benefits to ultra-poor households with vulnerable children. Sustained government commitment across party lines. Efficient, reliable operations. Community acceptance and support.

FINANCING: KES7.5 billion (US$85 million) allocated to the program in 2013–14.

SCALE: About 240,000 households and 480,000 individual beneficiaries (early 2015).

The death of a parent can spell a premature end to childhood. In the early years of the 21st century, 1.7 million Kenyan children had lost one or both parents—many from AIDS—and many more were struggling with serious family illness.[1] Deprived of parental love and protection in their formative years, while also losing financial support, orphans and vulnerable children faced physical, emotional, and economic risks: hunger, mental illness, school dropout, and exploitation.[2] Children already teetering on the edge of extreme poverty, who had few resources to weather such a huge shock, felt the loss deeply.

Concerned for the welfare of Kenya's most vulnerable young citizens, the United Nations Children's Fund (UNICEF) galvanized Kenyan public opinion, and subsequently the political will, to support a novel social protection program. Starting in 2004, 500 ultra-poor caregivers of orphans and vulnerable children received a modest stipend to help offset the cost of the children's basic health and schooling needs. Careful piloting and rigorous evaluation helped policymakers refine the program design and test its impact before staged national expansion. By 2014, more than 250,000 children were benefiting from the program, with plans for continued expansion.[3]

For many beneficiaries the program was life changing. In households receiving the transfer, children had more nutritious diets and were more likely to enroll in secondary school. They were less likely to experience absolute poverty or participate in paid labor, and they were substantially more likely to have official identity documents.[4] The program had different effects on boys and girls: girls were able to postpone marriage and pregnancy, while boys experienced better mental health and hope for the future. The transfer also had important implications for HIV prevention and broader public health: the benefit enabled adolescents to delay their sexual debut and reduced the likelihood that girls would engage in risky sexual behavior, probably by encouraging them to stay in secondary school and reducing their economic need for transactional sex.[5]

The Toll of Losing a Parent to AIDS

Before the broad introduction of lifesaving antiretroviral therapy (ART) in sub-Saharan Africa, an HIV diagnosis meant certain premature death. By 2003, the epidemic

This case was originally authored by Rachel Silverman.

133

was claiming about 2.3 million lives in the region each year.[6] This left 12.3 million children with at least one deceased parent (called orphans) and 4.6 million with no surviving parents (called double orphans).[7] Millions more had their childhoods prematurely cut short when ailing parents could no longer support them (one of many types of "vulnerable children").

Vulnerable children's hardship usually began long before their parents died. With primary breadwinners unable to work, household income and food security took a nosedive. Simultaneously, the family's healthcare costs rose exponentially, while HIV-related stigma could isolate children from broader community support. Too often, young children became caregivers to their own parents or went to work outside the home, forcing them to drop out of school and endanger their own futures.[8]

The combination of economic, health, and social vulnerability put children at serious risk. While the life prospects of orphans and vulnerable children naturally varied by household, region, and country, research from across the continent painted a consistently bleak picture of their physical and mental health. They were disproportionately affected by posttraumatic stress disorder, anxiety, anger, and depression, and were far more likely than nonorphans to experience physical and emotional abuse.[9] Suffering from emotional distress coupled with economic vulnerability, female orphans were three times more likely than nonorphaned girls to engage in transactional sex.[10] And in a cruel example of intergenerational disadvantage, orphans were almost twice as likely as nonorphans to engage in risky sexual behavior, contract HIV or other sexually transmitted infections, and experience an early pregnancy.[11]

Putting an Idea in Motion: Politicians Commit to a Stronger Safety Net

In the early years of the 21st century, HIV prevention programs had shown only limited impact and ART remained prohibitively expensive for most Kenyans. Hundreds of thousands of newly orphaned children needed care each year. And unlike other relatively constant causes of orphaning, the AIDS epidemic was growing, with no end in sight. International policymakers feared "the worst [was] yet to come."[12]

Kenya had community mechanisms in place to care for children following the loss of their parents or other serious trauma. In the late 1990s, about 85 percent of

Kenyan orphans were living with grandparents or other extended family.[13] Friends and neighbors would also chip in as needed. But the unprecedented scale of the epidemic, particularly in the hardest-hit communities, strained traditional safety nets. Orphans crowded into a dwindling number of available foster homes, led by a shrinking number of healthy working-age adults. Caregivers struggled to make ends meet as HIV stigma and the costs of food, healthcare, and school fees accumulated. Compounding these challenges, orphans could themselves be HIV positive, or they could be placed in the custody of ailing caregivers who were also living with HIV.

During this time, UNICEF country staff were directly confronted with the reality of an increasing number of Kenyan orphans and vulnerable children. Yet the national government had not yet intervened with an appropriately ambitious response. Meanwhile, Kenya's parliamentary elections, planned for late 2002, presented an ideal opportunity for UNICEF to raise awareness of the crisis and galvanize popular support for measures to address it. In the run-up to the election, UNICEF engineered a "Call to Action" campaign targeted toward parliamentary candidates. The campaign's leaders and staff bought TV and radio advertisements and blanketed public spaces with advocacy posters. Among their demands: free access to education and increased resources for social protection for orphans and vulnerable children.[14]

UNICEF's campaign led some aspiring parliamentarians to put their commitments in writing. To maximize candidate support, UNICEF's country director, Nicholas Alipui, took to the media to shame those who had not yet pledged their support. "There is no choice, only an imperative," Alipui told newspaper reporters. "We need official support to stand behind these children. . . . Is this part of your political agenda? And if so are you willing to rise to the occasion and do the things that matter for these children?"[15] In total, more than 350 parliamentary candidates signed the UNICEF pledge, including 100 successful candidates and incoming president Mwai Kibaki.[16]

The new administration followed through on its promise. Soon after taking office, the government abolished school fees for all children and began planning a series of steps to assess and pilot social protection policy options. Orphans and vulnerable children found a powerful advocate in "Uncle Moody"—then vice president and minister of home affairs Moody Awori, a successful Kenyan businessman turned popular politician. Awori held primary responsibility within the government for children's welfare and was the first to float the idea of cash transfers as a potential strategy.[17]

Other government officials and donors were cautious but intrigued by the idea. Some expressed concern that recipients might squander the funds instead of investing in the children's future; others countered that cash transfers were a relatively straightforward, cost-effective intervention.[18] Although direct cash transfers were untested in Kenya, they were supported by a wealth of evidence from Latin America that demonstrated wide-ranging educational and health benefits. Eventually, stakeholders agreed that a "prepilot" program was needed to assess operational feasibility and potential impact.[19]

By the end of 2004, UNICEF had helped the government set up a small pilot program in three districts, targeting 500 ultra-poor households caring for orphans and vulnerable children. These were households whose inhabitants were so poor that they could not afford to feed everyone living under their roof. The evaluation revealed that the monthly KES500 (US$6.50) transfer showed promise: although the funds were not enough to cover all needs, they helped families purchase much-needed food, school supplies, and other basic necessities. Beneficiary households were also less likely to sell off their few assets for desperately needed cash. Buttressing the formal evaluation results, many high-ranking government officials visited recipient households. Once there, their firsthand observations helped dispel fears about misuse of funds and crystallize their support for scale-up.[20]

Having demonstrated that cash transfers were feasible and likely beneficial, further support from the UK's Department for International Development (DFID) and UNICEF enabled the Kenyan government to increase the transfer amount to KES1,500 (about US$20) and embark upon a phase 2 expansion, reaching 15,300 households by 2008.[21] The results of the randomized phase 2 evaluation showed impressive gains in children's health and welfare, helping sustain donor and political commitment. At the same time, Kenya's booming economy and a subsequent rise in tax revenue enabled a growing government contribution to the program and continued expansion. With combined financing from the government, the World Bank, DFID, and UNICEF, transfers were reaching 280,000 children in 134,000 households annually by 2012.[22]

The Cash Transfer Program in Action

The cash transfer program was a highly collaborative effort, involving more than a dozen ministries and other government bodies. High-level leadership came from the National Steering Committee for Orphans and Vulnerable Children, whose members included officials from the Ministry for Home Affairs and representatives of international organizations.[23] Within the Department of Children's Services, a Central Program Unit was established to handle day-to-day operations. At the district and location levels, committees and subcommittees for orphans and vulnerable children supported targeting and follow-up.[24]

At the village level, local volunteer community representatives played an important role. Their role was neither official nor compensated—and their effectiveness varied. The best volunteers were proactive and knowledgeable; they proved invaluable for case management by telling families about the program and connecting them to the larger bureaucracy.[25]

Although the government aspired to eventually cover all orphans and vulnerable children in need, resource constraints meant it had to carefully prioritize to make the most of available funds. Program leaders thus developed a multistage targeting process to identify and enroll the neediest households with orphans or vulnerable children.[26]

First, policymakers selected districts and specific locations, prioritizing areas with the highest concentrations of poor orphans and vulnerable children. Members of local selection committees went door to door to identify potential beneficiaries below the poverty line who cared for at least one orphan or vulnerable child and did not yet benefit from a transfer or social protection scheme. Following initial selection, committee members again visited potential beneficiaries to administer an official poverty test and confirm the household's eligibility. Eligible families were then ranked by priority: households headed by very young or very old caregivers were accommodated first, whereas working-age caregivers would be enrolled only if sufficient resources remained available. Finally, the local community would approve the final selection at a public community meeting called a *baraza*.[27]

Every two months, beneficiaries picked up KES3,000 (about US$40) at their local post office. The amount was the same across households, diluting the impact in larger households with greater numbers of children.[28]

Between 2007 and 2009, the program experimented with the effect of imposing conditions. One group of beneficiaries received a no-strings-attached transfer, while the other had to ensure children's full vaccination and regular school attendance, among other conditions, to receive the full amount. Evaluation results showed that conditions were poorly understood and only loosely enforced; they were discontinued during further scale-up.[29]

The Payoff: Healthier, Happier Adolescents

By early 2015, about 240,000 households and 480,000 children were benefiting from the cash transfer.[30] The program's benefits—documented by a rigorous impact evaluation (Box 1)—were substantial and wide-ranging. Unsurprisingly, the transfer improved overall consumption, resulting in a 36 percent reduction in absolute poverty and an increase in food and health expenditure in the short term. Additional funds also translated into healthier diets: beneficiaries were more likely to consume milk, fish, and meat, and improve the diversity of their overall diets. However, recipient children's height and weight for age did not improve significantly over the time period studied.[31]

Adolescents and young adults benefited from the cash transfers. Four years after the program's introduction, the receipt of cash transfers had decreased the odds of sexual debut among adolescents and young adults by 30 percent among children of both sexes, and by more than 40 percent among girls. For girls who were already sexually active, the program was associated with an 80 percent reduction in the odds of having multiple sexual partners in the past year—an important statistic because having multiple partners is a strong driver of the HIV epidemic. Finally, girls and young women aged 12–24 were less likely to have had a pregnancy at follow-up, a result closely linked to continued school enrollment.[32]

Among boys, the transfer substantially improved mental health and life outlook. Boys whose caregivers had received the transfers were 26 percentage points less likely to exhibit signs of depression and 30 percentage points more likely to report hope for the future. These

---

Box 1. **Strength of the Evidence**

During the program's phase 2 expansion, starting in 2007, UNICEF and DFID selected 28 locations across seven districts to serve as a testing ground. Half of the locations were randomly assigned to receive the cash transfer intervention, while the remainder served as controls. Oxford Policy Management (OPM), a consulting group, was commissioned to conduct baseline and two-year follow-up surveys in both recipient and control locations. Impact was assessed by comparing the changes in the randomly selected intervention areas relative to changes in the control locations. A highly rigorous and robust "difference-in-differences" method was used to eliminate any statistical differences at baseline between the two areas. (With relatively small numbers of clusters, such baseline differences can persist even despite randomization.)

Due to limited program resources, only a portion of eligible households in the intervention areas were ultimately enrolled in the transfer program, which made identifying the suitable comparison group in control areas a challenge. The goal was to find the appropriate counterfactual group: households that *would* have been enrolled in the program if the program had been active in the control locations. The research team tried to closely replicate the program's selection process within the control areas and used statistical techniques to correct for differences at baseline. Nonetheless, due to substantial variation within the administrative selection process for program enrollment, there is a risk that unobservable differences between the two groups could bias the estimates of impact.

Other researchers have piggybacked on the original randomization and data collection to assess longer-term outcomes. Two years later, in 2011, surveyors revisited those households OPM had previously surveyed and asked questions about risky sexual behavior, mental health, pregnancy, and child labor.[36] As of 2015, results are forthcoming; future papers are expected to address the program's long-term effect on childhood vaccination, healthcare uptake, and consumption. In addition, the World Bank has sponsored an evaluation to assess the next phase of scale-up; baseline data were collected in 2012, with planned follow-up in later years.[37]

mental health gains, however, were not seen among girls—a result that warrants further investigation.[33]

Improved health was only one of many program goals. Above all, the program was a rights-based social protection scheme that aimed to ensure a minimum level of support to the most vulnerable and marginalized members of society. As policymakers hoped, the program helped keep vulnerable children in school, strengthened their overall legal status, and reduced child labor. The architects also designed the program to improve equity: the transfers targeted poor households within relatively deprived areas. The evaluation results showed that children in the poorest households reaped some of the largest gains in health, school enrollment, and the reduction of child labor.[34]

From a macroeconomic perspective, the transfers were an essential investment in the local economy via the increased economic activity of beneficiary households. To quantify this type of benefit, researchers at the Food and Agriculture Organization of the United Nations (FAO) developed a model to assess the macroeconomic impacts of cash transfers that calculates an economic multiplier—a number that represents the total benefit to the community that results from the initial injection of extra money. In two districts where the Kenya program was implemented, that multiplier ranged between 1.34 and 1.81. This means that for every KES1 transferred, the local economy benefited by between KES1.34 and KES1.81.[35]

Gains at What Price?

In the pilot phase of the program (2006–2009), the program spent a total of KES776.7 million (US$9.96 million) across seven districts. The government disbursed KES383.3 million (US$4.90 million) directly to 15,000 households and spent another KES393.4 million (US$5.04 million) on program setup, rollout, operational costs, and monitoring and evaluation. This translates to KES6,160 in total for each bimonthly payment—KES3,040 for the transfer itself, plus about KES3,100 in program management, administration, and delivery costs.[38]

The total cost of the program from 2009 to 2016 was initially projected at US$126 million.[39] But the scale (and cost) of the program quickly exceeded those projections. In the 2013–14 fiscal cycle, the Kenyan government allocated a total of KES7.5 billion (about US$85 million) to provide transfers to more than 310,000 Kenyan households.[40] This sum included about US$8 million from DFID, plus support from a second World Bank loan to expand Kenya's social safety net (a total value of US$250 million over the period 2013–2018).[41]

The balance of expenditure between the transfers themselves and the costs associated with their distribution sheds light on the efficiency of the program. A cost-transfer ratio compares a program's administrative expenses related to running the program with the actual value of the transfer itself; it is a common metric used to quantify the administrative efficiency of transfer programs. By 2008–09, the program's cost-transfer ratio was 0.34, meaning it cost about US$0.34 to transfer each dollar to a beneficiary. This is comparable to the cost-transfer ratio found the Programa de Asignación Familiar II in Honduras (see chapter 17 in this volume), but still higher than the cost-transfer ratio found for Mexico's Oportunidades program (described in the first *Millions Saved*).[42] Notably, the Mexican program, with a cost-transfer ratio of 0.11 and millions of beneficiaries, is considered to be one of the world's most efficient cash-transfer programs. As the Kenya program expands its coverage, its transfer ratio will likely decline.

The Keys to Lasting Success

The program of cash transfers offered a good solution for tackling the HIV-driven crisis of orphans and vulnerable children. Kenya had an indigenous support structure in place, but it was overburdened by the rapid increase and unprecedented volume of children in need. By supplementing the income of ultra-poor households that included vulnerable children, the transfer enabled caregivers to cover urgent expenses while keeping children in familiar homes within their own communities. Rigorous evaluations verified that the supplementary income was driving positive change, which helped spur and maintain political and donor support over many years.

Although it prospered with the help of donor financing and technical know-how, the program was a Kenyan initiative at heart. It was conceived, championed, and administered by Kenyan leaders, and expanded under the auspices of a 2010 constitutional revision guaranteeing Kenyans' right to social security.[43] Because it was essentially a homegrown intervention with broad support across party lines, it has been sustained and expanded despite political tumult and changes in national leadership. Kenyan buy-in was also financial: government funds covered more than 60 percent of program households by the 2013–14 fiscal year, helped along by a booming economy and rising tax revenue.[44]

Kenyan support for the program was bottom-up as well as top-down. Recipient communities had a favorable impression of the transfer and generally believed that the neediest families were benefitting.[45] *Baraza* community meetings helped sustain accountability and community support—albeit at the cost of recipients' privacy.

Still, general enthusiasm for the program was at times tempered by confusion and misinformation. Some beneficiaries misunderstood the program's basic parameters, including the conditions of their enrollment and the duration of support. On-the-ground communication could be inconsistent because case management depended heavily on the efforts of a single volunteer. Another occasional concern related to security; many in the community knew both the list of beneficiaries and the day of distribution, potentially putting beneficiaries at risk of robbery or harassment when they collected the money.[46]

In practice, however, few such incidents occurred. Most recipients were satisfied with the mode of distribution. Post office officials were courteous and competent, with minimal reported corruption or demands for unofficial payments.[47] The program later introduced biometric smart-card payment systems linked to participants' bank accounts, offering recipients control over when they collected the funds, which increased their sense of security.[48]

The program's targeting mechanism was also a success. The evaluation found that 97 percent of beneficiary households contained at least one orphan or vulnerable child, and 99 percent fell below the program's poverty threshold. On average, recipient households were also slightly poorer than nearby households with vulnerable children that did not receive the transfer. However, the first wave of expansion left many behind: only about a quarter of the poorest eligible households containing one or more orphans or vulnerable children were enrolled, even as some relatively better-off—albeit still poor—families received the benefit. Further expansion enabled more of the very poor to enroll, but ensuring equitable allocation of funds remains a pressing concern.[49]

Implications for Global Health

Cash transfers have had substantial success around the world, most notably in Latin America, but also in Asia and sub-Saharan Africa. But unlike many other programs, Kenya's social cash transfer program was born of the HIV crisis and implemented in a low-income setting, and it targeted a specific population, the ultra-poor caregivers of orphans and vulnerable children. Kenya successfully demonstrated that even low-income countries can afford modest social protection measures despite myriad constraints—tight budgets, weak infrastructure, sparse public services, and limited government capacity.

Although these cash transfers were not explicitly designed to improve children's health, they yielded broad overall gains in beneficiaries' quality of life. Children in need who received the transfer ate better, stayed in school, and reported higher levels of general well-being, even as no gains in vaccination rates or nutrition emerged in the short term. By keeping young, vulnerable Kenyans in homes with trusted adults in their communities and out of orphanages, the transfer helped avoid the many negative consequences of prolonged institutional care, including high costs and elevated risks of sexual abuse, school dropout, and stunted cognitive and emotional development.[50]

Improvements in children's overall welfare also spilled over into public health benefits. The economic boost appeared to ease the economic pressures pushing girls toward risky sexual behavior and early pregnancy—with likely knock-on benefits for HIV prevention and maternal and infant health. Further, the program modified risky sexual behavior in a high-risk population where many have failed and, in doing so, helped break the transfer of HIV susceptibility from mother to daughter.[51] Results from other settings have helped corroborate the protective effect of cash transfers for vulnerable groups. For example, the short-term risk of HIV infection among girls in Malawi dropped substantially when they and their caregivers received a modest monthly payment.[52]

Together, these results help illuminate the complex but critical ties between economic and social vulnerability and HIV risk that motivate the emergence and expansion of HIV-sensitive social protection. The development of HIV-sensitive social protection programming is responsive to the understanding, now widely shared, that even non-HIV programming can be adapted to alleviate the unique vulnerabilities faced by HIV-affected families.[53] Cash transfers and other social protection measures now feature prominently in the policy guidance regarding orphans and vulnerable children issued by major funders of HIV programs, including the President's Emergency Plan for AIDS Relief (PEPFAR) and the Joint United Nations Programme on HIV/AIDS (UNAIDS).[54] As cash transfer programs continue to take flight across sub-Saharan Africa, Kenya's program of cash transfers offers a model for affordable and well-targeted social protection, facilitated by deep government commitment and sensible donor support.

REFERENCES

Atwine, Benjamin, Elizabeth Cantor-Graae, and Francis Bajunirwe. 2005. "Psychological Distress Among AIDS Orphans in Rural Uganda." *Social Science and Medicine* 61 (3): 555–64. doi:10.1016/j.socscimed.2004.12.018.

Ayala Consulting Co. 2007. *Operational Manual Version 2.0: Cash Transfer Programme for Orphans and Vulnerable Children (CT-OVC)*. Nairobi, Kenya: Office of the Vice President and Ministry of Home Affairs. http://info. worldbank.org/etools/docs/library/243199/Ayala_ OperationsManual.pdf.

Baird, Sarah J., Richard S. Garfein, Craig T. McIntosh, and Berk Özler. 2012. "Effect of a Cash Transfer Programme for Schooling on Prevalence of HIV and Herpes Simplex Type 2 in Malawi: A Cluster Randomised Trial." *Lancet* 379 (9823): 1320–29. doi:10.1016/S0140-6736(11)61709-1.

Better Care Network. 2015. "Effects of Institutional Care." Accessed November 16. http://www.bettercarenetwork. org/library/particular-threats-to-childrens-care-and-protection/effects-of-institutional-care.

Cluver, Lucie, Frances Gardner, and Don Operario. 2007. "Psychological Distress amongst AIDS-Orphaned Children in Urban South Africa." *Journal of Child Psychology and Psychiatry* 48 (4): 755–63. doi:10.1111/j.1469-7610.2007. 01757.x.

Cluver, Lucie, Mark Orkin, Mark Boyes, Frances Gardner, and Franziska Meinck. 2011. "Transactional Sex amongst AIDS-Orphaned and AIDS-Affected Adolescents Predicted by Abuse and Extreme Poverty." *Journal of Acquired Immune Deficiency Syndromes* 58 (3): 336–43. doi:10. 1097/QAI.0b013e31822f0d82.

Handa, Sudhanshu, Carolyn Tucker Halpern, Audrey Pettifor, and Harsha Thirumurthy. 2014. "The Government of Kenya's Cash Transfer Program Reduces the Risk of Sexual Debut among Young People Age 15–25." *PLoS ONE* 9 (1): e85473. doi:10.1371/journal.pone.0085473.

Handa, Sudhanshu, Carolyn Huang, Kelly Kilburn, Carolyn Halpern, Audrey Pettifor, Molly Rosenberg, Harsha Thirumurthy, Peter Otienoh, Wanjiku Gacuru, and Paul Okewa. 2012. *Impact of the Kenya CT-OVC on the Transition to Adulthood*. Chapel Hill: University of North Carolina at Chapel Hill, Carolina Population Center.

Ikiara, Gerrishon K. 2009. *Political Economy of Cash Transfers in Kenya*. London: Overseas Development Institute. http:// www.odi.org/sites/odi.org.uk/files/odi-assets/publica-tions-opinion-files/5749.pdf.

Institute of Economic Affairs. 2013. *Budget 2013/14: The Onset of the Developed Government and the Hurdles Ahead,* edited by Otiato Guguyu, Oscar Ochieng', and Audi C. Zilper. Nairobi, Kenya: Institute of Economic Affairs. http://www.ieakenya.or.ke/downloads.php?page= Budget-Guide-2013-Very-Final.pdf.

Makame, V., C. Ani, and S. Grantham-McGregor. 2007. "Psychological Well-Being of Orphans in Dar es Salaam, Tanzania." *Acta Paediatrica* 91 (4): 459–65. doi:10.1111/j. 1651-2227.2002.tb01671.x.

McCoy, Sandra I., Rugare A. Kangwende, and Nancy S. Padian. 2010. "Behavior Change Interventions to Prevent HIV Infection among Women Living in Low and Middle Income Countries: A Systematic Review." *AIDS and Behavior* 14 (3): 469–82.

Ministry of Labour, Social Security and Services. n.d. *Achievements under the Jubilee Government*. Nairobi, Kenya: Ministry of Labour, Social Security and Services. http://www.labour.go.ke/downloads/MOLSSS%20 AchievemntsF.pdf.

Office of the Vice-President and Ministry of Home Affairs. 2005. *National Policy on Orphans and Vulnerable Children*. Draft. Vol. 3. Nairobi, Kenya: Office of the Vice-President and Ministry of Home Affairs.

Operario, Don, Kristen Underhill, Carolyn Chuong, and Lucie Cluver. 2011. "HIV Infection and Sexual Risk Behaviour among Youth Who Have Experienced Orphanhood: Systematic Review and Meta-Analysis." *Journal of the International AIDS Society* 14: 25. doi:10.1186%2F1758-2652-14-25.

Pearson, Roger, and Carlos Alviar. 2009. *Cash Transfers for Vulnerable Children in Kenya: From Political Choice to Scale-Up*. New York: United Nations Children's Fund. http://www.unicef.org/socialpolicy/files/Postscript_For-matted_PPCI_cash_transfers_in_Kenya_Final_Dec_15.pdf.

———. n.d. *The Evolution of the Government of Kenya Cash Transfer Programme for Vulnerable Children between 2002 to 2006 and Prospects for Nationwide Scale-Up*. New York: United Nations Children's Fund. http://www. unicef.org/infobycountry/files/The_Evolution_of_the_ Government_of_Kenya_Cash_Transfer_Programme_ for_Vulnerable_Children.pdf.

PEPFAR (President's Emergency Plan for AIDS Relief). 2012. *Guidance for Orphans and Vulnerable Children Programming*. Washington, DC: PEPFAR. http://www.pepfar.gov/ documents/organization/195702.pdf.

Republic of Kenya. 2010. *The Constitution of Kenya*. Niarobi, Kenya: National Council for Law Reporting. http://

REFERENCES, *continued*

kenyaembassy.com/pdfs/The%20Constitution%20of%20
Kenya.pdf.

Salmon, Katy. 2002. "HEALTH: Kenya's 1.2m AIDS Orphans at
the Centre of the 2002 Election Agenda." Inter Press
Service, November 27. http://www.ipsnews.net/2002/11/
health-kenyas-12m-aids-orphans-at-the-centre-of-the-
2002-election-agenda/.

Taylor, Edward, Justin Kagin, Mateusz Filipski, and Karen
Thome. 2013. *Evaluating General Equilibrium Impacts of
Kenya's Cash Transfer Programme for Orphans and
Vulnerable Children (CT-OVC).* Rome: Food and Agricul-
ture Organization of the United Nations. http://www.fao.
org/fileadmin/user_upload/p2p/Publications/Kenya_
LEWIE_2013.pdf.

UNAIDS (Joint United Nations Programme on HIV/AIDS).
2010a. *UNAIDS Expanded Business Case: Enhancing
Social Protection.* UNAIDS/JC1879E. Geneva: UNAIDS.
http://data.unaids.org/pub/BaseDocument/2010/
jc1879_social_protection_business_case_en.pdf.

———. 2010b. We Can *Enhance Social Protection for People
Affected by HIV.* Geneva: UNAIDS. http://www.unaids.
org/en/media/unaids/contentassets/documents/
unaidspublication/2010/20101031_JC1967_Social-
Protection_en.pdf.

———. 2011. *HIV and Social Protection Guidance Note.*
Geneva: UNAIDS. http://www.unicef-irc.org/files/
documents/d-3827-HIV-and-Social-Protection.pdf.

UNAIDS, United Nations Children's Fund (UNICEF), and
United States Agency for International Development
(USAID). 2004. *Children on the Brink 2004: A Joint Report
of New Orphan Estimates and a Framework for Action.*
New York: UNAIDS, UNICEF, and USAID.

UNAIDS and WHO (World Health Organization). 2003. *AIDS
Epidemic Update.* UNAIDS/03.39E. Geneva: UNAIDS.
http://data.unaids.org/pub/Report/2003/2003_epiupdate_
en.pdf.

UNICEF (United Nations Children's Fund). 2003. *Africa's
Orphaned Generations.* New York: UNICEF. http://
www.unicef.org/sowc06/pdfs/africas_orphans.pdf.

———. 2014. *UNICEF Annual Report 2013—Kenya.* New
York: UNICEF. http://www.unicef.org/about/annualreport/
files/Kenya_COAR_2013.pdf.

Ward, Patrick, Alex Hurrell, Aly Visram, Nils Riemenschneider,
Luca Pellerano, Clare O'Brien, Ian MacAuslan, and Jack
Willis. 2010. *Cash Transfer Programme for Orphans and
Vulnerable Children (CT-OVC), Kenya: Operational and
Impact Evaluation, 2007–2009.* Final Report. Oxford, UK:
Oxford Policy Management. http://www.unicef.org/
evaluation/files/OPM_CT-OVC_evaluation_report_
july2010-final_Kenya_2010-019.pdf.

World Bank. 2014. "Implementation Status and Results
Kenya: Kenya Cash Transfer for Orphans and Vulnerable
Children." ISR13091. http://www-wds.worldbank.org/
external/default/WDSContentServer/WDSP/AFR/2014/
01/17/090224b0821ee7a1/1_0/Rendered/INDEX/
Kenya000Kenya00Report000Sequence010.txt.

———. 2015. "Projects: National Safety Net Program for
Results." Accessed October 28. http://www.worldbank.
org/projects/P131305/national-integrated-safety-net-
program?lang=en.

———. 2016. "Kenya Cash Transfer for Orphans and
Vulnerable Children." Accessed February 5. http://www.
worldbank.org/projects/P111545/kenya-cash-transfer-
orphans-vulnerable-children?lang=en.

ENDNOTES

1. UNAIDS, UNICEF, and USAID (2004).
2. Office of the Vice-President and Ministry of Home
Affairs (2005).
3. Ministry of Labour, Social Security and Services (n.d.).
4. Ward et al. (2010).
5. Handa et al. (2014).
6. UNAIDS and WHO (2003).
7. UNAIDS, UNICEF, and USAID (2004).
8. UNICEF (2003).
9. Makame, Ani, and Grantham-McGregor (2007); Atwine,
Cantor-Graae, and Bajunirwe (2005); Cluver, Gardner,
and Operario (2007).
10. Cluver et al. (2011).
11. Operario et al. (2011).
12. UNICEF (2003, 10).
13. UNICEF (2003).
14. Salmon (2002).
15. Salmon (2002).
16. Pearson and Alviar (2009).
17. Ikiara 2009; Pearson and Alviar (2009).
18. Pearson and Alviar (n.d.).
19. Pearson and Alviar (2009).
20. Pearson and Alviar (2009).
21. Ward et al. (2010).
22. Handa et al. (2014).
23. Pearson and Alviar (2009).
24. Ayala Consulting Co. (2007, 9–11).
25. Ward et al. (2010).
26. Ayala Consulting Co. (2007).
27. Ward et al. (2010).
28. Ward et al. (2010).
29. Ward et al. (2010).
30. World Bank (2016).
31. Ward et al. (2010).
32. Handa et al. (2014).
33. Handa et al. (2012).
34. Ward et al. (2010).
35. Taylor et al. (2013).

REFERENCES, *continued*

36. Handa et al. (2012); Handa et al. (2014).
37. Joanne Bosworth, personal communication with the author, June 19, 2014.
38. Ward et al. (2010). The average transfer amount is higher than the standard KES3,000 payment because households in Garissa received supplementary payments each cycle to cover their additional transport costs.
39. World Bank (2016).
40. Institute of Economic Affairs (2013, 2).
41. UNICEF (2014); World Bank (2015).
42. Ward et al. (2010).
43. Republic of Kenya (2010, 43(1)(e)).
44. World Bank (2014).
45. Ward et al. (2010).
46. Ward et al. (2010).
47. Ward et al. (2010).
48. World Bank (2014).
49. Ward et al. (2010).
50. Better Care Network (2015).
51. McCoy, Kangwende, and Padian (2010).
52. Baird et al. (2012).
53. UNAIDS (2010a)
54. PEPFAR (2012); UNAIDS (2010b, 2011).

Protecting Childhood
Punjab's Female School Stipend Program

The Case at a Glance

HEALTH GOAL: To reduce the gender gap in schooling; specifically, to increase the percentage of girls who advance through school and complete at least middle school.[1]

STRATEGY: Payment of a quarterly stipend of PKR600 (around US$10) for girls' regular school attendance in grades 6 to 10.

HEALTH IMPACT: Increased age at marriage by 1.2 to 1.5 years and reduced total fertility by 0.4 children.

WHY IT WORKED: Gendered targeting of the incentive. Universal benefits within target districts (no means testing). Government commitment to education reform. Underlying increase in demand for education for girls.

FINANCING: Cost PKR1.5 billion (US$17.4 million) in stipends for 380,000 girls (2011–12).

SCALE: 393,000 girls (2014).

Punjab, in northeastern Pakistan, is the most populous of the country's four provinces. Until recently, almost half of girls in some Punjabi districts were denied their basic human right to education and the many benefits that schooling confers.[2] The predicament of these girls and their peers entered the international spotlight in 2012. That year, the Taliban tried to permanently silence one of the girls' fiercest advocates, Malala Yousafzai, who was just 13 at the time. In 2014 she won the Nobel Peace Prize for her persistence and bravery in the face of mortal danger.[3]

Instead of going to school, young girls help their families care for younger children and perform daily chores. When girls reach adolescence, many families and communities consider them ready for marriage.[4] Soon they have babies of their own; in Pakistan in the middle of the last decade, more than 40 percent of married young women had already given birth by age 19. But early childbearing is risky for mother and baby alike, and during the same period, 259 young Pakistani women under 20 died for every 100,000 live births. Early childbearing also extends the duration of a woman's reproductive years, paving the way for high fertility and population growth.

In 2003, the government of Punjab launched the Female School Stipend Program (FSSP) within a major package of education reforms, with support from the World Bank and others. To reduce the gender gap in schooling, the program provided a predictable sum of money to families whose girls regularly attended middle school. And the program worked: girls who participated in the program were more likely to complete middle school than girls who did not receive a stipend.

Already, researchers knew that education could serve as a "social vaccine" against HIV; studies consistently find an association between girls' schooling and lower HIV infection rates.[5] Punjab's FSSP demonstrated that girls' schooling could also protect against child marriage and early pregnancy, in turn protecting the girls' reproductive health. By offering a financial incentive for girls' education—cash transfers to families conditional on girls' school attendance—the government expanded their access to school, enabling more girls to delay marriage through a socially acceptable path. The Punjab experience thus shows that girls' education can be an excellent health investment, even in challenging settings.

This case was originally authored by Miriam Temin.

The Toll of School Dropout

In 2003, most Pakistani children faced bleak educational prospects. Nationwide, around one-third of primary school–age girls and boys did not attend school; among those who did, half dropped out before completing the fifth grade.[6] Despite long-standing efforts to combat gender inequity in schooling, the situation remained far worse for girls. In 2007, as a result of pervasive gender discrimination, 65 percent of all Pakistani women had never set foot in a classroom.[7]

Punjab boasts the country's highest school enrollment rate and smallest gender gap in schooling.[8] Even so, as of 2006, nearly 60 percent of Punjabi women still had never been to school.[9] Inequities became particularly acute at the postprimary level, where girls could access far fewer public high school facilities than their male peers.[10]

Low levels of girls' schooling went hand in hand with high rates of child marriage. In the middle of the first decade of the 21st century, the average Pakistani woman with no education married seven years earlier than a woman with postsecondary education. More than a third of Pakistani women were married by age 18.[11]

The situation in Pakistan was not unique. Child marriage is all too common across the world. According to the United Nations Children's Fund (UNICEF) and the advocacy group Girls Not Brides, 15 million girls under the age of 18 marry each year.[12] Some child brides marry under duress; others marry consensually after internalizing deeply inequitable social norms. Many child brides live restricted lives and face serious health, social, and economic problems. They often have limited mobility and little autonomy, and they may be cut off from friends and family. Their isolation affects their access to healthcare and mental health, increases their risk of gender-based violence, and limits their education and economic opportunity.[13] With no chance to build their knowledge and skills, they remain trapped in poverty and transmit their deprivation to their children—especially their own daughters.

Young brides soon become young mothers. In Pakistan in the middle of the last decade, nearly one-quarter of 19-year-old women had already given birth. More young women were delaying childbearing past their teenage years, but early pregnancy was still helping drive the country's high fertility rate.[14] In 2003, the national fertility rate was 3.3 births per woman—the second highest in the region after Afghanistan.[15]

Beyond its fertility effect, child marriage and early childbearing pose specific health risks. Maternal mortality from pregnancy-related complications is a leading cause of death for girls aged 15 to 19, and childbearing girls in this age group face up to 30 percent more risk of maternal mortality than women aged 20 to 24 years.[16] Babies of adolescent mothers may also have an increased risk of mortality and longer-term health problems. For example, a study from Uganda shows that infants born to adolescent girls were less likely to be vaccinated than those born to older mothers.[17]

Putting an Idea in Motion: Punjab Takes On Gender-Responsive Education Reform

Punjab had long-standing ambitions to strengthen its education system, as did Pakistan as a whole. In the 1990s and the following decade, national social action programs aimed to improve social services but rarely met their targets.[18] During the same period, the national government acknowledged gaps in girls' education, including at the middle-school level (grades 6 to 8). The National Education Policy for 1998–2010 addressed gender inequality and girls' access to formal and informal schooling. The World Bank had made funds available in 1992, under the Punjab Middle Schooling Project, to support public middle schools in Punjab, including scholarships for girls and recruitment of female teachers.[19] Despite these steps, a 2011 study of girls' schooling concluded that the federal government did not fully recognize the pivotal role of girls' education in growth and development, nor did it dedicate sufficient resources to education for girls.[20]

Punjab had the best record in Pakistan on gender equity in schooling; nonetheless, the provincial government was rightfully concerned about the persistent gender gap and other problems in the education sector. Insufficient resources; overall weak schools; management issues; and ongoing problems with education quality, access, and governance plagued the system.[21] And in the early years of this century, the government of Pakistan had decentralized the delivery of social services, including education, to the provinces. The provincial government became responsible for fixing these problems.

A combination of factors prompted the government of Punjab to take action: the provincial government's new mandate; growing evidence that the shortage and low quality of middle and high schools, especially in rural areas, exacerbated gender inequality; and recommendations from assessments undertaken in the 1990s.[22] In partnership with the World Bank, a major supporter, the government looked to design a reform package that would "improve access to services for all while ensuring equitable provision to boys and girls," among other objectives.[23] The Punjabi government decided to target its efforts to one clearly disadvantaged group: girls in the districts with the lowest literacy rates.[24]

The government focused on older girls—those in post-primary education—for several reasons. Younger girls' enrollment levels were increasing, but their dropout rates tended to increase significantly when the girls reached age 14.[25] Around the age that some girls were entering middle school, others had to stay at home; parents expected them to contribute more to the household or marry. A baseline survey showed that just 16 percent of girls were enrolled in middle school, compared with 24 percent of boys.[26] The focus on older girls also made sense because studies show that girls need more than eight years of schooling to reap the health and other gains from education.[27] When girls make it through middle school, they have more autonomy and sway over their marriages, household affairs, and reproduction than those with less schooling.

Another factor driving older girls' dropout rates was the distance between home and school. In Punjab, there were simply fewer schools at the postprimary level, forcing adolescents to travel farther. But when social norms strictly curtail girls' mobility, the distance can present an insurmountable barrier to school attendance. Restricting girls' freedom of movement can be common in some Muslim areas. These practices are in part influenced by *purdah*, which calls for the seclusion of adolescent girls and women to prevent men from looking at them. Research in Pakistan confirmed that the distance to school, coupled with availability of transport, were key factors among girls whose families limited their movement.[28]

Provincial education officials and World Bank staff considered a number of ways to narrow the gender gap. One proposal was to provide busing for girls to get to school.[29] Instead, they settled on regular cash payments to incentivize school attendance.

Stipends—a type of conditional cash transfer—already had a strong track record in the region.[30] In neighboring Bangladesh, the Female School Stipend Program, begun nationally in 1994, had increased girls' access to both public and private schools. The Bangladeshi program named fertility reduction and prevention of child marriage as its explicit objectives; evidence as of 2002 suggested that age at marriage was starting to move in the right direction.[31] Punjabi government officials drew on the Bangladeshi experience to shape their own approach.[32]

Punjab's FSSP was just one component of the larger Punjab Education Sector Reform Program (PESRP).[33] The PESRP's aims were ambitious: mutually reinforcing improvements in infrastructure, quality, capacity, oversight, and gender equity.[34] Broader education-sector improvements would increase the value of schooling for girls who stayed until later grades. At the same time, educated girls could later become teachers, expanding the pool of female educators and thus offering increased schooling opportunities for the next generation.[35] Empirical evidence bears this out: villages with a public girls' secondary school were 300 percent more likely to also have a private girls' school, thanks to the public school graduates available to staff it.[36]

The Female School Stipend Program in Action

The FSSP kicked off in 2003, targeting the 15 districts with the lowest literacy rates (less than 40 percent) in the province.[37] The stipend program initially targeted girls in grades 6 to 8, and in 2006 it expanded to cover grades 9 and 10. Expanded eligibility reportedly helped cool tensions between girls in different grades who did and did not receive stipends.[38] By 2014, stipend coverage had expanded to 393,000 girls across the target districts.[39]

Under the program, the government of Punjab gave families PKR600 (US$10) per quarter for each girl in a covered grade. In the program's initial year, 156,000 families received the stipend. The stipend was large enough to cover the costs of both schooling and transport—addressing one major barrier to girls' school attendance.

Critics of the program design questioned whether the stipend alone would overcome the many barriers to girls' schooling.[40] And the stipend amount remained static for nearly a decade, even as its value decreased due to inflation—the PKR2,400 was worth just US$25 by 2014, compared with US$43 in 2003. Beginning in 2013, pilot projects began testing larger stipends in selected districts.[41]

For families to receive the stipend, girls had to attend school at least 80 percent of the time. Unlike many other cash transfer programs, the stipend was not means tested—all girls could receive the stipend if they lived in an eligible district, enrolled in a target grade, and met the school attendance condition.

School headmasters and teachers played a key role in implementing the FSSP through their roles in recording girls' attendance. Schools submitted attendance records to the district's executive district office for education (EDO) every quarter, and then EDO staff requested the stipends from the PESRP's Program Monitoring and Implementation Unit (PMIU). The PMIU sent the requested funds to the EDO, which transferred the stipends to post offices and schools. Finally, girls collected the stipends from postal workers or received them at school.[42]

Regular program monitoring showed that the system was functioning smoothly, and an independent study found neither bribery nor withholding of stipends in the two years after its launch.[43] As of mid-2014, problems remained rare; nonetheless, the government was working to establish a beneficiary complaint mechanism.[44]

The Payoff: More School, Later Marriage and Pregnancy

An impact evaluation conducted by the Independent Evaluation Group of the World Bank measured the FSSP's effect (see Box 1).[45] Four years after the program began, it found that the program had increased beneficiaries' likelihood of school enrollment from 11 to 32 percent. Girls who received the stipends were more likely to stay in school through middle school and transition into high school.[46]

Even better, the study suggested benefits well beyond girls' education. According to the evaluation, transfer recipients postponed marriage until they were about 1.5 years older than their nonbeneficiary peers. Receiving the stipend for longer seemed to strengthen these effects.[47] Notably, the biggest benefits went to those most in need: the poorest girls saw the biggest increases in age at marriage.

Later marriage meant fewer pregnancies. Four years after receiving a stipend, the 17- to 19-year-old girls who had started their childbearing had fewer children than their nonbeneficiary peers. In other words, although there was no effect on the probability that these young women would become mothers, there was an effect on the likelihood that they would have more than one child (on average, they had 0.3 fewer children). The research-

Box 1. **Strength of the Evidence**

The FSSP was not set up for an impact evaluation, and its design, which used universal targeting by grade within districts, made randomization impossible. Instead, researchers from the World Bank's Independent Evaluation Group used a quasi-experimental method that looked at treatment and control groups over time.[50] The analysis contrasted outcomes between girls who benefited from the stipends for at least one year and similar girls in nonstipend districts. Researchers relied on school and household data from sources such as public school censuses, the Pakistan Social and Living Standards Measurement Survey, the Punjab Multiple Indicator Cluster Survey, and the Pakistan Integrated Household Survey.

The districts chosen for stipends differed from the rest of the province in important ways—the very features that led to their selection in the first place. They were poorer, they had fewer schools and lower enrollment levels than elsewhere in Punjab, and families there spent less on education. There is a chance that these characteristics could have biased the results. Another possible confounding factor was that the families that sent their girls to school likely differed from those that did not for reasons that were not isolated in the study.

These potentially confounding factors limit the reliability of the evaluation conclusions. However, the researchers attempted to minimize bias by controlling for a range of variables. Their models accounted for broader education reforms, including free textbooks for primary school students, new teachers, and new schools. These methods enabled them to confirm that the other new initiatives did not influence the results and to increase confidence that the observed changes resulted directly from the stipend program.

ers calculated that the marriage delay resulting from the stipend could translate to a total of 0.4 fewer children by the end of a woman's childbearing years.[48]

Several studies in Punjab have found that educated girls are helping bring down the province's fertility rate: women with a middle and high school education have almost two fewer children than those with less than a middle school education.[49] The government will be paying close attention to whether this trend is specifically attributable to the FSSP.

Gains at What Price?

The FSSP budget is part of the overall PESRP budget. The pool of girls enrolled in the stipend program has grown since its introduction in 2003, so program costs have increased over time. In 2007, a total of 245,000 girls were enrolled in grades 6 through 8, receiving around US$7.3 million in stipends.[51] In 2013, 411,000 girls in grades 6 to 10 were enrolled, receiving a combined US$14.2 million each year.[52]

The program's universal targeting design increased program costs—leaving some researchers to question its cost-effectiveness. Specifically, researchers from Learning and Educational Achievement in Punjab Schools estimate that the program cost a total of US$400 per newly enrolled girl.[53] This marginal cost is quite high, although it includes both the cost of the transfer and the cost of the program, taking into account economies of scale.

From a cost-benefit perspective, however, the investment might pay off. In Pakistan, girls see wage premiums of 24 percent for a middle school education and 157 percent for a high school education, representing an annual increase in earnings of US$16 and US$100, respectively. Over a lifetime, these returns would more than compensate for the program costs.[54] One caveat: the wage premium applies only to girls who ultimately work in the formal-sector economy, which is not the case for most girls in the FSSP. However, the stipend might still increase their private, informal-sector income.[55]

The Keys to Lasting Success

All signs suggest that the program improved girls' education outcomes, increased their age at marriage, and decreased their fertility. These impressive gains resulted from several factors, chief among them the targeting strategy, programmatic design, political will, and complementary supply-side reforms.

The government's targeting decisions paid off. First, channeling stipends to all girls in the target grades was a good political and financial move. Although benefits were universal, the program still had its largest effect on the poorest girls, thus increasing equity. The FSSP benefit helped alleviate the cost of private transport—a particularly potent contribution for the poorest girls with constrained mobility.[56]

Second, the program prioritized older adolescent girls over those in primary school. Incentivizing older girls to

stay in school made a difference for those enrolled at the time and had a ripple effect for girls in primary school, whose families were newly motivated to keep them in school by the promise of tangible future benefits.

Third—and ultimately of greatest significance—was the priority placed on tackling gender inequity. Evidence from diverse settings has shown the merit of structuring educational cash transfer programs with gender in mind. Directly targeting women and girls can overcome household-level sex discrimination and undo historic underinvestment in girls' education.[57] Meanwhile, background cultural shifts meant Pakistani girls and young women increasingly gained higher social status from being educated.[58]

The PESRP's massive education reforms signaled the government's commitment to education, which was another important factor for the program's success. Governance of the education sector improved, which enabled monitoring and validation of the stipends.[59] With a smoother flow of information, the PMIU could respond to problems by adjusting aspects of program design. For example, when the PMIU learned about payment delays in remote areas, it decided to use schools to disburse stipends to those who could not access the postal system.

In addition, the PMIU initiated a pilot study in 2013 in three districts. The pilot combined branchless banking with a rural focus, higher stipend levels to account for inflation, and increased stipends for those in higher grades.[60] The results of the pilot will inform the next phase of the program.

Demand-side transfers such as the FSSP have more impact when combined with supply-side investments, and other PESRP reforms helped the FSSP achieve its goals.[61] For instance, the construction of toilets in girls' schools, when combined with the stipend, may have made schooling more acceptable to parents.[62]

Implications for Global Health

Stipends have become a popular instrument for increasing girls' schooling in Punjab, throughout Pakistan, and beyond. In Khyber-Pakhtunkhwa province, bordering Punjab to the north, a similar program seeks to replicate Punjab's success.[63] And the Punjab Education Foundation's public-private voucher scheme increases access to private schooling for children from low-income families.[64]

Despite its impact on education and health, there are indications that the stipend program did not change underlying social norms about the value of educating girls or about their position in the family. Gender-sensitive cash transfers can keep adolescent girls in school and reduce the most popular alternative path in this setting: the premature end of childhood that comes with child marriage and early childbearing. Yet the desire for educated girls can also play into long-standing inequitable gender roles. The father of a stipend girl explained: "Yes, of course there is a use of her education [even] if she cannot get a proper job, because she is responsible for many generations if she is educated."[65] Parents also continued to invest more in their sons' education, sending them to private schools—where children learn more— while sending their daughters to public schools.[66]

What else is needed to increase the underlying demand for girls' education? Some researchers suggest that opposition to female education is less a reflection of cultural values and more a reflection of parents' distrust of schools. In this setting, schools must be culturally acceptable to families and communities.[67] Ensuring that schools and the routes to them are safe, and that schools are staffed with female teachers to maintain *purdah*, is paramount.[68]

The Punjab experience shows the potential of stipends in combination with girls' education to raise marriage age and reduce fertility. This would be an untold story if evaluators had not collected data on marriage and fertility impacts. More evidence on the interaction between

girls' schooling and marriage is needed to assess the strength of the connections among efforts to improve education access and quality, end child marriage, and protect reproductive health. A comparison between the stipend program and other, cheaper ways to boost girls' school enrollment (such as hiring more female teachers) would be a valuable contribution.

Child marriage is declining worldwide, albeit slowly. Building on efforts to combat child marriage and early pregnancy is of utmost importance to ensure that millions of girls can access their basic human rights and thrive. But there is no agreement among advocates and political leaders on the best ways to chip away at child marriage cost-effectively and at scale.[69] Approaches that involve education deserve further consideration in the push to end child marriage, especially approaches that take aim at gender barriers.

In 2010, the government drafted an amendment to Pakistan's constitution that promised free and compulsory education for all Pakistani children up to age 16. In 2013, an editorial in the Punjabi newspaper the *Express Tribune* lauded the provincial government for increasing spending on education in Punjab by 900 percent in just five years. The writer argued that "for any country to have consistent and sustainable growth, it is imperative to invest in education."[70] While the remaining challenges are significant, there is considerable momentum to sustain and accelerate gains for girls.

REFERENCES

Ahmed, Vaqar, Muhammad Zeshan, and Muhammad Tahir Ali. 2013. *Poverty and Social Impact Analysis of Stipend Program for Secondary School Girls of Khyber Pakhtunkhwa*. Policy Brief 32. Islamabad, Pakistan: Sustainable Development Policy Institute. http://www.sdpi.org/publications/files/Policy%20Brief%2032.pdf.

Alam, Andaleeb, Javier E. Baez, and Ximena V. Del Carpio. 2011. *Does Cash for School Influence Young Women's Behavior in the Longer Term?* Policy Research Working Paper 5669. Washington, DC: World Bank. http://ftp.iza.org/dp5703.pdf.

Andrabi, Tahir, Jishnu Das, Asim Ijaz Khwaja, Tara Vishwanath, Tristan Zajonc, and the LEAPS Team. 2007. *Pakistan: Learning and Educational Achievements in Pubjab Schools (LEAPS): Insights to Inform the Education Policy Debate*. Washington, DC: World Bank. http://www-wds.worldbank.

org/external/default/WDSContentServer/WDSP/IB/2008/05/20/000333038_20080520040840/Rendered/PDF/437500WP0PAK021Box0327368B01PUBLIC1.pdf.

Atuyambe, Lynn, Florence Mirembe, Nazarius M. Tumwesigye, Johansson Annika, Edward K. Kirumira, and Elisabeth Faxelid. 2008. "Adolescent and Adult First Time Mothers' Health Seeking Practices during Pregnancy and Early Motherhood in Wakiso District, Central Uganda." *Reproductive Health* 5 (1): 13. doi:10.1186/1742-4755-5-13.

Bano, Masooda. 2007. *Pakistan Country Case Study*. Paris: United Nations Educational, Scientific and Cultural Organization (UNESCO). http://unesdoc.unesco.org/images/0015/001555/155503e.pdf.

Biography.com. 2015. "Malala Yousafzai Biography." Accessed November 19. http://www.biography.com/people/malala-yousafzai-21362253#early-life.

REFERENCES, *continued*

Blanc, Ann K., William Winfrey, and John Ross. 2013. "New Findings for Maternal Mortality Age Patterns: Aggregated Results for 38 Countries." *PLoS ONE* 8 (4): e59864. doi:10.1371/journal.pone.0059864.

Callum, Christine, Zeba Sathar, and Minhaj ul Haque. 2012. "Is Mobility the Missing Link in Improving Girls' Schooling in Pakistan?" *Asian Population Studies* 8 (1): 5–22. doi:10.108 0/17441730.2012.646805.

Chaudhury, Nazmul, Jeffrey Hammer, Michael Kremer, Karthik Muralidharan, and F. Halsey Rogers. 2006. "Missing in Action: Teacher and Health Worker Absence in Developing Countries." *Journal of Economic Perspectives* 20 (1): 91–116.

Chaudhury, Nazmul, and Dilip Parajuli. 2006. *Conditional Cash Transfers and Female Schooling: The Impact of the Female School Stipend Program on Public School Enrollments in Punjab, Pakistan.* Impact Evaluation Series WPS4102. Washington, DC: World Bank.

Government of Punjab. 2013. "Expressions of Interest for Consulting Services—Hiring of Firms for Evaluation of the Supplemental Stipend Pilot and Branchless Banking Pilot: School Surveys." dgMarket Tenders Worldwide, January 2. http://www.dgmarket.com/tenders/np-notice. do?noticeId=8827419.

Hasan, Amer. 2010. *Gender-Targeted Conditional Cash Transfers: Enrollment, Spillover Effects and Instructional Quality.* Policy Research Working Paper 5257. Washington, DC: World Bank.

ICRW (International Center for Research on Women) and Girls Not Brides. 2013. Solutions to End Child Marriage: Summary of the Evidence. Washington, DC: ICRW. http:// www.icrw.org/sites/default/files/publications/19967_ ICRW-Solutions001%20pdf.pdf.

IHME (Institute for Health Metrics and Evaluation). 2013. GBD 2010 Arrow Diagram. Accessed December 15. http:// vizhub.healthdata.org/gbd-compare/arrow.

Independent Evaluation Group. 2011. *Do Conditional Cash Transfers Lead to Medium-Term Impacts? Evidence from a Female School Stipend Program in Pakistan.* Washington, DC: World Bank. http://ieg.worldbank.org/Data/reports/ pakistancctimpacteval2011.pdf.

Lloyd, Cynthia B., and Juliet Young. 2009. *New Lessons: The Power of Educating Adolescent Girls.* New York: Population Council. http://www.girleffect.org/media/1119/ new-lessons-the-power-of-educating-adolescent-girls.pdf.

Malik, Allah Bakhsh. 2011. *Policy Analysis of Education in Punjab Province.* Islamabad, Pakistan: UNESCO Islamabad. http://unesco.org.pk/education/documents/ situationanalysis/Education_Policy_Analysis_for_Punjab.pdf.

Mohammad, Zubair. 2013. "Punjab Government's Performance." *Express Tribune,* March 7. http://tribune.com.pk/ story/516706/punjab-governments-performance/.

Mushtaq, Shahzad, and Mariam Abbas Soharwardi. 2013. "The Gender Disparity in Education (A Case Study of Regional Punjab)." *International Journal of Research in Humanities, Arts and Literature* 1 (2): 57–68.

NIPS (National Institute of Population Studies) and Macro International. 2008. *Pakistan Demographic and Health Survey 2006–07.* Islamabad, Pakistan: NIPS and Macro International. http://dhsprogram.com/pubs/pdf/FR200/ FR200.pdf.

Oppenheim, Willy. 2013. "Why Should Girls Go to School? Qualitative Aspects of 'Demand' for Girls' Schooling in Rural Pakistan." *St. Antony's International Review* 8 (2): 106–26.

PESRP (Punjab Education Sector Reform Program). 2015a. "Distribution of Stipend to Girl Students." Accessed October 21. http://www.pesrp.edu.pk/pages/Stipend-to-Girl.

———. 2015b. "Mission Statement." Accessed October 21. http://www.pesrp.edu.pk/pages/mission.

Qureshi, Sabina. 2003. *Pakistan: Education and Gender Policy. Girl's Education: A Lifeline to Development.* Budapest, Hungary: Central European University, Center for Policy Studies and Open Society Institute.

Sarwar, M.B. 2006. *Documenting Educational Innovations. Sharing Practices for Educational Change.* Karachi, Pakistan: Sindh Education Foundation.

Schurmann, Anna T. 2009. "Review of the Bangladesh Female Secondary School Stipend Project Using a Social Exclusion Framework." *Journal of Health, Population, and Nutrition* 27 (4): 505–17.

UK DFID (Department for International Development). 2014. "The Girl Summit Charter on Ending FGM and Child, Early and Forced Marriage." https://www.gov.uk/ government/uploads/system/uploads/attachment_ data/file/346027/GS-CharterEnglish.pdf.

UNFPA (United Nations Population Fund). 2012. *Marrying Too Young: End Child Marriage.* New York: United Nations Population Fund. https://www.unfpa.org/sites/ default/files/pub-pdf/MarryingTooYoung.pdf.

UNICEF (United Nations Children's Fund). 2014. *Ending Child Marriage: Progress and Prospects.* New York: UNICEF. http://data.unicef.org/corecode/uploads/ document6/uploaded_pdfs/corecode/Child-Marriage-Brochure-HR_164.pdf.

Vandelmoortele, Jan, and Enrique Delamonica. 2000. "The 'Education Vaccine' Against HIV." *Current Issues in Comparative Education* 3 (1): 6–13.

World Bank. 2001. *Implementation Completion Report on a Credit in the Amount of US$115 Million Equivalent to the Islamic Republic of Pakistan for the Punjab Middle Schooling Project.* Implementation Completion Report 21496. Washington, DC: World Bank.

REFERENCES, *continued*

———. 2002. *Pakistan—Poverty Assessment: Poverty in Pakistan—Vulnerabilities, Social Caps, and Rural Dynamics.* Report 24296-PAK. Washington, DC: World Bank. http://documents.worldbank.org/curated/en/2002/10/2050407/pakistan-poverty-assessment-poverty-pakistan-vulnerabilities-social-caps-rural-dynamics.

———. 2013. "Invest in Fertility Decline to Boost Development in Pakistan," June 14. http://www.worldbank.org/en/news/feature/2013/06/14/invest-in-fertility-decline-to-boost-development-in-pakistan.

———. 2016. "IDA and Girls' Education in South Asia." Accessed February 9. http://go.worldbank.org/K9L01MQLO0.

Zaidi, Batool, Zeba Sathar, Minhaj ul Haque, and Fareeha Zafar. 2012. *The Power of Girls' Schooling for Young Women's Empowerment and Reproductive Health.* New York: Population Council.

Zia-ur-Rahman, Mohammad. 2014. "Pakistan's Slow but Steady Progress on Ending Child Marriage." *Guardian,* June 2. http://www.theguardian.com/global-development/2014/jun/02/pakistan-progress-ending-child-marriage.

ENDNOTES

1. The Female School Stipend Program did not include health improvement as an explicit objective. Nonetheless, by increasing gender equity in education, the program significantly reduced early marriage and childbearing—two widely recognized social determinants of health.
2. Independent Evaluation Group (2011).
3. Biography.com (2015).
4. UNFPA (2012).
5. Vandelmoortele and Delamonica (2000).
6. Qureshi (2003).
7. NIPS and Macro International (2008).
8. Zaidi et al. (2012).
9. NIPS and Macro International (2008).
10. Malik (2011).
11. NIPS and Macro International (2008); Zia-ur-Rahman (2014).
12. UNICEF (2014).
13. UNFPA (2012).
14. NIPS and Macro International (2008).
15. World Bank (2013).
16. IHME (2013); Blanc, Winfrey, and Ross (2013).
17. Atuyambe et al. (2008).
18. Zaidi et al. (2012).
19. World Bank (2001).
20. Zaidi et al. (2012).
21. Chaudhury and Parajuli (2006).
22. Alam, Baez, and Del Carpio (2011).
23. Independent Evaluation Group (2011, 6).
24. Alam, Baez, and Del Carpio (2011).
25. Zaidi et al. (2012).
26. Independent Evaluation Group (2011).
27. Lloyd and Young (2009); Zaidi et al. (2012).
28. Callum, Sathar, and ul Haque (2012).
29. Dhushyanth Raju, personal communication with the author, August 26, 2014.
30. Alam, Baez, and Del Carpio (2011).
31. Schurmann (2009).
32. Dhushyanth Raju, personal communication with the author, August 26, 2014.
33. The FSSP was paid for from the overall PESRP budget, which the government of Punjab funded with donor support from the World Bank, the UK Department for International Development, and the Canadian International Development Agency. For further information on the PESRP, see PESRP (2015a).
34. PESRP (2015b).
35. Chaudhury and Parajuli (2006, 4).
36. Andrabi et al. (2007, xvi).
37. Alam, Baez, and Del Carpio (2011, 8).
38. Dhushyanth Raju, personal communication with the author, August 26, 2014.
39. World Bank (2014).
40. Hasan (2010).
41. PESRP (2015a).
42. Independent Evaluation Group (2011).
43. Independent Evaluation Group (2011).
44. Dhushyanth Raju, personal communication with the author, August 26, 2014.
45. Alam, Baez, and Del Carpio (2011).
46. Alam, Baez, and Del Carpio (2011); Independent Evaluation Group (2011).
47. Independent Evaluation Group (2011).
48. Alam, Baez, and Del Carpio (2011).
49. Alam, Baez, and Del Carpio (2011, 21).
50. Independent Evaluation Group (2011).
51. Alam, Baez, and Del Carpio (2011, 8).
52. Using December 2013 exchange rate: US$1 = PKR105.84 (PESRP 2015a).
53. Andrabi et al. (2007).
54. Alam, Baez, and Del Carpio (2011).
55. Dhushyanth Raju, personal communication with the author, August 26, 2014.
56. World Bank (2016).
57. Chaudhury and Parajuli (2006).
58. Oppenheim (2013).
59. Mushtaq and Soharwardi (2015).
60. For the pilot, 68 schools were selected by the World Bank across six tehsils (the level below district); see PESRP (2015a). For information on recent revisions, see Government of Punjab (2007).
61. Alam, Baez, and Del Carpio (2011).
62. Chaudhury et al. (2006).

ENDNOTES, *continued*

63. Vaqar, Zeshan, and Tahir Ali (2013).
64. Zaidi et al. (2012).
65. Oppenheim (2013).
66. Alam, Baez, and Del Carpio (2011, 25).

67. World Bank (2002); Bano (2007); Sarwar (2006).
68. ICRW and Girls Not Brides (2013).
69. ICRW and Girls Not Brides (2013).
70. Mohammad (2013).

A Step Up for the Children Apartheid Left Behind
South Africa's Child Support Grant

The Case at a Glance

HEALTH GOAL: To protect children in poor households, reduce poverty, and decrease inequality.

STRATEGY: State-provided cash transfers for poor households with young children.

HEALTH IMPACT: Improved height-for-age scores and decreased likelihood of illness, especially for boys. Reduced adolescent risky sexual activity, pregnancy, and drug and alcohol use.

WHY IT WORKED: Sustained government commitment and civil society advocacy. Flexible design. Dedicated effort to identify and reduce barriers to enrollment. Loosened eligibility requirements. Use of technology to increase efficiency and reduce fraud. Accountability.

FINANCING: Cost nearly ZAR31 billion (US$4.2 billion) in 2010–11.

SCALE: 11.2 million children, around 75 percent of those eligible (2012).

When democracy came to South Africa in 1994, many children were suffering the cumulative effects of years of disadvantage—the legacy of apartheid. One-quarter of young children had stunted growth and nearly one-fifth were underweight, signs of enduring deprivation despite South Africa's relative wealth.[1] Although the government had sufficient funds to finance a national welfare program, the existing state system was inadequate and reinforced strict racial divides. State Maintenance Grants had been introduced in the 1930s to give assistance to poor white families and had been extended over the years to certain racial and demographic groups. However, few Africans ever received the grants, and by the early 1990s this grant system covered just a small fraction of eligible young citizens: 5 percent of "colored" children (under apartheid, a term referring to people of mixed racial descent), 1.5 percent of white children, and only 0.2 percent of children of African ethnicity.[2]

Upon taking power in 1994, Nelson Mandela's new egalitarian government set out to rebuild a nation that had been torn apart by apartheid. Recognizing the long-term benefits of investing in young children, in 1998 the government created the Child Support Grant (CSG). In recent years, programs for cash transfers to poor families have gained worldwide traction, but at that time the CSG was among the first such programs in low- or middle-income countries to reach national scale. As of 2015 the CSG provided regular monthly payments to nearly three-quarters of South African children living in poverty.

The CSG has been surveyed, studied, and evaluated, and research results time and again have confirmed major gains in beneficiaries' health and well-being. The CSG is no magic bullet; alone, it cannot close South Africa's deep-seated economic and racial divides. But as a serious government investment in reducing intergenerational inequities, it offers important lessons for other countries aiming to improve the life prospects of children born into entrenched poverty.

The Toll of Racialized Poverty

Despite South Africa's national wealth, in the apartheid era systematic racial oppression prevented many children from thriving. In 1993, more than 40 percent of South Africans were poor[3]—and poverty followed stark racial

This case was originally authored by Miriam Temin and was reviewed by Michael Samson.

divisions. The government rationed high-skill, high-wage jobs to whites, leaving only low-wage, low-skill jobs to nonwhites. In 1993, white South Africans enjoyed living standards comparable to those in developed countries, while black South Africans struggled to get by on slightly more than one-tenth of white people's per capita income.[4]

Children's health status reflected their meager diets and unsanitary living conditions in the areas where black South Africans were forced to live, often the crowded informal townships. Malnourishment left many children vulnerable to a host of health problems, including cognitive delays and long-term impairment.[5] It also weakened children's ability to fight infection.[6] In the early 1990s, lower respiratory infections and diarrhea, both diseases of poverty, accounted for well over one-third of all under-five deaths.[7]

The harsh environment also jeopardized adolescent health. As former president Mandela explained, "The apartheid state . . . ignored the special needs and concerns of youth. Young people were left to find their own way in a divided and volatile society—to varying degrees brutalized as master and servant alike."[8] Adolescent substance abuse, smoking, suicide attempts, unsafe driving, and violent behavior were common. So was unprotected sex, with its many associated risks. In 1995, 40 percent of all pregnancies were among teenage girls.[9]

HIV compounded adolescents' vulnerability, especially for girls. A 2012 national survey reported that up to four young women were living with HIV for every one young man living with HIV.[10] This shocking gender imbalance reflected the frequency of age-disparate sex. Young women would enter sexual relationships with older men to receive gifts and money—and HIV infection would often follow.[11] These myriad threats prompted some researchers to declare a state of emergency for South African adolescents.[12]

Putting an Idea in Motion: The "New" South Africa Confronts Entrenched Racial Poverty

In 1994, South Africans of all races elected their first democratic and egalitarian government. But their elation soon faced a reality check as leaders began to govern a divided nation.

Among its first moves, the new government looked to address widespread poverty and to reform unfairly distributed social services. In 1994, a new South African constitution guaranteed citizens the right to "social secu-rity, including, if they are unable to support themselves and their dependents, appropriate social assistance."[13] Reforming the child welfare system became a top priority, made even more urgent by the growing burden of AIDS within already disadvantaged communities.[14]

To kick-start reform, the minister of welfare and provincial leaders convened an expert committee. Francie Lund, a professor of social policy at the University of KwaZulu in Natal, was asked to chair what became the Lund Committee on Child and Family Support. The Lund Committee issued its recommendations and submitted them for parliamentary approval in 1997. It proposed a new social welfare program, the Child Support Grant, which would provide ZAR70 (around US$15) each month to the poorest 30 percent of children under seven years old.[15] The South African parliament ultimately approved the committee's recommendations, with one notable modification: an increase in the amount of the grant to ZAR100 (roughly US$21).[16] Conditions initially were set for receipt of the grant, including participation in development programs and proof of immunization status.[17] Once they submitted paperwork to confirm eligibility, applicants could enroll for regular receipt of the grant.

The launch of the CSG in 1998 got off to a slow start, reaching only 22,000 children in its first year. Concern about the low uptake soon reached the highest levels of government. Amid heavy advocacy from civil society organizations, in 2000 the South African cabinet approved the Committee of Inquiry into a Comprehensive System of Social Security (the Taylor Committee) to explore needed reforms to the social security system. The committee documented several problems with the existing system, including widespread misinterpretation of CSG eligibility criteria and people's inability to meet the necessary conditions, leading the government to tweak some key programmatic elements and increase its efforts to expand enrollment. Three years later, the government increased the age cutoff from 7 to 14, which quickly doubled the program's pool of eligible beneficiaries.[18]

The Child Support Grant in Action

The CSG program offered regular, predictable payments to the caregivers of eligible children. This core has remained constant over the years, even as the CSG has become more inclusive. By 2012, more than 11 million children, three-quarters of all eligible children nationwide, were enrolled in the CSG.[19]

Children's eligibility for the CSG was determined by their age, household income, and residency status (they had to be permanent residents, citizens, or refugees). At first, only children under seven years old could apply. The age cutoff gradually increased, contributing to massive expansion (see Figure 1).[20] In addition, children could qualify only if they lived in poverty. When the CSG was first launched, the government set a household income threshold of ZAR800 (US$170) in rural areas and ZAR1,100 (US$234) in urban areas. In 2008, thanks to a long-overdue policy change, the government increased the income threshold, pegging the cutoff at 10 times the value of the grant.[21]

At first, receipt of the grant was conditional on meeting health requirements, which in practice meant possession of a Road to Health card—a record of a child's immunization and growth rate. However, it soon became clear that those requirements penalized eligible children who lacked the card, leading the CSG to eliminate its conditions.[22] In 2010, the government recommended conditioning receipt on children's schooling, but to little effect—the system was not set up to collect the information needed to link school attendance with receipt of the grant.[23]

The government has regularly adjusted the size of the transfer (Figure 1). The grant is relatively large compared with poverty-reducing grants in some other countries, and this served as a strong incentive for South Africans to enroll. Many millions of South Africans now rely on the transfer to top up their meager household incomes.

The CSG is one of several government social grants; South Africa also provides disability grants, foster-care grants, pensions, and others. As of 2014, nearly 16 million South Africans benefited from publicly provided grants.[24] The ballooning welfare system gained structure in 2005 with the creation of the South African Social Security Agency (SASSA), which administers social grants at the national level. The agency oversees essential aspects of the CSG design, including eligibility, the grant amount, the delivery strategy, and accountability systems. SASSA is part of the Department of Social Development (DSD), which oversees the comprehensive national social protection system.

The application process for the CSG can be daunting. But structures are in place to help South Africans access the grant and to hold DSD and SASSA accountable. An SASSA hotline is available to assist callers with CSG

Figure 1. Eligibility for the Child Support Grant Shifts and Increases Enrollment

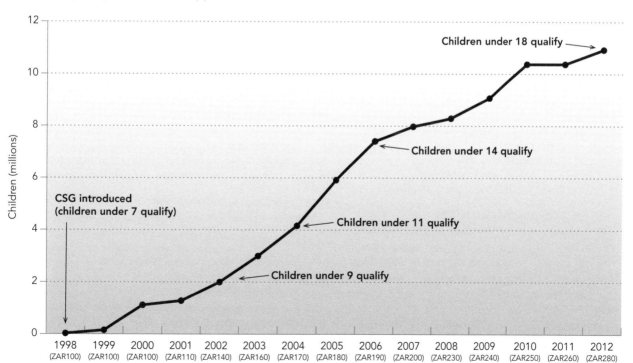

Source: DSD, SASSA, and UNICEF (2012a).

applications and delivery, and DSD social workers also help some families through the CSG application process. Civil society organizations such as Black Sash, an established human rights organization, also offer a hand to CSG-eligible families, for example, by directing them to advice hotlines if they encounter problems when applying for or accessing the grant.[25]

SASSA has also implemented measures to reduce fraud—a major concern for all social grants. Grantees receive cards that link directly to their bank accounts, which streamlines delivery and also helps minimize cheating.

The Payoff: Healthier Childhood, Safer Adolescence

A wealth of evidence shows that CSG receipt is good for children's health and other dimensions of welfare: improved nutrition, more schooling, legally documented identities, and less labor-force participation. The earlier children receive the grant, the more it helps. Receipt before age 2 provides the most durable benefits, though receiving the grant during adolescence (the cutoff age is now 18) also seems to help.[26]

A large impact assessment conducted by the DSD, SASSA, and the United Nations Children's Fund (UNICEF) in 2012 concluded that early receipt of the CSG helped keep children healthy (see Box 1). Researchers found that, for some children, the grant reduced the risk of flu, cold, stomachache, cough, and other common illnesses.[27] Children who received the CSG early and had educated mothers reaped significant health and growth benefits; this subgroup of children was less likely to be ill and more likely to grow taller than children who received the grant later in life.[28]

The grant appears to have improved the quality and quantity of food in recipient households, contributing to the observed improvements in nutrition and growth.[29] The precise pathway to other health benefits is less clear. Caregivers paid for health services, transport, medicine, and early childhood development services with the grant, which certainly helped. Some recipients borrowed against future CSG payments to pay for large unanticipated expenses such as a health crisis, transforming the CSG into a form of informal health insurance.[30]

In addition, the CSG reduced several adolescent-specific risks. Children who received the grant early in life reported less alcohol and drug use during their teenage years.[31] Adolescents in households where a child received

---

Box 1. Strength of the Evidence

Cash transfers are a relatively well-studied policy instrument, and they are often found to improve beneficiaries' health. In South Africa, many studies have examined the CSG's impact on a wide range of health and welfare outcomes.

Most health results presented in this chapter come from a mixed-method impact assessment of the grant scheme that was commissioned and funded by the DSD, SASSA, and UNICEF South Africa, and led by researchers from the South African Economic and Policy Research Institute. Researchers used a cross-sectional design that compared eligible households that received the cash transfer (the treatment group) with a group of eligible households that did not receive the transfer. The two groups had similar demographic and economic characteristics. Within households that received the grant, researchers also compared earlier with later receipt to understand the importance of duration and timing.[36] They also conducted a qualitative study to contextualize the quantitative findings, which provided policymakers with valuable insight into the reach of grant cover-

age, how recipients used the income, and what they valued and disliked about the CSG system.[37]

Additional research by Cluver and others[38] explored the connection between receipt of CSG and changes in risky sexual behavior. Using statistical techniques, they matched otherwise similar adolescents from recipient and nonrecipient households and compared their responses to a structured interview.

The introduction of the CSG was not randomized, so impact evaluations had to rely on quasi-experimental methods. It is thus conceivable that some bias persists and that the CSG's observed health impact is due to other forces unrelated to transfer receipt. However, researchers have used a number of different methods to control for the confounding factors that could result in selection bias. Although it is impossible to eliminate alternative explanations entirely, the study designs and consistency with results from other countries suggest that the CSG was indeed responsible for the observed health gains.

the grant were more likely to abstain from sex than their nonbeneficiary peers, even when they were not themselves enrolled to receive the grant.[32] The CSG has also been found to reduce adolescent pregnancy.[33] This is particularly important in light of conservative opposition to the program expressed in the common assertion that "the Child Support Grant encourages teenagers to literally 'breed' [to get] grants."[34] Rigorous research disproves this charge.

A separate study found that the CSG reduced the types of sexual behavior that put adolescent girls at extreme risk of HIV. Girls in CSG households had significantly less transactional and age-disparate sex than similar girls who had not received the transfer, muting two important drivers of HIV transmission. Effects on adolescent boys' sexual behavior were more modest: namely, the share of boys who reported having had sex with multiple sexual partners within the past year decreased, although this benefit was not sustained over time. (Fortunately, the study found no evidence that the grant increased boys' risky sexual behavior.)[35]

Gains at What Price?

Every year, the government has increased the size of the grant. The initial grant was ZAR100 (US$21) monthly; as of 2012, it had grown to ZAR280 (US$34).

The government has funded the extensive social grants system through taxation. The total public expenditure on social assistance was approximately 3.5 percent of gross domestic product in 2011, an increase of 1.5 percent since 1994.[39] The CSG is by far the largest of South Africa's grant programs.[40] In 2010–11, the government's expenditure on the CSG totaled nearly ZAR31 billion (US$4.2 billion).[41] Thanks to South Africa's economic growth and its expanding tax base, the share of national income that the CSG absorbs has remained relatively constant in recent years despite its increasing coverage.[42]

The Keys to Lasting Success

When the program was first launched, finance minister Trevor Manuel worried that the system was wholly unsustainable and would turn South Africa into a welfare state. Over time he became a firm supporter.[43] The evidence clearly shows its benefits for human development and confirms its critical role within the government's broader strategy to roll back structural inequality.[44] The level of public investment in the social grants overall, and the CSG in particular, is a testament to the government's dedication.

The government has had to be flexible in order to fulfill the social security commitment of the 1994 constitution. It has adjusted the CSG system along the way to respond to slow uptake, need, inflation, and concerns about equity. Beneficiaries report their appreciation for simplified documentation requirements, widely publicized information about procedures, a faster application process, and an expanded range of options for collecting grant money. A new procedure for issuing birth certificates helps facilitate enrollment and also reflects cross-sectoral cooperation: hospitals now give new parents birth certificates for their newborns directly rather than requiring them to make an extra trip to the Home Office to get them.[45]

Despite the CSG's widespread coverage, the most vulnerable children are still falling through the cracks. Surprisingly, the largest number and proportion of excluded eligible children live in formal urban areas, possibly reflecting the intensity of outreach activities in relatively deprived rural and informal urban settings.[46] Eligible babies and adolescents are excluded more often than children of other ages. Education level, employment, refugee status, and the presence of a mother also influence whether eligible children will be enrolled.[47]

In addition, to apply for a grant, the caregiver for eligible children must provide SASSA with documentation to conduct the eligibility tests. A national survey revealed that this prevented more than one in four caregivers of eligible children from applying in 2008, a challenge that the government has worked hard to address.[48] Ironically, a 2010 National Income Dynamics Survey found that the most common reason for nonenrollment was caregivers' belief that their income level was too high to qualify.[49]

SASSA has embraced technology as a way to increase efficiency and reduce fraud. For example, online birth registration facilitates the CSG application process. SASSA is rolling out a biometric voice-activated telephone system to shorten waiting times at pay points. With the new system, beneficiaries will be able call a number once a month to confirm their identity and release that month's payment.[50]

Every major change in the system for enrollment, verification, and payment has been accompanied by a communication campaign to minimize panic and other transition pains. SASSA used road shows, radio, schools, and traditional rural authority figures called *indunas* to help spread the word about the new age cutoff after each expansion.[51] The government acknowledges that the communication process still has room to improve, and some caregivers still miss critical information about important changes to the program. To combat this, SASSA has introduced a toll-free advice line and special provisions for particularly vulnerable families.[52]

Showing a strong commitment to learning, the DSD and SASSA have played an active role in commissioning studies of the program's impact, drawing on South Africa's strong cadre of domestic researchers. The evidence has enabled SASSA and the DSD to identify problems and guide reforms accordingly. Information on the CSG is publicly available for those with Internet access, promoting accountability.

South Africa's active civil society has played a crucial role. Organizations with roots in the apartheid struggle have now turned their sights on South Africa's rampant inequality. The human rights organization Black Sash informs visitors to its website about eligibility criteria for the grant and the application process. GroundUp, a web-based community news outlet, gives township residents a place to publicize their user experiences and helps maintain pressure on the government to live up to its commitments.[53]

The level of public expenditure has risen as the grant's coverage has expanded, which has led to questions about the CSG's sustainability. Demographic predictions indicate that the number of eligible children should remain steady,[54] yet researchers emphasize that sustainability depends on continuing to broaden the tax base as coverage expands to reach more children in need.[55]

Implications for Global Health

The most basic lesson of the CSG is that government-provided cash transfers can improve health. This is possible even when health goals are not explicit, benefits are not conditional, and the transfer income is shared among household members. Cash transfers can improve health directly by helping to pay for services, transport, and medicine; they can improve health indirectly by reducing poverty and influencing the social determinants of health. By helping children overcome the constraints of their parents' disadvantage and continue their schooling, the CSG's benefits are likely to extend to the next generation.

Predictable cash transfers can be a powerful weapon against HIV in a generalized epidemic such as South Afri-

ca's. (A generalized epidemic is one in which HIV prevalence is more than 1 percent in the general population.) Signs suggest that by increasing household income, the CSG reduces the motivation for risky sexual behaviors—transactional and age-disparate sex—that are driven by girls' deprivation and material need.[56]

South Africa's experience shows how the interaction between cash transfers and other social investments can amplify health impact (see also chapter 11 in this volume, on Brazil's family health program). For example, according to the evaluation, enrolled children with educated mothers reaped greater health benefits from the transfer than children whose mothers had minimal schooling. In addition, social workers in South Africa helped caregivers access the grant, extended the reach of the CSG program to the most marginalized children, and prepared children for the inevitable process of becoming too old for—or "aging out" of—grant eligibility. Unfortunately, despite the critical role government social workers play, they are few in number, overstretched, and rarely able to follow up with individual families.[57] Increasing the number of government social workers and expanding support for them as part of the comprehensive social protection system could further amplify the benefits of the transfer.

The method of payment is a design feature with broad implications. Enrolled children's primary caregivers—not heads of household—are responsible for picking up the CSG payments. Since most primary caregivers are women, this arrangement channels income directly to them: mothers, aunts, and grandmothers. Most studies have found that women invest more in their children than men do.[58] So even though the CSG program design was not explicitly gendered, by empowering female caregivers with the cash rather than male heads of households, it may have had a greater impact than if it had been designed differently.

Another CSG design feature with broad implications is the level of conditionality associated with the grant. The hot topic of whether to condition cash transfers remains unresolved in South Africa—and globally—as researchers and advocates find evidence to support both positions. Conditional cash transfers may be more politically palatable than what some view as a "handout." However, conditionality can keep the most disadvantaged residents from accessing transfers where social services are limited and when the requirements are too big a hurdle.

Proponents of cash transfer programs recognize that national government–administered transfer programs can have wide reach but uneven implementation. South Africa's experience is an example of the challenge: the need for the cash transfer is concentrated among the approximately one-quarter of children, especially newborns, who are eligible but not yet enrolled, but the CSG program's information management system is not nuanced enough to track specific groups of eligible vulnerable children. Many of those who stand to benefit the most miss out because their caregivers are unaware of or unable to access the grant.[59]

One possible solution could be universal provision of the CSG. Universal provision would mean that all children receive the grant regardless of their families' means, as opposed to the current means-tested targeting. Program evaluators have pointed out that "universal provi-sion of the Child Support Grant will reduce many barriers to access and help include millions of poor children currently erroneously excluded from the program."[60] Another possibility: a Basic Income Grant (BIG), which would provide a basic income for every South African.[61] A universal CSG seems likely, and it may be the first incremental step toward a BIG.

The CSG is one important and successful step toward addressing the legacy of apartheid, but it is not a panacea. Deeply entrenched problems remain, such as high and inequitable HIV prevalence and endemic violence. Ensuring that all eligible children receive their grant entitlements from the earliest days of life will help propel continued progress toward a safer, healthier, and more just South Africa.

REFERENCES

Agüero, Jorge M., Michael R. Carter, and Ingrid Woolard. 2007. *The Impact of Unconditional Cash Transfers on Nutrition: The South African Child Support Grant.* Working Paper 39. Brasilia, Brazil: International Poverty Centre. http://www.ipc-undp.org/pub/IPCWorkingPaper39.pdf.

Black Sash. 2015. "You and Your Rights: Child Support Grant." Accessed October 29. http://www.blacksash.org.za/index.php/your-rights/social-grants/item/you-and-your-rights-2.

Cluver, Lucie, Mark Boyes, Mark Orkin, Marija Pantelic, Thembela Molwena, and Lorraine Sherr. 2013. "Child-Focused State Cash Transfers and Adolescent Risk of HIV Infection in South Africa: A Propensity-Score-Matched Case-Control Study." *Lancet Global Health* 1 (6): e362–70. doi:10.1016/S2214-109X(13)70115-3.

Counter, Peter B. 2014. "Voice ID Biometric Deployment in South Africa among the Largest in the World." *FindBiometrics*, August 28. http://findbiometrics.com/voice-id-biometric-deployment-in-south-africa-among-the-largest-in-the-world/.

Department of Health. 1999. *Draft Policy Guidelines for Adolescent and Youth Health.* Pretoria, South Africa: Department of Health.

DSD (Department of Social Development), SASSA (South African Social Security Agency), and United Nations Children's Fund (UNICEF). 2011. *Child Support Grant Evaluation 2010: Qualitative Research Report.* Pretoria, South Africa: UNICEF South Africa.

———. 2012a. *The South African Child Support Grant Impact Assessment: Evidence from a Survey of Children, Adolescents and Their Households.* Pretoria, South Africa: UNICEF South Africa.

———. 2012b. *South Africa's Child Support Grant: Overall Findings from an Integrated Qualitative-Quantitative Evaluation.* Pretoria, South Africa: UNICEF South Africa. http://www.unicef.org/southafrica/SAF_resources_csg2012findings.pdf.

Finn, Arden, Murray Leibbrandt, Ingrid Woolard, and Jonathan Argent. 2010. *Trends in South African Income Distribution and Poverty since the Fall of Apartheid.* OECD Social, Employment and Migration Working Papers 101. Paris: OECD Publishing. http://www.oecd-ilibrary.org/social-issues-migration-health/trends-in-south-african-income-distribution-and-poverty-since-the-fall-of-apartheid_5kmms0t7p1ms-en.

GroundUp. 2015. "About GroundUp." Accessed October 29. http://www.groundup.org.za/about/.

Haarmann, Claudia, and Dirk Haarmann. 1996. *A Contribution towards a New Family Support System in South Africa.* Report for the Lund Committee on Child and Family Support. Pretoria, South Africa: Government of South Africa.

Hall, Katharine, Ingrid Woolard, Lori Lake, and Charmaine Smith. 2012. *South African Child Gauge 2012.* Cape Town, South Africa: University of Cape Town, Children's Institute. http://www.ci.org.za/depts/ci/pubs/pdf/general/gauge2012/sa_child_gauge2012.pdf.

Heinrich, Carolyn, John Hoddinott, and Michael Samson. 2012. "Reducing Adolescent Risky Behaviors in a High-Risk Context: The Impact of Unconditional Cash Transfers in South Africa." Presentation at Center for Global Development, Washington, DC, December 17.

REFERENCES, *continued*

IHME (Institute for Health Metrics and Evaluation). 2015. GBD Compare. Accessed October 29. http://vizhub.healthdata.org/gbd-compare.

Kelly, Gabrielle. 2013. "We Need to Change How We Think (and Talk) about Social Grants." *GroundUp*, October 7. http://www.groundup.org.za/content/we-need-change-how-we-think-and-talk-about-social-grants.

———. 2014. "Everything You Need to Know about Social Grants." *GroundUp*, May 7. http://groundup.org.za/article/everything-you-need-know-about-social-grants_820.

Kruger, John. 1998. "From Single Parents to Poor Children: Refocusing South Africa's Transfers to Poor Households with Children." Paper presented at ISSA's 2nd International Research Conference on Social Security, Summing Up the Evidence: The Impact of Incentives and Targeting on Social Security. Jerusalem, January 25–28. https://www.issa.int/html/pdf/jeru98/theme1/1-1d.pdf.

Laryea-Adjei, Stephen Devereux, and Maureen Motepe. 2011. "Impact Evaluation of South Africa's Child Support Grant on Child Protection: A Qualitative Review." PowerPoint presentation, Pretoria, South Africa, May 25. http://www.thepresidency.gov.za/MediaLib/Downloads/Home/Ministries/DepartmentofPerformanceMonitoringandEvaluation3/TheMELearningNetwork/Impact%20Evaluation%20of%20the%20Child%20Support%20Grant%20in%20South%20Africa.pdf.

Leibbrandt, Murray, Ingrid Woolard, and Christopher Woolard. 2007. "Poverty and Inequality Dynamics in South Africa: Post-apartheid Developments in the Light of the Long-Run Legacy." Draft paper, University of Cape Town. http://www.ipc-undp.org/conference/ems/papers/ENG/Leibbrandt_Woolard_Woolard_ENG.pdf.

Mabugu, Ramos, and Margaret Chitiga-Mabugu. 2013. "Are Social Grants a Threat to Fiscal Sustainability?" Human Sciences Research Council. http://www.hsrc.ac.za/en/review/hsrc-review-november-2013/social-grants-fiscas.

Makiwane, Monde, Eric Udjo, Linda Richter, and Chris Desmond. 2006. *Is the Child Support Grant Associated with an Increase in Teenage Fertility in South Africa? Evidence from National Surveys and Administrative Data.* Pretoria, South Africa: Human Sciences Research Council.

McEwen, Hayley, and Ingrid Woolard. 2012. "The Fiscal Cost of Child Grants in the Context of High Adult Mortality in South Africa: A Simulation to 2015." *Development Southern Africa* 29 (1): 141–56. doi:10.1080/0376835X.2012.645648.

PHILA (Public Health Intervention through Legislative Advocacy). 1997. "The Report of the Lund Committee on Child and Family Support," April 22. http://www.healthlink.org.za/pphc/Phila/lundsum.htm.

SASSA (South African Social Security Agency) and United Nations Children's Fund (UNICEF). 2013. *Preventing Exclusion from the Child Support Grant: A Study of Exclusion Errors in Accessing CSG Benefits.* Pretoria, South Africa: UNICEF South Africa.

Seekings, Jeremy. 2007. *Deserving Individuals and Groups: Justifying the Shape of South Africa's Welfare State.* Working Paper 193. Cape Town, South Africa: Centre for Social Science Research and Public Policy.

Simbayi, L.C., O. Shisana, T. Rehle, D. Onoya, S. Jooste, N. Zungu, and K. Zuma. 2014. *South African National HIV Prevalence, Incidence and Behaviour Survey, 2012.* Pretoria, South Africa: Human Sciences Research Council. http://www.hsrc.ac.za/en/research-outputs/view/6871.

SouthAfrica.info. 2014. "Increases in Old Age, Child Support Grants," February 27. http://www.southafrica.info/business/economy/policies/budget2014h.htm#.VHy2izGjNiQ.

Tiberti, Luca, Hélène Maisonnave, Margaret Chitiga, Ramos Mabugu, Véronique Robichaud, and Steward Ngandu. 2013. *The Economy-wide Impacts of the South African Child Support Grant: A Micro-Simulation-Computable General Equilibrium Analysis.* Working Paper 13-03. Montreal, QC: Centre Interuniversitaire sur la Risque les Politiques Economiques at l'Emploi. http://www.cirpee.org/fileadmin/documents/Cahiers_2013/CIRPEE13-03.pdf.

UNICEF (United Nations Children's Fund). 1998. *The State of the World's Children 1998.* Oxford, UK: Oxford University Press.

Williams, Martin J. 2007. "The Social and Economic Impacts of South Africa's Child Support Grant." Thesis, Williams College, Williamstown, MA. http://web.williams.edu/Economics/Honors/2007/Williams_thesis.pdf.

Woolard, Ingrid, Thabani Buthelezi, and Jonathan Bertscher. 2012. *Child Grants: Analysis of the NIDS Wave 1 and 2 Datasets.* Working Paper 84. Cape Town, South Africa: Southern Africa Labour and Development Research Unit.

Woolard, Ingrid, and Murray Leibbrandt. 2010. "The Evolution and Impact of Unconditional Cash Transfers in South Africa." Working paper, University of Cape Town, Southern Africa Labour and Development Research Unit. http://siteresources.worldbank.org/DEC/Resources/84797-1251813753820/6415739-1251815804823/Ingrid_Woolard_paper.pdf.

World Bank. 2011. *Gender Equality and Development.* Washington, DC: World Bank. https://siteresources.worldbank.org/INTWDR2012/Resources/7778105-1299699968583/7786210-1315936222006/Complete-Report.pdf.

Zembe, Yanga Z., Loraine Townsend, Anna Thorson, and Anna Ekström. 2013. "'Money Talks, Bullshit Walks' Interrogating Notions of Consumption and Survival Sex among Young Women Engaging in Transactional Sex in Post-Apartheid South Africa: A Qualitative Enquiry." *Globalization and Health* 9 (1): 28. doi:10.1186/1744-8603-9-28.

REFERENCES, *continued*

Zere, Eyob, and Diane McIntyre. 2003. "Inequities in Under-Five Child Malnutrition in South Africa." *International Journal for Equity in Health* 2:7. doi:10.1186/1475-9276-2-7.

ENDNOTES

1. Zere and McIntyre (2003).
2. Kruger (1998).
3. Finn et al. (2010).
4. Leibbrandt, Woolard, and Woolard (2007).
5. UNICEF (1998); Agüero, Carter, and Woolard (2007).
6. UNICEF (1998).
7. IHME (2015).
8. Department of Health (1999, 6).
9. Department of Health (1999).
10. Simbayi et al. (2014).
11. Zembe et al. (2013).
12. Heinrich, Hoddinott, and Samson (2012).
13. PHILA (1997).
14. Kruger (1998).
15. Haarmann and Haarmann (1996).
16. Michael Samson, personal communication with the author, August 21, 2014.
17. Woolard and Leibbrandt (2010).
18. Woolard and Leibbrandt (2010).
19. Hall et al. (2012).
20. In subsequent years the age cutoff was raised to 18, in steps, starting in 2003 (to 8), then again in 2004 (to 11), 2005 (to 14), 2009 (to 15), 2010 (to 16), 2011 (to 17), and finally, 2012 (to 18) (Michael Samson, personal communication with the author, August 21, 2014).
21. DSD, SASSA, and UNICEF (2012a).
22. Woolard and Leibbrandt (2010)
23. Lack of school attendance is supposed to trigger social services for CSG beneficiaries (Michael Samson, personal communication with the author, August 21, 2014).
24. SouthAfrica.info (2014).
25. Black Sash (2015); Kelly (2014).
26. DSD, SASSA, and UNICEF (2012a).
27. DSD, SASSA, and UNICEF (2012a).
28. DSD, SASSA, and UNICEF (2012a).
29. Williams (2007).
30. DSD, SASSA, and UNICEF (2011).
31. DSD, SASSA, and UNICEF (2012a).
32. Heinrich, Hoddinott, and Samson (2012).
33. Makiwane et al. (2006).
34. Kelly (2013).
35. Cluver et al. (2013).
36. DSD, SASSA, and UNICEF (2012a).
37. DSD, SASSA, and UNICEF (2011).
38. 2013.
39. Laryea-Adjei, Devereux, and Motepe (2011); Seekings (2007, 2).
40. Tiberti et al. (2013).
41. Laryea-Adjei, Devereux, and Motepe (2011).
42. McEwen and Woolard (2012).
43. Michael Samson, personal communication with the author, August 21, 2014.
44. Michael Samson, personal communication with the author, August 21, 2014.
45. DSD, SASSA, and UNICEF (2011).
46. SASSA and UNICEF (2013).
47. SASSA and UNICEF (2013).
48. DSD, SASSA, and UNICEF (2012a).
49. Woolard, Buthelezi, and Bertscher (2012).
50. Counter (2014).
51. DSD, SASSA, and UNICEF (2011).
52. SASSA and UNICEF (2013).
53. Black Sash (2015); GroundUp (2015).
54. McEwen and Woolard (2012).
55. Mabugu and Chitiga-Mabugu (2013).
56. Cluver et al. (2013).
57. DSD, SASSA, and UNICEF (2011).
8. World Bank (2011).
59. SASSA and UNICEF (2013).
60. DSD, SASSA, and UNICEF (2012b, 2).
61. Michael Samson, personal communication with the author, August 21, 2014.

CASE 17

Learning from Disappointment
Honduras's Programa de Asignación Familiar II

The Case at a Glance

HEALTH GOAL: To instruct mothers in feeding and hygiene practices; promote proper diets; build demand for and access to health services for pregnant women, nursing mothers, and children under age three; and ensure timely and suitable healthcare for Programa de Asignación Familiar II (PRAF-II) beneficiaries.

STRATEGY: Conditional cash transfers, targeting families with pregnant women or young children in deprived rural areas, supplemented by supply-side interventions to improve health service quality and promote breast-feeding and better hygiene.

HEALTH IMPACT: Increased health service utilization for young children and expectant mothers. No change in prenatal visits. No improvements in diarrhea prevalence, anemia, or stunting. Likely caused an unintended 2 to 4 percentage-point increase in fertility.

WHY IT DIDN'T WORK: Small transfer size and weakly enforced conditions. Weak institutional capacity that impeded efforts to strengthen the quality of health services. The design of the transfer, which possibly led to a perverse incentive for increased childbearing.

FINANCING: Cost about US$18 million over four years for the health and nutrition component.

SCALE: 109,649 beneficiary families annually.

For Hondurans living in extreme poverty, survival can be a daily challenge. In the country's poor, rural western region, a family's meager income may depend upon forces far beyond its control: the vagaries of the coffee harvest and global prices for coffee. Food is scarce and often insufficient to share among family members, forcing many children to live with chronic malnutrition. Many parents put their sons to work in the coffee fields. Their daughters marry young and give birth early, contributing to high fertility rates and completing the cycle of poverty. Far from cities and high-quality health services, and lacking modern infrastructure, electricity, and improved sanitation, the daily toil and deprivation are difficult to escape.

Facing deep poverty in the country's rural regions, the Honduran government began experimenting with cash transfers for social protection in 1990, well before they became popular in other low- and middle-income countries. In 1990 Honduras introduced the first iteration of its Programa de Asignación Familiar ("Family Allowance

Program"), aiming to compensate the poorest families for losses incurred under structural adjustment policies. When PRAF-I, as it was called, failed to make a dent in overall poverty, the Inter-American Development Bank (IDB) moved forward with a new and improved pilot program, called PRAF-II, which was designed to boost human capital and replace the foundering PRAF-I. Yet missteps begot more missteps: although PRAF-II corrected some of PRAF-I's deficiencies, new design flaws created new and unanticipated problems, with mixed and even adverse consequences for beneficiaries' health.

The PRAF experience shows how cash transfers can lead to unintended consequences, mainly related to poor design choices. Regular monitoring of program implementation is critical to avoid pitfalls and identify adverse effects early, so that program design can be modified and corrected. The Honduran story is one of learning while doing and constant iteration over two decades—while still achieving mixed results.

This case was originally authored by Rachel Silverman (based on a draft by Alix Beith).

The Toll of Rural Poverty

With more than half the population living in the rolling hills and mountainous terrain of the country's rural areas, Honduras has long struggled to achieve the growth that many of its neighbors attained. In 1999, Hondurans were scraping by on just US$890 per year in today's (2015) dollars, making Honduras the poorest country in Central America and second only to Haiti in the Latin America and Caribbean region.[1]

Honduras's Gini index, a standard metric indicating the degree of income inequality, was among the highest in Latin America, with 42 percent of the country's scarce wealth concentrated in the hands of its richest 10 percent.[2] The poorest Hondurans, predominantly indigenous families and those living in rural areas, struggled to stretch their lempiras to survive: almost 70 percent of all Hondurans lived below the poverty line, with 25 percent in extreme poverty (less than US$1.25 [purchasing power parity] per day).[3]

Living in entrenched poverty with little access to secondary education—an important gateway to smaller family sizes and better life prospects—rural Honduran women gave birth early and often. In rural Honduras, a 2001 survey found that the average woman would have 5.62 children over the course of her life, a surprisingly high figure compared with the fertility rate in urban areas of Honduras, 3 to 3.5 children per woman, and that of the Latin America and Caribbean region as a whole, 2.6 children.[4] At that time, 60 percent of rural Honduran women ages 20 to 24 had already given birth by age 20, and 36 percent by age 18.[5] And the rural-urban divide in the use of modern contraceptives was stark: a little more than one-third of married or in-union adolescent girls used modern family-planning methods in rural areas, compared with almost half of their urban peers and two-thirds or more of urban women in union aged 20 and up.[6]

For these girls and women in rural Honduras, often far from quality health services, childbearing was risky business. Just 38 percent of rural women delivered their babies in a clinic or hospital, and one in five received no prenatal care whatsoever.[7]

Rural poverty also took a heavy toll on children. Of every 1,000 babies born, 38 did not survive infancy and another 13 died before their fifth birthdays. Most succumbed to entirely preventable causes of death such as diarrhea, acute respiratory infection, and complications during childbirth.[8] Of the surviving children, many failed to thrive. About 14 percent of all Honduran babies were born with low birth weight; 35 percent of children under age five were stunted, and 34 percent suffered from anemia.[9]

Putting an Idea in Motion: An Old Cash Transfer Responds to New Crises

The 1990s in Honduras were marked by relative peace throughout the country and a fairly strong civilian government.[10] Despite ups and downs over the previous decades and an incredibly low baseline gross domestic product (GDP), the Honduran economy was slowly but steadily expanding. There was reason for cautious optimism.[11]

In the late 1990s, a few years of slow but encouraging progress were quickly wiped out by twin crises. In 1998, the landfall of Hurricane Mitch took a tremendous human and economic toll, killing almost 6,000 people and causing US$3.8 billion in material damages.[12] Compounding Mitch's impact, Honduras also suffered through a collapse in global prices for coffee—its staple export. From 1997 through the early years of the following decade, those plummeting prices jeopardized the livelihoods of the nearly one-third of rural Hondurans who drew at least part of their income from coffee.[13]

Teetering on the brink of disaster, many rural families were desperate for a helping hand. The good news was that Honduras had a long tradition of social protection programs targeted to its most vulnerable citizens. Starting in 1950, the Honduran government had offered food aid to the poor, and by the early 1990s, more than a quarter of the population benefited from this assistance.[14] Things changed, however, in 1990, when Honduras began implementing structural adjustment policies to maintain eligibility for International Monetary Fund and World Bank loans. Acknowledging that the "shock" of privatization and the social spending cuts associated with structural adjustment would cause near-term pain, the World Bank and Honduran government agreed to establish and expand a strong social safety net. Thus, with financial support from the World Bank and the IDB, PRAF-I began operations in 1990.[15]

PRAF-I was an ever-evolving program with multiple aims, including the improvement of nutrition, healthcare access, and health among the poorest Hondurans. The program provided mothers with vouchers exchangeable for food or money if they met specific eligibility requirements and conditions. Health-related benefits distributed as part of this scheme included maternal and child health vouchers for pregnant women, nursing mothers, and those with young or developmentally disabled children, contingent on regular visits to health centers; and no-strings-attached nutritional vouchers for children under five at risk of malnutrition. Other types of vouchers were available to encourage school attendance and help build entrepreneurial capacity among Honduran women. By 1998, 318,000 people were receiving PRAF-I vouchers each year.[16]

By the time of the twin crises of the late 1990s, however, it had become clear that PRAF-I was not fulfilling its potential. The IDB placed the blame on design and implementation flaws. The nominal conditions lacked bite because enforcement was nonexistent, and even when mothers fulfilled the health conditions they often arrived at understaffed and underresourced facilities. With most beneficiaries lacking access to banking services, distribution of cash benefits took place through health workers and teachers, which left the process vulnerable to waste and theft. The health vouchers accounted for just 12 percent of the cost of a basic food basket—too small to realistically influence behavior or make much difference in consumption.[17]

Targeting, or the lack thereof, also presented a major problem. PRAF-I distribution sites, schools and health centers, had been selected on the basis of child malnutrition rates within their catchment areas. Yet at each site, selection of beneficiaries was delegated to the judgment of health workers and teachers and thus made the program vulnerable to subjective decision making. Two-fifths of the maternal and child health benefit was captured by the richest 40 percent of Hondurans, while many of the poorest Hondurans were left out.[18]

The IDB theorized that a new approach was needed—one explicitly focused on increasing human capital among the very poorest Hondurans, with clear metrics for success and a sound strategy to evaluate whether it was achieving its objectives.[19] In 1998, the government of Honduras and the IDB negotiated a US$45 million loan to Honduras to help initiate a new version of the PRAF, a pilot program known as PRAF-II.

PRAF-II in Action

PRAF-II targeted 70 municipalities in deeply impoverished rural western Honduras. It provided cash transfers for health and education, coupled with supply-side interven-

tions such as quality improvement in health services and education in a focused effort to help break the cycle of poverty. Working with government officials, the IDB spearheaded the new design and its evaluation in partnership with the International Food Policy Research Institute (IFPRI), a highly respected international research group based in Washington, DC, whose focus is agricultural development, food security, and alleviating poverty.[20]

The pilot program was funded via a concessional loan from the IDB and a small amount of cofinancing from the Honduran government. The new and improved PRAF-II increased the value of the transfer benefit, created clear and objective criteria for beneficiary selection, added a supply side-strengthening component, and created a new procedure for distributing transfers.[21] PRAF-II also built in rigorous evaluation from the start. To help study the impact of various program components, the 70 municipalities were randomly split into four different groups: just cash transfers, just the supply-side interventions, both program components, and a control group (see Box 1).[22] PRAF-I continued to operate nationwide, including in the 70 municipalities selected for the PRAF-II pilot.[23]

Similar to PRAF-I, PRAF-II targeted 70 municipalities with the highest rates of malnutrition, a proxy for extreme poverty. Home to about 660,000 people, these municipalities in western Honduras performed dismally on human development indicators: nearly 80 percent of residents lived in poverty, more than 70 percent in extreme poverty, and one in three adults were illiterate.[24] About half the children were stunted, and roughly 30 percent were underweight.[25] Only 40 percent or so of women attended at least five prenatal visits, and about four in five women received no postpartum checkup.[26]

Because targeting on the basis of poverty took place at the municipal level, eligibility for the cash transfer was open to all households with a pregnant or nursing woman or a child under age three in the target areas. Households with one or more eligible residents qualified for at least US$48 in transfers per year, delivered in twice-yearly installments. If a household had more than one eligible member, it could receive up to two transfers simultaneously, for a total value of US$96 per year. This amount was calculated to be roughly one-third of the average annual cost of staple food for a rural family. In addition, families could receive a bonus of another US$38 per year for each child 13 or younger attending school in grades one through four, up to a maximum of three children per family.[27] Enrollment for both transfers remained open during the program, so families could add additional beneficiaries when their household composition changed—most often due to a new pregnancy.[28]

In theory, receipt of the transfers was conditional. (Conditional cash transfers are often called CCTs.) To qualify for the health-related transfer, eligible children had to attend nutritional and health checkups, while mothers had to make five prenatal visits during pregnancy and attend a postpartum checkup.[29] Beginning in late 2001, a system was introduced to monitor compliance with the conditions via bar-coded attendance slips, submitted by beneficiaries during health center visits. In practice, however, the program evaluation stated that "no beneficiary was actually suspended for noncompliance." To qualify for the bonus education transfer, eligible children were expected to attend school regularly; in practice, only enrollment in school was enforced.[30] Ultimately, an average of 109,649 Honduran families received PRAF-II transfers each year.[31]

For the supply-side component, the government gave health facilities in program areas roughly US$5,000 per year to facilitate quality improvements, contingent on managers' participation in the quality improvement process and the provision of requisite health services.[32] At each health center, teams were established from within the local community to craft a work plan for improving quality and to oversee its implementation. The plans could involve structural repairs to the facility, equipment or drug procurement, or payments to community health workers.[33]

PRAF-II also included community-based nutrition and education programs. Catering to infants and children under two years old, staffers trained community members to conduct monthly growth monitoring and counsel mothers on hygiene and feeding practices.[34] Finally, PRAF-II offered transfers of about US$4,000 per school to strengthen local educational quality, funds that parents' associations and local nongovernmental organizations controlled.[35]

IFPRI conducted its intermediate assessment of the PRAF-II pilot from 2000 to 2002, after which the IDB and Honduran government tweaked several dimensions of the program design. Starting in 2003, PRAF-II extended eligibility to children up to age five but discontinued the per-child basis of calculating total payment. Instead, the program offered a set transfer amount to all eligible families. The distribution mechanism also changed; instead of delivery via PRAF-II staff, as of 2003 the program contracted with Banco Hondureño del Café,

a private Honduran bank, to distribute the transfers at local branches. Finally, the program added a component to cover delivery costs for mothers who gave birth in hospitals and registered the birth in the national registry (see also chapter 13 in this volume).[36]

The Payoff: From Mixed Effects to Unintended Health Impacts

IFPRI designed a multiarm randomized impact evaluation, which should have yielded high-quality results. Yet PRAF-II ran into unforeseen roadblocks from the beginning, which complicated the evaluation. Fiscal and legal barriers prohibited the prompt transfer of supply-side payments to community-based teams, preventing the researchers from measuring the effects, if any, of the supply-side program components.[37] Later, a dispute led PRAF-II to cancel IFPRI's contract, and the planned final evaluation was never completed.[38] Evidence of program impact is thus based on the midterm impact assessment for 2000 to 2002.[39] The bottom line: evidence is robust but covers a shorter time period than was originally planned.

The midterm assessment suggested a mixed bag of effects. In areas that received the CCTs, families used more health services than families in the control groups. Members of those households were more likely to make five or more prenatal care visits, and their children were more likely to visit a health center, receive the DTP1/pentavalent vaccine, and get weighed regularly.[40] They also saw educational gains: attendance among beneficiary children rose by about 4.5 percentage points, which translated to about 10 extra days of school per year. But the transfers failed to make a difference for postpartum checkups—and perhaps surprisingly, they generated no significant improvements in consumption or dietary composition.[41]

More disappointing was that the modest gains in the utilization of health services among CCT recipients failed to result in improved health. After two years, children in households that received the transfer were just as likely to be stunted or anemic as those that did not. The prevalence of wasting and diarrhea increased across treatment and control groups alike, and the increase in diarrhea prevalence was even more pronounced in areas that received the transfer.[42]

Then, in 2007, a research team led by Hebrew University's Guy Stecklov revealed that PRAF-II may have induced an unintended negative effect. After two years, already sky-high birth rates were 2 to 4 percentage points higher in PRAF-II treatment areas than in control municipalities—a significant difference. Researchers hypothesized that the structure of the transfer may have inspired some families to either increase their total fertility or bring forward the timing of their next pregnancy.[43]

Some question this hypothesis, suggesting that the amount of the transfer was too small to generate this kind of fertility effect. (In South Africa, the Child Support Grant—with a relatively large transfer size—reduced fertility. The program had a similar structure to the Honduran CCT. See chapter 16 of this volume.)

At What Price?

The original cash transfer program, PRAF-I, cost roughly US$9.8 million per year and accounted for about 7 percent of the government's aggregate spending on health and education in 1997. The original budget for PRAF-II was comparable, totaling about US$12.6 million each year, or US$50.3 million from 2000 to 2004. It was mostly funded by an IDB loan, with US$5.1 million in counterpart funding from the Honduran government.[45] Ultimately, just US$40.3 million of the approved loan was spent, leaving about US$5 million undisbursed.[46]

The nutrition and health component was expected to cost US$17.7 million over the project's four-year duration, including US$11.6 million for the demand-side cash transfers. US$2.7 million went to supply-side strengthening and the remainder to administrative expenses and other miscellaneous costs. Other major components of the PRAF-II budget included education (US$22.6 million), targeting of beneficiaries (US$3.2 million), and monitoring and evaluation (US$5.2 million).[47]

Why PRAF-II Fell Short in Honduras

Despite PRAF-II's effect on care-seeking behavior, the program failed to improve health and nutrition outcomes and may have prompted an unintended fertility bump. The sources of PRAF-II disappointment are manifold, but the small transfer size, the possible creation of a perverse incentive, and weak institutional capacity deserve much of the blame.

Box 1. Strength of the Evidence

A rigorous impact evaluation of PRAF-II was planned from the program's start, with a clever design to tease out both overall program effects and the impact of specific program components, both alone and in combination.[44] Seventy municipalities were randomized into four groups: 20 received the household-level package (cash transfers) only, 10 received supply-side strengthening only, and 20 received both cash transfers and supply-side strengthening, while the final 20 municipalities served as a control group. IFPRI conducted a baseline survey during the second half of 2000 and a first follow-up survey in 2002. A second follow-up survey was planned for 2004. Based on advance planning alone, program leaders could expect strong evidence on whether or not the program worked.

Yet the researchers' best-laid plans met serious challenges that compromised the quality and utility of their evaluation. Implementation of the demand-side component began before the baseline survey had been completed, while baseline data collection in two of the other study arms was delayed by several months into the coffee harvest season, with potentially important implications for some consumption and school enrollment variables. The net result was skewed baseline data that may have introduced bias into the evaluation's estimates of program impact. In addition, the supply-side component was slow to get off the ground because of legal difficulties in transferring funds to community groups. This made it nearly impossible to measure the impact of the supply-side components, essentially voiding the results from the two groups that had been assigned to supply-side interventions.

The final nail in the coffin came from a dispute between PRAF officials and IFPRI that ultimately led to the cancellation of IFPRI's contract. The final survey and evaluation were never completed, so the available evidence reflects just two years of implementation. Notwithstanding these limitations, the rigorous initial planning still led to strong evidence on program impact based on the midterm assessment. However, interpretation of the evidence should take into account the relatively (and unexpectedly) short duration of the intervention period under study and the inability to appropriately account for the supply-side component.

First, many of the program's core limitations stemmed from the small size of the transfer. The US$48 per year health transfer was likely insufficient to improve children's diets or boost their nutritional status substantially.[48] This amount seems meager when compared with South Africa's Child Support Grant of around US$250 per person per year (see chapter 16 in this volume). Yet the program structure enabled Honduran families to receive an additional small benefit with each new pregnancy—up to two active beneficiaries in total—which appears to have introduced a small but potentially meaningful incentive for women to increase their fertility.

Limited institutional capacity and politicization of the program staff were also major stumbling blocks. Problems began early on for PRAF-II, when the inability to legally transfer funds to health facilities brought the supply-side component to a halt. Weak institutional capacity also prevented the enforcement of the conditions, watering down the potential for health impact. And in 2002, midway through the program, the inauguration of a new Honduran president, Ricardo Maduro, led to the prompt dismissal of all PRAF employees, which destabilized program implementation. A similar mass exodus occurred with another change in administration just four years later.[49]

In response to the disappointing midterm evaluation, and with the election of President Maduro, a freshly installed PRAF-II staff realized that major reforms were needed. By 2003, they had introduced an updated banking system and decoupled the amount of the benefit from the number of children; they also expanded coverage to children up to five years old and offered an incentive for institutional births. Nonetheless, PRAF-II had lost much of its momentum, and its woes were further exacerbated by the decision to abandon the planned final evaluation. In 2006, the IDB officially closed out the PRAF-II loan.[50]

Yet even as PRAF-II ended, cash transfers continued via PRAF-I, which still operated nationwide with domestic funding. In 2008 PRAF-I underwent major changes based on PRAF-II's policy lessons. Targeting improved substantially with the introduction of a more sophisticated formula to identify the very poorest rural villages, and program administrators actually began to enforce the conditions for receipt of the transfer. Meanwhile, following the 2006 election, incoming president Manuel Zelaya and the IDB agreed to another PRAF loan—PRAF-III—with a design informed by the PRAF-II experience. PRAF-III increased the transfer amount, doubled the frequency of disbursements, enforced conditions, and corrected problems that had arisen with supply-side strengthening.[51] Perhaps most important, the PRAF-III loan also laid the groundwork to finally integrate PRAF-I and PRAF-III into a single, unified CCT program, now dubbed Bono Vida Mejor, meaning "Better Life Voucher."[52]

Implications for Global Health

CCT programs have a long track record in Latin America and are expanding rapidly in other regions. Advocates of these programs have much to learn from PRAF-II's experience. Getting the design details right is paramount, including targeting arrangements, the amount of the transfer, eligibility criteria, and monitoring measures. Regular monitoring is essential to quickly catch and correct for unintended consequences. Changes in fertility deserve particular attention, given the common charge that people will change their behavior in order to access the benefits.

Poverty and inequality continue to pose immense challenges in Honduras. Modest economic gains achieved between 2006 and 2009 had been reversed by 2013, owing to both the global recession and a drop in government social spending. Poverty has worsened, unemployment has risen, and underemployment has also increased since 2010. By 2013, Honduras had the most unequal income distribution of all countries in Latin America.[53]

Although overall poverty decreased slightly during the lifetimes of PRAF I–III, these programs cannot take the credit. Researchers attribute most poverty reduction to remittances from abroad, which grew from 7.5 percent of GDP in 2001 to more than 20.8 percent in 2007.[54] Hondurans voted with their feet, leaving the country in droves beginning in the late 1990s, primarily heading north toward the United States.[55] For them, migration may have been the way out of poverty, not CCTs.

In 2010, PRAF-III was absorbed into a new CCT program, now named Bono Vida Mejor. Bono Vida Mejor's designers have attempted to learn from earlier mistakes and offer a transfer amount far larger than any of the PRAF predecessors. Early findings suggest mixed program impact: while beneficiary children were more likely to receive regular checkups and regular weight monitoring, researchers observed no change in women's use of prenatal or postnatal services.[56]

Cash transfers have done an enormous amount of good in the world, but their benefits are still far from guaranteed. Their impact depends on their design and adaptation to contextual realities. Over the past two decades, and despite the best of intentions, the Honduran government learned this lesson the hard way. But that lesson is also the silver lining: without a rigorous evaluation and follow-up studies, Honduras might still be in the dark about PRAF's ineffectiveness and potential adverse consequences. Now, with insight from evaluation, the government is fine-tuning a still developing but potentially important program so the next generation can reap the benefits.

REFERENCES

Adato, Michelle, and John Hoddinott. 2010. *Conditional Cash Transfers in Latin America.* Baltimore, MD: Johns Hopkins University Press for International Food Policy Research Institute. http://ebrary.ifpri.org/cdm/ref/collection/p15738coll2/id/127902.

Benedetti, Fiorella, Pablo Ibarrarán, and Patrick J. McEwan. 2015. *Do Education and Health Conditions Matter in a Large Cash Transfer? Evidence from a Honduran Experiment.* IDB Working Paper Series IDB-WP-577. Washington, DC: Inter-American Development Bank. http://publications.iadb.org/handle/11319/6816.

CEMLA (Center for Latin American Monetary Studies), MIF (Multilateral Investment Fund), and IDB (Inter-American Development Bank). 2008. *International Remittances in Honduras.* Mexico City: CEMLA. http://www.cemla-remesas.org/informes/report-honduras.pdf.

Coady, David, Pedro Olinto, and Natalia Caldes. 2003. *Coping with the Coffee Crisis in Central America: The Role of Social Safety Nets in Honduras.* Washington, DC: World Bank. http://siteresources.worldbank.org/EXTLACREGTOPPOVANA/Resources/Coady CaldescopingwiththecoffeecrisisinCA.pdf.

Corrales, Gustavo, Suyapa Pavón, Ramón Enamorado, Paul Stupp, Mariaelena Jefferds, Laurence Grummer-Strawn, Stephen McCracken, Jennifer Ballentine, Mary Goodwin, and Richard Monteith. 2002. *Encuesta Nacional de Epidemiologia y Salud Familiar ENESF-2001.* Tegucigalpa, Honduras: Secretaria de Salud.

IDB (Inter-American Development Bank). 1998. *Family Allowances Program—Phase II.* HO-0132. Washington, DC: IDB. http://idbdocs.iadb.org/wsdocs/getdocument.aspx?docnum=454963.

———. 2000. "Central America after Hurricane Mitch: The Challenge of Turning a Disaster into an Opportunity: Honduras." http://www.iadb.org/regions/re2/consultative_group/backgrounder2.htm.

———. 2006. *Programa de Asignación Familiar Fase II.* Washington, DC: IDB. http://idbdocs.iadb.org/wsdocs/getdocument.aspx?docnum=865397.

IFPRI (International Food Policy Research Institute). 2003. *Proyecto PRAF/BID Fase II: Impacto Intermedio.* Washington, DC: IFPRI. http://idbdocs.iadb.org/wsdocs/getdocument.aspx?docnum=335841.

Johnston, Jake, and Stephan Lefebvre. 2013. "Honduras since the Coup: Economic and Social Outcomes." London: Centre for Economic and Policy Research. http://www.cepr.netwww.conservativenannystate.org/documents/publications/Honduras-2013-11.pdf.

Merril, Tim, ed. 1995. *Honduras: A Country Study.* Washington, DC: US Government Publishing Office for the Library of Congress. http://countrystudies.us/honduras/.

Moore, Charity. 2008. *Assessing Honduras' CCT Programme PRAF, Programa de Asignación Familiar: Expected and Unexpected Realities.* Country Study 15. Brasilia, Brazil: International Poverty Centre.

Morris, Saul S., Rafael Flores, Pedro Olinto, and Juan Manuel Medina. 2004. "Monetary Incentives in Primary Health Care and Effects on Use and Coverage of Preventive Health Care Interventions in Rural Honduras: Cluster Randomised Trial." *Lancet* 364 (9450): 2030–37. doi:10.1016/S0140-6736(04)17515-6.

Reichman, Daniel. 2013. "Honduras: The Perils of Remittance Dependence and Clandestine Migration." Migration Policy Institute, April 11. http://www.migrationpolicy.org/article/honduras-perils-remittance-dependence-and-clandestine-migration.

Sabonge, Kenia, Deirdre Wulf, Lisa Remez, and Elena Prada. 2006. *Early Childbearing in Honduras: A Continuing Challenge.* In Brief 4, 2006 Series. New York: Guttmacher Institute. https://www.guttmacher.org/pubs/2006/10/13/rib_Honduras_en.pdf.

Sistema de las Naciones Unidas en Honduras. 2003. *Informe sobre las Metas del Milenio: Honduras 2003.* Tegucigalpa, Honduras: Sistema de las Naciones Unidas en Honduras.

Stecklov, Guy, Paul Winters, Jessica Todd, and Ferdinando Regalia. 2007. "Unintended Effects of Poverty Programmes on Childbearing in Less Developed Countries: Experimental Evidence from Latin America." *Population Studies* 61 (2): 125–40. doi:10.1080/00324720701300396.

UCP (Unidad Coordinadora del Proyecto) and IFPRI (International Food Policy Research Institute). 2000. *Segundo*

REFERENCES, *continued*

Informe: Propuesta de Implementación del Proyecto PRAF/ BID-Fase II. Washington, DC: Inter-American Development Bank. http://publications.iadb.org/ bitstream/handle/11319/4534/Honduras%20PRAF%20 II%20-%20Segundo%20Informe%3a%20Propuesta%20 de%20Implementaci%C3%B3n.pdf?sequence=1.

UN (United Nations). 2015. UN Data. Accessed October 27. http://data.un.org/.

World Bank. 2015. Data. Accessed November 10. http://data. worldbank.org/.

ENDNOTES

1. World Bank (2015).
2. World Bank (2015).
3. Sistema de las Naciones Unidas en Honduras (2003); UN (2015).
4. Corrales et al. (2002; World Bank (2015).
5. Sabonge et al. (2006).
6. Corrales et al. (2002).
7. Corrales et al. (2002).
8. Corrales et al. (2002).
9. World Bank (2015).
10. Although Honduras did not suffer from the devastating civil wars in neighboring El Salvador, Guatemala, and Nicaragua during the 1980s, it experienced considerable instability during that decade (see Merril 1995).
11. Merril (1995).
12. IDB (2000).
13. Coady, Olinto, and Caldes (2003).
14. Moore (2008).
15. Adato and Hoddinott (2010).
16. Moore (2008).
17. Moore (2008).
18. Moore (2008).
19. IDB (1998).
20. Moore (2008).
21. Moore (2008).
22. Morris et al. (2004).
23. Moore (2008).
24. UCP and IFPRI (2000).
25. IFPRI (2003).
26. Morris et al. (2004).
27. IDB (1998).
28. Stecklov et al. (2007).
29. Moore (2008).
30. Morris et al. (2004).
31. Moore (2008).
32. Moore (2008).
33. Morris et al. (2004).
34. Morris et al. (2004).
35. IDB (1998).
36. Moore (2008).
37. Morris et al. (2004).
38. Moore (2008).
39. Morris et al. (2004).
40. Morris et al. (2004).
41. Moore (2008).
42. IFPRI (2003).
43. Stecklov et al. (2007).
44. Morris et al. (2004).
45. IDB (1998).
46. IDB (2006).
47. IDB (1998).
48. Moore (2008).
49. Moore (2008).
50. Moore (2008).
51. Moore (2008).
52. Adato and Hoddinott (2010).
53. Johnston and Lefebvre (2013).
54. CEMLA, MIF, and IDB (2008).
55. Reichman (2013).
56. Benedetti, Ibarrarán, and McEwan (2015).

PART IV

Changing Behavior Population-wide to Reduce Risk

Many people closely associate health with doctors and hospitals. Yet sometimes the biggest health impact is attained not in a clinical setting but instead in the world of everyday life: on the road or in homes, schools, and bars, where people make choices that can put their health at risk.

Clinicians and policymakers alike increasingly recognize the importance of healthy habits for longer lives and better health; however, nudging people toward health-promoting behaviors has proven a tough nut to crack. People are often aware of the potential health consequences of their choices, but knowledge alone is not enough to overcome psychological, social, financial, or environmental barriers to changing their behavior.

Even though the role of prevention and public health measures in changing behavior is generally recognized, establishing the norms and creating the needed infrastructure is a huge challenge. This section profiles five policies or programs that aimed to improve population health by encouraging people to adopt healthier habits and behaviors in their everyday lives. Four of these programs achieved notable successes: real health improvements were detected when critical masses quit smoking in Thailand, donned helmets on motorbikes in Vietnam, ceased open defecation in Indonesia, and used condoms in India. But in Peru, a promising initiative to increase handwashing with soap fell flat, failing to significantly reduce the frequency of diarrhea or other ailments transmitted through feces.

These cases prove that governments and their partners can make a real dent in the behavioral drivers of disease and other medical conditions with the right strategy; thoughtful program design; and sustained, intense attention. Behavior change interventions are among the few programs in low- and middle-income countries to make a difference in the burden of noncommunicable diseases such as heart disease. Treating these requires intensive clinical care and places tremendous stress on already stretched health systems.

What makes for successful behavior change? Policymakers seeking a quick fix should think again: the most successful behavior change programs require all hands on deck, typically combining intense formative work, aggressive new legislation and enforcement, ubiquitous educational and promotional campaigns, intense person-to-person outreach, and sustained changes to the enabling environment. And group dynamics matter. Uptake of healthy habits is most likely when communities rally around a new social norm—for example, the use of condoms in sex work and latrines for defecation—that drives individual behavior change.

Cracking Down on Lighting Up
Thailand's Campaign for Tobacco Control

The Case at a Glance

HEALTH GOAL: To reduce smoking rates and thereby lower the burden of lung cancer, heart disease, respiratory illness, and other tobacco-related illness, and prevent death.

STRATEGY: Sustained series of tax increases, laws, regulations, and health promotion campaigns to reduce tobacco demand and availability.

HEALTH IMPACT: Smoking prevalence dropped from 59 percent in 1991 to 42 percent in 2007 among men, and from 5 percent to 2 percent among women. At the population level, rates of new lung cancer cases plateaued and emphysema deaths dropped substantially. 32,000 lives saved between 1991 and 2006, estimated to rise to 320,000 lives saved by 2026. 542,000 disability-ty-adjusted life years (DALYs) averted by 2006.

WHY IT WORKED: Broad public support to take on transnational tobacco companies. Cost-saving or revenue-neutral measures that sustained government commitment. A highly organized and effective advocacy community. An agile and responsive government and regulatory framework.

FINANCING: Cost saving: increased taxation raised almost US$2 billion each year by 2011. Administration of the tobacco tax was also highly cost-effective. Estimated cost-effectiveness ratio for administration of the tobacco tax: US$75.40 per DALY averted.

SCALE: National, targeting 11.4 million smokers in 1991.

In the time it takes to read this sentence, someone will have died from a tobacco-related illness. Each year, tobacco use claims almost six million lives—a rate of one death every six seconds. And the global burden of smoking-related disease continues to grow, driven by the massive spread of tobacco use in low- and middle-income countries.[1]

Smoking is proven to cause an astounding array of diseases, from lung cancer to heart disease, emphysema, and low birth weight in infants. Inspired by a growing understanding of tobacco's health toll, international institutions such as the World Health Organization (WHO), the World Bank, and the International Monetary Fund are beginning to help countries strengthen measures to limit and control the use of tobacco.[2] Yet approximately one billion smokers around the world continue to light up each day—a habit that will literally be the death of many of them.[3]

Across the globe, Big Tobacco[4] spent the second half of the 20th century using aggressive, clever advertising to

increase its reach and snare new customers, targeting children and adolescents.[5] It also used international trade agreements such at the General Agreement on Tariffs and Trade (GATT) to force access to new markets across the globe. Many low- and middle-income countries already had domestic tobacco industries and popular indigenous tobacco products, but as smoking (particularly the smoking of manufactured cigarettes) gained popularity, their governments were unprepared to counter the onslaught of marketing and lobbying by multinational companies.

Bolstered by the growing body of scientific evidence and changing public opinion, backlash against multinational tobacco companies eventually galvanized global action. By the time the international response to the tobacco threat gained momentum in the early years of the 21st century, one Southeast Asian country—Thailand—already had more than a decade of experience in implementing serious tobacco control measures, paving the way for its neighbors.[6]

This case was originally authored by Rachel Silverman.

Starting in the 1990s, Thailand introduced a series of restrictions on the sale and use of tobacco products, including advertising bans, aggressive health warnings, prohibitions on public smoking, and high excise taxes. (These measures later gained global popularity under the WHO's Framework Convention on Tobacco Control.) The result of Thailand's campaign: smoking among men fell by roughly a third between 1991 and 2007, hundreds of thousands of lives will likely be saved by 2026, and an additional US$2 billion in annual excise taxes on tobacco products have helped fill government coffers. And while Thailand still faces challenges, including a resurgence of tobacco use among adolescents, the Thai model of tobacco control has proved itself as a feasible and cost-saving approach with important lessons for other governments.

The Toll of Tobacco Use

Smoking's fleeting pleasures are countered by a harsh reality: smokers are gradually self-administering an addictive and highly dangerous cocktail of poisons. Cigarette smoke contains 250 toxic chemicals, including 69 known carcinogens such as arsenic, cyanide, and carbon monoxide.[7] The consequences of smoking are numerous and severe. Half of all smokers will die prematurely as a result of a tobacco-related illness, while many more will suffer from nonfatal health problems that will substantially reduce their quality of life.[8]

Smoking affects almost all essential human anatomical functions. Smokers are 25 times as likely to develop lung cancer as those who abstain from tobacco use, and smoking is causally linked to many other common and lethal cancers. Tobacco is the culprit behind much of the world's growing burden of chronic disease, more than doubling smokers' risk of stroke and coronary heart disease and causing a 12-fold increase in the risk of death from chronic obstructive pulmonary disease.[9] At the same time, smoking-related lung damage increases vulnerability to major infectious diseases, particularly influenza, tuberculosis, and pneumonia.[10] Even secondhand smoke is a killer—especially to fetuses and young children. Smoke exposure during pregnancy heightens the risk of low birth weight and sudden infant death syndrome, and infants in a smoke-filled home are at increased risk of respiratory illness.[11] All these conditions place a mammoth strain on health systems.

In aggregate, the global burden of tobacco-related disease is staggering: 6.3 million deaths and 156 million disability-adjusted life years (DALYs) were attributed to tobacco use in 2010, making tobacco the single largest behavioral or environmental risk factor for mortality at the global level.[12] The burden is concentrated in low- and middle-income countries, home to 80 percent of all smokers, and disproportionately borne by society's poorest strata.[13] People pay a high cost for their addiction; smokers living in poverty use scarce resources that could otherwise pay for food, healthcare, education, or housing. The poor also suffer disproportionately from tobacco-related illnesses and the high medical costs that result, helping perpetuate health inequity.[14]

In Thailand as elsewhere in Southeast Asia, smoking grew in popularity during the 20th century. By 1991, nearly 60 percent of adult men and 5 percent of adult women (older than 15) were regularly lighting up cigarettes.[15] Smoking was far more common among the poorest quintile of Thai households, where men were almost twice as likely to smoke as their counterparts among the richest fifth of Thais.[16]

Ubiquitous tobacco use took a serious health toll in Thailand, particularly for men who smoked heavily. By 1990, lung cancer was the second most common cancer among men (eclipsed only by liver cancer), and the rate of new cases was more than twice as high for men as for women.[17] Chronic and respiratory diseases were also on the rise, leading the eminent Oxford epidemiologist Sir Richard Peto to predict in 1988 that one million Thai children would eventually die from the effects of smoking.[18] Smokeless tobacco use also harmed women. In 1990, for example, the incidence of lip cancer was seven times higher among Thai women than among men.[19]

Putting an Idea in Motion: Thailand Counters Big Tobacco

Beginning in the 1940s, Thailand's government kept the Thai tobacco industry under tight control. The Tobacco Monopoly Act, passed in 1943, protected the government-owned Thai Tobacco Monopoly (TTM) and outlawed foreign products. For nearly half a century, the relatively passive TTM manufactured low-quality cigarettes but eschewed advertising and promotion of its products.[20] By the 1970s, the Thai Medical Association had also secured early victories for tobacco control, including health warnings on cigarette packets and Bangkok-wide smoking bans in movie theaters and on buses.[21]

In the mid-1980s, however, those early tobacco control wins encountered a dangerous adversary: multinational tobacco companies intent on entering the Thai market. Thailand and its fellow "Asian tigers," with their large populations and booming economies, were attractive targets for the expansionist tobacco industry. Big Tobacco saw an opportunity to use international trade rules to force open the Thai market.[22]

First came advertising. Although the Thai government had prohibited foreign tobacco companies from selling in Thailand, international brands could still flood Thai media with advertisements for their products. Frightened by the sudden specter of competition, the TTM itself began advertising.[23]

Antitobacco activists saw the coming storm and realized it was time to get organized. In 1986, a small band of dedicated advocates joined forces to create the Thai Anti-smoking Campaign Project (TASCP, also known as ASH Thailand). In its formative years, TASCP pursued two strategies to lead a Thai antismoking movement. First, its members educated the public about the dangers of smoking and mobilized broad support for tobacco control. TASCP proved adept at generating media coverage of people suffering from pulmonary disease to illustrate the human cost of tobacco addiction. The group's subsequent initiatives were similar: a documentary on the life of an emphysema patient, a poster campaign to counter a harmful tradition ("Offering cigarettes to monks is a sin"), and a press conference calling for legislation to prevent the eventual deaths of a million children. Second, TASCP facilitated public lobbying by building relationships with government officials and helping shape public and media discourse on relevant legislation.[24]

TASCP's approach quickly paid off. In 1988, TASCP pressure led the government to revoke its previous approval for the TTM to build a new factory, and its lobbying helped secure a ban on cigarette advertising the following year. But poor enforcement of the advertising ban meant that international tobacco companies continued to flout the regulation. Big Tobacco made another stride when, in 1989, it successfully petitioned GATT to strike down Thailand's import ban, forcing Thailand to allow the first sales of foreign tobacco products in 1991. However, the trade dispute had mobilized public opinion against tobacco companies. Over the following two decades, the coalition of advocates led by TASCP seized the public momentum and pushed for a series of tough new laws to curb tobacco use and distribution.[25]

In the meantime, the WHO's 2003 Framework Convention on Tobacco Control (FCTC) provided a strong foundation for international tobacco control.[26] By the time Thailand ratified the FCTC in 2004, it had already implemented almost all of the FCTC's recommended tobacco control measures.

Thailand's Tobacco Control Policy in Action

Thailand's approach to tobacco control was multifaceted and comprehensive, targeting both supply and demand while also tackling the problem of secondhand smoke. The extensive set of restrictions and control measures can be loosely grouped into seven approaches:

1. *Tax increases.* Between 1991 and 2009, Thailand progressively raised excise taxes on cigarettes, from 55 percent to 85 percent of the factory price. Tobacco products were also subject to normal value-added tax (VAT), a special "health tax" of 2 percent to fund antitobacco health promotion (as of 2001), and later an additional surcharge to fund the Thai Public Broadcasting Service.[27]

2. *Restrictions on sales and distribution.* Major restrictions on tobacco sales and distribution came into force with the 1992 Tobacco Products Control Act. The legislation prohibited the sale of cigarettes to children under 18, banned distribution of free samples of tobacco products, and forbade the sale of tobacco products via vending machines.[28]

3. *Restrictions on advertising and marketing.* Thailand had already banned most forms of tobacco advertising. Now, the Tobacco Products Control Act also outlawed advertisements for nontobacco products using tobacco brand names and the use of contests and promotions that could incentivize tobacco purchases.[29] In 2005, Thailand further strengthened the ban by prohibiting tobacco advertising at the point of sale—no more flashy signs and displays.[30]

4. *Aggressive health warnings.* New health warnings ensured that smokers would recognize the health consequences of smoking. Starting in 1993, Thailand's modest cigarette carton warnings grew progressively larger and more gruesome. New regulations required that graphic health warnings cover at least a quarter of the total package surface, a portion that increased to more than half by 2009.[31]

5. *Restrictions on public smoking.* Measures to reduce demand were coupled with laws to shield nonsmokers from secondhand smoke. In 1992 the Thai government passed an act that gave the Ministry of Health authority to limit smoking in specific public places at its discretion.[32] The first completely smoke-free locations included public transport and cinemas, and smokers were limited to private rooms or designated areas in schools, hospitals, stores, government offices, and other public institutions.[33] The Ministry of Health has expanded the list of smoke-free zones repeatedly over time.

6. *Innovative financing for health promotion.* In 2001, the Thai government established the Thai Health Promotion Foundation, called ThaiHealth for short, as an autonomous state agency. ThaiHealth receives about US$120 million a year from a specially earmarked 2 percent tax on all tobacco and alcohol sales.[34] The organization works with nongovernmental organizations and the public to support antitobacco and other health campaigns. ThaiHealth has demonstrated a savvy approach to promoting healthy behavior. For example, it attracted international acclaim for a 2012 advertising campaign that enlisted young child actors to ask adult smokers for a light. The adults universally refused, citing the dangers of smoking. "If you smoke you die faster," replied one man. "Don't you want to live and play?" The child responded by chiding him: "You worry about me—but why not about yourself?"[35]

7. *Monitoring and evaluation.* Since 1976, regular household surveys have assessed smoking prevalence and trends.[36] As a signatory to the FCTC, Thailand submits regular reports on progress to the WHO.[37] In 2009, Thailand also became one of 16 low- and middle-income countries to participate in the WHO's Global Adult Tobacco Survey (GATS), helping to monitor tobacco use, secondhand smoke, attitudes, enforcement of smoking bans, and illicit advertising.[38]

The Payoff: Fewer Smokers, Healthier Thais

Even with aggressive tobacco control measures, change in Thailand took time. Tobacco's addictive qualities mean that major changes in smoking behavior are most likely to occur when new generations avoid getting hooked in the first place. Further, the health effects of tobacco are long term and cumulative, meaning that population-level health gains from tobacco control will only appear after a decade or more.

The long-term trends are clear: following Thailand's crackdown on Big Tobacco, smoking rates declined significantly, and the health gains are now starting to emerge. Between 1991 and 2007, smoking prevalence among Thai adults aged 15 and older declined from 59 percent to 42 percent for men, and from 5 percent to 2 percent for women (Figure 1).[39]

Figure 1. Adult (15+) Smoking Prevalence in Thailand, 1991–2007

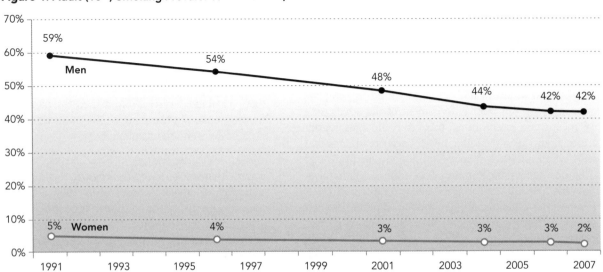

Source: WHO Country Office for Thailand (2015a).

Using the widely validated SimSmoke model (Box 1), researchers estimated that Thailand's smoking rates in 2006 were 25 percent lower among men and 24 percent lower among women than they would have been if not for the implementation of new laws and regulations.[40] Given scientific estimates of the link between smoking and heightened risk of death, they calculate that Thai tobacco policies saved about 32,000 lives between 1991 and 2006—and that if current trends continue, a total of almost 320,000 lives will be saved by 2026.[41]

Thailand's reductions in smoking prevalence have started to improve health. Between 1987 and 1997, the adult male mortality rate—the likelihood that a 15-year-old male will die before his 60th birthday—had gradually increased from 21 percent to 27 percent; meanwhile,

adult mortality among women had remained relatively constant between 13 percent and 14 percent. But over the following decade and a half, those trends reversed: by 2012, the adult mortality rate had fallen to 21 percent among men and 11 percent among women.[42] Many factors underlie Thais' lengthening life span, and reductions in smoking undoubtedly played a key role.

The health payoff also shows in incidence trends for many diseases attributable to smoking. For example, lung cancer incidence in men skyrocketed from 4 cases per 100,000 people in 1985 to 27 cases per 100,000 people in 1997. But incidence plateaued over the next decade and was less than 25 cases per 100,000 from 2001 to 2003.[43] Emphysema deaths peaked at 6 per 100,000 in 2003 but fell to 4 per 100,000 by 2009.[44]

Box 1. **Strength of the Evidence**

The evidence for tobacco control is extensive and robust. However, policy impact is difficult to trace due to the absence of a comparable counterfactual—that is, we do not know for sure what smoking prevalence and health status would have been in Thailand if not for its antitobacco campaign. As a result, the WHO and others rely heavily on the SimSmoke model to tease apart the effects of specific policy changes from long-term tobacco use trends. The SimSmoke model works by measuring the number of current smokers, ex-smokers, and never-smokers in the population and tracking these groups over time. Through its inclusion of parameters for policy measures, SimSmoke can be used to predict how tobacco use will evolve in the future under different policy scenarios. It can also retrospectively construct a counterfactual of how tobacco use would have evolved if policy changes had not gone into effect.

David Levy, of Georgetown University, is the architect of the SimSmoke model. Levy and his colleagues applied the model in Thailand to estimate the impact of the tobacco control campaign.[45] To ensure that the model was calibrated appropriately for the Thai context, they compared predicted results from the model with the observed data on smoking status from past surveys. They then set the model to reflect the 1991 policy scenario and projected forward to 2006, assuming no changes in the policy environment. Subtracting actual observed tobacco use from the projected rates, researchers found that smoking rates in 2006 were roughly a quarter lower than they would have been if Thailand had stuck with its 1991 status quo.

The researchers' next step was to translate changes in smoking behavior into differences in mortality, comparing the relative risk of death for current smokers, ex-smokers, and never-smokers over time. In the absence of needed risk data from Thailand, the researchers were obliged to use cause-specific risk-of-death data from an epidemiologically and economically similar setting, Taiwan, and apply them to the total deaths in Thailand. The result: the researchers estimated that Thailand's tobacco control measures saved 32,000 lives between 1991 and 2006 and will save another 288,000 lives by 2026.

Can we believe the modeled results? Ultimately, their validity depends on whether the underlying assumptions hold true for the Thai population. The authors' validation exercise increases confidence that the model accurately reflects the role of policy change on tobacco use. But the second step, the jump from smoking to death, is less certain. In particular, the authors note that different estimates of the relationship between tobacco use and death would dramatically change their findings. In the United States, smoking more than doubles the risk of death. If that held true in Thailand, the estimated lives saved would leap to 540,000. But if the real relative risk for Thailand is closer to the relationship between smoking and death observed in China—just a 35 percent increase in risk—their estimates will overstate the impact. In the latter case, the real figure would be closer to 221,000 deaths averted.

Gains at What Price?

Many tobacco control measures are actually *cost saving* due to the revenue generated from increased taxes, the low cost of legislative interventions, and the reduced burden on the health system. Other effective measures, such as mass media campaigns and the creation of government agencies to enforce tobacco laws, require a substantial up-front investment.[46] Nonetheless, they are highly cost-effective: the WHO has estimated that the price tag for a comprehensive tobacco control package is just US$0.11 per person per year, making these interventions among their "best buys" to reduce noncommunicable diseases.[47]

In Thailand, the only major expense came via the ThaiHealth health promotion fund, which was financed through an additional dedicated surcharge on alcohol and tobacco. Even better, tobacco taxes provided a major source of revenue for the government, money that helped solidify the government's political commitment and could be reinvested in improving population health. As tax rates went up, total government revenue from the excise tax increased roughly fourfold, from less than US$500 million in 1992 to nearly US$2 billion in 2011.[48] The excise tax also became an increasingly significant contributor to the overall budget, accounting for about 3.5 percent of total tax revenue in 2011.[49]

Analysis of the health impact of Thailand's aggressive approach to tobacco control done by researchers for *Millions Saved* suggests that the government and its partners averted 125,000 DALYs from lung cancer, 86,000 DALYs from chronic obstructive pulmonary disease, and 330,000 DALYs from cardiovascular disease, for a combined total of 541,695 DALYs by 2006. We then estimated the cost-effectiveness of one part of the approach—the administration of the taxation—based on changes in death and disability from three major tobacco-related health outcomes: lung cancer, chronic obstructive pulmonary disease, and cardiovascular disease.[50] Working from previous studies that price the administration of tobacco tax increases at about 0.005 percent of gross national product, we estimate that administration of Thailand's tobacco tax cost around US$25 million from 1991 to 2006.[51] These figures yielded an estimated cost-effectiveness ratio of US$75.40 per DALY averted—this is highly cost-effective in relation to Thailand's gross domestic product per capita of US$3,143.[52]

The Keys to Lasting Success

The Thai government had a solid foundation of favorable public opinion for its tobacco control policies—including surprisingly strong support among smokers. The trade dispute with Big Tobacco had ignited a public outcry, and Thai citizens accepted increasingly strict measures. For example, a 1993 poll of Bangkok residents found that 70 percent supported an increase in the tax rate on tobacco products—including 60 percent of current smokers. This evidence was used to lobby government officials who feared public backlash, helping advocates overcome institutional inertia and secure the first major tax increase later that year.[53]

Even better, support for stricter tobacco laws increased even after the first control measures were introduced. Survey data from 2006 showed that Thai smokers were more amenable to tobacco control laws than smokers in other countries. For example, 90 percent of Thai smokers supported a complete ban on indoor smoking at restaurants, compared with only 40 percent of smokers in France and 21 percent of smokers in China.[54] Over time, the level of public support empowered policymakers to resist lobbying from the tobacco industry and strengthen regulations.

Another key to Thailand's success was the comprehensive nature of the intervention package. Successful health promotion campaigns, including pictorial warnings on cigarette boxes, supplemented the restrictive regulations on tobacco sales, advertising, and use. By 2011, 97 percent of Thai adults knew that smoking was addictive and caused serious illness and 94 percent correctly identified the dangers of secondhand smoke.[55]

The win-win economics of tobacco control also helped maintain political commitment. Antismoking activists proposed a new source of government revenue, which helped garner support from the minister of finance.[56] With proceeds from the tobacco tax forming an increasing share of government revenue, opposition within the government receded. Likewise, advocates were able to secure funding for ThaiHealth by proposing an earmarked surcharge on top of the existing excise tax, rather than appealing for a share of existing funds.[57]

But the fight isn't over. Big Tobacco is a formidable enemy that continues to buy political influence and identify loopholes to gain market share and increase its hold.[58] Roll-your-own cigarettes are the preferred tobacco product for about half of Thai smokers, yet these cigarettes have remained largely outside the scope of tobacco control legislation.[59] Cigarette smugglers evade taxes and other control measures but are rarely prosecuted; their wares accounted for as much as 20 percent of Thailand's cigarette market in 2011.[60] Plus, enforcement remains uneven, particularly outside Bangkok, and consumers' exposure to point-of-sale advertisements almost tripled from 2009 to 2011.[61] These challenges have kept smoking prevalence stubbornly high among men despite recent declines.

Perhaps more worrisome, survey data suggest an uptick in smoking prevalence among young people ages 15 to 24, from 20 percent in 2009 to 22 percent in 2011. Younger smokers are far more likely than their elders to smoke cigarettes rather than smoke-free tobacco products, to purchase "loose" individual cigarettes instead of full packs, and to prefer manufactured cigarettes to roll-your-own varieties.[62] Together, these trends suggest Thais' shift away from indigenous forms of tobacco use toward the blandishments of international consumerism.

In response to these emerging challenges, the Thai government has sustained its commitment to the fight against tobacco. For example, in 2004 a cabinet directive prohibited tobacco company interference with policymaking, including a ban on gifts of any kind from representatives of tobacco companies to public officials.[63]

Implications for Global Health

By 2015, the WHO's FCTC had been ratified by 178 United Nations member states. Although the prevalence of global tobacco use has dipped in recent years, the absolute number of smokers and the global burden of tobacco-related illness have continued to rise.[64]

Big Tobacco is a savvy, relentless enemy whose profits depend on developing, manufacturing, and marketing products that cause ill health and death. Thailand was one of the first low- and middle-income countries to take tobacco control seriously, which meant that Thailand was also among the first to confront this transnational foe. Thailand's story shows that with sustained political commitment, aggressive tobacco control measures can push back Big Tobacco and substantially reduce the prevalence of tobacco. It also demonstrates the need for constant vigilance: as Thailand cracked down, the tobacco industry adapted and fought back. Governments must recognize that tobacco control is a long-term fight and that successful antismoking measures require adaptability, constant monitoring, and an aggressive defensive strategy.

Thailand's approach to tobacco control may have implications for other leading drivers of noncommunicable disease. One obvious candidate for a coordinated approach is alcohol, a significant risk factor for liver disease, cardiovascular problems, and cancer.[65] Many staples of Thailand's tobacco control program—such as high taxation, health warnings, and a ban on media or point-of-sale advertising—could be equally well applied to alcohol. Already, the Philippines (see Box 2) has levied "sin taxes" on alcohol in an attempt to deter harmful overconsumption. Ultimately, other countries should continue to look to Thailand for inspiration, both to identify concrete measures to fight 21st-century vices and as a shining example of sustained political will to improve citizens' health.

Box 2. Alcohol: The Next Frontier?

Inspired by the success of tobacco taxation in Thailand, some countries have begun to explore so-called sin taxes to deter the consumption of alcohol, another product that is bad for its consumers. In 2012 the Philippines enacted a major tax increase on alcohol products (alongside tobacco products), designed to lower alcohol consumption and raise resources to expand the country's national health insurance program and health promotion campaigns.[66] The tax is planned to increase automatically every year until 2017.[67]

It remains to be seen whether the new sin tax will help reduce alcohol consumption and boost health. In the tax's first year, the sales volume of fermented drinks dropped 12 percent, but the sales volume of distilled spirits skyrocketed 26 percent, possibly indicating consumers' pivot toward higher-proof, more potent forms of alcohol.[68]

Although the long-term effect of the sin tax on the country's health will be clear only over time, its positive effect on the government's treasury is already obvious: in 2013, the new alcohol and tobacco taxes provided additional revenues of PHP34 billion (about US$758 million).[69]

REFERENCES

Adulyadej, Bhumibol. 1992a. *Non-smokers' Health Protection Act B.E. 2535.* http://www.tobaccocontrollaws.org/files/live/Thailand/Thailand%20-%20Non-smokers%20HPA%20.pdf.

———. 1992b. *Tobacco Products Control Act B.E. 2535.* http://www.tobaccocontrollaws.org/files/live/Thailand/Thailand%20-%20TPCA%20B.E.%202535.pdf.

Arcavi, Lidia, and Neal L. Benowitz. 2004. "Cigarette Smoking and Infection." *Archives of Internal Medicine* 164 (20): 2206. doi:10.1001/archinte.164.20.2206.

Bureau of Policy and Strategy, Ministry of Public Health. 2011. *Thailand Health Profile Report 2008–2010.* Bangkok, Thailand: Bureau of Policy and Strategy, Ministry of Public Health. http://wops.moph.go.th/ops/thp/thp/en/index.php?id=288&group_=05&page=view_doc.

Campaign for Tobacco-Free Kids. 2010. *Big Tobacco: Exposing Its Deadly Tactics.* Washington, DC: Campaign for Tobacco-Free Kids. http://global.tobaccofreekids.org/files/pdfs/en/ExposeBigTobac_Final.pdf.

Charoenca, Naowarut, Jeremiah Mock, Nipapun Kungskulniti, Sunida Preechawong, Nicholas Kojetin, and Stephen L. Hamann. 2012. "Success Counteracting Tobacco Company Interference in Thailand: An Example of FCTC Implementation for Low- and Middle-Income Countries." *International Journal of Environmental Research and Public Health* 9 (4): 1111–34.

Chisholm, Dan, Dele Abegunde, and Shanthi Mendis. 2011. *Scaling Up Action against Noncommunicable Diseases: How Much Will It Cost?* Geneva: World Health Organization.

Diaz, Jess. 2013. "Higher Sin Taxes Take Effect Today." *Philippine Star,* January 1.

Dorotheo, Ulysses, Sophapan Ratanachena, Bungon Ritthiphakdee, Mary Assunta, Domilyn Villarreiz, and Jennie Lyn Reyes. 2013. *ASEAN Tobacco Tax Report Card: Regional Comparisons and Trends.* Bangkok, Thailand: Southeast Asia Tobacco Control Alliance. http://seatca.org/dmdocuments/ASEANTaxReportCardMay13forWEB.pdf.

Fernandez, Aaron Neil. 2014. "Revisiting the Sin Tax Law." *Business World Online,* June 12.

GATS (Global Adult Tobacco Survey). 2012. *Fact Sheet: Thailand 2011.* http://global.tobaccofreekids.org/files/pdfs/en/GATS_thailand_2011.pdf.

———. n.d. *Comparison Fact Sheet: Thailand 2009 and 2011.* http://www.who.int/tobacco/surveillance/survey/gats/thailand_fact_sheet_thailand_2009_2011.pdf?ua=1.

IHME (Institute for Health Metrics and Evaluation). 2015. Global Health Data Exchange. Accessed November 3. http://ghdx.healthdata.org/.

ITC Project (International Tobacco Control Policy Evaluation Project). 2009. *ITC Thailand Summary.* Bangkok, Thailand: Thai Health Promotion Foundation. http://www.itcproject.org/files/Report_Publications/National_Summary/itcthailand4pagesummaryenglish.pdf.

Levy, D.T., S. Benjakul, H. Ross, and B. Ritthiphakdee. 2008. "The Role of Tobacco Control Policies in Reducing Smoking and Deaths in a Middle Income Nation: Results from the Thailand SimSmoke Simulation Model." *Tobacco Control* 17 (1): 53–59. doi:10.1136/tc.2007.022319.

Ministry of Public Health. 2005. *Directive Procedures for Distribution of Tobacco Products.* Bangkok, Thailand: Ministry of Public Health. http://www.tobaccocontrollaws.org/files/live/Thailand/Thailand%20-%202005%20POS%20Directive.pdf.

———. 2009. "Ministry of Public Health Notice of Rules, Procedures, and Conditions for the Display and Content of Cigarette Labels." *Government Gazette,* September 30, sec. 143 D. http://www.tobaccocontrollaws.org/files/live/Thailand/Thailand%20-%20Cigarette%20Label%20Regs%202009.pdf.

Mirelman, Andrew, Amanda Glassman, and Miriam Temin. 2016. *Estimating the Avertable Disease Burden and Cost-Effectiveness in* Millions Saved *Third Edition.* CGD Working Paper. Washington, DC: Center for Global Development.

National Cancer Institute. 2015. "Harms of Cigarette Smoking and Health Benefits of Quitting." Accessed July 30. http://www.cancer.gov/cancertopics/factsheet/Tobacco/cessation.

National Institute on Alcohol Abuse and Alcoholism. 2015. "Alcohol's Effects on the Body." Accessed July 30. http://www.niaaa.nih.gov/alcohol-health/alcohols-effects-body.

Neal, Meghan. 2012. "Heartbreaking Thai 'Smoking Kids' Anti-Smoking Ad Goes Viral." *New York Daily News,* June 21. http://www.nydailynews.com/news/world/heartbreaking-thai-smoking-kids-anti-smoking-ad-viral-article-1.1100062.

Ranson, M. Kent, Prabhat Jha, Frank J. Chaloupka, and Son N. Nguyen. 2002. "Global and Regional Estimates of the Effectiveness and Cost-Effectiveness of Price Increases and Other Tobacco Control Policies." *Nicotine and Tobacco Research: Official Journal of the Society for Research on Nicotine and Tobacco* 4 (3): 311–19. doi:10.1080/14622200210141000.

Rivera, Danessa O. 2014. "PHL Exceeds Revenue Goal for Sin Tax in First Year with P34-B Collection." *GMA News Online,* January 23. http://www.gmanetwork.com/news/story/342322/money/personalfinance/phl-exceeds-revenue-goal-for-sin-tax-in-first-year-with-p34-b-collection.

Savedoff, William. 2014. "What's New in Tobacco Control?" *Views from the Center / Global Health Policy Blog,* Center for Global Development, June 2. http://www.cgdev.org/blog/what%E2%80%99s-new-tobacco-control.

REFERENCES, *continued*

Thai Health Promotion Foundation. 2015. "About Thai Health." Accessed August 4. http://en.thaihealth.or.th/WHO_WE_ARE/THAIHEALTH_INTRO/.

Thanasitthichai, Somchai. n.d. "National Cancer Institute and Cancer Epidemiology in Thailand." Presentation. http://hp.anamai.moph.go.th/download/%E0%B8%A7%E0%B8%B1%E0%B8%A2%E0%B8%97%E0%B8%B3%E0%B8%87%E0%B8%B2%E0%B8%99/Meeting13_14Mar.2557/EPI.breast.central.%E0%B8%99%E0%B8%9E.%E0%B8%AA%E0%B8%A1%E0%B8%8A%E0%B8%B2%E0%B8%A2.pdf.

Tobacco Control Research and Knowledge Management. n.d. *Thailand's Tobacco Use Surveillance: Smoking Prevalence, 1991–2006.* Bangkok, Thailand: Tobacco Control Research and Knowledge Management. http://www.trc.or.th/e15/images/upload/files/tobaccoinformation/Thailands_Tobacco_Use_Surveillance__Smoking_Prevalence_1991_-_2006.pdf.

US HHS (Department of Health and Human Services). 2014. *The Health Consequences of Smoking: 50 Years of Progress. A Report of the Surgeon General.* Atlanta, GA: HHS, Centers for Disease Control and Prevention, National Center for Chronic Disease Prevention and Health Promotion, Office on Smoking and Health.

Vatanasapt, V., N. Martin, and H. Sriplung. 1995. "Cancer Incidence in Thailand, 1988–1991." *Cancer Epidemiology, Biomarkers and Prevention* 4 (August): 475–83.

Vateesatokit, Prakit. 2003. "Tailoring Tobacco Control Efforts to the Country: The Example of Thailand." In *Tobacco Control Policy: Strategies, Successes, and Setbacks.* Washington DC: World Bank. http://siteresources.worldbank.org/INTPH/Resources/ch7.pdf.

Vateesatokit, Prakit, Benjamin Hughes, and Bungon Ritthphakdee. 2000. "Thailand: Winning Battles, but the War's Far from Over." *Tobacco Control* 9 (2): 122–27. doi:10.1136/tc.9.2.122.

Vateesatokit, Prakit, Tan Yen Lian, and Bungon Ritthiphakdee. 2011. *Lessons Learned in Establishing a Health Promotion Fund.* Bangkok, Thailand: Southeast Asia Tobacco Control Alliance.

Vateesatokit, Prakit, and Bung-on Ritthiphakdee. 1997. "Tobacco Control in Thailand." *Mahidol Journal* 4 (2): 73–82.

Visaruthvong, Chonlathan. 2010. *Thailand Tobacco Tax Report Card.* Bangkok, Thailand: Southeast Asia Tobacco Control Alliance. http://www.smoke-free.ca/trade-and-tobacco/Thailand/Thailand%20Tax%20Report%20Card%202010.pdf.

WHO (World Health Organization). 2004. *Tobacco and Poverty: A Vicious Circle.* Geneva: WHO.

———. 2011. *Joint National Capacity Assessment on the Implementation of Effective Tobacco Control Policies in Thailand.* Geneva: WHO.

———. 2015a. "GATS (Global Adult Tobacco Survey)." Accessed August 4. http://www.who.int/tobacco/surveillance/gats/en/.

———. 2015b. "Parties to the WHO Framework Convention on Tobacco Control." Accessed February 12. http://www.who.int/fctc/signatories_parties/en/.

———. 2015c. "Tobacco." *Fact Sheet 339.* July 6. http://www.who.int/mediacentre/factsheets/fs339/en/.

WHO Country Office for Thailand. 2015a. "Prevalence of Tobacco Use." Accessed October 27. http://www.searo.who.int/thailand/areas/tobaccoprevalence/en/.

———. 2015b. "Tobacco Taxation." Accessed August 4. http://www.searo.who.int/thailand/areas/tobaccotax/en/.

WHO FCTC (Framework Convention on Tobacco Control). 2015. "Thailand." Accessed August 4. http://www.who.int/fctc/reporting/party_reports/tha/en/.

World Bank. 2016. World DataBank. Accessed February 9. http://databank.worldbank.org/data/home.aspx.

ENDNOTES

1. WHO (2015c).
2. Savedoff (2014).
3. WHO (2015c).
4. "Big Tobacco" is a common colloquial term that refers to the largest transnational tobacco companies, primarily Phillip Morris, British American Tobacco, Japan Tobacco International, Reemstra, and Altadis (see http://www.who.int/tobacco/en/atlas18.pdf).
5. Campaign for Tobacco-Free Kids (2010).
6. Starting in 1995, Poland also introduced comprehensive tobacco control. Its successful campaign is featured in the original *Millions Saved.*
7. National Cancer Institute (2015).
8. WHO (2015c).
9. US HHS (2014).
10. Arcavi and Benowitz (2004).
11. US HSS (2014).
12. Arcavi and Benowitz (2004).
13. WHO (2015c, 339).
14. WHO (2004).
15. WHO Country Office for Thailand (2015a).
16. Tobacco Control Research and Knowledge Management (n.d.).
17. Vatanasapt, Martin, and Sriplung (1995).
18. Vateesatokit (2003).
19. Vatanasapt, Martin, and Sriplung (1995).
20. Vateesatokit, Hughes, and Ritthphakdee (2000).
21. Vateesatokit (2003).

REFERENCES, *continued*

22. Vateesatokit, Hughes, and Ritthphakdee (2000).
23. Vateesatokit (2003).
24. Vateesatokit (2003); Vateesatokit, Hughes, and Ritth- phakdee (2000).
25. Vateesatokit (2003); Vateesatokit, Hughes, and Ritth- phakdee (2000).
26. WHO (2015b).
27. Visaruthvong (2010).
28. Adulyadej (1992b).
29. Adulyadej (1992b).
30. Ministry of Public Health (2005).
31. Vateesatokit and Ritthiphakdee (n.d.); Ministry of Public Health (2009).
32. Adulyadej (1992a).
33. Vateesatokit and Ritthiphakdee (1997).
34. Thai Health Promotion Foundation (2015).
35. Neal (2012).
36. Vateesatokit (2003).
37. WHO FCTC (2015).
38. WHO (2015a).
39. WHO Country Office for Thailand (2015a).
40. Levy et al. (2008).
41. Levy et al. (2008).
42. World Bank (2015).
43. Thanasitthichai (n.d.).
44. Bureau of Policy and Strategy, Ministry of Public Health (2011).
45. Levy et al. (2008).
46. Levy et al. (2008).
47. Chisholm, Abegunde, and Mendis (2011).
48. Dorotheo et al. (2013); WHO Country Office for Thailand (2015b).
49. Author's calculations based on figures above; World Bank (2015).

50. IHME (2015).
51. Ranson et al. (2002); Levy et al. (2008).
52. Estimation of total DALYs averted through tobacco taxation came from lung cancer, chronic obstructive pulmonary disease, and cardiovascular disease in people older than 30 (IHME 2015). Averted deaths figures were from Levy et al. (2008), and associated parameters of attribution, duration, and disability weights were used. Final DALY estimates were validated against the WHO Global Health Estimates. Costs came from literature on costs of fiscal tax policies (Ranson et al. 2002). See Mirelman, Glassman, and Temin (2016).
53. Vateesatokit (2003).
54. ITC Project (2009).
55. ITC Project (2009).
56. Vateesatokit (2003).
57. Vateesatokit, Lian, and Ritthiphakdee (2011).
58. Vateesatokit, Hughes, and Ritthphakdee (2000).
59. GATS (2012).
60. WHO (2011).
61. GATS (2012, n.d.).
62. GATS (2012).
63. Charoenca (2012).
64. National Institute on Alcohol Abuse and Alcoholism (2015).
65. National Institute on Alcohol Abuse and Alcoholism (2015).
66. Diaz (2013); Fernandez (2014).
67. Diaz (2013); Fernandez (2014).
68. Fernandez (2014).
69. Rivera (2014).

CASE 19

Improving Road Safety
Vietnam's Comprehensive Helmet Law

The Case at a Glance

HEALTH GOAL: To reduce road-traffic head injuries and deaths.

STRATEGY: Coordinated, multipronged plan building on national Helmet Day to change helmet-wearing behavior at scale, including expanded enforcement and a large financial penalty for noncompliance.

HEALTH IMPACT: 1,557 lives saved and 2,495 serious injuries prevented (2008).

WHY IT WORKED: Careful preplanning and coordination of multiple elements. Strengthened traffic police force for effective enforcement. Hefty fines to deter noncompliance. Widespread compliance with the new law on Helmet Day. High-level government leadership. Hard-hitting information campaigns. Local availability of affordable helmets appropriate to the hot, humid climate.

FINANCING: Cost about US$24 million for new helmets and police salaries. Estimated cost-effectiveness ratio: US$1,248 per disability-adjusted life year averted.

SCALE: National.

Some motorcyclists walk away from a crash with a few scratches and bruises, but others suffer lifelong consequences or even death. Head injuries are common in motorcycle accidents; brain trauma can leave injured motorcyclists with personality changes, cognitive impairment, and disabilities that force them to use a wheelchair for life.

In a motorcycle accident, high-quality helmets can reduce the risk of death by 40 percent and the risk of serious injury by more than 70 percent.[1] Riders who forgo a helmet put their lives at risk with every ride, a common scenario where helmet laws are weak, not comprehensive, or nonexistent. This was the situation in the mid-1990s in Vietnam, where a booming economy prompted many Vietnamese to upgrade from bicycles to motorcycles.[2] As of 2014, more than 40 million motorbikes filled Vietnam's busy streets every day, accounting for nearly 95 percent of all Vietnamese road traffic.[3] And these numbers are rising further as the economy continues to grow.

Mandatory helmet laws can persuade riders to wear helmets and thus reduce the frequency and severity of head injuries.[4] Yet in the early years of the 21st century, despite Vietnam's efforts to require helmet use, less than one-third of motorcyclists were donning helmets.[5] With so many unprotected drivers and passengers on Vietnam's crowded streets, the country had a sky-high traffic fatality rate.[6]

In mid-2007, Prime Minister Nguyen Tan Dung announced a new, simple law: starting December 15 of that year—"Helmet Day"—all motorcycle riders would be required to wear helmets on all roads. Those who did not would be subject to a hefty fine from traffic police. A wide range of partners worked with the national government to put the law in place, communicate its contents, and enforce it, including the World Health Organization (WHO), the Asia Injury Prevention Foundation, and private corporations. Thanks to government leadership, the deterrent effect of fines, and policy changes to close loopholes, more than 90 percent of Vietnamese motorcyclists were wearing helmets by 2013.[7]

This case was originally authored by Miriam Temin, with contributions by Jonathan Passmore.

The Toll of Road Traffic Injuries

The most serious disabilities and deaths following motor-cycle crashes are from head and neck injuries.[8] Even after a minor crash, a motorcyclist may feel the effects of a hard knock to the head: severe headache, nausea, dizziness, and blurred vision in the short term; memory loss, depression, and a host of other life-changing problems in the long term.[9] The injured rider may be left unable to perform daily tasks; make decisions; or see, hear, or speak. Traumatic brain damage is often debilitating; it can also be fatal.

The rising toll of motorcycle deaths in low- and middle-income countries is part of a global trend that has accompanied economic growth, increased urbanization, and the desire for personal motorized transport. In some of these countries, head injuries caused nearly 90 percent of motorcycle deaths in 2013.[10] Road traffic injuries account for an increasing proportion of all deaths worldwide.[11] If current trends continue, road traffic deaths are predicted to be the fifth leading cause of death worldwide by 2030.[12] In absolute terms, the total number of road traffic deaths is surprisingly high: around 1.24 million every year—about the same as the number of deaths from tuberculosis and twice the number of deaths caused by malaria.

Vietnam's traffic is among the most dangerous in the world.[13] The roads themselves are extremely hazardous. Dangerous habits such as drunk driving are common, and the roads are packed with drivers and riders who often flout the rules. Important traffic laws are in place but not consistently enforced.[14] In 2007, traffic accidents were the leading cause of death among working-age Vietnamese. That year, around 14,000 people, including 2,000 children, lost their lives in traffic accidents.[15] In addition, traffic accidents caused more than 30,000 head and severe brain injuries. And the real toll may be up to a third higher, given underreporting.[16]

Experts estimated that nearly 60 percent of those who lost their lives were motorcycle riders.[17] Despite their risks, motorcycles had become ubiquitous in Vietnam as the economy took off and the pace of life sped up. From the early 1990s to the early years of the following decade, the number of motorcycles on the road climbed steadily. The recorded number quadrupled in just five years, from 5 million in 2002 to more than 20 million by 2007—about one for every four Vietnamese people.[18] As motorcycle ownership boomed, laws covering helmet use remained out of date.

The toll of motorcycle injuries was emotional as well as economic—especially when accidents ended in death or traumatic brain injury. A study by the Asian Development Bank found that as early as 2003, road accidents and their consequences were costing Vietnam at least US$900 million each year, equal to 2.7 percent of the country's gross domestic product (GDP).[19]

Putting an Idea in Motion: Vietnam Takes Action as Traffic Injuries Take Off

The government had begun to take on motorcycle safety as early as the mid-1990s, yet the toll of motorcycle-related deaths continued to grow. In 2001, the first mandatory helmet use law required helmets on national highways and provincial roads. This covered less than a quarter of the country's road system and excluded cities, where motorcycle use was most common. And the law imposed only a minor fine for noncompliance.[20]

In subsequent years, the government continued to expand helmet legislation, for example, to mandate helmet use on all roads.[21] However, the regulations encountered major implementation and enforcement barriers.[22] Traffic police struggled to keep up with the explosion of motorcycle ownership as drivers routinely disregarded the laws—which was somewhat understandable, given the cost of purchasing a helmet and the discomfort of wearing one in the hot climate. According to one journalist, motorcycle riders dubbed helmets "rice cookers"; even after new legislation took hold, he reported that the government's "warnings, celebrity entreaties, and grainy pictures of people drooling from head injuries just unleashed angry protests by riders."[23] With just a small chance of receiving a minor penalty, most motorcyclists did without.[24] Traffic accidents reached an all-time high in 2002.

Then, in 2002, new leadership in the government's National Traffic Safety Committee (NTSC) and other factors created a window for action. Bui Huynh Long, the incoming director of the NTSC, had come from the Ministry of Transport, where he had a track record of support for helmet legislation.[25] His passionate, committed leadership gave international supporters in the Global Road Safety Partnership and other organizations a solid government partner for collaboration.[26]

Long's arrival at the NTSC coincided with helmet initiatives from several international partners. Among them was the Hanoi-based Asia Injury Prevention (AIP)

Foundation, founded by Greig Craft, an American who suspected that a law would change behavior only if people had helmets they were willing to wear. In 2002 the AIP Foundation had opened a factory in Hanoi that produced high-quality helmets for use in tropical settings. The Vietnam Safety Products and Equipment Company produced roughly half a million Protec Tropical Helmets in its first dozen years of operation.[27]

It took several more years to develop the comprehensive helmet law—"Resolution 32"—but by 2007 it was ready. Prime Minister Dung helped announce the new law, which made helmet use mandatory in Vietnam for all motorcycle drivers and passengers on all roads. The law would go into effect on December 15, 2007, the first-ever Helmet Day.[28] In August, in preparation, the government required all its employees—around four million people—plus members of the armed forces to don helmets.[29]

Unlike previous helmet reforms, this new law had support from the Communist Party. Party leadership had become convinced that improving road safety was a sufficiently urgent goal to require mass action. Provincial party chairs got involved by heading local NTSC chapters, and they became responsible to the government and the party leadership for traffic accidents in their localities.[30] Party leaders and other government workers also signed their own "commitments" to wear helmets themselves and to comply with other traffic safety rules.

Helmet Legislation in Action

Helmet Day signaled the launch of the comprehensive helmet law. The law was unambiguous: all riders and passengers needed to wear helmets on all roads—no exceptions.[31] But the strong legislation needed more than a flashy kickoff to improve compliance. Ongoing enforcement, penalties, adjustments, communications, and measurement were paramount to its successful implementation.

The law gave riders an incentive to comply: a substantial fine more than 10 times previous penalties. If caught, bareheaded motorcyclists were fined VND100,000–VND200,000 (US$6–US$12), one-third of the average monthly income.[32] This could be more than the price of some helmets, making it more economical to buy a helmet than to go without.[33] The traffic police were responsible for catching offenders and received training to do so effectively. In the year after the new law took force, police ticketed nearly 680,000 riders for their failure to comply, generating revenue for the state treasury.[34]

But riders already knew all about the new law. The groundwork for Helmet Day had been laid earlier in 2007 by a public education campaign spearheaded by the AIP Foundation with Ogilvy & Mather (Vietnam) dubbed "Enough Is Enough" and "No Excuses . . . Wear a Helmet." The hard-hitting, award-winning campaign used concerts, billboards, and television commercials to educate people about the benefits of helmets and the penalties for noncompliance.[35] The public education campaign didn't focus on helmet safety basics—riders already understood the dangers. Instead it focused on the "real" reasons for noncompliance: "It ruins my hair" and "It will look awful with my trendy clothes." The campaign countered these complaints by demonstrating that the effects of a serious head injury look far worse.[36]

The motorcycle helmet market expanded quickly as demand grew, but quality did not follow suit. Young people were soon seen wearing trendy yet flimsy helmets with cartoon and sports logos on them, "and equally dubious products with special holes at the back for . . . ponytails."[37] Helmet quality is still a major concern. A 2012 study found that fewer than one in five helmets passed safety tests, despite stricter regulatory standards starting in 2008.[38]

With the jump in helmet use, riders found new loopholes to exploit. For example, many riders would wear helmets but leave the chin straps unhooked. The government caught on, and in 2008 a new policy imposed a penalty for an unhooked strap, equal to the fine for riding without a helmet.[39]

Another challenge was presented by earlier legislation, which made it illegal to fine children under 16 for not wearing a helmet.[40] (About 80 percent of urban Vietnamese children rode motorcycles as passengers.[41]) Again, the government adjusted its policy: in 2010 it introduced helmet legislation making helmets mandatory for children ages six and older, with a fine for noncompliance.[42] Acquiring the helmets created a financial burden for some families, and the AIP Foundation stepped in to help families comply, distributing more than a quarter million free child-sized helmets through its Helmets for Kids campaign.[43]

The Payoff: Safer Riders, Fewer Head Injuries

Observational studies confirm that widespread behavior change followed the launch of Resolution 32. In the first days following Helmet Day, police and volunteers from the Youth Union monitored compliance on street corners;

95,000 commune police workers stepped in to help.[44] Starting in 2007, researchers from the Hanoi School of Public Health and the WHO collaborated to track helmet use before and after the law. They observed more than half a million motorcycle riders and passengers in 45 randomly selected sites across three provinces. Before Helmet Day in 2007, 40 percent of the observed riders wore helmets. By early 2011, they found that 93 percent of all observed riders were wearing helmets.[45]

Although Resolution 32 was released without specific plans for an impact evaluation, the Ministry of Health established a hospital-based surveillance system to track road traffic injuries and deaths. The data suggest that the helmet law and related initiatives achieved public health success. Researchers from the WHO and Ministry of Health estimate that Vietnam saw a 16 percent reduction in road traffic head injuries and an 18 percent reduction in road traffic deaths in the three months after the law's enactment.[46] Unfortunately, several hospitals stopped participating in the surveillance system over time, limiting analysis of the law's long-term impact.[47] According to ongoing surveillance at Hanoi's Viet Duc Hospital, one of the country's largest surgical centers, there were nearly 8 percent fewer head injuries among traffic-accident patients in 2010 than before the law, a statistically significant difference.[48]

The police also monitored implementation of the law. National police data suggest that Resolution 32 saved 1,600 lives and averted 2,500 serious injuries in its first year.[49] Given that police data often miss unreported injuries and fatalities, the real impact may be greater.[50] Another assessment, undertaken by the AIP Foundation, suggests that the law prevented 20,609 deaths and 412,175 serious injuries from 2008 to 2013 (see Box 1).[51]

Since these data were not generated through experimental methods, they should be interpreted with caution. Nonetheless, the evidence of declining head injuries in the context of ever-expanding motorcycle ownership strongly suggests that Resolution 32 prevented more injuries and saved more lives than Vietnam's previous helmet legislation.

Resolution 32 also helped Vietnam outperform its neighbor, Cambodia. Cambodia's 2009 law made helmets mandatory for motorcycle drivers—but not for their passengers. As of 2010, only 65 percent of Cambodian drivers and 9 percent of passengers wore helmets, and Cambodia had the highest vehicular fatality rate of any country in Southeast Asia.[52] In 2014 the Cambodian government expanded its helmet law to cover passengers.

Box 1. Strength of the Evidence

It is common sense that helmets protect motorcyclists' heads during a crash, so it is no surprise that evidence from a handful of countries suggests that laws to mandate helmet use decrease head injuries and death. However, high-quality studies of national road traffic measures are hard to find, and methodological challenges limit the scope for quasi-experimental designs. A Cochrane systematic review found 61 studies, but none were randomized, most relied on observational designs, and all but a handful focused on helmet laws in high-income countries.[53]

The question remains: can national-level behavior change sustain the consistent, correct use of motorcycle helmets? In Vietnam, the main source of potential data is a hospital-based surveillance system of road traffic injuries, put in place by the Ministry of Health in 2007. Using a before-and-after study design in which numbers of injuries were assessed three months before and after Helmet Day, the system drew data from a total of 20 provincial and central hospitals around the country.[54] The sample consisted of more than 80,000 injury patients (injuries that resulted in death were counted only if death occurred after the accident, in the hospital, not at the scene of the accident). The data suggest that the risk of head injury and death as a result of a traffic accident decreased following the introduction of the law, by 16 percent and 18 percent, respectively.[55] Another study, by the AIP Foundation, estimated a much larger impact.[56]

Several limitations prevent full confidence in the results of the analysis. Hospitals counted all road traffic injuries, not just those among motorcycle riders, and did not record whether the patients had been wearing helmets or whether there were any weather-related variations. There was no validation of staff reporting to prevent undercounting, biased reporting, or other inconsistencies in data collection. Other estimates also face limitations because of the risks of underreporting.

Gains at What Price?

Brain injury is the most common injury from motorcycle crashes, and hospital care to treat such injuries can be expensive.[57] One study found that the average medical costs in Vietnam for a person suffering from a severe head trauma came to US$2,370, which exceeded the national GDP per capita of US$1,910 in 2013.[58] Treatment for catastrophic conditions can impoverish entire families and thus magnify the economic effects of a crash.[59] As many as 70 percent of traffic accident victims lose income, and two-thirds of them must take on debt to compensate.[60]

Studies from countries of all income levels have found significant evidence that mandatory helmet laws, combined with enforcement, can greatly reduce the burden of traffic injuries on families, the health system, and the economy. They conclude that legislation is among the most cost-effective interventions available.[61]

In the first year after passage of the decree, researchers for *Millions Saved* estimate that the law averted 90,582 disability-adjusted life years (DALYs) from prevented deaths and nonfatal injuries.[62] This is a conservative estimate because prevented deaths are likely to be concentrated among young adult males; their deaths or permanent injuries would result in more life years lost than death or injury incurred by the average, older person on the standard age distribution. In addition, number of deaths is estimated from police data—a source that is subject to underreporting. The estimated cost of the initiative was the cost of helmets and of hiring new police officers to enforce the law. The calculation yielded a cost-effectiveness ratio of US$1,248 per DALY averted.

This ratio falls above the range reported elsewhere, of US$467 to US$769 per DALY averted, likely because the data source and methods used underestimated impact. Nonetheless, the cost-effectiveness ratio is close to the GDP per capita for Vietnam.

The Keys to Lasting Success

The success of the 2007 law was made possible by strong leadership, a vibrant partnership, a hefty fine for non-compliance, and culturally appropriate approaches.[63] The prime minister and his party threw their weight behind simple legislation that reduced confusion about enforcement: all riders and passengers were covered on all roads. Since then, policy adjustments have closed loopholes and given the helmet law sharper teeth.

Resolution 32 had broad-based support across the Communist Party, the government, and a range of other organizations, and communication campaigns helped it take hold across the country. Political leaders featured prominently in media spots to promote the new legislation, supported by groups like the Youth Union.[64] Traditional and new international partners supported the government's effort. The AIP Foundation's engagement with the Global Road Safety Partnership, initiated by the World Bank, brought private-sector funding from automobile manufacturers Ford Motors and Toyota.[65] Meanwhile, Bloomberg Philanthropies supported social marketing and legislative action to increase police enforcement.[66]

The hefty fine was one of the law's essential design elements. Even with the considerable effort put into other activities, the fear of getting a penalty may have been riders' deciding factor. The consistency of enforcement by traffic police made the threat feel real and helped spur compliance.[67] The paperwork was a nuisance, and paying the fine required taking time off from work. A further disincentive was that riders stopped by the police for not wearing a helmet also risked being cited for other traffic violations.

To achieve behavior change, planners knew that their approach had to be culturally appropriate. In Vietnam, where conformity is highly valued, planners leveraged the power of conformity to ensure adoption of the helmet decree. Through the population-wide launch, everyone adopted the new behavior all at once, thus motivating helmet wearing through peer pressure.[68] It worked: helmet use seems to have become a new social norm.

To be able to comply with the law, the Vietnamese also needed access to affordable helmets. High-quality, climate-appropriate helmets were available to those who could afford them, and the government had progressively strengthened helmet quality standards as of 2008. But low-quality helmets, some costing as little as US$2.40, still flooded the market.[69] Identifying and discouraging the sale and use of substandard helmets remained a major challenge.[70] The NTSC and its partners have worked hard to take substandard helmets off the streets, and their efforts are beginning to pay off. Trade and customs officials are clamping down on the import of Chinese helmets, whose manufacturers falsely claim that their products adhere to quality standards.[71]

Children's safety is still a serious concern. Initial legislative inconsistencies made it easy for helmeted parents to tote around unprotected kids. Even when the policy changed to cover children over the age of six, many parents still failed to put helmets on their children's heads. As of 2010, just 18 percent of primary school children wore helmets while riding as motorcycle passengers in major cities.[72] Partly to blame is a widely quoted media report that erroneously suggested that helmets injure children's necks.[73] Despite the lack of evidence, this common myth deters well-intentioned parents from protecting their small children. The Helmets for Kids campaign, led by the AIP Foundation, attempts to counteract this false claim through education and donations of children's helmets.

Implications for Global Health

Vietnam's helmet law experience suggests that a law can successfully change behavior—perhaps especially in a country where the government exercises strong control, as in Vietnam. But even there, the law needed effective enforcement with high penalties to ensure compliance.

The government still faces several persistent challenges: children's helmet wearing, helmet quality, and correct usage. There are clear steps the government can take to overcome these challenges. People who cannot afford helmets need donated ones, and babies and young children need small tropical helmets. And everyone needs a helmet that meets the national safety standard. Substandard helmets must attract the same penalty as no helmet, and riders must learn that chin straps are essential to their protection in a crash.[74]

The AIP Foundation is helping other countries learn about the lessons from Vietnam. It now has offices around the region, in Cambodia, China, and Thailand, and has expanded to Uganda and Tanzania. Its factory has sparked particular interest. A delegation of government officials from Cambodia visited the facility and considered plans to open an in-country helmet plant to support their country's new passenger helmet requirement.[75]

Legislation mandating helmet use has advanced globally, yet only one-third of countries rate enforcement of their helmet laws as "good."[76] Encouraging helmet wearing is a central goal of the Global Plan for the Decade of Action for Road Safety,[77] and a 2014 United Nations General Assembly resolution, "Improving Global Road Safety," asks member states to enact legislation on motorcycle helmets and take other measures to reduce risk.[78] One clear priority: to collect and disseminate more and better evidence from low- and middle-income countries on how to improve road traffic safety at scale.

REFERENCES

ADB (Asian Development Bank). 2012. *Road Safety Action Plan.* Mandaluyong, the Philippines: ADB. http://www.adb.org/sites/default/files/institutional-document/33427/files/road-safety-action-plan.pdf.

ADB and ASEAN (Association of Southeast Asian Nations). 2003. *Regional Road Safety Program Accident Costing Report: The Cost of Road Traffic Accidents in Vietnam.* Manila, the Philippines: ABD and ASEAN.

AIP (Asia Injury Prevention) Foundation. 2013. "Trade Your Used Helmet for a Standard Quality Helmet at Protec." News release, March. http://aip-foundation.org/wp-content/uploads/2013/05/Protec-Exchange-Program-March-2013-English.pdf.

———. 2014. *Developing an Integrated Campaign to Address Child Helmet Use in Vietnam: A Case Study.* New York: Atlantic Philanthropies. http://issuu.com/aipfoundation/docs/case_study_-_vietnam_national_helme.

Asian Scientist. 2012. "Vietnam's Baseball Cap 'Helmets,'" December 3. http://www.asianscientist.com/2012/12/health/vietnam-baseball-cap-helmets-2012/.

Bishai, David M., and Adnan A. Hyder. 2006. "Modeling the Cost Effectiveness of Injury Interventions in Lower and Middle Income Countries: Opportunities and Challenges." *Cost Effectiveness and Resource Allocation* 4 (2).

Bloomberg Philanthropies. *2013 Leading the Worldwide Movement to Improve Road Safety.* New York: Bloomberg Philanthropies. http://www.mikebloomberg.com/content/uploads/sites/10/2015/06/Bloomberg_Philanthropies_Leading_the_Worldwide_Movement_to_Improve_Road_Safety.pdf.

Britton, Eric. 2009. "Lessons from a Helmet Wearing Campaign in Vietnam." *World City Bike Forum*, February 6. https://groups.yahoo.com/neo/groups/WorldCityBike/conversations/topics/597.

Center for Injury Prevention and Policy Research. 2008. *Study Report on Traffic Injury Situation in Provinces of Yen Bai, Da Nang and Binh Duong.* Hanoi, Vietnam: Ha Noi School of Public Health.

Dribben, Melissa. 2008. "Vietnam Shows Effect of Motorcycle Helmets: Injuries Dropped up to 30% after Their Use

REFERENCES, *continued*

Became Mandatory." Philly.com, June 28. http://articles. philly.com/2008-06-28/news/25249036_1_helmet-law-head-injury-deaths-helmet-legislation.

Hansen, Arve. 2014. "Hanoi's Looming Traffic Nightmare." *Diplomat,* September 7. http://thediplomat.com/2014/09/ hanois-looming-traffic-nightmare/.

Hiep, Dinh Van, and Pham Thi Quyen. 2009. "Road Traffic Accidents in Vietnam." *Road Research* (January): 6. http:// www.academia.edu/209613/Analysis_of_road_traffic_accidents_in_Vietnam.

Hill, P.S., A.D. Ngo, T.A. Khuong, H.L. Dao, H.T.M. Hoang, H.T. Trinh, L.T.N. Nguyen, and P.H. Nguyen. 2009. "Mandatory Helmet Legislation and the Print Media in Viet Nam." *Accident Analysis and Prevention* 41 (4): 789–97.

Hoang, Hanh T.M., Tran L. Pham, Thuy T.N. Vo, Phuong K. Nguyen, Christopher M. Doran, and Peter S. Hill. 2008. "The Costs of Traumatic Brain Injury Due to Motorcycle Accidents in Hanoi, Vietnam." *Cost Effectiveness and Resource Allocation: C/E* 6 (August): 17. doi:10.1186/ 1478-7547-6-17.

Huu, Nguyen, Duong Thi Mai, Nguyen Thien, and Nguyen Ngoc. 2011. "Study on Vietnam Traffic Accident Situation via Data of Health Sector." *Journal of the Eastern Asia Society for Transportation Studies* 9: 2011–21.

Hyder, A.A., H. Waters, T. Phillips, and J. Rehwinkel. 2007. "Exploring the Economics of Motorcycle Helmet Laws Implications for Low and Middle-Income Countries." *Asia-Pacific Journal of Public Health* 19 (2): 16–22. doi:10.1177/10105395070190020401.

Le, Duy. 2008. "Mother Weighs Dangerous Options." Vietnam News, January 30. http://vietnamnews.vn/talk-aroundtown/173392/mother-weighs-dangerous-options.html.

Le, L., C. Pham, M. Linnan, V.D. Dung, N.L. Phuong, H.L. Hanh, and V.L. Anh. 2002. "Vietnam Profile on Traffic-Related Injury: Facts and Figures from Recent Studies and Their Implications for Road Traffic Injury Policy." Paper presented at the Road Traffic Injuries and Health Equity Conference, Cambridge, MA, April 10–12.

Liu, Bette C., Rebecca Ivers, Robyn Norton, Soufiane Boufous, Stephanie Blows, and Sing Kai Lo. 2008. "Helmets for Preventing Injury in Motorcycle Riders." *Cochrane Database of Systematic Reviews* 2008 (1): Article CD004333. http:// doi.wiley.com/10.1002/14651858.CD004333.pub3.

Magnier, Mark. 2010. "Helmets Are a Fashion Must-Have in Vietnam; The Law Says So." *Los Angeles Times,* May 25. http://articles.latimes.com/2010/may/25/world/la-fgvietnam-helmets-20100526.

Mason, Margie. 2007. "Vietnam Enacts Motorbike Helmet Law." *USA Today,* October 3. http://usatoday30.usatoday. com/news/world/2007-10-03-469093791_x.htm.

Mayo Clinic Staff. 2015. "Diseases and Conditions: Traumatic Brain Injury." Mayo Clinic, May 15. http://www.mayoclinic.

org/diseases-conditions/traumatic-brain-injury/basics/ symptoms/con-20029302.

McDonnell, Mary Byrne, Van Bich Thi Tran, and Nina R. McCoy. 2010. *Helmet Day: Lessons Learned on Vietnam's Road to Healthy Behavior.* Brooklyn, NY: Social Science Research Council.

Minh, Hung. 2014. "Vietnam Shares Road Traffic Safety Experiences with Cambodia." *Thanhnien Daily,* October 17. http://www.thanhniennews.com/society/ vietnam-shares-road-traffic-safety-experiences-withcambodia-32688.html.

Mirelman, Andrew, Amanda Glassman, and Miriam Temin. 2016. *Estimating the Avertable Disease Burden and Cost-Effectiveness in* Millions Saved *Third Edition.* CGD Working Paper. Washington, DC: Center for Global Development.

National People's Assembly of Socialist Republic of Viet Nam. 2002. *Ordinance on Handling of Administrative Violations.* Ordinance No. 44/2002/PL-UBTVQH10, July 2. http:// www.wipo.int/wipolex/en/details.jsp?id=6682.

Ngo, Anh D., Chalapati Rao, Nguyen Phuong Hoa, Damian G. Hoy, Khieu Thi Quynh Trang, and Peter S. Hill. 2012. "Road Traffic Related Mortality in Vietnam: Evidence for Policy from a National Sample Mortality Surveillance System." *BMC Public Health* 12 (1): 561. doi:10.1186/ 1471-2458-12-561.

Nguyen, Ha Trong, Jonathon Passmore, Pham Viet Cuong, and Nam Phuong Nguyen. 2013. "Measuring Compliance with Viet Nam's Mandatory Motorcycle Helmet Legislation." *International Journal of Injury Control and Safety Promotion* 20 (2): 192–96. doi:10.1080/17457300.2012. 706617.

O'Flaherty, Bridget. 2012. "Traffic: Vietnam's Silent Killer." *Diplomat,* August 28. http://thediplomat.com/2012/08/ traffic-vietnams-silent-killer/.

Olson, Zachary, John A. Staples, Charles Mock, Nam Phuong Nguyen, Abdulgafoor M. Bachani, Rachel Nugent, and Stéphane Verguet. 2016. "Helmet Regulation in Vietnam: Impact on Health, Equity and Medical Impoverishment." *Injury Prevention.* doi:10.1136/injuryprev-2015-041650.

Passmore, Jonathon W., Lan Huong Nguyen, Nam Phuong Nguyen, and Jean-Marc Olivé. 2010. "The Formulation and Implementation of a National Helmet Law: A Case Study from Viet Nam." *Bulletin of the World Health Organization* 88 (10): 783–87. doi:10.2471/BLT.09.071662.

Pham, K.H., Q.X. Le Thi, D.J. Petrie, J. Adams, and C.M. Doran. 2008. "Households' Willingness to Pay for a Motorcycle Helmet in Hanoi, Vietnam." *Applied Health Economics and Health Policy* 6 (2–3): 137–44.

Prime Minister. 2012. *Approval of the National Road Safety Strategy by 2020 and a Vision to 2030.* Decision 1586/ QD-TTg. http://www.who.int/roadsafety/decade_of_ action/plan/vietnam_plan.pdf?ua=1.

REFERENCES, *continued*

Protec. 2011. "Helmet Structure: Frequently Asked Questions," October 17. http://protec.com.vn/web/en/frame/faq_category/q-a.html.

Stokes, Connla. 2012. "Letter from Vietnam: Hard-Headed Motorcyclists." *Guardian*, March 20. http://www.theguardian.com/world/2012/mar/20/letter-from-vietnam-motorcycle-helmets.

Talk Vietnam. 2010. "Elevating Awareness of Need for Helmets among Children," September 16. http://www.talkvietnam.com/2010/09/elevating-awareness-of-need-for-helmets-among-children/.

United Nations General Assembly. 2014. *Improving Global Road Safety.* New York: United Nations General Assembly. http://www.who.int/roadsafety/news/2014/Final_draft_UN_General_Assembly_resolution_improving_global_road_safety.pdf?ua=1.

US CDC (Centers for Disease Control and Prevention). n.d. *Motorcycle Safety: How to Save Lives and Save Money.* Atlanta, GA: CDC. http://www.cdc.gov/motorvehiclesafety/pdf/mc2012/motorcyclesafetybook.pdf.

WHO (World Health Organization). 2006. "How to Design and Implement a Helmet Programme." In *Helmets: A Road Safety Manual for Decision-Makers and Practitioners.* Geneva: WHO. http://www.who.int/roadsafety/projects/manuals/helmet_manual/3-How%20to.pdf?ua=1.

———. 2013. *Global Status Report on Road Safety 2013: Supporting a Decade of Action.* Geneva: WHO. http://www.who.int/violence_injury_prevention/road_safety_status/2013/en/.

———. n.d. *Global Plan for the Decade of Action for Road Safety 2011–2020.* Geneva: WHO. http://www.who.int/roadsafety/decade_of_action/plan/en/.

World Bank. 2015. Data. Accessed November 10. http://data.worldbank.org/.

———. 2016. "GDP per Capita (Current US$)." Data. Accessed February 8. http://data.worldbank.org/indicator/NY.GDP.PCAP.CD.

ENDNOTES

1. Liu et al. (2008).
2. McDonnell, Thi Tran, and McCoy (2010); Hoang et al. (2008).
3. Hansen (2014).
4. US CDC (n.d.); Liu et al. (2008).
5. Passmore et al. (2010).
6. WHO (2013).
7. Nguyen et al. (2013).
8. WHO (2013).
9. Mayo Clinic Staff (2015).
10. WHO (2013).
11. Hoang (2015).
12. Hoang (2015).
13. Dribben (2008).
14. O'Flaherty (2012).
15. Center for Injury Prevention and Policy Research (2008).
16. Le et al. (2002).
17. Le et al. (2002).
18. McDonnell, Thi Tran, and McCoy (2010).
19. ADB and ASEAN (2003), quoted in McDonnell, Thi Tran, and McCoy (2010).
20. McDonnell, Thi Tran, and McCoy (2010).
21. WHO (2006).
22. Hill et al. (2009).
23. Magnier (2010).
24. McDonnell, Thi Tran, and McCoy (2010).
25. McDonnell, Thi Tran, and McCoy (2010).
26. Hill et al. (2009).
27. Hoang (2015). See the Protec website for technical and other information on the company's helmets (Protec 2011); AIP Foundation (2013).
28. McDonnell, Thi Tran, and McCoy (2010).
29. McDonnell, Thi Tran, and McCoy (2010).
30. McDonnell, Thi Tran, and McCoy (2010).
31. Passmore et al. (2010).
32. Passmore et al. (2010).
33. Pham et al. (2008).
34. Passmore et al. (2010).
35. AIP Foundation (2013); Britton (2009).
36. Mason (2007).
37. Stokes (2012).
38. Passmore et al. (2010); *Asian Scientist* (2012).
39. Passmore et al. (2010).
40. National People's Assembly of Socialist Republic of Viet Nam (2002).
41. Talk Vietnam (2010).
42. McDonnell, Thi Tran, and McCoy (2010).
43. McDonnell, Thi Tran, and McCoy (2010).
44. McDonnell, Thi Tran, and McCoy (2010).
45. Nguyen et al. (2013).
46. Based on risk ratios (Passmore et al. 2010).
47. Jonathan Passmore, personal communication with the author, April 10, 2015.
48. Jonathan Passmore, personal communication with the7author, April 10, 2015.
49. Passmore et al. (2010).
50. Huu et al. (2011).
51. AIP Foundation (2014).
52. WHO (2013); Hiep and Thi Quyen (2009).
53. Liu et al. (2008).
54. Passmore et al. (2010).
55. Passmore et al. (2010).
56. AIP Foundation (2014).
57. Hoang et al. (2008).
58. World Bank (2015, 2016).
59. Hill et al. (2009).

ENDNOTES, *continued*

60. ADB (2012).
61. Hyder et al. (2007).
62. Estimation of total DALYs averted was calculated for injuries and deaths from traffic accidents. The helmet policy was found to avert 1,557 deaths and 2,495 injuries (Passmore et al. 2010). The costs of implementing the policy were calculated as US$24 million, including police salaries and costs of helmets (Bishai and Hyder 2006; Olson et al. 2016). The cost-effectiveness is US$1,248 per DALY averted. This puts it right around the GDP per capita of Vietnam in 2008. Adding in treatment costs averted means that there are likely to be many cost savings. See Mirelman, Glassman, and Temin (2016).
63. Hill et al. (2009).
64. Hill et al. (2009).
65. McDonnell, Thi Tran, and McCoy (2010).
66. Bloomberg Philanthropies (2013).
67. AIP Foundation (2014).
68. McDonnell, Thi Tran, and McCoy (2010).
69. Passmore et al. (2010).
70. Stokes (2012); *Asian Scientist* (2012).
71. Jonathan Passmore, personal communication with the author, April 10, 2015.
72. AIP Foundation (2014).
73. For example, see Le (2008).
74. WHO (2013).
75. Minh (2014).
76. WHO (2013).
77. WHO (n.d.).
78. United Nations General Assembly (2014).

CASE 20

A Persuasive Plea to Become "Open Defecation Free"

Indonesia's Total Sanitation and Sanitation Marketing Program

The Case at a Glance

HEALTH GOAL: To reduce childhood deaths by halting the spread of diarrheal diseases through feces-contaminated water and food sources.

STRATEGY: Educate rural communities on the dangers of open defecation and increase demand for hygienic sanitation while boosting the supply and availability of affordable hygienic products and services through consumer research and market interventions.

HEALTH IMPACT: Prevalence of diarrhea decreased 30 percent. 2,200 communities verified as "open defecation free." 220 lives saved and nearly 19,000 disability-adjusted life years (DALYs) from diarrhea averted (2007 to 2011).

WHY IT WORKED: Intervention design that leveraged Indonesia's highly decentralized political system. Reliance on communities' natural cohesion and intrinsic motivation to be healthier. Incorporation of complementary demand- and supply-side components.

FINANCING: Cost of US$14 million over four years, including costs to households. Estimated cost-effectiveness ratio: US$749 per DALY averted, reduced to US$213 per DALY averted when excluding costs to households.

SCALE: 6,250 communities in 29 rural districts, covering approximately 9.2 million people. 1.4 million people gained latrine access as a result of the program.

Around the world, more than one billion people lack basic sanitary facilities—they have no clean, private, and sanitary place to go when "nature calls."[1] Whereas the better-off can enjoy privacy and take their time on the "porcelain throne," many of the poor are forced to defecate in the open, in public spaces such as fields and streets. The practice of open defecation is not only unattractive but also downright dangerous: pathogens from expelled fecal matter often find their way into food and drinking water, causing diarrhea and other illnesses.

In Indonesia—a huge and highly diverse archipelago with a population exceeding 200 million—the scope of the sanitation crisis was daunting. As of 2005, an estimated 27 percent of Indonesians—37 percent in rural areas—practiced open defecation.[2] A series of previous government and donor initiatives to improve sanitation had fallen flat, in large part because they failed to convince poor rural households that open defecation posed real health risks.[3]

It was time for Indonesia to try a new approach, one that simultaneously promoted the construction of latrines and boosted demand for their introduction. The Total Sanitation and Sanitation Marketing program (TSSM) did both: it persuaded communities to ditch unhygienic practices while also introducing measures to increase access to improved sanitation. Just two years after the program began, recipient communities were transformed: residents exposed to the program were 17 percent less likely to practice open defecation than comparable individuals who were not, and even better, their communities experienced a 30 percent reduction in the prevalence of diarrhea.

The Toll of Open Defecation

For men, women, and children without access to a toilet or latrine, the call of nature can sound more like a call of

This case was originally authored by Rachel Silverman.

distress. Absent safe, hygienic, and private places to seek relief, people must take to fields, rivers, streets, or forests. This daily indignity—"open defecation"—is the norm in many poor rural communities around the world, affecting one billion of the world's poorest inhabitants.[4]

Open defecation also poses a major threat to health and well-being. Human excrement is home to a cornucopia of pathogens, including those that cause polio, cholera, typhoid, schistosomiasis, and cryptosporidiosis; when people ingest fecal matter, these microbes find new hosts. Modern sanitation systems work by containing or treating these harmful pathogens, preventing them from entering groundwater, bodies of fresh water, and the food supply.[5] But open defecation offers no such safeguards; as a result, feces spread diarrheal and other diseases to surrounding households and communities, particularly poor ones that lack piped water and draw drinking water from contaminated rivers and water wells. A cholera outbreak in Haiti illustrates the potentially tragic consequences: nearly 745,000 cases and 9,000 deaths from 2010 to 2015.[6] Researchers have estimated that inadequate sanitation is to blame for about one-fifth of the global diarrhea burden, accounting for 280,000 deaths and 18.6 million disability-adjusted life years (DALYs) each year.[7]

The lack of private sanitation facilities leads to additional dangers for women and girls. To avoid defecating in public, many wait until night to seek relief.[8] Darkness offers some privacy, but it also cloaks potential threats: unwanted attention, harassment, and even the specter of rape and other forms of violence. In 2014, for example, two teenage girls in India were gang-raped and hanged after leaving their dwelling to relieve themselves.[9]

Indonesia is the fourth most populous country in the world and has been a middle-income economy since 2003.[10] The country extends across more than 17,000 islands, home to dozens of ethnic groups speaking upward of 700 languages.[11] Yet, as of 2005, about 60 million Indonesians—more than a quarter of the country's population—had something in common: they practiced open defecation.[12] The problem was particularly acute in poorer rural areas, where infrastructure lagged and many people were unaware of the attendant health risks. The cost of the status quo was unacceptable. Each year, 50,000 deaths and 120 million illnesses were attributed to poor sanitation practices and inadequate sanitation facilities in Indonesia. And according to one estimate, this public health crisis was causing US$6.3 billion in annual economic losses.[13]

Putting an Idea in Motion: Indonesia Imports Community-Led Sanitation

Water and sanitation projects had been a staple of Indonesian development efforts throughout the 20th century. As early as 1920, Dutch colonial authorities had launched sanitation campaigns to promote hygiene practices, and by the 1960s the construction of free and subsidized toilets had become a core strategy of the government and its donor partners.[14] Through the 1990s and into the following decade, the World Bank provided loans for construction and financing of communal and private sanitary facilities.[15]

But lack of sanitary facilities was not the only driver of open defecation. Nonmaterial drivers included erroneous beliefs and even some preferences. One common belief among the poor, for example, was that defecating in rivers was hygienic because the water swept excrement far away. Early supply-side efforts neglected these nonmaterial drivers and so failed to prompt the level of behavior change needed to generate major health gains.[16] Efforts to construct hygienic latrines were particularly criticized for exacerbating social inequities; the poorest were almost universally left behind as wealthier households and elites benefited from government subsidies for toilet construction. Indonesian government officials and members of the international policy community continued to wrestle with "deep frustration over the continued lack of progress in the sanitation sector."[17]

It was clear that the challenge required a different approach. Any new effort, however, would face serious implementation difficulties. This was especially true given Indonesia's major decentralization in 2001, which had shifted most development authority to local government leaders who had no obligation to comply with national policies.[18]

Despite these challenges, Indonesia field staff from the World Bank's Water and Sanitation Program (WSP) found one potential solution during a visit to villages in Bangladesh: Community-Led Total Sanitation (CLTS), a new approach that focused on self-motivated, community-level behavior change. Following a conference in late 2003, a small group from the WSP visited several communities that had been declared "open defecation free," meaning the practice of open defecation had been completely eradicated—an achievement attributed to the CLTS approach. The WSP team was eager to share its findings with Indonesian government officials. The following year, the team invited a leading CLTS researcher to visit Indonesia and present the approach to high-level stakeholders. Three months later, WSP flew a group of Indonesian officials to Bangladesh to show them CLTS in action.[19]

The trip was a success: Indonesian policymakers agreed that they had found a valuable new approach to sanitation improvement. Previous Indonesian efforts had focused on expanding the supply of toilets and sanitation facilities under the belief that "if you build it, they will come." Yet results had been disappointing. CLTS operated under a different theory of change. The starting point was increasing demand for good sanitation. CLTS programs were designed to "trigger" feelings of shame in people who practiced open defecation, leading them to seek access to improved sanitation. And instead of targeting individual households through a top-down approach, CLTS attempted to mobilize entire villages, drawing on their collective community identity and exploiting existing social connections to change social norms.[20]

Immediately upon their return, the Indonesian officials began pushing for adoption of the new approach. By the first half of 2005, donor-supported field trials of CLTS had begun in 17 Indonesian communities; others joined soon thereafter. The program showed early success, with several participating communities quickly achieving "open defecation free," or ODF, status. In 2006, impressed by the initiative's rapid achievements, minister of health Ibu Siti Fadilah elevated CLTS as one of two "twin pillars" for sanitation policy.[21]

Some within the government and donor organizations were skeptical, wondering whether these successes would translate at scale. In 2007, they were slated to find out: the Indonesian government partnered with the WSP and the Bill & Melinda Gates Foundation to test a scaled TSSM program based on the CLTS methodology and complementary social marketing techniques. The WSP planned to test the TSSM approach in three countries— India, Indonesia, and Tanzania.[22]

In Indonesia, the coalition zeroed in on East Java, a diverse and largely poor and rural province of almost 37 million people.[23] East Java was already home to a small but successful CLTS pilot program, earning respect and support from local doctors and policymakers. At the same time, the province lacked any ongoing large-scale sanitation programs, making it a relatively blank slate for testing the new approach during scale-up (2007–2009).[24] Once started, the program quickly went to scale: by 2011 it had reached 6,250 communities, and nearly 2,200 of them had achieved the ODF designation.[25]

The Total Sanitation and Sanitation Marketing Program in Action

To kick off the scaled-up initiative and recruit participating communities, TSSM team members embarked on "road shows" throughout East Java to introduce the new approach to local authorities. Originally, program designers hoped to adopt a demand-based approach, offering the intervention only where communities asked for it. However, most village leaders had little incentive to actively pursue a program that offered no material rewards or subsidies. As a result, stakeholders at the district and subdistrict levels were often charged with selecting the target communities and implementing the intervention.[26]

Implementers created a staged rollout plan in 29 districts, to take place in three phases from 2007 to 2010. Importantly, in phase 2, a World Bank team randomized the rollout at the village level to facilitate a rigorous impact evaluation, as described below.[27]

The TSSM program consisted of three core components designed to simultaneously address both demand- and supply-side impediments to sanitation improvements:

1. CLTS
2. Sanitation marketing
3. Development of an enabling environment

In addition, a routine monitoring system recorded sanitation access in each hamlet and noted whether it had achieved ODF status.[28]

Community-Led Total Sanitation

CLTS focused on "triggering" sessions, designed to motivate communities to abandon open defecation in favor of latrines and other sanitation facilities. To determine the targets for these sessions, district officials identified hamlets with a high prevalence of open defecation and diarrhea that were not yet benefiting from other sanitation programs, especially subsidies for toilet construction.[29]

During each triggering session, a trained facilitator met with community leaders and residents. The sessions varied but typically started with a mapping exercise showing where community members lived, drew water, and defecated. The facilitator would then lead community members on a walk through the hamlet, identifying human waste along the way and attempting to trigger community members' feelings of shame and disgust by modeling fecal contamination of drinking water. For example, a facilitator might first dip a hair in feces, and then dip that same hair in a glass of drinking water. When asked to drink the contaminated water, community members would of course refuse. In such ways, they were led to recognize the consequences of open defecation.[30]

The facilitator would educate community members on the health risks of open defecation, creating a sense of urgency to fix the problem. In some communities, the message was later reinforced through complementary social messaging or home visits. The facilitator would not prescribe a particular sanitation solution or strategy but instead would leave the community to independently mobilize and plan the next steps.[31]

Sanitation Marketing

To complement CLTS, the program included a sanitation marketing component that addressed consumers' attitudes toward sanitation. First, the TSSM commissioned market research on the barriers to sanitation uptake. The researchers found that individuals often misunderstood the connection between open defecation and disease, and consequently saw latrines as an unnecessary and unaffordable expense. Community members often overestimated the actual cost of installing a latrine. At the same time, few suppliers had experience with low-cost latrine construction and rarely marketed cheaper options to potential buyers. The TSSM team took follow-up steps to boost demand for and supply of affordable sanitation solutions. For example, it printed and distributed promotional materials to dissuade open defecation, and catalogues featuring the pros, cons, and costs of different sanitation options. It also trained local masons in the construction of low-cost latrines.[32]

Enabling Environment

To sustain progress and broaden coverage, the TSSM included dedicated activities to create an enabling environment for sanitation expansion. This component included advocacy and policy outreach to national and local government representatives. Its aims were to secure support, increase funding for sanitation, and incentivize sanitation achievements, all within a favorable regulatory regime.[33]

The TSSM team enlisted *Jawa Pos,* one of Indonesia's leading daily newspapers, as a partner to help drive local government accountability. Already, *Jawa Pos* was monitoring the achievements of local governments in various categories, offering "autonomy awards" to recognize high performance and good governance. TSSM convinced *Jawa Pos* to include measures of sanitation progress among its award indicators, which helped motivate district-level stakeholders and inspire action.[34]

The Payoff: Less Open Defecation, Less Diarrhea

By 2011, the TSSM program had held trigger events in 6,250 communities in 29 rural districts of East Java, and 2,200 of these communities had been verified as ODF. In total, 1.4 million Javanese enjoyed newfound access to improved sanitation facilities, all of which had been constructed and fully financed by the households themselves.[35]

The program's impact, according to the evaluation results, was more modest but still impressive (see Box 1). Compared with a group of randomly selected control hamlets that were not targets of the intervention, residents of the communities selected for triggering were 23 percent more likely to build a toilet and 9 percent less likely to practice open defecation. These behavioral changes were sufficiently large to translate into a 30 percent drop in the prevalence of diarrhea among people living in the target communities.[36] Our own estimate suggests that the program averted 220 deaths over four years; those life years gained, combined with the diarrhea morbidity averted, translate to approximately 18,666 DALYs averted.

Despite its notable health impact, the program unfortunately did not increase equity in sanitation access. The bulk of toilet construction and increased use occurred among relatively better-off families; poor households remained unable to afford improved sanitation—so they saw no statistically significant improvements in toilet ownership. Still, poor families benefited from community-wide sanitation advances. For example, poor children without access to sanitation at baseline saw disproportionately large decreases in the prevalence of diarrhea and lower respiratory infections. This possibly reflected decreases fecal contamination of food and water supplies that resulted from toilet construction elsewhere in the community.[37]

Gains at What Price?

TSSM program costs totaled about US$14 million, including the private cost to households of toilet and latrine construction. In total, each additional latrine required a US$65 investment. Of that sum, local governments spent

Box 1. Strength of the Evidence

During phase 2 of TSSM program expansion in East Java, from September 2008 to June 2009, the evaluation team asked each of eight participating districts to create a list of potential villages to receive the intervention. From that list, the team randomly selected a total of 160 villages—10 sets of matched pairs per district, with one treatment village and one control village in each pair. One hamlet in each study village was selected as the focus of the intervention and measurement. Then in each hamlet the team randomly selected 13 households from a list of families with young children. Baseline surveys were conducted in mid-2008, with follow-up a little more than two years later. The analysis used an "intent-to-treat" approach: researchers compared the mean outcome of all households in the treatment villages with that of the households in the control villages, rather than focusing only on households that changed their sanitation status. This decision was based on the assumption that sanitation improvements in even a portion of village households would have spillover effects on their neighbors.[38]

The evaluation showed important gains in treatment hamlets: households were less likely to practice open defeca-tion, children had lower prevalence of diarrhea, and the pace of toilet construction was faster than in control communities. Yet when compared with the results reported to the routine program monitoring system—particularly the huge reported number of newly ODF communities—these improvements seemed relatively modest.

Amin, Rangarajan, and Borkum[39] offered several potential explanations for the apparent discrepancy. Routine monitoring data showed relatively poor performance during phase 2, with just 17 percent of program communities achieving ODF status (compared with 58 percent in phase 1 and 54 percent in phase 3). The estimated impact may also have been diluted by con-tamination in the assignment to treatment and intervention groups; several intended treatment hamlets were never trig-gered, while a number of control villages received the inter-vention despite instructions to the contrary. Finally, some of the sampled families may have lived outside the neighbor-hoods where triggering occurred, limiting their exposure to the intervention. Notwithstanding these limitations, the analy-sis strongly suggests that the program drove the behavioral changes that led to the measured health benefits.[40]

---

about US$5 per latrine, mostly on training and triggering activities; the WSP spent US$14 per latrine, mostly for program management costs; and private households spent US$46 per latrine on the latrine construction itself.[41] District governments did contribute small amounts from their own budgets. Their contributions varied substantially, but averaged IDR118 million (US$13,100) annually between 2007 and 2010.[42]

Were the TSSM investments in sanitation worth it? The United Nations Development Programme has esti-mated that each dollar invested in water and sanitation yields US$8 in return.[43] We estimated the specific cost-effectiveness of the East Java program, which had the potential to influence diarrhea, helminth infections, and acute respiratory infection. Only the averted burden from diarrhea was modeled for cost-effectiveness because this was the only statistically significant health impact identi-fied in the evaluation.[44] We find that the program cost US$749 per DALY averted, decreasing to US$213 per DALY averted after excluding the costs to households.[45]

This is much lower than the gross domestic product (GDP) per capita threshold for assessing whether an intervention is "very cost-effective," as recommended by the World Health Organization. In 2010, the GDP per cap-ita for Indonesia was US$2,947.

However, despite sanitation's cost-effectiveness, Indonesian government funding for sanitation remains insufficient to meet international goals. To reach the rel-evant Millennium Development Goal target—a halving of those without access to basic sanitation by 2015—the Indonesian government would have needed to invest an estimated US$600 million each year. The available resources did not match the clear urgency of the situa-tion. In the 30 years prior to 2007, government and donor funds for sanitation together totaled just US$27 million annually, and most funds flowed to relatively privileged urban areas.[46] Overall public expenditure on sanitation was only 0.04 percent of total public spend-ing in 2009.[47]

The Keys to Lasting Success

Despite impressive CLTS results elsewhere in the world, Indonesia faced a number of initial hurdles that had to be overcome to achieve impact. East Java had limited experience with at-scale sanitation programs and hence limited capacity to implement the new initiative. The country's decentralization in 2001 had resulted in fragmentation of authority and complex lines of accountability, presenting a major challenge for any large-scale program. And since the TSSM program offered no subsidies or material benefits, requiring local governments to front the funds and human resources instead, it was a hard sell for district and village officials.[48]

The program was able to transform these hurdles into facilitating factors that enabled rapid scale-up. By working primarily through district governments, the TSSM team leveraged the highly decentralized East Javanese policy environment.[49] The road shows helped introduce the program to skeptical district officials and secure their commitment. From there, stakeholders could adapt the delivery strategy to fit the local context. In addition, the lack of an existing large-scale sanitation program in East Java allowed the program to avoid bureaucratic confusion and muddled messaging. As the WSP adviser Nalajana Mukherjee writes, Indonesia's blank slate meant that "vast amounts of efforts and time did not have to be wasted on battling and adjusting political agendas attached to high-profile national programs with contradictory provisions."[50]

Still, devolved control over the program led to uneven implementation and mixed results. Some local authorities immediately stepped up to the plate with the needed resources and follow-up support to triggering sessions. Others provided only limited post-triggering activities. Areas abutting lakes, rivers, and beaches were among the biggest laggards; there, the longstanding and socially sanctioned practice of water defecation proved difficult to change.[51] To incentivize the achievement of ODF status in such areas, program leaders and district governments stepped in with a number of responsive initiatives, including the partnership with *Jawa Pos,* cash rewards, and "clustering" intervention sites to increase motivation for a collective ODF achievement.[52]

As the program progressed, it became clear that supply-side interventions had not kept pace with the increased demand for sanitation. After nearly two years, the program's marketing component was up and running—but even then, local markets still suffered from a shortage of suppliers of low-cost sanitation solutions.[53] And even where lower-cost options were available, costs could still exceed what the poorest and most vulnerable households could afford.

Many of poorest families were stuck between a rock and hard place: their communities pressured them to give up open defecation, but they could not afford to drain their scarce household savings on a big-ticket purchase like a toilet or latrine. Some communities overcame this roadblock by pooling funds for a shared latrine or offering within-hamlet subsidies to assist poor families.[54] Nonetheless, the inability of many poor families to fund latrine construction remains an important barrier to sanitation expansion and a source of inequity.

Implications for Global Health

The TSSM program in East Java should be lauded for the results it has already achieved. Motivated by evidence of this success, Indonesia's national government adopted the TSSM design as "the backbone of Indonesia's national rural sanitation program."[55] Similar programs are now under way in rural communities nationwide.[56] Yet Indonesian officials rightly worry that increased demand for sanitation is of limited value for the most deprived people, who may demand improved sanitation but cannot afford latrines.[57] This concern is validated by the evaluation results showing that the intervention had little to no impact on latrine construction among the poorest families.[58] Finding solutions to this conundrum is no easy task; while some have suggested that the government expand construction subsidies, research has shown that external subsidies may actually impede communities' attainment of ODF status by eroding their intrinsic desire for change.[59] As in Indonesia, countries everywhere must consider how to overcome the real resource constraints impeding sanitation uptake by the poorest.

Others express concerns about some of the program's tactics. Critics have attacked its focus on shaming people who practice open defecation, suggesting that even if the approach is effective, a program built on such a premise cannot be considered fully community-led and participatory. They note that some of its promotional messages cross the fine line between persuasive communication and divisive propaganda that blames the poor for their poverty.[60] For example, posters depict the misadventures of a character named Lik Telek—Uncle Feces.

In one version, Lik Telek appears filthy and fly-covered while clean, respectable-looking Indonesians shy away in disgust. "Defecating in the open makes you the talk of the whole village," the caption reads. "The stench is . . . Yuck! Ugh! Flies follow everywhere you go!"[61] The results of these messages can be devastating: those too poor or otherwise reluctant to defecate in latrines may experience public shaming or fines.[62] These serious ethical quandaries must be carefully considered when moving forward with the scale-up of similar interventions in other contexts.

Global interest in sanitation has exploded, with CLTS at the forefront of the worldwide movement. In 2013, United Nations deputy secretary-general Jan Eliasson launched a high-profile campaign to end open defecation, aiming to completely eliminate the practice by 2025.[64] Dozens of countries across Asia, Africa, and Latin America have introduced CLTS initiatives, albeit with mixed results (see Box 2). And recognizing the importance of better sanitation options, the Bill & Melinda Gates Foundation has challenged the world to "reinvent the toilet," so far funding 16 innovative projects that transform human waste into energy or fertilizer.[65] Will the Indonesian experience inform a global sanitation revolution? Only time will tell—but it's clear the world is finally mobilizing to move the "call of nature" indoors.

Box 2. India's Experience with TSSM

Around the same time that Indonesia's program geared up, the World Bank's WSP tried a similar experiment in India under the TSSM project, blending CLTS behavior-change methods with subsidies for latrine construction and financial incentives for villages to achieve ODF status. In India, a randomized rollout of the TSSM program occurred in Madhya Pradesh between 2009 and 2011. An evaluation of the program was released in 2014. Researchers found that communities receiving the intervention saw a decrease in open defecation of about 10 percent among adults and 6 percent among children.

The gains in sanitation were accompanied by modest health improvements—small but statistically significant reductions in the prevalence of acute lower respiratory illness and *Giardia lamblia* infections (which can cause diarrheal illness) in children. But unlike in East Java, the evaluation was unable to identify any corresponding changes in other dimensions of child health such as diarrhea, anemia, and stunting. One possible reason for the limited health impact was the relatively short time between the intervention and follow-up, which was unable to capture any longer-term health gains that emerged. Imperfect compliance with the intervention, evidence that some designated control villages did indeed receive program activities (contamination), and possible bias associated with self-reported outcomes presented further limitations.[63]

REFERENCES

Amin, Samia, Anu Rangarajan, and Evan Borkum. 2011. *Improving Sanitation at Scale: Lessons from TSSM Implementation in East Java, Indonesia*. Final Report 4993/18136 (11). Princeton, NJ: Mathematica Policy Research. http://www.mathematica-mpr.com/~/media/publications/PDFs/international/TSSM_implementation.pdf.

Bill & Melinda Gates Foundation. 2015. "Water, Sanitation and Hygiene." Accessed July 8. http://www.gatesfoundation.org/What-We-Do/Global-Development/Water-Sanitation-and-Hygiene.

Cameron, Lisa, Manisha Shah, and Susan Olivia. 2013. *Impact Evaluation of a Large-Scale Rural Sanitation Project in Indonesia*. Policy Research Working Papers. Washington, DC: World Bank. http://elibrary.worldbank.org/doi/book/10.1596/1813-9450-6360.

Carr, Richard. 2001. "Excreta-Related Infections and the Role of Sanitation in the Control of Transmission." In *Water Quality: Guidelines, Standards and Health*. London: IWA Publishing.

CIA (Central Intelligence Agency). 2015. "The World Factbook: Indonesia." Accessed November 11. https://www.cia.gov/library/publications/the-world-factbook/geos/id.html.

Eliasson, Jan. 2013. "About." United Nations End Open Defecation Campaign. Accessed November 11. http://opendefecation.org/news/about/.

Engel, Susan, and Anggun Susilo. 2014. "Shaming and Sanitation in Indonesia: A Return to Colonial Public Health Practices?" *Development and Change* 45 (1): 157–78. doi:10.1111/dech.12075.

Kosek, Margaret, Caryn Bern, and Richard L. Guerrant. 2003. "The Global Burden of Diarrhoeal Disease, as Estimated from Studies Published between 1992 and 2000." *Bulletin of the World Health Organization* 81: 197–204.

McCarthy, Julie. 2014. "How a Lack of Toilets Puts India's Women at Risk of Assault." NPR, June 9. http://www.npr.org/sections/parallels/2014/06/09/319529037/indias-rape-uproar-ignites-demand-to-end-open-defecation.

Mirelman, Andrew, Amanda Glassman, and Miriam Temin. 2016. *Estimating the Avertable Disease Burden and Cost-Effectiveness in Millions Saved Third Edition*. CGD Working Paper. Washington, DC: Center for Global Development.

Mukherjee, Nilanjana, Amin Robiarto, Saputra, Effentrif, and Djoko Wartono. 2012. *Achieving and Sustaining Open Defecation Free Communities: Learning from East Java*. Washington, DC: Water and Sanitation Program. http://www.wsp.org/sites/wsp.org/files/publications/WSP_Indonesia_Action_Research_Report.pdf.

Mukherjee, Nilanjana, and Nina Shatifan. 2009. *The CLTS Story in Indonesia: Empowering Communities, Transforming Institutions, Furthering Decentralization*. Brighton, UK: Institute of Development Studies. http://www.communityledtotalsanitation.org/resource/clts-story-indonesia-empowering-communities-transforming-institutions-furthering.

PAHO (Pan American Health Organization) and WHO (World Health Organization). 2015. *Epidemiological Update: Cholera*. August 12. Washington, DC: PAHO and WHO. http://www.paho.org/hq/index.php?option=com_docman&task=doc_view&gid=31105+&Itemid=999999&lang=fr.

Patil, Sumeet R., Benjamin F. Arnold, Alicia L. Salvatore, Bertha Briceno, Sandipan Ganguly, John M. Colford Jr., and Paul J. Gertler. 2014. "The Effect of India's Total Sanitation Campaign on Defecation Behaviors and Child Health in Rural Madhya Pradesh: A Cluster Randomized Controlled Trial." *PLoS Med* 11 (8): e1001709. doi:10.1371/journal.pmed.1001709.

Prüss-Ustün, Annette, Jamie Bartram, Thomas Clasen, John M. Colford, Oliver Cumming, Valerie Curtis, Sophie Bonjour, et al. 2014. "Burden of Disease from Inadequate Water, Sanitation and Hygiene in Low- and Middle-Income Settings: A Retrospective Analysis of Data from 145 Countries." *Tropical Medicine and International Health* 19 (8): 894–905. doi:10.1111/tmi.12329.

Rhee, Changyong. 2012. "Indonesia Risks Falling into the Middle-Income Trap—Changyong Rhee." Op-ed/editorial, Asian Development Bank, March 27. http://www.adb.org/news/op-ed/indonesia-risks-falling-middle-income-trap-changyong-rhee.

Robinson, Andy. 2011. *Enabling Environment Endline Assessment: Indonesia*. Washington, DC: Water and Sanitation Program. https://www.wsp.org/sites/wsp.org/files/publications/WSP-Indonesia-Enabling-Environment-Endline.pdf.

Rosensweig, Fred, Eddy Perez, and Andy Robinson. 2012. *Policy and Sector Reform to Accelerate Access to Improved Rural Sanitation*. Washington, DC: Water and Sanitation Program. http://www.wsp.org/sites/wsp.org/files/publications/WSP-Policy-and-Sector-Reform-to-Accelerate-Access-to-Improved-Rural-Sanitation.pdf.

UNDP (United Nations Development Programme). 2006. *Beyond Scarcity: Power, Poverty and the Global Water Crisis*. Human Development Report 2006. New York: UNDP.

UN Water. 2014. "Open Defecation, Women and Violence Centre Stage for World Toilet Day," August 18. http://www.unwater.org/news-events/news-details/en/c/241040/.

WHO (World Health Organization) / UNICEF (United Nations Children's Fund) JMP (Joint Monitoring Programme for Water Supply and Sanitation). 2014. *Progress on Drinking Water and Sanitation: 2014 Update*. Geneva: WHO and UNICEF.

REFERENCES, *continued*

———. 2015. "Indonesia: Estimates on the Use of Water Sources and Sanitation Facilities (1980–2015)." Accessed November 11. http://www.wssinfo.org/documents/?tx_displaycontroller%5Bregion%5D=19&tx_displaycontroller%5Bsearch_word%5D=&tx_displaycontroller%5Btype%5D=country_files.

WSP (Water and Sanitation Program). 2008. *Economic Impacts of Sanitation in Indonesia: A Five-Country Study Conducted in Cambodia, Indonesia, Lao PDR, the Philippines, and Vietnam under the Economics of Sanitation Initiative (ESI).* Jakarta, Indonesia: World Bank. http://www.wsp.org/sites/wsp.org/files/publications/esi_indonesia.pdf.

———. 2009. *Urban Sanitation in Indonesia: Planning for Progress.* Jakarta, Indonesia: WSP. http://www.wsp.org/sites/wsp.org/files/publications/Urban_San_Indonesia.pdf.

———. 2013a. *Impact Evaluation of a Large-Scale Rural Sanitation Project in Indonesia.* Washington, DC: World Bank.

———. 2013b. *Results, Impacts, and Learning from Improving Sanitation at Scale in East Java, Indonesia.* Field Note 85200. Washington, DC: World Bank. http://www-wds.worldbank.org/external/default/WDSContentServer/WDSP/IB/2014/02/25/000333037_20140225143456/Rendered/PDF/852000WSP0Box30valuation0Field0Note.pdf.

———. 2015. Lik Telek posters. http://www.wsp.org/content/lik-telek-posters.

ENDNOTES

1. WHO/UNICEF JMP (2014).
2. WHO/UNICEF JMP (2015).
3. Amin, Rangarajan, and Borkum (2011).
4. WHO/UNICEF JMP (2014).
5. Carr (2001).
6. PAHO and WHO (2015).
7. Prüss-Ustün et al. (2014).
8. UN Water (2014).
9. McCarthy (2014).
10. Rhee (2012).
11. CIA (2015).
12. WHO/UNICEF JMP (2015).
13. WSP (2008).
14. Engel and Susilo (2014).
15. Amin, Rangarajan, and Borkum (2011).
16. Amin, Rangarajan, and Borkum (2011).
17. Mukherjee and Shatifan (2009).
18. Mukherjee and Shatifan (2009).
19. Mukherjee and Shatifan (2009).
20. Mukherjee and Shatifan (2009).
21. Mukherjee and Shatifan (2009).
22. Mukherjee and Shatifan (2009).
23. Amin, Rangarajan, and Borkum (2011).
24. Rosensweig, Perez, and Robinson (2012).
25. WSP (2013b).
26. Amin, Rangarajan, and Borkum (2011).
27. Amin, Rangarajan, and Borkum (2011).
28. Amin, Rangarajan, and Borkum (2011).
29. Amin, Rangarajan, and Borkum (2011).
30. Amin, Rangarajan, and Borkum (2011).
31. Amin, Rangarajan, and Borkum (2011).
32. Amin, Rangarajan, and Borkum (2011).
33. Cameron, Shah, and Olivia (2013).
34. Amin, Rangarajan, and Borkum (2011).
35. WSP (2013b).
36. Cameron, Shah, and Olivia (2013).
37. Cameron, Shah, and Olivia (2013).
38. Cameron, Shah, and Olivia (2013).
39. 2011.
40. Amin, Rangarajan, and Borkum (2011).
41. Amin, Rangarajan, and Borkum (2011).
42. Robinson (2011).
43. UNDP (2006).
44. Cameron, Shah, and Olivia (2013).
45. Estimated DALYs averted were calculated for diarrhea only (helminth infection and respiratory infection excluded). The efficacy of the program for reducing diarrhea (Cameron 2013), the under-five population, the case-fatality rate (Kosek et al. 2003), and the severity distribution of diarrhea were inputs to the model. The four-year costs of the program were reported with and without costs to the household (Amin 2011) and combined with DALY estimates to derive cost-effectiveness. See Mirelman, Glassman, and Temin (2016).
46. Mukherjee and Shatifan (2009).
47. WSP (2009).
48. Amin, Rangarajan, and Borkum (2011).
40. WSP (2013b).
50. Mukherjee and Shatifan (2009, 15–16).
51. Mukherjee et al. (2012).
52. Amin, Rangarajan, and Borkum (2011).
53. Amin, Rangarajan, and Borkum (2011).
54. Amin, Rangarajan, and Borkum (2011).
55. WSP (2013b, 2).
56. WSP (2013b).
57. Mukherjee and Shatifan (2009).
58. Cameron, Shah, and Olivia (2013).
59. Mukherjee et al. (2012).
60. Engel and Susilo (2014).
61. WSP (2015).
62. Engel and Susilo (2014).
63. Patil et al. (2014).
64. Eliasson (2013).
65. Bill & Melinda Gates Foundation (2015).

Empowering Communities to Tackle HIV
India's Avahan Program

The Case at a Glance

HEALTH GOAL: To prevent new HIV infections in India, particularly among key population groups: female sex workers and their partners, men who have sex with men, injection drug users, and transgender individuals.

STRATEGY: Community-based HIV prevention interventions designed to change risky behavior among groups with high HIV prevalence and vulnerability.

HEALTH IMPACT: Increased correct and consistent condom use, decreased sharing of needles among injection drug users, and increased use of the program's clinical services. Averted 202,000 HIV infections and 3.5 million disability-adjusted life years (2004–2008).

WHY IT WORKED: A focus on behavior change in key populations at heightened risk, particularly sex workers. A balance between high standards for success and programmatic agility. Strong management driven by robust data collection and review. Leveraging of local nongovernmental organizations and peer educators to access marginalized communities.

FINANCING: The program cost US$258 million from 2004 to 2009. Estimated cost-effectiveness ratio: US$46 per disability-adjusted life year averted.

SCALE: When combined with the complementary efforts of India's National AIDS Control Organization, Avahan reached 86 percent of female sex workers, 91 percent of men who had sex with men, and 84 percent of people who used intravenous drugs in the six target areas (2009).

For female sex workers, simply going to work can be a daily risk. Often driven by extreme poverty, many women pursue the only available option for supporting their families. Each transaction brings much-needed funds, but it may also bring a sexually transmitted infection or unwanted pregnancy. Many sex workers suffer abuse from their clients, ranging from minor insults to brutal physical assault or rape.[1] Life at home may offer little relief; intimate partner violence can be common and severe.[2] Too frequently, these women find little recourse when victimized; fear can prevent them from seeking police assistance, and police themselves may engage in harassment or violence.[3]

A biomedical threat compounds the social vulnerability of sex workers: an elevated risk of infection with HIV, the human immunodeficiency virus. As the virus continued to spread across Asia and Africa in the 1990s and early years of the following decade, global health activ-ists feared that the epidemic was only in its first phase. The thought was enough to incite panic: while medical advances meant that HIV could be treated, the high cost of antiretroviral therapy (ART) prohibited most people living with HIV in low- and middle-income countries from accessing effective care.[4] In India, new infections were concentrated among society's most marginalized, stigmatized, and even criminalized groups: female sex workers, men who have sex with men, transgender people, and people who inject drugs. These groups were politically invisible, and they faced substantial barriers to advocating for their own health and safety.

The spread of HIV among key populations at height-ened risk drove fears about a looming epidemic in India. National figures from 2001 showed an overall national prevalence of less than 1 percent—relatively low com-pared with the rates seen in sub-Saharan Africa. Even so, India's billion-plus population meant the absolute

This case was originally authored by Rachel Silverman.

numbers were staggering: nearly four million Indians were already believed to be living with HIV, and many believed the epidemic would soon spread from concentrated pockets to become a generalized epidemic.[5]

By helping scale up HIV interventions led by the Indian government and others, the 2003 introduction of Avahan ("Call to Action" in Sanskrit) contributed to a positive trend in HIV prevention programming. Using a community-based approach to gain access and build trust, Avahan offered proven prevention services in six of India's states with the highest HIV prevalence and along national trucking routes. By 2009, Avahan was providing monthly services to more than 300,000 individuals from India's most vulnerable key populations and roughly five million male clients and partners of female sex workers.[6] Studies estimate that Avahan averted hundreds of thousands of infections by 2013. However, controversy remains about the scale of Avahan's impact and its cost-effectiveness compared with that of other HIV programs in India.

The Toll of HIV in Key Affected Populations

HIV and AIDS were first recognized in the 1980s, and health professionals soon realized that the pandemic had already reached global scale. The virus primarily spreads through unprotected sex and other exposure to infected bodily fluids, such as shared needles or contaminated blood transfusions. During any single encounter, the risk of acquiring HIV is low. But with frequent repeated exposure, particularly during the most virulent phase of the infection, HIV can rapidly circulate among certain occupational, demographic, or behavioral groups. Those infected can transmit the virus to their spouses and other sexual partners—so-called "bridge groups"—who can pass it on to others. This can quickly cause an epidemic that is concentrated in certain groups to spread to the general population.

Groups with particularly high vulnerability to HIV include female sex workers, men who have sex with men, transgender people, and people who inject drugs. People in these key population groups, alongside their sexual partners, consistently account for a substantial proportion of infections across countries.[7] Studies from low- and middle-income countries suggest that the odds of HIV infection are 14 times as high for female sex workers as for other similarly aged women, and 19 times as high for men who have sex with men as for the general adult population.[8] High infection rates among key populations often signal an impending generalized epidemic.

The elevated risk within key populations is part biological, part social. For example, sex workers often have encounters with multiple clients each day, which exposes these women to high biological risk. Social forces heighten their vulnerability: they are often stigmatized, unable to seek help from health workers or police, and susceptible to abuse. They may lack access to condoms and the skills to demand their use by clients, or be so desperate as to accept a premium payment for unprotected sex.[9]

In the 1990s and into the next decade, India faced high infection rates among key populations, but prevalence remained relatively low in the general population. By 2003, the Indian government estimated national prevalence rates of less than 1 percent in the general population and 8 to 13 percent in key population groups. But several states and districts had disastrously high prevalence rates in these groups—for example, 54 percent among female sex workers in Mumbai.[10] Later modeling suggested that the government's estimates were too high—the epidemic was never as big as was feared, and prevalence rates in South India were actually declining by the early years of the 21st century.[11]

Putting an Idea in Motion: Dire Predictions Shine Light on Key Populations

In 2002, there was major concern that India would soon become ground zero for the global AIDS pandemic—although it is now clear that fears of HIV exceeded the actual trajectory of India's epidemic. Despite relatively low national prevalence, the US National Intelligence Council issued a doomsday prediction that India would see 20 to 25 million cases by 2010—more infections than predicted in any other country.[12]

The Indian government had already recognized the threat. In 1992, India implemented the first phase of a World Bank–financed National AIDS Control Program (NACP-I). And in 1999, the expanded program (NACP-II) devoted 14 percent of its budget to key populations.[13] The Indian government's AIDS control program, coupled with donor-funded interventions, made strides in changing norms about condom use among sex workers, among other prevention wins.[14] Yet despite its notable successes, the national program left large coverage gaps even in the states with highest prevalence.[15]

The US National Intelligence Council's prediction spurred action. Soon after its release, the document reached the desk of philanthropist Bill Gates. In late 2002, he announced that the Bill & Melinda Gates Foundation would pledge US$100 million to fight HIV in India. At the time, this grant was the foundation's largest investment focused on a single country (it doubled the commitment to US$200 million in 2003, and added another US$58 million in 2006).[16]

Indian nongovernmental organizations (NGOs) and activists welcomed the foundation's commitment, but more broadly the announcement met a mixed reception.[17] The Indian government had already planned to expand its work with key populations, and there were reports of some tensions between public officials and Avahan staff when it was confirmed that the foundation would not channel its funds through the national program.[18] Despite this, Avahan forged ahead, tapping Indian national Ashok Alexander to bring his private-sector expertise to drive the new initiative forward.[19] To facilitate hands-on management, the foundation opened its first field office in New Delhi.[20]

Avahan's activities were concentrated in India's highest-HIV-prevalence states and along national trucking routes, where sex workers and their clients congregate.[21] Within those states, Avahan coordinated with the National AIDS Control Organization (NACO) to identify areas with high HIV prevalence and few prevention services for female sex workers, men who have sex with men, transgender people, and people who inject drugs.[22] Avahan used a competitive bidding process to recruit NGO "implementing partners" for day-to-day program management. Funds began to flow in late 2003 and early 2004, signaling that operations had begun in earnest.

Avahan in Action

Avahan's approach was two-pronged, targeting short- and long-term sources of HIV risk. As a short-term measure to meet immediate needs, it filled gaps in the delivery of preventive and health services among its target groups. To promote long-term change, it empowered key populations to advocate for their own health and interests, while encouraging the government to reduce harmful policies that could create barriers or disincentives to preventive behavior, and to create an enabling environment for HIV prevention.[23]

As a starting point, Avahan planners understood they had to "know the epidemic" to "know the response."

Avahan's local partners worked in 83 target districts to identify entry points into wary communities. Local NGOs recruited peer educators from within key population groups; these insiders helped map beneficiary networks and took on outreach and service delivery responsibilities.[24]

For key populations at heightened risk of infection, the Avahan package included three core components. First, Avahan distributed free condoms at a massive scale—up to 10 million each month by 2007—and needles. Second, peer educators worked within their own networks on the ground to distribute products and collect information on beneficiaries. Third, Avahan opened a network of free clinics to diagnose and treat sexually transmitted infections (STIs).[25]

In addition to its core constituencies, Avahan targeted the clients and regular partners of female sex workers. Program staff helped open new condom outlets in non-traditional locations near transmission hot spots, such as tobacco shops and truck stops. Men at risk were exposed to health education and behavior change campaigns in areas where they congregated. Finally, staff developed a network of franchised clinics in the highest-risk areas, offering fee-based STI treatment and prepackaged prescription kits.[26]

Avahan also served as a platform for community mobilization of "bottom-up" activism to spark change within local communities. Local NGO partners and peer-group educators helped empower community groups to fight police abuse of sex workers and other vulnerable groups and to advocate for their interests by providing skills training and facilitation to self-help groups. Meanwhile, Avahan staff undertook mass media outreach and "top-down" lobbying of leaders and policymakers to help create an enabling environment.[27]

Avahan enlisted large international agencies to help tie together the diverse efforts of the program's many implementing partners and NGO subgrantees. In that role, organizations such as Family Health International, CARE International, and the World Health Organization drafted guidelines, trained grantees in community mobilization, and developed advocacy and communication plans.[28]

To track progress, Avahan staff relied on a dedicated monitoring and evaluation system. Although program managers did not conduct a baseline survey, they made frequent and rigorous data collection a central goal. Routine monitoring data were collected and reviewed at every level, complemented by population-based surveys.[29]

Avahan rapidly expanded and by late 2007 had undeniably achieved scale: 7,500 peer educators across 605 towns were reaching 280,000 members of key population groups (out of about 500,000) in targeted urban areas and distributing 10 million condoms each month.[30] Avahan and NACO reported that their combined efforts covered 86 percent of female sex workers, 91 percent of men who had sex with men, and 84 percent of people who used intravenous drugs in the six target areas.[31]

The Payoff: Communities Protect Themselves from HIV

Avahan's rollout was not randomized, making it difficult to definitively attribute the health impact to Avahan alone (see Box 1). Nonetheless, a host of observational studies and modeled impact evaluations paint a positive picture. They suggest that Avahan, working alongside government initiatives, curbed the drivers of HIV, even as the epidemic was already declining.

Across Avahan's target area, key populations adopted proven strategies to decrease their HIV risk. Rates of correct and consistent condom use skyrocketed among female sex workers, their male clients and partners, and men who have sex with men.[32] Likewise, injection drug users were less likely to share needles and more likely to use condoms with casual partners.[33] Two major evaluations and several smaller studies indicate that Avahan played a role in promoting these changes.[34]

Over time, the use of Avahan's clinical services increased and the STI picture improved. By the end of

---

Box 1. Strength of the Evidence

Avahan did not conduct a baseline survey and, in the interest of speed, it did not stagger or randomize the rollout. As a result, evaluators jumped through statistical hoops to assess the program's impact. Although Avahan is widely considered to have been a success, the evaluations do have limitations, prompting considerable debate about whether the observed trends can be attributed to Avahan's interventions.

In a 2011 article published in *The Lancet*, Ng and others attempted to work around these constraints by constructing a measure of program "intensity" based on Avahan's per capita spending in each district. In three of the six target states, higher program intensity was strongly associated with lower HIV prevalence, suggesting that Avahan averted roughly 100,000 new infections between 2003 and 2008. The intensity measure accounted only for Avahan spending and ignored complementary government-funded programs that were often operating in the same districts.[39] For this reason, some have noted that it might be a conservative estimate.[40] But the distribution of funding was nonrandom, so the findings could also reflect underlying differences between districts at the program's start.

In 2013, a second evaluation painted an even brighter picture of Avahan's impact. Using a mathematical model and Avahan-funded surveys, Pickles and others calculated HIV prevalence trends among key populations in the four southern states. They then linked the decline in prevalence to a plausible cause: increased self-reported condom use. The authors estimated that more than 200,000 infections had been averted between 2003 and 2007–2008, rising to more than 600,000 by 2013. However, because their method used modeled projections as the control group and relied on self-reported data, the researchers also could not prove attribution.[41]

Adding to the controversy, another study found that while HIV and syphilis prevalence in pregnant women fell significantly in Avahan program areas, the rates of decline were faster in areas funded by India's less expensive NACO. Further, the authors found no significant associations between the density of Avahan spending or sex worker interventions and the decline in HIV prevalence, whereas significant associations were identified in NACO-financed areas.[42]

Some view Avahan's inability to definitely prove population-level impact as a cautionary tale. They argue that Avahan could have more convincingly demonstrated its impact with better baseline data, designated control districts, or a randomized phase-in of activities, particularly given the cost of the monitoring and evaluation component. In the absence of those measures, critics contend that the program's results are "promising and highly suggestive, but not definitive."[43]

Others forcefully disagree, reiterating perceived practical and ethical barriers to randomizing the program's introduction. The co-chairs of Avahan's Evaluation Advisory Group argued in 2011, in *The Lancet*, that "rapid rollout and ethical discussions" precluded more rigorous evaluation methods.[44] Others argued that a randomized design would have gotten in the way of the context-specific nature of the activities—forcing more uniformity in the intervention—and prevented the ongoing program adjustments made on the basis of monitoring results.[45]

2009, a beneficiary would visit an Avahan clinic more than eight times per year on average, a significant increase from 1.2 visits in the program's first year. As health seeking improved, the prevalence of STIs observed during clinic visits declined. Between 2005 and 2009, prevalence went from 39 percent to 11 percent among female sex workers and from 12 percent to 3 percent among men who had sex with men.[35] Because some STIs facilitate HIV transmission, these gains may also have helped slow the HIV infection rate.

Did Avahan in fact slow the spread of HIV in its target districts in India? Most likely it did. While the specifics vary substantially, experts estimate that Avahan averted between about 100,000 to 200,000 infections in its first phase, a figure that may have risen to 600,000 by 2013.[36] Put differently, Avahan may have prevented up to 42 percent of potential HIV infections in its target districts within its first 4 years, possibly rising to 57 percent of potential HIV infections over the entire 10-year period.[37] That said, whether and to what extent Avahan has made an impact is not undisputed: the evaluations lack a strong counterfactual, and HIV transmission was already falling. Some studies also suggest that the government's HIV program achieved similar and possibly greater gains at a lower cost.[38]

Gains at What Price?

Between 2004 and 2009, Avahan's budget totaled US$258 million, including US$19 million for monitoring and evaluation.[46] These funds were provided by the Bill & Melinda Gates Foundation. Subgrantees spent about US$45 per beneficiary on program activities; Avahan's middle management and senior oversight expenses added another US$32 to the total per person cost. Notably, while the program cost compared favorably with the government's per-beneficiary spending for similar programs, Indian officials feared that the central overhead expenses would prove unaffordable if the Avahan program were to be taken over by the government.[47]

Avahan staff have published an analysis of the program's cost-effectiveness in 22 districts.[48] On the basis of their data, we calculated that Avahan averted 202,000 infections and an average of 17.19 disability-adjusted life years (DALYs) per HIV infection averted, for 3,471,973 total DALYs averted between 2004 and 2008. Using the total DALYs averted calculation done for *Millions Saved* led to the same cost-effectiveness ratio as the published study: US$46 per DALY averted.[49]

The Keys to Lasting Success

Avahan's strategy was to fight the virus in its "strongholds"—and it did so at a time when many HIV prevention programs shied away from working directly with these key marginalized populations. Peer educators from target communities had firsthand experience with the challenges their friends faced. A competitive bidding process enabled Avahan to select the best local NGOs for the job, ones with existing connections in target communities and with the capacity to deliver results.

Avahan was steadfast about its programming standards but also remained flexible. Rigorous clinical guidelines and a "common minimum program" of required elements kept Avahan firmly grounded in science.[50] But local implementers were empowered to tweak programmatic components to meet local needs. For example, in Bangalore, the partner NGO created "crisis response teams" to support people who experienced violence and help them file a police report; the strategy was so successful that it was eventually rolled out programwide.[51]

Another defining feature of the program was its leadership: a team of business-minded Indian nationals, steered by Ashok Alexander. Their hands-on management and "execution focus" helped jump-start the program and achieve rapid scale.[52] They also set ambitious goals, regularly reviewed program data, and often visited program sites, which promoted accountability. Grantees sometimes bristled at the demands and unrealistic targets managers placed on them. But Avahan's leaders paired high ambitions with understanding management; they were accepting of failures as long as everyone learned lessons from them.[53]

As the program progressed, it became clear that Avahan would need more than five years to achieve lasting impact and that its long-term success depended on a transition to ownership by the government and beneficiary communities.[54] In 2009 the Avahan program was renewed for a second phase, from 2009 to 2013. A written agreement with the Indian government stipulated that 10 percent of Avahan programs would transition to government control by 2009, another 20 percent two years later, and the final 70 percent by 2013.

This transition proved challenging. As the government assumed increasing responsibility for the project, Avahan planners had to compromise in some areas to meet government guidelines and budgets. For example, implementing partners had to lower staff salaries and increase the size of the catchment population served by each STI clinic.[55] But smart planning helped ease transition pains. For example, early on Avahan had pushed its grantees to forge ties with state-level AIDS control entities. And a growing government budget for AIDS enabled the government to assume increasing financial responsibility for Avahan activities. Under the third NACP, from 2007 to 2013, NACO's budget increased fivefold, to US$2.5 billion, with 70 percent dedicated to prevention.[56]

Throughout Avahan's lifespan, the criminalization of key population groups has been a barrier to success. Even as NACO and Avahan implemented interventions to reduce beneficiaries' social and medical vulnerabilities, restrictive legislation remained in place. In particular, sex work continues to have tenuous legal standing; although sex work per se is not illegal, solicitation, organized sex work, and buying or selling sex near public places are crimes.[57] As a result, individuals from key population groups and the health workers who serve them fear prosecution while organizing to improve safety, access to care, and community empowerment.

Implications for Global Health

The launch of the Avahan program in 2003 coincided with the global increase in HIV funding. Yet Avahan differed in important ways from many other programs that were expanding around the same time. Starting in 2002, the Global Fund to Fight AIDS, Tuberculosis and Malaria distributed significant funds to countries for HIV prevention and treatment, but country proposals rarely prioritized marginalized or criminalized people.[58] Likewise, in the United States, the President's Emergency Plan for AIDS Relief (PEPFAR) began operations in 2003 and quickly became the world's largest AIDS funder. Yet PEPFAR focused its resources on care and treatment, not prevention. Meanwhile, the US Congress had prohibited the use of government funds for many harm-reduction initiatives, including HIV prevention services for sex workers and needle exchange.[59]

While the global rate of new infections eventually slowed, the total population living with HIV continued to rise, leading to a general perception that HIV prevention was foundering worldwide.[60] Within this context, some cite Avahan as an exception; building on preexist-

ing government efforts, the program bucked global trends by focusing on those most at risk without judging their lifestyles. India's preexisting support for key population programs and funding from a flexible private donor made this possible.

The approach of many international agencies has since shifted toward the proactive, nonjudgmental approach pioneered by India's NACP and Avahan, reflecting broad agreement that governments and funders have both a moral and pragmatic obligation to serve key populations. For instance, key populations featured prominently in PEPFAR's 2012 "blueprint" for an AIDS-free generation and in the Global Fund's 2014 key-population action plan.[61] While the focus on key populations is now mainstream, one aspect of Avahan has not been fully embraced: behavior change as a strategy for prevention. Proven biomedical interventions like voluntary male circumcision and treatment-as-prevention consume most donor funding despite the promising results from Avahan.

Avahan's programmatic legacy is mostly positive, although the missed opportunity to conclusively demonstrate the impact of a behavioral approach has limited Avahan's influence on other HIV prevention programs. Avahan did spend substantially on monitoring and evaluation, but most of the funds went to one-off surveys. A more sustainable alternative could have been to strengthen routine government surveys to track ongoing progress. Many also express frustration that results from Avahan's stand-alone surveys were not shared with external researchers and policymakers, limiting their use.

The ultimate lesson of Avahan, when paired with the government of India's preexisting AIDS program, is twofold. First, targeting key populations can likely help alter the course of a country's HIV epidemic. Second, only rigorous, prospective evaluation—facilitated by transparent measurement—can definitively confirm that finding and tell us by how much. Now under full government ownership, Avahan has the potential to sustain and expand the quality and sensitivity that characterized its first decade. Yet potentially threatening that quest for sustainability, one development is worth watching closely: 2015 administrative changes and budget cuts that, some say, may be affecting the availability of prevention and treatment interventions.[62]

REFERENCES

amfAR. 2013. *Tackling HIV/AIDS Among Key Populations: Essential to Achieving an AIDS-Free Generation*. Washington, DC: amfAR. http://www.amfar.org/uploadedFiles/_amfarorg/Articles/On_The_Hill/2013/Key%20Populations%20Issue%20Brief%20-%20Final%20(2).pdf.

amfAR and Johns Hopkins Bloomberg School of Public Health. 2012. *Achieving an AIDS-Free Generation for Gay Men and Other MSM: Financing and Implementation of HIV Programs Targeting MSM*. New York and Baltimore, MD: amfAR and Johns Hopkins Bloomberg School of Public Health. http://www.amfar.org/uploadedFiles/_amfar.org/In_The_Community/Publications/MSM-GlobalRept2012.pdf.

Armstrong, Gregory, Chumben Humtsoe, and Michelle Kermode. 2011. "HIV Risk Behaviours among Injecting Drug Users in Northeast India Following Scale-Up of a Targeted HIV Prevention Programme." *BMC Public Health* 11 (Suppl 6): S9. doi:10.1186/1471-2458-11-S6-S9.

Armstrong, Gregory, Gajendra K. Medhi, Michelle Kermode, Jagadish Mahanta, Prabuddhagopal Goswami, and R.S. Paranjape. 2013. "Exposure to HIV Prevention Programmes Associated with Improved Condom Use and Uptake of HIV Testing by Female Sex Workers in Nagaland, Northeast India." *BMC Public Health* 13 (1): 476. doi:10.1186/1471-2458-13-476.

Arora, P., N.J.D. Nagelkerke, R. Moineddin, M. Bhattacharya, and P. Jha. 2013. "Female Sex Work Interventions and Changes in HIV and Syphilis Infection Risks from 2003 to 2008 in India: A Repeated Cross-Sectional Study." *BMJ Open* 3 (6): e002724. doi:10.1136/bmjopen-2013-002724.

AVERT. 2015. "Needle and Syringe Programmes (NSPs) for HIV Prevention." Accessed July 8. http://www.avert.org/needle-and-syringe-programmes-nsps-hiv-prevention.htm.

Baral, Stefan, Chris Beyrer, Kathryn Muessig, Tonia Poteat, Andrea L. Wirtz, Michele R. Decker, Susan G. Sherman, and Deanna Kerrigan. 2012. "Burden of HIV among Female Sex Workers in Low-Income and Middle-Income Countries: A Systematic Review and Meta-Analysis." *Lancet Infectious Diseases* 12 (7): 538–49. doi:10.1016/S1473-3099(12)70066-X.

Baral, Stefan, Frangiscos Sifakis, Farley Cleghorn, and Chris Beyrer. 2007. "Elevated Risk for HIV Infection among Men Who Have Sex with Men in Low- and Middle-Income Countries 2000–2006: A Systematic Review." *PLoS Medicine* 4 (12): e339. doi:10.1371/journal.pmed.0040339.

Bertozzi, Stefano M., Nancy Padian, and Tyler E. Martz. 2010. "Evaluation of HIV Prevention Programmes: The Case of Avahan." *Sexually Transmitted Infections* 86 (Suppl 1): i4–5. doi:10.1136/sti.2009.039263.

Bill & Melinda Gates Foundation. 2008a. *Avahan—The India AIDS Initiative: The Business of HIV Prevention at Scale*. New Delhi, India: Bill & Melinda Gates Foundation. https://docs.gatesfoundation.org/Documents/Avahan_HIVPrevention.pdf.

———. 2008b. *Use It or Lose It: How Avahan Used Data to Shape Its HIV Prevention Efforts in India*. New Delhi, India: Bill & Melinda Gates Foundation.

———. 2009. "Avahan—The India AIDS Initiative." Fact sheet. https://docs.gatesfoundation.org/Documents/Avahan_FactSheet.pdf.

———. 2010. *Breaking through Barriers: Avahan's Scale-Up of HIV Prevention among High-Risk MSM and Transgenders in India*. New Delhi, India: Bill & Melinda Gates Foundation. https://docs.gatesfoundation.org/Documents/breaking-thru-barriers.pdf.

Boerma, Ties, and Isabelle de Zoysa. 2011. "Beyond Accountability: Learning from Large-Scale Evaluations." *Lancet* 378 (9803): 1610–12. doi:10.1016/S0140-6736(11)61519-5.

Business Standard. 2003. "Gates Foundation Hikes AIDS Grant to $200 Million," October 14. http://www.business-standard.com/article/economy-policy/gates-foundation-hikes-aids-grant-to-200-million-103101401088_1.html.

Cole, Claire, Maria May, Julie Rosenberg Talbot, Rebecca Weintraub, and Michael Porter. 2012. *The Avahan India AIDS Initiative: Managing Targeted HIV Prevention at Scale*. Cases in Global Health Delivery. Boston: Global Health Delivery Project at Harvard University.

Deering, Kathleen N., Marie-Claude Boily, Catherine M. Lowndes, Jean Shoveller, Mark W. Tyndall, Peter Vickerman, Jan Bradley, et al. 2011. "A Dose-Response Relationship between Exposure to a Large-Scale HIV Preventive Intervention and Consistent Condom Use with Different Sexual Partners of Female Sex Workers in Southern India." *BMC Public Health* 11 (Suppl 6): S8. doi:10.1186/1471-2458-11-S6-S8.

Gezari, Vanessa. 2002. "Gates Giving $100 Million to Fight HIV: Indian Officials Say Billionaire Spreading 'Panic.'" *Chicago Tribune*, November 12. http://articles.chicagotribune.com/2002-11-12/news/0211120154_1_national-aids-control-organization-hiv-and-aids-aids-sufferers.

Global Fund to Fight AIDS, Tuberculosis and Malaria. 2014. *Key Populations Action Plan 2014–2017*. Geneva: Global Fund to Fight AIDS, Tuberculosis and Malaria. http://www.theglobalfund.org/documents/publications/other/Publication_KeyPopulations_ActionPlan_en/.

Gordon, David F. 2002. *The Next Wave of HIV/AIDS: Nigeria, Ethiopia, Russia, India, and China*. ICA 2002-04D. Washington, DC: National Intelligence Council. http://fas.org/irp/nic/hiv-aids.html.

Goswami, P., H.K. Rachakulla, L. Ramakrishnan, S. Mathew, S. Ramanathan, B. George, R. Adhikary, et al. 2013. "An Assessment of a Large-Scale HIV Prevention Programme

REFERENCES, *continued*

for High-Risk Men Who Have Sex with Men and Transgenders in Andhra Pradesh, India: Using Data from Routine Programme Monitoring and Repeated Cross-Sectional Surveys." *BMJ Open* 3 (4): e002183. doi:10.1136/bmjopen-2012-002183.

Gurung, Anup, Prakash Narayanan, Parimi Prabhakar, Anjana Das, Virupax Ranebennur, Saroj Tucker, Laxmi Narayana, et al. 2011. "Large-Scale STI Services in Avahan Improve Utilization and Treatment Seeking Behaviour amongst High-Risk Groups in India: An Analysis of Clinical Records from Six States." *BMC Public Health* 11 (Suppl 6): S10. doi:10.1186/1471-2458-11-S6-S10.

Izugbara, Chimaraoke O. 2007. "Constituting the Unsafe: Nigerian Sex Workers' Notions of Unsafe Sexual Conduct." *African Studies Review* 50 (03): 29–49. doi:10.1353/arw.2008.0025.

Jha, P., R. Kumar, A. Khera, M. Bhattacharya, P. Arora, V. Gajalakshmi, P. Bhatia, et al. 2010. "HIV Mortality and Infection in India: Estimates from Nationally Representative Mortality Survey of 1.1 Million Homes." *BMJ* 340 (2): c621. doi:10.1136/bmj.c621.

Kuriakose, Dhiya. 2012. *Violence against SexWorkers in Chennai.* YouTube video, 6:56. Posted April 30. https://www.youtube.com/watch?v=PlpdO8lrrec.

Laga, Marie, and Rob Moodie. 2012. "Avahan and Impact Assessment." *Lancet* 379 (9820): 1003–4. doi:10.1016/S0140-6736(12)60426-7.

Lipovsek, V., A. Mukherjee, D. Navin, P. Marjara, A. Sharma, and K.P. Roy. 2010. "Increases in Self-Reported Consistent Condom Use among Male Clients of Female Sex Workers Following Exposure to an Integrated Behaviour Change Programme in Four States in Southern India." *Sexually Transmitted Infections* 86 (Suppl 1): i25–32. doi:10.1136/sti.2009.038497.

Mainkar, Mandar M., Dilip B. Pardeshi, Jayesh Dale, Sucheta Deshpande, Shirin Khazi, Abhishek Gautam, Prabuddhagopal Goswami, et al. 2011. "Targeted Interventions of the Avahan Program and Their Association with Intermediate Outcomes among Female Sex Workers in Maharashtra, India." *BMC Public Health* 11 (Suppl 6): S2. doi:10.1186/1471-2458-11-S6-S2.

Mirelman, Andrew, Amanda Glassman, and Miriam Temin. 2016. *Estimating the Avertable Disease Burden and Cost-Effectiveness in* Millions Saved *Third Edition.* CGD Working Paper. Washington, DC: Center for Global Development.

NACO (National AIDS Control Organization). 2007. *HIV Fact Sheets: Based on HIV Sentinel Surveillance Data in India 2003–2006.* New Delhi, India: Ministry of Health and Family Welfare. http://naco.gov.in/upload/NACO%20PDF/HIV_Fact_Sheets_2006.pdf.

———. 2016. "About NACO." Accessed February 5. http://www.naco.gov.in/NACO/About_NACO/.

Ng, Marie, Emmanuela Gakidou, Alison Levin-Rector, Ajay Khera, Christopher J.L. Murray, and Lalit Dandona. 2011. "Assessment of Population-Level Effect of Avahan, an HIV-Prevention Initiative in India." *Lancet* 378 (9803): 1643–52. doi:10.1016/S0140-6736(11)61390-1.

Office of the Global AIDS Coordinator. 2012. *PEPFAR Blueprint: Creating an AIDS-Free Generation.* Washington, DC: Office of the Global AIDS Coordinator. http://www.pepfar.gov/documents/organization/201386.pdf.

One Hundred Eighth Congress of the United States of America. 2003. H.R.1298. Washington, DC: United States Congress. http://www.state.gov/documents/organization/30368.pdf.

Over, Mead, Peter Heywood, Julian Gold, Indrani Gupta, Subhash Hira, and Elliot Marseille. 2004. *HIV/AIDS Treatment and Prevention in India: Modeling the Cost and Consequences.* Health, Nutrition, and Population Series. Washington, DC: World Bank.

Panchanadeswaran, Subadra, Sethulakshmi C. Johnson, Sudha Sivaram, A.K. Srikrishnan, Carla Zelaya, Suniti Solomon, Vivian F. Go, and David Celentano. 2010. "A Descriptive Profile of Abused Female Sex Workers in India." *Journal of Health, Population, and Nutrition* 28 (3): 211–20.

Pandey, Arvind, Ram Mishra, Damodar Sahu, Sudhir Benara, Uttpal Sengupta, Ramesh S. Paranjape, Abhishek Gautam, Satya Lenka, and Rajatshurva Adhikary. 2011. "Heading towards the Safer Highways: An Assessment of the Avahan Prevention Programme among Long Distance Truck Drivers in India." *BMC Public Health* 11 (Suppl 6): S15. doi:10.1186/1471-2458-11-S6-S15.

Parliament of the Republic of India. 1956. *The Immoral Traffic (Prevention) Act.* http://www.hyderabadpolice.gov.in/acts/immoraltraffic.pdf.

Pickles, Michael, Marie-Claude Boily, Peter Vickerman, Catherine M. Lowndes, Stephen Moses, James F. Blanchard, Kathleen N. Deering, et al. 2013. "Assessment of the Population-Level Effectiveness of the Avahan HIV-Prevention Programme in South India: A Preplanned, Causal-Pathway-Based Modelling Analysis." *Lancet Global Health* 1 (5): e289–99. doi:10.1016/S2214-109X(13)70083-4.

Rao, P.J.V.R. 2010. "Avahan: The Transition to a Publicly Funded Programme as a next Stage." *Sexually Transmitted Infections* 86 (Suppl 1): i7–8. doi:10.1136/sti.2009.039297.

Seale, Andy. 2015. "Global Fund HIV Investments: MSM, Transgender and Human Rights." PowerPoint presentation. Accessed July 8. http://www.amfar.org/uploadedFiles/Articles/Articles/Around_The_World/MSM/HumanRights.pdf?n=135.

Sgaier, S.K., A. Ramakrishnan, N. Dhingra, A. Wadhwani, A. Alexander, S. Bennett, A. Bhalla, et al. 2013. "How the Avahan HIV Prevention Program Transitioned from the

REFERENCES, *continued*

Gates Foundation to the Government of India." *Health Affairs* 32 (7): 1265–73. doi:10.1377/hlthaff.2012.0646.

Shannon, Kate, Steffanie A. Strathdee, Shira M. Goldenberg, Putu Duff, Peninah Mwangi, Maia Rusakova, Sushena Reza-Paul, et al. 2015. "Global Epidemiology of HIV among Female Sex Workers: Influence of Structural Determinants." *Lancet* 385 (9962): 55–71. doi:10.1016/S0140-6736(14)60931-4.

Sharma, Dinesh C. 2015. "Budget Cuts Threaten AIDS and Tuberculosis Control in India." *Lancet* 386 (9997): 942. doi:10.1016/S0140-6736(15)00114-2.

Shetty, Priya. 2002. "Gates Offers $100 M Grant to Fight AIDS." *Tribune* (India), November 11. http://www.tribuneindia.com/2002/20021112/biz.htm#1.

———. 2005. "Ashok Alexander: Taking on the Challenge of AIDS in India." *Lancet* 366 (November): 1843.

Subramanian, Thilakavathi, Lakshmi Ramakrishnan, Santhakumar Aridoss, Prabuddhagopal Goswami, Boopathi Kanguswami, Mathew Shajan, Rajat Adhikary, et al. 2013. "Increasing Condom Use and Declining STI Prevalence in High-Risk MSM and TGs: Evaluation of a Large-Scale Prevention Program in Tamil Nadu, India." *BMC Public Health* 13 (1): 857. doi:10.1186/1471-2458-13-857.

Thilakavathi, S., K. Boopathi, C.P. Girish Kumar, A. Santhakumar, R. Senthilkumar, C. Eswaramurthy, V. Ilaya Bharathy, et al. 2011. "Assessment of the Scale, Coverage and Outcomes of the Avahan HIV Prevention Program for Female Sex Workers in Tamil Nadu, India: Is There Evidence of an Effect?" *BMC Public Health* 11 (Suppl 6): S3. doi:10.1186/1471-2458-11-S6-S3.

UNAIDS (Joint United Nations Programme on HIV/AIDS). 2002. *Report on the Global HIV/AIDS Epidemic.* UNAIDS/02.26E. Geneva: UNAIDS.

———. 2013. *Global Report: UNAIDS Report on the Global AIDS Epidemic 2013.* Geneva: UNAIDS.

Vassall, Anna, Michael Pickles, Sudhashree Chandrashekar, Marie-Claude Boily, Govindraj Shetty, Lorna Guinness, Catherine M. Lowndes, et al. 2014. "Cost-Effectiveness of HIV Prevention for High-Risk Groups at Scale: An Economic Evaluation of the Avahan Programme in South India." *Lancet Global Health* 2 (9): e531–40. doi:10.1016/S2214-109X(14)70277-3.

ENDNOTES

1. Panchanadeswaran et al. (2010).
2. Panchanadeswaran et al. (2010).
3. Kuriakose (2012).
4. See also chapter 2 in this volume.
5. UNAIDS (2002).
6. Bill & Melinda Gates Foundation (2009).
7. amfAR (2013).
8. Baral et al. (2007, 2012).
9. Izugbara (2007).
10. NACO (2007).
11. Jha et al. (2010).
12. Gordon (2002).
13. NACO (2016); Cole et al. (2012).
14. Over and World Bank (2004).
15. Bill & Melinda Gates Foundation (2008a).
16. *Business Standard* (2003); Shetty (2002); Gezari (2002).
17. Shetty (2002).
18. Cole et al. (2012).
19. Shetty (2005).
20. Cole et al. (2012).
21. Bill & Melinda Gates Foundation (2009).
22. Bill & Melinda Gates Foundation (2008b).
23. Bill & Melinda Gates Foundation (2008a).
24. Bill & Melinda Gates Foundation (2008b).
25. Bill & Melinda Gates Foundation (2008a)
26. Bill & Melinda Gates Foundation (2008a)
27. Bill & Melinda Gates Foundation (2008a)
28. Cole et al. (2012)
29. Bill & Melinda Gates Foundation (2008a)
30. Bill & Melinda Gates Foundation (2008a)
31. Bill & Melinda Gates Foundation (2008a). The figures for female sex workers and men who have sex with men are for Karnataka, Andhra Pradesh, Maharashtra, and Tamil Nadu only. Injection drug user figures are for Manipur and Nagaland only.
32. Mainkar et al. (2011); Deering et al. (2011); Thilakavathi et al. (2011); Lipovsek et al. (2010); Pandey et al. (2011); Armstrong et al. (2013); Goswami et al. (2013); Subramanian et al. (2013).
33. Armstrong, Humtsoe, and Kermode (2011).
34. Ng et al. (2011); Pickles et al. (2013).
35. Gurung et al. (2011).
36. Ng et al. (2011); Pickles et al. (2013).
37. Pickles et al. (2013).
38. Arora et al. (2013).
39. Ng et al. (2011).
40. Pickles et al. (2013).
41. Pickles et al. (2013).
42. Arora et al. (2013).
43. Bertozzi, Padian, and Martz (2010).
44. Boerma and de Zoysa (2011).
45. Laga and Moodie (2012).
46. Cole et al. (2012).
47. Rao (2010).
48. Vassall et al. (2014).
49. Estimated costs, DALYs averted, and cost-effectiveness are from the *Lancet Global Health* study (Vassall et al. 2014). The extrapolation of study results to the scaled-up scenario in all program districts was done linearly, and a similar cost-effectiveness ratio was obtained. See Mirelman, Glassman, and Temin (2016) for details of calculations and assumptions.

ENDNOTES, *continued*

50. Bill & Melinda Gates Foundation (2008a).
51. Bill & Melinda Gates Foundation (2010).
52. Bill & Melinda Gates Foundation (2008a).
53. Cole et al. (2012).
54. Cole et al. (2012).
55. Cole et al. (2012).
56. Sgaier et al. (2013).
57. Shannon et al. (2015); Parliament of the Republic of India (1956).
58. amfAR and Johns Hopkins Bloomberg School of Public Health (2012); Seale (2015).
59. One Hundred Eighth Congress of the United States of America (2003); AVERT (2015).
60. UNAIDS (2013).
61. Office of the Global AIDS Coordinator (2012); Global Fund to Fight AIDS, Tuberculosis and Malaria (2014).
62. Sharma (2015).

Learning from Disappointment
Peru's Handwashing Initiative

The Case at a Glance

HEALTH GOAL: To improve the health of children under five by reducing childhood diarrhea and acute respiratory infection.

STRATEGY: Mass media, community, and school-based promotion of handwashing with soap.

HEALTH IMPACT: No impact on diarrhea, anemia, growth, or acute lower respiratory tract infection.

WHY IT DIDN'T WORK: Insufficiently intensive and personalized interventions in communities, schools, and facilities. Uneven implementation through partners. Uneven quality of frontline workers. Insufficient training and other materials.

FINANCING: No dedicated budget: programming integrated into multiple government programs at different levels, plus corporate social responsibility programs in the private sector.

SCALE: Implemented in 24 of Peru's 25 regions; reached an estimated 640,000 people through public events and direct contact with frontline workers (2010).

Since the mid-19th century, when a Viennese doctor recognized the importance of handwashing to halt the spread of disease, the health benefits of handwashing with soap have been common knowledge in many countries. Poor hygiene is a major contributor to diarrhea and acute respiratory infection, two of the most common killers of children in low- and middle-income countries. Yet in these countries an average of just 17 percent of mothers wash their hands with soap after defecating.[1] But improving handwashing habits is hard, even when knowledge about the benefits is widespread and soap and water are readily available.[2] Most efforts to make handwashing universal have been sporadic, small-scale, and often ineffective.[3]

In Peru, the government began a handwashing initiative (HWI) in 2003 as a multisectoral effort to increase handwashing among mothers and young children. The HWI, which was a collaboration with the Global Public-Private Partnership for Handwashing with Soap, used public education and media messaging to spread the word in 14 of the country's 25 regions.

The program got a major boost in 2007 when the World Bank's Water and Sanitation Program (WSP)

added its resources and know-how through the Global Scaling Up Handwashing Project, an evidence-based program to improve handwashing behavior in real-world settings. The initiative reached its target audience, increased their knowledge, and improved self-reported handwashing behavior. However, as of 2015, the combination of efforts has been neither potent nor consistent enough to significantly improve child health—a finding that may also reflect Peru's rapid economic growth and improved living conditions over the past decade.

The Global Scaling Up Handwashing Project provided the first-ever opportunity to study the impact of a large-scale, real-world handwashing program on a range of health outcomes. The experience yields important lessons on sanitation and hygiene promotion efforts for Peru and beyond.

The Toll of Dirty Hands

Human excrement hosts a range of harmful pathogens, including those that cause diarrhea and lower respiratory infections (see also chapters 5 and 20 in this volume).

This case was originally authored by Miriam Temin.

When mothers or their children wipe themselves after defecating and then prepare or eat food, their own hands can become a potent disease vector.

Peruvian mothers viewed diarrhea as a normal part of childhood, much like teething.[4] This reflected its frequency; in a study conducted in 2000, an average of 15 percent of children under five had experienced diarrhea within the previous two weeks.[5] Diarrhea can be deadly serious; it was the cause of 6 percent of Peru's under-five deaths that same year. Between the 1990s and 2010, however, the situation improved significantly. Helped by a dramatic increase in exclusive breast-feeding—breast milk provides babies with immunological support and prevents mothers from feeding babies contaminated fluids and food instead[6]—and living standards during the 1990s, the burden of diarrhea-related disease in Peru fell more than the burden of any other single disease.[7] In contrast, lower respiratory infection remained the biggest single killer of Peruvian children, responsible for one-quarter of under-five deaths in 2000.[8]

Many factors made Peruvian children sick, and poor handwashing habits were one of them. As of 2004, a mere 14 percent of mothers washed their hands with soap after using the toilet, and only 6 percent of mothers did so before cooking.[9] More than one-fifth of households had no access to sanitation, compounding the hygiene risk.[10]

Hygiene promotion is a relatively uncontroversial strategy, unsullied by the debates surrounding many other health promotion enterprises such as condom campaigns or sin taxes. It is widely accepted that washing hands with soap removes viruses and bacteria and thus prevents nasty pathogens from entering people's systems.[11] Systematic reviews have likewise confirmed the potential of handwashing with soap to prevent disease. When done at critical times—before eating and cooking, and after using the toilet or cleaning a baby's bottom—it can prevent a third to nearly half of childhood diarrhea cases, and nearly a quarter of respiratory infections.[12]

Studies on the impact of handwashing with soap make for compelling reading, but they must be interpreted with caution. Most evidence comes from small, tightly controlled projects that measured a program's impact after a short period of time, rarely documenting whether behavior changes were sustained in the long run.[13] In addition, the handwashing projects investigated have typically been intense, often including weekly visits from health promoters and free soap distribution, and have been difficult to replicate in large-scale settings.[14]

Putting an Idea in Motion: Peru Adds Soap to Water

To test different strategies for translating handwashing efficacy into handwashing effectiveness, the World Bank's WSP initiated a Global Scaling Up Handwashing Project in 2006, with the support of the Bill & Melinda Gates Foundation. Since the 1970s, the World Bank has been a leader in promoting access to water and sanitation services; it administers the WSP on behalf of multiple donors. Peru was one of several sites selected for the Global Scaling Up Handwashing Project, along with Vietnam, Tanzania, and Senegal.

Peru had a national HWI under way since 2003, in collaboration with the Global Public-Private Partnership for Handwashing with Soap.[15] The HWI also worked closely with the Ministry of Health, which strongly championed handwashing from the start. Over time the Ministry of Education added its support.[16] By 2005 the HWI was up and running in 14 regions of the country. The HWI supported a variety of activities, including engaging mothers in small group discussions and a mass media campaign called Manos Limpios, Niños Sanos ("Clean Hands, Healthy Children") to promote handwashing messages.

By 2008, sanitation practices had indeed improved: nearly 50 percent of caregivers reported washing their hands with soap after using the toilet, and 68 percent reported doing so before cooking and preparing food, although only a third washed with soap before feeding children. There was still considerable room for improvement, but the HWI had provided a solid foundation for a serious scale-up effort.

Broader political trends in Peru facilitated a stronger nationwide push on handwashing. Around the time the HWI kicked off, the government had made childhood malnutrition a priority, providing a natural entry point for handwashing promotion given the link between malnutrition, diarrhea and other childhood illnesses, and poor sanitation. In addition, the government was moving toward a more decentralized structure. It devolved funding and decision making to provincial, district, and regional levels. This made it possible for politicians at every level of government to embrace handwashing promotion.[17]

The Handwashing Initiative in Action

By 2007 the HWI was ready to test whether the results of small-scale efficacy studies on handwashing could be scaled up. With the support of World Bank funding and Global Scaling Up Handwashing Project staff, the HWI set out to reach nearly 800 districts across 104 provinces in Peru.[18] The initiative's scale-up approach was grounded in a solid theory of change: by using innovative promotional approaches to influence the behavioral determinants of handwashing, it should be possible to break the chain between poor hygiene and childhood illness.[19]

The HWI strategy was to surround the target group— mothers, caregivers, and children under 12—with consistent messages using mass media, direct consumer contact, and community- and school-based activities. Across a wide variety of media outlets—radio, posters, comic books, and events—the HWI delivered a single core message: soap and water should be available and used immediately before cooking or eating, and after going to the toilet or changing a baby.

Planners targeted the determinants of handwashing as suggested by formative research and the latest developments in behavior change theory. The initiative's "FOAM" framework—Focus, Opportunity, Ability, and Motivation (see Figure 1)—departed from the assumption that knowledge of germs and disease is sufficient to change behavior.[20] Instead, it conveyed how dirty and disgusting hands can get in the toilet, a potent psychological motivation. It also addressed other determinants of handwashing, such as ready access to soap and water. Primary school teachers integrated handwashing into their classrooms and mobilized students as "change agents," training them to insistently remind their mothers about handwashing at home.[21]

At the forefront of the HWI's expanded efforts was a newly minted superhero, Super Jaboncin ("Super Soapy"), a germ fighter powered by soap and water.[22] Through colorful public theater, parades, and games, Super Jaboncin figures stressed the importance of handwashing with soap. For the many Peruvians without a convenient place to wash their hands, Super Jaboncin lent his name to simple handwashing stations made available by Duraplast, a private-sector partner.[23] The stations held repurposed plastic bottles containing soap and water. In total, considerably more than 80,000 Super Jaboncin handwashing stations appeared in schools and households.[24] The initiative also encouraged households to build their own versions.

Beyond Duraplast, the HWI had several other partners and many participating entities. National, regional, and local governments integrated the HWI into ongoing health promotion, school education, environmental education, and water and sanitation programs run by the Ministry of Women and the Ministry of Social Development, Health, and Education.[25] In 2008, handwashing promotion was incorporated into Juntos, Peru's large-scale conditional cash transfer program targeting poor households. By 2010, the HWI had engaged more than 16,000 frontline workers from a range of organizations.

Figure 1. FOAM Behavior Change Framework

FOCUS	OPPORTUNITY	ABILITY	MOTIVATION
Target behavior	Access/availability	Knowledge	Belief and attitudes
Target population	Product attributes	Social support	Outcome expectations
	Social norms		Threat
			Intention

Source: Coombes and Devine (2010).

The HWI's complex structure made knowledge management, monitoring, and evaluation of paramount importance. A management information system monitored implementation. Progress was also tracked with supervisory visits and periodic intercept studies (which collect data from passersby using short interviews) around markets, which helped inform an impact evaluation.[26] The HWI used a website, newsletters, meetings, and reports to facilitate information flow between partners and to disseminate guidance and technical assistance.

The Payoff: No Difference for Child Health

The HWI's scale-up phase was designed to facilitate an impact evaluation (Box 1): some districts received only the mass media campaign and direct consumer contact events, whereas others received these interventions plus community-based activities such as training of change agents and additional school-based activities.

The impact evaluation revealed disappointing results. Evaluators found that the partial set of interventions—the mass media and direct consumer contact only—had no measurable impact on the determinants of handwashing with soap. But there was a glimmer of hope: Peruvians' exposure to the full set of interventions—mass media, direct consumer contact, training for change agents, and school-based activities—had some impact. More people in this arm heard promotional messages, learned about correct handwashing practice, and improved household availability of soap and water.

But the good news ended there. Researchers found that even with the full set of interventions, the HWI had no impact on the living environment, nor on the bacterial prevalence in drinking water or parasite prevalence in stools.[27] There was also no evidence of changes in diarrhea, micronutrient malnutrition, anemia, acute lower respiratory infection, or anthropometric measures of children's physical growth.[28] The HWI's impact may have been muted by the fact that diarrhea, one of the main targets of the initiative, was much less frequent than it had been a decade before. Still, the bottom line didn't move: the HWI did not improve health.

At What Price?

Many public and private institutions in Peru allocated resources to the HWI as they integrated handwashing activities into their programs. This made it extremely difficult to calculate the overall budget for the national program. Nevertheless, the HWI appeared to be inexpensive. Rather than massive costs for infrastructure, goods, and service delivery, the bulk of the technical assistance budget supported cheaper activities such as advocacy, coordination, information and knowledge dissemination, monitoring and evaluation, and the development of key methodologies and tools.

Notably, in other studies, handwashing has been identified as cost-effective for disease prevention. In Burkina Faso, for example, researchers estimated that hygiene promotion through handwashing with soap reduced diarrhea in children for less than 1 percent of the Ministry of Health budget and less than 2 percent of household budgets.[32] A comprehensive review ranked hygiene promotion (including handwashing) as a highly cost-effective intervention to prevent disease, costing around US$3.40 for each disability-adjusted life year (DALY) averted.[33]

But despite its likely low cost in Peru, the HWI was not cost-effective for health because it was not effective in improving health.

Why the Handwashing Initiative Fell Short in Peru

The WSP and HWI architects carefully designed a strategy for scale-up based on sophisticated research and the latest learning on behavior change communications. And the evaluation found that intense, local exposure implemented collaboratively with communities was more successful than a hands-off approach. In the districts with more comprehensive programming, the HWI did affect the determinants of handwashing, but not enough to improve children's health.

Why did it fall short? Evidence has suggested that aspects of delivery, commitment, and capacity limited the impact. The HWI's flexible design enabled provincial-level planners to adjust their strategy according to their findings on supervisory visits and to reflect cultural, demographic, and geographic diversity.[34] However, the structure and membership of the provincial-level partnerships to promote handwashing varied, which led to inconsistent

Box 1. Strength of the Evidence

Systematic reviews have confirmed the importance of hand-washing with soap to prevent infectious diseases, but whether handwashing promotion can be effective in a real-world setting remains an open question.[29] From 2008 to 2011, evaluators explored whether handwashing could work at scale in Peru by deploying a randomized study to scrutinize the provincial and district-level components of its HWI.[30]

In one study arm, people were exposed to a provincial-level intervention, which included mass media and direct consumer contact through radio, posters, and promotional events. In the second, HWI added community-level interventions, particularly training for change agents and school-based activities in selected primary schools. A final study arm served as the control group.[31]

Using quantitative and qualitative data from a broad range of sources, the evaluation measured a range of outcomes that mirrored the program's theory of change. The results chain moved from program exposure to beliefs and knowledge about handwashing to self-reported and observed handwashing behavior and, finally, to effect on bacteria prevalence in drinking water and child health metrics. The result: the mass media and direct consumer contact cam-

paigns alone failed to even get off the ground, prompting no discernible change in exposure to messages promoting handwashing. Community- and school-based interventions did slightly better, creating statistically significant changes in message exposure, knowledge about handwashing, and some measures of handwashing behavior—but even they failed to make a dent in environmental contamination or child health.

The robust experimental design of the impact evaluation provides confidence in the results, and the researchers took smart steps to limit the potential for bias or measurement error. For example, it can be a challenge to accurately measure a socially desirable behavior such as handwashing—people are liable to misreport their own behavior to match the surveyor's perceived expectations, leading to overestimates. The evaluation could not avoid this problem entirely, but it mitigated bias by using several different measures to assess handwashing frequency, including observation of household facilities, direct structured observations of handwashing, and the cleanliness of caregivers' hands, in addition to their self-reported behavior.

---

implementation of the behavior change strategy across provinces.[35] For example, participating schools did not approach handwashing uniformly, and some avoided the HWI entirely. Teacher turnover was high—reducing the effect of teacher training—and some teachers resisted spending class time on handwashing promotion.

Compounding these challenges were a variety of other implementation problems. The HWI lacked a system of quality assurance for the diverse network of frontline workers, so it was not possible to enforce the right communication methods and messages. Materials were not always available, and print materials were not consistently translated into different dialects, which required frontline workers to translate on the spot—again putting consistency of messaging at risk—or exclude speakers of some indigenous languages. In addition, demand for the Super Jaboncin handwashing stations well outstripped supply.[36]

Beyond behavior change and physical supplies, the HWI sought to promote an enabling environment—a critical factor in sustaining widespread action on hand-

washing.[37] However, while national commitment to the HWI was consistently high, provincial leaders' commitment varied. One implication of this was that despite the HWI's integration within programs at all levels of the government, the national government had to continue dedicating resources to coordinate partnerships and oversee progress.[38]

Implications for Global Health

Short-term, small-scale projects have shown that handwashing with soap can reduce childhood diarrhea; the problem is in scaling up those programs. As the Peru experience shows, a major challenge is that individuals' personal hygiene habits result from a complex combination of economic, cultural, and social forces that cannot be fully changed in the short term. Health promotion requires personalized treatment to take on these forces over time and move from knowledge to sustained behavior to health impact. (See also Box 2).

The HWI in Peru highlights the importance of impact evaluations. Program managers can begin to pinpoint the reasons for success or failure only when rigorous qualitative research is accompanied by quantitative evidence. And this is possible only when programs are well planned and have sufficient budget to monitor key outcomes that track an explicit results chain.

Entire academic departments and countless experts are dedicated to health promotion through behavior change. And it is now clear that handwashing promotion faces similar challenges to other well-studied behavior change efforts, for example, to increase condom use and encourage healthy eating. As with condom promotion, changing knowledge and beliefs about handwashing and increasing access to the necessary products alone will not improve health. To effect change, efforts must translate these products into new behaviors that are correct, consistent, and sustained over the long term.[39]

The Global Scaling Up Handwashing Project has also found that there are difficult trade-offs between effectiveness, scale, and sustainability in strategies to promote widespread behavior change. For example, experts have learned that a new behavior is more likely to be taken up by someone facing a major life change. Thus, targeting a specific group, such as women expecting their first child, may work better than targeting all mothers—but such a strategy will necessarily cover a smaller segment of the population.[40]

Another promising strategy is to integrate handwashing into other healthy habits that mothers instill in their children, for example, brushing their teeth. Doing and seeing a behavior often enough, over time, can turn it into a habit for children. Specific visual cues, like a Super Jaboncin handwashing station at the toilet exit, help remind people to take the healthy step, laying the groundwork for an automatic behavior.[41] A socioecological approach that changes social norms could play a valuable role.

Based on the evaluations and other findings, the World Bank no longer intensively supports handwashing as a stand-alone intervention—it has been integrated into a Scaling Up Rural Sanitation program (see also chapter 20 in this volume). However, handwashing promotion is ongoing in Peru. Five regional governments have allocated their own funding to continue dedicated activities. And at the national level, the Ministries of Health and Education organized a massive handwashing event in 2011 to show government commitment. Thanks to their efforts and plenty of popular buy-in, Peru won the Guinness World Record for the greatest "number of people washing their hands in multiple locations" that year.[42]

Although the specific reasons for disappointment remain unclear, evidence provides a basis for improving the national handwashing strategy. It also reinforces the importance of careful continued tracking as Peru moves forward to implement a new ministerial resolution on handwashing calling for more involvement by local government, implementation by community networks, results-based funding, and better monitoring of behavior and information feedback.[43] Ongoing learning will be necessary to replicate the success of small handwashing initiatives at scale, both in Peru and around the world.

Box 2. Handwashing Promotion in Vietnam: Another Tough Challenge

In Vietnam, the Global Scaling Up Handwashing Project built on an existing national effort to improve handwashing in seven provinces.[44] Specifically, it worked with the Vietnam Women's Union to emphasize key times for handwashing and to promote handwashing with soap as something that "good mothers" do to ensure the health and development of their young children. In provinces where activities were implemented, people's knowledge about handwashing grew. However, this did not increase self-reported handwashing with soap and, similar to the experience in Peru, the program failed to reduce prevalence of diarrhea and acute respiratory infection.[45]

The reasons? Complementary interventions were ongoing nationwide, potentially diluting the initiative's impact. In addition, characteristics of the study population may have interfered. The participants were relatively advantaged; for them, childhood illness may not have posed a sufficiently severe risk to motivate behavior change. Implementation also ran into unanticipated challenges. For example, busy women did not have the time to attend educational sessions, and the Vietnam Women's Union may have emphasized traditional but outdated didactic approaches over participatory training methods.

REFERENCES

Ansari, Shamim A., Syed A. Sattar, V. Susan Springthorpe, George A. Wells, and Walter Tostowaryk. 1989. "In Vivo Protocol for Testing Efficacy of Hand-Washing Agents against Viruses and Bacteria: Experiments with Rotavirus and Escherichia Coli." *Applied and Environmental Microbiology* 55 (2): 3113–18.

Banerjee, Abhijit V., and Esther Duflo. 2011. *Poor Economics: A Radical Rethinking of the Way to Fight Global Poverty*. New York: PublicAffairs.

Borghi, J., L. Guinness, J. Ouedraogo, and V. Curtis. 2002. "Is Hygiene Promotion Cost-Effective? A Case Study in Burkina Faso." *Tropical Medicine and International Health* 7 (11): 960–69. doi:10.1046/j.1365-3156.2002.00954.x.

Cairncross, Sandy, Jamie Bartram, Oliver Cumming, and Clarissa Brocklehurst. 2010. "Hygiene, Sanitation, and Water: What Needs to Be Done?" *PLoS Medicine* 7 (11): e1000365. doi:10.1371/journal.pmed.1000365.

Chumpitazi, Mario. 2010. "Super Jaboncín al Rescate." *Boletin Jabocín* 3. Image, February 26. https://infografiasos.wordpress.com/tag/boletin-informativo/.

Coombes, Yolande, and Jacqueline Devine. 2010. *Introducing FOAM: A Framework to Analyze Handwashing Behaviors to Design Effective Handwashing Programs*. Washington, DC: Water and Sanitation Program. http://www.wsp.org/sites/wsp.org/files/publications/WSP_IntroducingFOAM_HWWS.pdf.

Curtis, Val, and Sandy Cairncross. 2003. "Effect of Washing Hands with Soap on Diarrhoea Risk in the Community: A Systematic Review." *Lancet Infectious Diseases* 3 (5): 275–81. doi:10.1016/S1473-3099(03)00606-6.

Curtis, V.A., L.O. Danquah, and R.V. Aunger. 2009. "Planned, Motivated and Habitual Hygiene Behaviour: An Eleven Country Review." *Health Education Research* 24 (4): 655–73. doi:10.1093/her/cyp002.

Dutton, Pennelope, Rocio Florez Paschiera, and Nga Kim Nguyen. 2011. *The Power of Primary Schools to Change and Sustain Handwashing with Soap among Children: The Cases of Vietnam and Peru*. Lima, Peru: Water and Sanitation Program.

Ejemot-Nwadiaro, Regina I., John E. Ehiri, Dachi Arikpo, Martin M. Meremikwu, and Julia A. Critchley. 2015. "Hand Washing Promotion for Preventing Diarrhea." *Cochrane Database of Systematic Reviews* 2015 (9). Article CD004265. doi:10.1002/14651858.CD004265.pub3.

Faix, R.G. 1987. "Comparative Efficacy of Handwashing Agents against Cytomegalovirus." *Infection Control* 8 (4): 158–62.

Fan, Victoria Yue-May, and Ajay Mahal. 2011. "What Prevents Child Diarrhoea? The Impacts of Water Supply, Toilets, and Hand-Washing in Rural India." *Journal of Development Effectiveness* 3 (3): 340–70. doi:10.1080/19439342.2011.596941.

Favin, Michael. 2011. *Endline Assessment of the Enabling Environment in Peru*. Washington, DC: Water and Sanitation Program.

Fewtrell, Lorna, Rachel B. Kaufmann, David Kay, Wayne Enanoria, Laurence Haller, and John M. Colford. 2005. "Water, Sanitation, and Hygiene Interventions to Reduce Diarrhoea in Less Developed Countries: A Systematic Review and Meta-Analysis." *Lancet Infectious Diseases* 5 (1): 42–52. doi:10.1016/S1473-3099(04)01253-8.

Galiani, Sebastian, Paul Gertler, and Alexandra Orsola-Vidal. 2012. *Promoting Handwashing Behavior in Peru: The Effect of Large-Scale Mass-Media and Community Level Interventions*. Policy Research Working Paper 6257. Washington, DC: Water and Sanitation Program.

Galiani, Sebastian, and Alexandra Orsola-Vidal. 2010. *Scaling Up Handwashing Behavior: Findings for the Impact Evaluation Baseline Survey in Peru*. Washington, DC: Water and Sanitation Program.

Gibson, L.L., J.B. Rose, C.N. Haas, C.P. Gerba, and P.A. Rusin. 2002. "Quantitative Assessment of Risk Reduction from Hand Washing with Antibacterial Soaps." *Journal of Applied Microbiology* 92 (s1): 136S–143S. doi:10.1046/j.1365-2672.92.5s1.17.x.

IHME (Institute for Health Metrics and Evaluation). 2015. GBD Compare. Accessed December 9. http://vizhub.healthdata.org/gbd-compare/.

———. 2013b. GBD Profile: Peru. Seattle, WA: IHME. http://www.healthdata.org/sites/default/files/files/country_profiles/GBD/ihme_gbd_country_report_peru.pdf.

Jamison, Dean T., Joel G. Breman, Anthony R. Measham, George Alleyne, Mariam Claeson, David B. Evans, Prabhat Jha, et al., eds. 2006. *Disease Control Priorities in Developing Countries*. 2nd ed. New York and Washington, DC: Oxford University Press and World Bank.

Lamberti, Laura M., Christa L. Fischer Walker, Adi Noiman, Cesar Victora, and Robert E. Black. 2011. "Breastfeeding and the Risk for Diarrhea Morbidity and Mortality." *BMC Public Health* 11 (Suppl 3): S15. doi:10.1186/1471-2458-11-S3-S15.

Larson, Elaine, Allison Aiello, Lillian V. Lee, Phyllis Della-Latta, Cabilia Gomez-Duarte, and Susan Lin. 2003. "Short- and Long-Term Effects of Handwashing with Antimicrobial or Plain Soap in the Community." *Journal of Community Health* 28 (2): 139–50.

Luby, Stephen P., Mubina Agboatwalla, Daniel R. Feikin, John Painter, Ward Billhimer, Arshad Altaf, and Robert M. Hoekstra. 2005. "Effect of Handwashing on Child Health: A Randomised Controlled Trial." *Lancet* 366 (9481): 225–33. doi:10.1016/S0140-6736(05)66912-7.

Madajewicz, Malgosia, Alexander Pfaff, Alexander van Geen, Joseph Graziano, Iftikhar Hussein, Hasina Momotaj,

REFERENCES, *continued*

Roksana Sylvi, and Habibul Ahsan. 2007. "Can Information Alone Change Behavior? Response to Arsenic Contamination of Groundwater in Bangladesh." *Journal of Development Economics* 84:731–54.

MINSA (Ministry of Health of Peru). 2012. Resolución Ministerial. Vol. 773–2012/MINSA. Lima, Peru: Republic of Peru.

Montville, Rebecca, Yuhuan Chen, and Donald W. Schaffner. 2002. "Risk Assessment of Hand Washing Efficacy Using Literature and Experimental Data." *International Journal of Food Microbiology* 73 (2–3): 305–13. doi:10.1016/S0168-1605(01)00666-3.

NDTV. 2015. "Guinness Book Recognises Madhya Pradesh's World Record in Washing Hands," July 4. http://www.ndtv.com/india-news/guinness-book-recognises-madhya-pradeshs-world-record-in-washing-hands-778023.

Reyes, Jorge, and Luis H. Ochoa. 2001. *Encuesta Demográfica Y de Salud Familiar 2000.* Lima, Peru: Instituto Nacional de Estadística e Informática.

Rocio, Flores. 2012. *Making the Hard-to-Reach . . . Reachable: Experiences on Public Private Partnerships for Hygiene Promotion in Peru.* Lima, Peru: World Bank, Water and Sanitation Program. https://www.wsp.org/sites/wsp.org/files/publications/WSP-Making-the-Hard-to-Reach-Reachable.pdf.

Waddington, Hugh, Birte Snilstveit, Howard White, and Lorna Fewtrell. 2009. *Water, Sanitation and Hygiene Interventions to Combat Childhood Diarrhoea in Developing Countries. Synthetic Review 001.* New Delhi, India: International Initiative for Impact Evaluation (3ie). http://www.3ieimpact.org/media/filer_public/2012/05/07/17-2.pdf.

Whitby, Michael, Mary-Louise McLaws, and Michael W. Ross. 2006. "Why Healthcare Workers Don't Wash Their Hands: A Behavioral Explanation." *Infection Control and Hospital Epidemiology* 27 (5): 484–92.

WHO (World Health Organization). 2013. "Protecting Breastfeeding in Peru," July. http://www.who.int/features/2013/peru_breastfeeding/en/.

WHP (World Hygiene Programme). 2015. "Handwashing." Accessed August 10. http://cargocollective.com/whp/Handwashing.

World Bank. 2005. *The Handwashing Handbook: A Guide for Developing a Hygiene Promotion Program to Increase Handwashing with Soap.* Document 32302. Washington, DC: World Bank. http://documents.worldbank.org/curated/en/2005/01/5794173/handwashing-handbook-guide-developing-hygiene-promotion-program-increase-handwashing-soap.

WSP (Water and Sanitation Program). 2010. *Peru: A Handwashing Behavior Change Journey.* Washington, DC: Water and Sanitation Program. http://www.wsp.org/sites/wsp.org/files/publications/WSP_PeruBehaviorChange_HWWS.pdf.

ENDNOTES

1. Curtis, Danquah, and Aunger (2009).
2. Whitby, McLaws, and Ross (2006).
3. WHP (2015).
4. Curtis, Danquah, and Aunger (2009).
5. Reyes and Ochoa (2001).
6. Lamberti et al. (2011).
7. IHME (2013b); WHO (2013).
8. IHME (2013a).
9. WSP (2010).
10. Galiani and Orsola-Vidal (2010).
11. Curtis and Cairncross (2003); Faix (1987); Ansari et al. (1989); Luby et al. (2005); Gibson et al. (2002); Montville, Chen, and Schaffner (2002); Fewtrell et al. (2005); Larson et al. (2003).
12. Curtis, Danquah, and Aunger (2009); Cairncross et al. (2010); Waddington et al. (2009).
13. Cairncross et al. (2010); Fan and Mahal (2011); Galiani, Gertler, and Orsola-Vidal (2012).
14. Jacqueline Devine, personal communication with the author, September 4, 2014.
15. World Bank (2005).
16. Favin (2011).
17. Favin (2011).
18. Galiani and Orsola-Vidal (2010).
19. Galiani, Gertler, and Orsola-Vidal (2012).
20. WSP (2010); Curtis, Danquah, and Aunger (2009).
21. Dutton, Paschiera, and Nguyen (2011).
22. Chumpitazi (2010).
23. Galiani and Orsola-Vidal (2010).
24. Favin (2011).
25. Favin (2011).
26. WSP (2010).
27. Fewer *E. coli* and other microorganisms were found in drinking water in the treatment group, but the amount was not statistically significant.
28. Studies in selected provinces found a reduction in children's diarrhea following handwashing promotion activities, but the studies did not use experimental designs, which made it difficult to attribute the cause of the change (Rocio 2012).
29. Ejemot-Nwadiaro et al. (2015); Curtis and Cairncross (2003).
30. Galiani, Gertler, and Orsola-Vidal (2012).
31. Galiani, Gertler, and Orsola-Vidal (2012).
32. Borghi et al. (2002).
33. Jamison et al. (2006).
34. WSP (2010).
35. Favin (2011).
36. WSP (2010).
37. Favin (2011).
38. Favin (2011).
39. Madajewicz et al. (2007); Banerjee and Duflo (2011).

ENDNOTES, *continued*

40. Jacqueline Devine, personal communication with the author, September 4, 2014.
41. Curtis, Danquah, and Aunger (2009); NDTV (2015).
42. NDTV (2015).
43. MINSA (2012).
44. Dutton, Paschiera, and Nguyen (2011).
45. Dutton, Paschiera, and Nguyen (2011).

Methods Used in Selecting and Analyzing *Millions Saved* Cases

Here we describe and discuss the process used to select the new *Millions Saved* cases, briefly review the evaluation methods used in the case studies, and set out our approach to estimating the real-world cost-effectiveness of *Millions Saved* programs.

Running the Case Selection Process

Millions Saved cases describe large-scale efforts to improve health that have mostly succeeded, saving millions of lives and preventing unnecessary suffering. Each case met many of the criteria set out in the introduction (these criteria are restated in Box 1); most important, each case had to address a major health problem, achieve attributable health impact, and operate at scale for several years. Together, the cases constitute an evidence-based portfolio of successful investments to improve health—alongside a few that didn't meet expectations.

Finding and selecting these cases proved challenging. Despite the recent surge in impact evaluation, relatively few studies show that particular health policies or programs actually caused the observed changes in health outcomes. Even fewer assess the costs of interventions alongside their impact. Of course, not all policies or programs require such rigorous evaluation. But where the stakes are high—in terms of lives, suffering, or politics—and where public and donor investment is significant, this kind of impact evaluation is needed to inform the allocation of limited resources, to enable policymakers to improve programs, and to motivate greater investments from those who control the purse strings.

The *Millions Saved* case selection process was rigorous, open, and transparent. We partnered with the Dis-

ease Control Priorities Network (dcp-3.org) to find cases and studies; issued public calls for submissions via the Center for Global Development and Disease Control Priorities Network websites; conducted interviews with subject-matter experts; and searched the literature, particularly Cochrane (cochrane.org), the International Initiative for Impact Evaluation (3ieimpact.org/evidence), and other evaluation and systematic review databases.

We relied on an external expert advisory group and an internal advisory group of economists to consider a list of cases that met at least some of the *Millions Saved* criteria. Finally, we enlisted people directly involved in the design, implementation, or evaluation of the particular program or policy to review each case. When we faced tough choices—on malaria, for example—we publicly aired our dilemmas on the Center for Global Development blog, which provided new perspectives on the issues, and additional evidence.[1]

Through this process we generated a short list of cases, each informed by a collection of evidence and references, plus interviews with experts or participants. Among the references were one to three key evaluation reports or systematic review studies—which had been peer reviewed in the process of preparation for publication in a journal or as a working paper—that isolated the impact of the featured program or policy on health outcomes.

Our selection process led us to eliminate several strong candidates. A number of programs to tackle noncommunicable diseases came close: in India, visual inspection of the cervix with acetic acid to screen for cervical cancer; in South Africa, reducing dietary salt by creating a national bread supply; and in multiple sites, the use of a polypill to prevent cardiovascular disease. Although these and other promising programs demonstrated that they could improve health, they fell short on at least one of the key selection criteria, most often duration or scale. Other programs—for instance, promoting dietary zinc in Bangladesh—met these criteria but were unable to demonstrate attributable health impact at scale.

No selection process is perfect, and the one used by *Millions Saved* is no exception. In particular, we are limited by the relative newness of many included programs. Although we considered the best available evidence at the time of writing, every passing day offers new insight into the programs' health impacts. Replication studies, longer-term evaluations, evolving disease and risk factor patterns, and new technologies, among other factors, will continuously influence our understanding and assessment of these policies and programs. For example, one of our "learning from disappointment" cases, government financing for facility-based births in Gujarat, India, is still under study as of 2015. The results of this evaluation may show new or different health effects over the longer time frame.

Establishing Attributable Health Impact

One of the selection criteria used by *Millions Saved* was—not surprisingly—that cases establish the attributable health impact of the included programs and policies. To do so, evaluation researchers had to estimate the "counterfactual" for each policy or program—that is, the health status that participants would have had if they had not participated in the program. Methods to establish a robust counterfactual are the backbone of good impact evaluation.

Without an appropriate impact evaluation design, establishing the counterfactual is difficult because of selection bias (when underlying differences between program beneficiaries and nonbeneficiaries result in too high or too low an estimate of impact). For example, people who choose to seek care or participate in a program are likely to be quite different from those who do not. They may be more motivated to improve their situation, more empowered, or better educated, or they might simply have more free time. Researchers often try to control for these differences, but they may miss some important factors; motivation, for example, can be difficult or impossible to measure. These factors mean that differences in outcomes may result from these unobserved characteristics rather than the intervention itself.

To avoid these biases that emerge from studies without rigorous estimation of the counterfactual, *Millions Saved* focuses on some programs whose results were assessed as part of a randomized controlled trial (RCT). In an RCT, researchers randomly assign people, facilities, or geographical areas to treatment and control groups. Randomization helps mitigate selection bias by assuring that beneficiaries and nonbeneficiaries start off in roughly similar conditions (on average), thus enabling researchers to attribute any later differences between the groups to the intervention.

In the field of global health, many worry about the ethics of randomized evaluations for scaled programs. One adviser to *Millions Saved* noted, "In a situation where the resources exist to scale up more broadly, it would be unethical to withhold lifesaving interventions for the purposes of an evaluation design." Yet *Millions Saved* cases (and many that did not make the cut) clearly show that an impact detected during an RCT (efficaciousness) does not automatically translate into an impact at scale (effectiveness)—and understanding the mechanisms of better service delivery is a worthwhile investment. Further, given the extreme scarcity of resources in low-income countries, resources to cover the entire population in need usually do not exist; as a result, gradual rollouts accompanied by an RCT are both feasible and ethical.

Where an RCT cannot be used—where it is not appropriate to the policy question, where a program or policy is already nationwide in scope, or where it is not feasible—quasi-experimental approaches offer an alternative to evaluate attribution of health impact. Quasi-experimental methods include controlled before-and-after studies, regression discontinuity designs, and matched comparisons (such as difference-in-differences). These designs are described in more detail in reference textbooks, for example, from the Abdul Latif Jameel Poverty Action Lab (povertyactionlab.org, formerly the MIT Poverty Action Lab) and the *Handbook on Impact Evaluation*.[2]

This new edition of *Millions Saved* features all of these evaluation approaches. RCTs were used to evaluate cash transfer and sanitation programs, while researchers deployed a difference-in-differences design to evaluate Thailand's universal coverage scheme. Where impact evaluations were not available, *Millions Saved* evaluators also used empirically verified increases in coverage of proven interventions alongside modeled counterfactuals to establish impact—for example, hepatitis B vaccination in China, tobacco control in Thailand, and HIV prevention in India (the Avahan program). These evaluation approaches are clearly less watertight than RCT and quasi-experimental study designs, but they do illustrate a program's likely impact with reference to a counterfactual. A final case, in Haiti, illustrates the successful elimination of a disease, polio. Here, the small number of polio cases and the large scale of the program make it difficult to directly attribute health impacts to the intervention. Instead, we consider the range of factors that contributed to elimination, including vaccination and adherence to the World Health Organization's and the Pan American Health Organization's disease elimination protocols.

Infectious disease prevention and control presents particular challenges for the establishment of cause and effect, even when quasi-experimental methods are used; this is especially the case when it is difficult or impossible to assess disease incidence or cause-specific deaths. In malaria, for example, all-cause child mortality (ACCM) is used as a primary impact measure in lieu of direct malaria mortality, both because of the difficulty in measuring malaria-specific mortality and because ACCM reflects both directly attributable and indirect deaths from malaria (via anemia, low birth weight, impaired immu-

nity, and other causes).[3] Even in this case, however, efforts can be made to assess whether changes in ACCM resulted from program effort or from weather patterns, housing improvements, or economic growth at the population level. And there is still room to learn about service delivery using RCTs or related evaluation methods—for example, which bed net distribution strategy is best for health impact?

Finally, this edition of *Millions Saved* includes several programs that met a high standard of evidence but did not demonstrate a significant health gain. Yet in interpreting these results, it is important to distinguish evidence of zero impact from limitations in the study design. For example, the Matlab, Bangladesh, evaluation of Integrated Management of Childhood Illness (IMCI), a program consisting of efficacious interventions delivered effectively and actions to improve the utilization of these same interventions, did not show a significant impact on mortality. Researchers were unable to determine whether IMCI really made no difference, or whether, owing to a surprisingly quick reduction in overall infant mortality in Bangladesh, they lacked sufficient statistical power to identify relatively small effect sizes. In contrast, other disappointments are easier to interpret because studies were adequately powered and appropriately controlled: Gujarat's subsidy for institutional delivery disappointed because of flaws in the program design, and Peru's handwashing promotion program was not intensive enough to change disease outcomes.

These issues are discussed in the "Strength of the Evidence" boxes within the specific cases. We include these boxes to allow you, the reader, to make your own judgments about the available data and the study methods used and to weigh the evidence yourself as to what worked in that particular case and what that means for global health generally.

Assessing Cost-Effectiveness

Resources are finite, and policymakers must make hard choices and set clear priorities. In doing so, they face an inconvenient truth: even the most carefully considered decisions imply real opportunity costs. For example, choosing to invest in one intervention, benefiting a particular group, inevitably means less is available to spend on another.

As a result, no matter how effective a particular intervention is for health, information on costs alongside benefits is required to establish whether the investment's health impact was "worth" the money spent in its achievement—in other words, were the benefits achieved worth the benefits forgone because the money was not spent on something else? Cost-effectiveness analyses allow policymakers to answer this essential question. Yet cost-effectiveness analysis is rarely performed as part of program implementation and impact evaluation; only a few of the evaluations underlying the case studies included their own original estimates of cost-effectiveness.

To help close the gap, we conducted our own assessment of cost-effectiveness for a subset of *Millions Saved* cases. We selected all but one of the successful programs from the "Rolling Out Medicine and Technology" and "Changing Behavior Population-wide to Reduce Risk" categories for this analysis, as they were most likely to deal with a single health problem and have an attributable health impact that could be converted to disability-adjusted life years (DALYs); only one case from each of the other two categories—"Expanding Access to Health Services" and "Using Targeted Cash Transfers to Improve Health"—was selected, Plan Nacer in Argentina and Kenya's social cash transfer program for orphans and vulnerable children. These programs not only had an attributable positive impact on one or more health outcomes but also conferred many benefits beyond those measured in the study.

These estimates are not intended to be the final word on the burden averted or the cost-effectiveness of each program—nor are they intended to be used as a guide for resource allocation. Instead, they simply provide a relative indication of possible health gains and their per-unit costs, and ways one might go about calculating this. These examples highlight that there is a lack of economic evaluation and that more formal evaluations should be conducted. There are other economic evaluation approaches that could be used as well, such as cost-benefit analysis, which would quantify the benefit in terms of monetary units and accommodate the inclusion of broader, non-health benefits that may be monetized as well.

To develop cost-effectiveness estimates, we first assessed the attributable disease and health impacts for each case study in terms of deaths and DALYs averted. We followed the World Health Organization's recommended methodology for DALY calculation. We also assessed the costs in terms of the financial resources required to carry out a given activity from the perspective of the health system. In general, we did not estimate costs related to averting future illness or from the

perspective of patients and caregivers. Thus the "costs" of a program included only financial (and not economic) costs, and for simplicity we assumed that private costs to patients and caregivers are static, or inconsequential to decision making.

It is generally recommended that cost-effectiveness be expressed as an incremental ratio, that is, a quantification of how much more health is gained for every additional dollar spent as assessed against comparator interventions, or the status quo of no intervention with existing standards of treatment. In making decisions about introducing an intervention, incremental ratios allow comparison either with maintaining the status quo or with other intervention options.[4] In our analysis, we approximated the incremental cost-effectiveness ratio (ICER) by using the attributable health impact and additional budget outlays required. Our estimates are approximations, however, and many assumptions were made in the calculations.

To determine whether or not an intervention is cost-effective, ICERs are sometimes compared with a predefined cost-effectiveness threshold. One threshold that has been historically recommended is a country's gross domestic product (GDP) per capita. Here, any intervention with an ICER (a ratio expressed as dollars per DALY averted) less than the GDP per capita is deemed "very cost-effective," and any estimate less than three times the GDP per capita is deemed "cost-effective."[5] Many global health analyses use the GDP per capita threshold, despite theoretical and practical problems with its use.[6] We employ it in our estimates to provide a context for the results. One of the lessons from the *Millions Saved* cases is that there is no guarantee that what worked in one setting will succeed or be as cost-effective in another. In other words, the generalizability of the *Millions Saved* cases and their lessons is limited. For similar reasons, the ICERs should not be compared across cases but should instead be used to signal the financial cost of health gains resulting from each program.

The results of the disease burden and cost-effectiveness estimation can be found in Table 1 (see page 224). For each case study, we list our findings on deaths and DALYs averted, the costs, and the ICERs. We also reviewed relevant literature for each intervention, including studies of cost-effectiveness found for similar interventions in settings other than the one featured in the case.

For the "Rolling Out Medicine and Technology" category, most ICERs were less than or equal to US$100 per DALY averted. This result highlights that the cost-effectiveness of small-scale interventions can be retained when the intervention is implemented at large scale, but this is not always the case. Effectiveness and cost-effectiveness can decline or even disappear in larger programs, as has been documented in education interventions.[7]

Mexico's Piso Firme program, which upgraded flooring material, was the one case in the medicine and technology rollout category in which an ICER could not be calculated because of the difficulty of estimating the total costs and health impacts. We have provided a modeled estimate of the DALYs averted from improvements in diarrhea mortality and morbidity, but clearly additional health benefits have been gained from the intervention. As one point of comparison, though, the authors of the impact evaluation in a single state estimate that Piso Firme cost about US$150 per household, which compares favorably with the cost of achieving nutrition outcomes of similar magnitude in a Latin American cash transfer program.[8]

In the "Expanding Access to Health Services" category, Argentina's Plan Nacer had an original cost-effectiveness estimate calculated as part of the impact evaluation, which we were able to use because the impact evaluation was conducted during the project scale-up instead of just during a pilot or in a single state. The study is notable because it is one of the only ones in which the cost-effectiveness of a structural health systems intervention, here a performance-based incentive program, was estimated. This is in fact rarely done, even in high-income countries.[9]

Calculating the cost-effectiveness of the programs described in the "Using Targeted Cash Transfers to Improve Health" section is problematic because of their multiple development objectives. In this case, efficiency is measured in terms of the cost-transfer ratio (CTR), a measure of administrative efficiency that divides the cost of the program by the amount of the transfer. A CTR below 1 means that the administrative costs of the program are at least less than the amount of money disbursed. In comparison with the CTRs of other cash transfer programs, the CTR of the Kenya cash transfer program falls within an acceptable range of 0.1 to 0.5.[10] But the CTR may change depending on when in the program life it is calculated. For example, at the start of a program, the CTR will be much higher because of fixed capital and other start-up costs.[11]

In the "Changing Behavior Population-wide to Reduce Risk" category, we found that all the interventions appeared to be relatively cost-effective. Thailand's national tobacco control program and India's Avahan each fell under US$100 per DALY averted, sanitation promotion in Indonesia was between US$200 and US$800 per DALY averted, and Vietnam's motorcycle helmet policy was around US$1,200 per DALY averted. These results were similar to estimates found in the literature, although our estimate for helmets was higher than those seen in other studies. This may be due to differences in the cost and impact data that we used for this case, which were particularly difficult to obtain.[12]

Finally, most programs had ICERs well under the GDP per capita; Vietnam's helmet program just barely exceeded that threshold. Although the GDP per capita threshold is only a rough indication of the cost-effectiveness of any given health intervention, these results suggest that most of the *Millions Saved* programs selected were good buys in terms of implementation.[13]

In Summary

Establishing cause and effect and cost-effectiveness in health policies and programs is essential to the process of deciding where the next peso, pound, or pula can be spent to improve global health. The *Millions Saved* cases show that this kind of rigor in evaluation at scale is possible, that there are several techniques available to assess the impact, and that the *Millions Saved* programs represent good investments.

REFERENCES

Bold, Tessa, Mwangi Kimenyi, Germano Mwabu, Alice Ng'ang'a, and Justin Sandefur. 2013. *Scaling Up What Works: Experimental Evidence on External Validity in Kenyan Education.* Working Paper 321. Washington, DC: Center for Global Development. http://papers.ssrn.com/sol3/papers.cfm?abstract_id=2241240.

Cattaneo, Matias D., Sebastian Galiani, Paul J. Gertler, Sebastian Martinez, and Rocio Titiunik. 2009. "Housing, Health, and Happiness." *American Economic Journal: Economic Policy* 1 (1): 75–105. doi:10.1257/pol.1.1.75.

Commission on Macroeconomics and Health. 2001. *Macroeconomics and Health: Investing in Health for Economic Development.* Geneva: World Health Organization. http://apps.who.int/iris/bitstream/10665/42435/1/924154550X.pdf.

Eijkenaar, Frank. 2012. "Pay for Performance in Health Care: An International Overview of Initiatives." *Medical Care Research and Review* 69 (3): 251–76. doi:10.1177/1077558711432891.

Glassman, Amanda, and Kate McQueston. 2014a. "What Works in Malaria Control?" Center for Global Development blog, April 30. http://www.cgdev.org/blog/what-works-malaria-control.

———. 2014b. "What Works in Malaria Control? Part 2." Center for Global Development blog, May 9. http://www.cgdev.org/blog/what-works-malaria-part-2.

Hutubessy, Raymond, Dan Chisholm, and Tessa Tan-Torres Edejer. 2003. "Generalized Cost-Effectiveness Analysis for National-Level Priority-Setting in the Health Sector." *Cost Effectiveness and Resource Allocation: C/E* 1 (1): 8. doi:10.1186/1478-7547-1-8.

Khandker, Shahidur R., Gayatri B. Koolwal, and Hussain A. Samad. 2010. *Handbook on Impact Evaluation: Quantitative Methods and Practices.* Washington, DC: World Bank Publications.

Marseille, Elliot, Bruce Larson, Dhruv S. Kazi, James G. Kahn, and Sydney Rosen. 2015. "Thresholds for the Cost-Effectiveness of Interventions: Alternative Approaches." *Bulletin of the World Health Organization* 93 (2): 118–24.

McCabe, Christopher, Karl Claxton, and Anthony J. Culyer. 2008. "The NICE Cost-Effectiveness Threshold: What It Is and What That Means." *PharmacoEconomics* 26 (9): 733–44.

Mirelman, Andrew, Amanda Glassman, and Miriam Temin. 2016. *Estimating the Avertable Disease Burden and Cost-Effectiveness in* Millions Saved *Third Edition.* CGD Working Paper. Washington, DC: Center for Global Development.

Passmore, Jonathon W., Lan Huong Nguyen, Nam Phuong Nguyen, and Jean-Marc Olivé. 2010. "The Formulation and Implementation of a National Helmet Law: A Case Study from Viet Nam." *Bulletin of the World Health Organization* 88 (10): 783–87. doi:10.2471/BLT.09.071662.

Samson, Michael, Ingrid van Niekerk, and Kenneth Mac Quene. 2006. *Designing and Implementing Social Transfer Programmes.* Cape Town, South Africa: EPRI Press. http://www.unicef.org/socialpolicy/files/designing_and_implementing_social_transfer_programmes.pdf.

Ward, Patrick, Alex Hurrell, Aly Visram, Nils Riemenschneider, Luca Pellerano, Clare O'Brien, Ian MacAuslan, and Jack Willis. 2010. *Cash Transfer Programme for Orphans and Vulnerable Children (CT-OVC), Kenya: Operational and Impact Evaluation, 2007–2009.* Final Report. Oxford, UK: Oxford Policy Management. http://www.unicef.org/evaluation/files/OPM_CT-OVC_evaluation_report_july2010-final_Kenya_2010-019.pdf.

ENDNOTES

1. Glassman and McQueston (2014a, 2014b).
2. Khandker, Koolwal, and Samad (2010).
3. Erin Eckert, comment on "What Works in Malaria Control?" blog post (Glassman and McQueston 2014a).
4. Hutubessy, Chisholm, and Edejer (2003).
5. Commission on Macroeconomics and Health (2001).
6. Marseille et al. (2015).
7. Bold et al. (2013).
8. Cattaneo et al. (2009).
9. Eijkenaar (2012).
10. Ward et al. (2010); Samson, van Niekerk, and Mac Quene (2006).
11. Ward et al. (2010).
12. Passmore et al. (2010).
13. Marseille et al. (2015) have criticized the use of the GDP per capita threshold as a measure for making cost-effectiveness conclusions. The cost-effectiveness threshold, as conceived as an opportunity cost given a health budget constraint, provides guidance for the amount of health that can be gained or lost when one intervention is invested in, compared with the most cost-effective intervention currently in the budget. That is, interventions found to be cost-effective below this threshold are health gaining, but interventions above this threshold represent a health loss due to the need for disinvestment (McCabe, Claxton, and Culyer 2008). For further information on the approach used to calculate the cost-effectiveness ratios used in this book, see Mirelman, Glassman, and Temin (2016).

Table 1. Estimated Health Impact and Incremental Cost-Effectiveness Estimates for a Selection of *Millions Saved* Cases

PROGRAM, COUNTRY, PER CAPITA GROSS DOMESTIC PRODUCT (GDP)	TIME HORIZON	TARGET POPULATION	KEY HEALTH OUTCOMES	DEATHS AVERTED	DISABILITY-ADJUSTED LIFE YEARS (DALYS) AVERTED	PUTTING DALYS INTO CONTEXT
ROLLING OUT MEDICINE AND TECHNOLOGY						
MenAfriVac in Chad (2012 GDP per capita: US$1,053)	2011–2013	Under-30 population of Chad	Morbidity and mortality from acute meningitis	12,469	875,844	World Health Organization (WHO) Global Health Estimates (GHE) states 456,700 DALYs lost from acute meningitis in under-30 population in 2012 in Chad (1).
Anti-retroviral therapy (ART) in Botswana (2012 GDP per capita: US$7,255)	2002–2010	Over-18 population of Botswana	Morbidity and mortality from HIV/AIDS	143,637	8,116,079	WHO GHE estimates 1,078,100 DALYs lost from HIV/AIDS in 2000 and 324,600 DALYs lost from HIV/AIDS in 2012 in Botswana (1).
Hepatitis B (hep B) vaccine in China (2012 GDP per capita: US$6,092)	2003–2009	Western and central provinces of China, under-5s	Morbidity and mortality from hepatocellular carcinoma, cirrhosis, and acute infection	93,200	3,100,000	WHO GHE estimates 1,479,400 DALYs lost from acute hep B; 9,757,700 DALYs lost from liver cancer; and 4,857,500 DALYS lost from cirrhosis in all ages in 2000 in China. WHO GHE also estimates 761,600 DALYs lost from acute hep B; 8,540,000 DALYs lost from liver cancer; and 1,875,100 DALYs lost from cirrhosis in all ages in 2012 in China (1).
Malaria in Zambia (2012 GDP per capita: US$1,771)	2001–2010	All newborns in Zambia	Morbidity and mortality from acute malaria	29,900	2,500,000	WHO GHE estimates 760,100 DALYs lost from malaria in 2000 in all ages (697,800 of these are in children 0–4 years) in Zambia (1).
Piso Firme in Mexico (2012 GDP per capita: US$9,817)	2007–2013	Mexican households with dirt floors, population under 6 years old	Diarrhea morbidity and mortality	408	34,248	WHO GHE estimates 178,100 DALYs lost from diarrheal disease in 2012 in Mexico (1).
Deworming in Kenya (2012 GDP per capita: US$1,165)	2012 (year of scale-up)	All school-age children in Kenya	Morbidity from soil-transmitted helmiths and schistosomiasis	NA	99,568	WHO GHE estimates 154,934 DALYs lost in children ages 5–14 in 2000. This declined to 40,267 DALYs lost in children ages 5–14 in 2012 (1).

COST/UNIT (US$)	COST PER DALY RATIO—INCREMENTAL COST-EFFECTIVENESS RATIO (ICER) ($FINANCIAL/DALY)	PUTTING ICER INTO CONTEXT
Budget: US$70 million for MenAfriVac vaccine project creation and to develop vaccine; US$1.40 per vaccinated person (2)	US$96.36	Routine polysaccharide vaccination is about US$50 per QALY (quality-adjusted life year) and about US$1,200 per fatal case in sub-Saharan Africa (6). Evidence that switching to conjugate vaccine is cost saving because of improved duration of effect over polysaccharide vaccine (2).
US$813 million	US$475	*Disease Control Priorities* (DCP2) finds ART range of US$350–US$1,494 per DALY averted (7). A South African study finds that the range is anywhere from cost saving to US$1,400 per DALY averted (8). Another South African study finds an estimate of US$200 per DALY averted (9).
US$10,345,200 Budget: Initial 5-year estimated project cost = US$76 million	US$3.33	DCP2 reports estimate of US$23,520 per DALY averted from deaths averted only (7). A study in Mozambique finds estimates of US$36 per DALY averted (undiscounted DALY) and US$47 per DALY averted (discounted DALY) (10).
Budget: Total budget of US$60 million	US$13.50	DCP2 finds estimates for the following interventions: insecticide-treated net (ITN): US$11 per DALY averted, range US$5–US$17 per DALY averted; indoor residual spraying (IRS): US$17 per DALY averted, range US$9–US$24 per DALY averted; intermittent preventive treatment in infants (IPTI): US$19 per DALY averted, range US$13–US$24 per DALY averted (with sulfadoxine pyrimethamine, with other drug US$2–US$11 per DALY averted); artemisinin combined therapy (ACT): < US$150 per DALY averted (change from chloroquine; will get worse over time, though) (7). A review of IPTI finds cost-effectiveness in the range of US$2.90–US$39.63 per DALY averted (11). A review of the cost-effectiveness of intermittent preventive treatment during pregnancy (IPTp) finds an estimate of US$1 per DALY averted (12). Another systematic review finds evidence of the following provider-perspective cost-effectiveness: ITN: US$27 per DALY averted (US$8.15–US$110); IRS: US$143 per DALY averted (US$135–US$150); IPTp: US$24 per DALY averted (US$1.08–US$44.24) (13).
NA	NA	NA
$5,638,902 (modeled based on unit costs from Jonah Sinick at GiveWell (3))	US$56.63	DCP2: US$3 per DALY averted, range US$2–US$9 per DALY averted (albendazole for *Trichuris* and hookworm); US$336–US$692 per DALY averted (praziquantel only for schistosomiasis); US$8–US$19 per DALY (albendazole + praziquantel) (7). A study in Uganda finds an estimate of US$3.19 per case of anemia averted (14). GiveWell's estimates are US$28.19–US$70.48 per DALY averted for schistosomiasis and US$82.54 per DALY averted for soil-transmitted helminth (3). J-PAL's estimate is US$4.55 per DALY averted (15).

continued

Table 1. *continued*

PROGRAM, COUNTRY, PER CAPITA GROSS DOMESTIC PRODUCT (GDP)	TIME HORIZON	TARGET POPULATION	KEY HEALTH OUTCOMES	DEATHS AVERTED	DISABILITY-ADJUSTED LIFE YEARS (DALYS) AVERTED	PUTTING DALYS INTO CONTEXT
EXPANDING ACCESS TO HEALTH SERVICES						
Plan Nacer in Argentina (2012 GDP per capita: US$13,693)	2005–2008	Newborn population in seven provinces in northern Argentina	Neonatal mortality and low-birth-weight morbidity	733	72,800	WHO GHE estimates 237,800 DALYs lost from neonatal conditions in children 0–4 years in 2000 (all, not specific for deaths) (1).
USING TARGETED CASH TRANSFERS TO IMPROVE HEALTH						
CT-OVC in Kenya (2012 GDP per capita: US$1,165)	2007–2009	Households with an orphan or vulnerable child	Sexual debut, likelihood of multiple sexual partners and early pregnancy among girls, and mental health among boys	NA	NA	NA
CHANGING BEHAVIOR POPULATION-WIDE TO REDUCE RISK						
Tobacco in Thailand (2012 GDP per capita: US$5,479)	1991–2006	Entire Thailand population ages 15 and over	Deaths and morbidity from chronic obstructive pulmonary disease (COPD), lung cancer, and cardiovascular disease (CVD)	29,357	541,695	WHO GHE estimates 340,000 DALYs lost from lung cancers; 675,000 DALYs lost from COPD; and 2,738,000 DALYs lost from CVD in 2000. WHO GHE estimates 467,000 DALYs lost from lung cancers; 739,000 DALYs lost from COPD; and 3,151,000 DALYs lost from CVD in 2012 (1).
Helmets in Vietnam (2012 GDP per capita: US$1,755)	2008 (single year)	Entire country, all ages	Injuries and deaths from traffic accidents	1,557	90,582	WHO GHE estimates 1,270,400 DALYs lost from road injury in all ages in 2012 in Vietnam (1).
Sanitation in Indonesia (2012 GDP per capita: US$3,551)	2007–2010	East Java, Indonesia, population under 5	Diarrhea morbidity and mortality	220	18,666	WHO GHE estimates 930,100 DALYs lost from diarrhea in children 0–4 years in 2012 in Indonesia (1).
Avahan in India (2012 GDP per capita: US$1,503)	2004–2008	Entire Avahan area, 83 districts	Morbidity and mortality from HIV/AIDS	202,000 HIV infections averted	3,471,973	WHO GHE estimates 6,377,000 DALYs lost from HIV/AIDS in 2000 in India. WHO GHE estimates 8,041,000 DALYs lost from HIV/AIDS in 2012 in India (1).

COST/UNIT (US$)	COST PER DALY RATIO— INCREMENTAL COST-EFFECTIVENESS RATIO (ICER) ($FINANCIAL/DALY)	PUTTING ICER INTO CONTEXT
US$20,450,000 (4)	US$814[a]	NA
Budget: US$9,960,000 for 2006–2009 pilot	CTR of US$0.34[b]	NA
NA	US$75.40	DCP2 finds the following cost-effectiveness results for tobacco price interventions: US$22 per DALY averted, range US$13–US$195 per DALY averted globally, range US$3–US$142 per DALY averted in low- and middle-income countries. For nonprice interventions (e.g., advertising bans, smoking restrictions, supply reduction, and health information), the DCP2 results are US$353 per DALY averted. Last, for nicotine replacement therapy, the DCP2 results are US$396 per DALY averted, range US$54–US$674 per DALY averted (16).
NA	US$1,248	A study from Thailand found the cost-effectiveness to be US$467 per DALY averted (7).
US$13,989,000	US$213[c]	DCP2 finds that cost-effectiveness for improved infrastructure for at least 5 years is US$4,185 per DALY averted, range US$1,974–US$6,390 per DALY averted. The cost-effectiveness for low-cost latrines is US$141 per DALY averted, range US$11–US$270 per DALY averted (7).
US$158,570,000 US$327 per person reached in the 4 years of the program (5).	US$46[d]	DCP2 finds the following cost-effectiveness results for HIV/AIDS. Voluntary testing and counseling: US$14–US$261 per DALY averted; peer education for high-risk groups (sex workers and intravenous drug users): US$1–US$74 per DALY averted; social marketing of condoms: US$19–US$205 per DALY averted; prevention of mother-to-child transmission with nevirapine: US$192 per DALY averted, range US$7–US$377 per DALY averted; sexually transmitted infection treatment: US$57 per DALY averted, range US$9–US$105 per DALY averted; antiretroviral therapy (ART): US$10–US$500 per DALY averted; home care: US$673 per DALY averted; ART in low adherence: US$922 per DALY averted, range US$350–US$1,494 per DALY averted; treating opportunistic infections: US$156 per DALY averted, range US$3–US$310 per DALY averted (7).

continued

Notes:

[a] In situ estimate (4).

[b] CTR (cash-transfer ratio) is the ratio of resources to the total amount of the transfer (Ward et al. 2010).

[c] Here, we were able to include household costs, which bring the cost-effectiveness ratio to 749.

[d] ICER (incremental cost-effectiveness ratio) from Vassall et al. (2014); disease burden estimates assume scale-up to all Avahan districts.

Table references:

1. World Health Organization. 2014. Global Health Estimates. Accessed September 3. http://www.who.int/healthinfo/global_burden_disease/en/.
2. LaForce, F.M., and J.M. Okwo-Bele. 2011. "Eliminating Epidemic Group A Meningococcal Meningitis in Africa through a New Vaccine." *Health Affairs* 30 (6): 1049–57.
3. Sinick, J. 2014. "Cost-Effectiveness in $/DALY for Deworming Interventions." Accessed August 19. http://www.givewell.org/print/1579.
4. Gertler, P., P. Giovagnoli, and S. Martinez. 2014. *Rewarding Provider Performance to Enable a Healthy Start to Life.* Policy Research Working Paper. Washington, DC: World Bank.
5. Vassall, A., M. Pickles, S. Chandrashekar, M.C. Boily, G. Shetty, L. Guinness, C.M. Lowndes, et al. 2014. "Cost-Effectiveness of HIV Prevention for High-Risk Groups at Scale: An Economic Evaluation of the Avahan Programme in South India." *Lancet Global Health* 2 (9): e531–40.
6. Bovier, P.A., K. Wyss, and H.J. Au. 1999. "A Cost-Effectiveness Analysis of Vaccination Strategies against *N. meningitidis* Meningitis in Sub-Saharan African Countries." *Social Science and Medicine* 48 (9): 1205–20.
7. Laxminarayan, R., J. Chow, and S.A. Shahid-Salles. 2006. "Intervention Cost-Effectiveness: Overview of Main Messages." In *Disease Control Priorities in Developing Countries,* edited by D.T. Jamison, J.G. Breman, A.R. Measham, G. Alleyne, M. Claeson, D.B. Evans, P. Jha, et al. Washington, DC: World Bank.
8. Granich, R., J.G. Kahn, R. Bennett, C.B. Holmes, N. Garg, C. Serenata, M.L. Sabin, et al. 2012. "Expanding ART for Treatment and Prevention of HIV in South Africa: Estimated Cost and Cost-Effectiveness 2011–2050." *PLoS One* 7 (2): e30216.
9. Kahn, J.G., E.A. Marseille, R. Bennett, B.G. Williams, and R. Granich. 2011. "Cost-Effectiveness of Antiretroviral Therapy for Prevention." *Current HIV Research* 9 (6): 405–15.
10. Griffiths, U.K., G. Hutton, and E. Das Dores Pascoal. 2005. "The Cost-Effectiveness of Introducing Hepatitis B Vaccine into Infant Immunization Services in Mozambique." *Health Policy and Planning* 20 (1): 50–9.
11. van Vugt, M., A. van Beest, E. Sicuri, M. van Tulder, and M.P. Grobusch. 2011. "Malaria Treatment and Prophylaxis in Endemic and Nonendemic Countries: Evidence on Strategies and Their Cost-Effectiveness." *Future Microbiology* 6 (12): 1485–500.
12. Conteh, L., E. Sicuri, F. Manzi, G. Hutton, B. Obonyo, F. Tediosi, P. Biao, et al. 2010. "The Cost-Effectiveness of Intermittent Preventive Treatment for Malaria in Infants in Sub-Saharan Africa." *PLoS One* 5 (6): e10313.
13. White, M.T., L. Conteh, R. Cibulskis, and A.C. Ghani. 2011. "Costs and Cost-Effectiveness of Malaria Control Interventions: A Systematic Review." *Malaria Journal* 10:337.
14. Brooker, S., N.B. Kabatereine, F. Fleming, and N. Devlin. 2008. "Cost and Cost-Effectiveness of Nationwide School-Based Helminth Control in Uganda: Intra-country Variation and Effects of Scaling-Up." *Health Policy and Planning* 23 (1): 24–35.
15. Abdul Latif Jameel Poverty Action Lab. 2012. *Deworming: A Best Buy for Development.* Cambridge, MA: Abdul Latif Jameel Poverty Action Lab.
16. Jha, P., F.J. Chaloupka, J. Moore, V. Gajalakshmi, P.C. Gupta, R. Peck, S. Asma, and W. Zatonski. 2006. "Tobacco Addiction." In *Disease Control Priorities in Developing Countries,* edited by D.T. Jamison, J.G. Breman, A.R. Measham, G. Alleyne, M. Claeson, D.B. Evans, P. Jha, et al. Washington, DC: World Bank.

Index

Center
for
Global
Development

The Center for Global Development works to reduce global poverty and inequality through rigorous research and active engagement with the policy community to make the world a more prosperous, just, and safe place for us all.

The policies and practices of the rich and the powerful—in rich nations, as well as in the emerging powers, international institutions, and global corporations—have significant impacts on the world's poor people. We aim to improve these policies and practices through research and policy engagement to expand opportunities, reduce inequalities, and improve lives everywhere.

By pairing research with action, CGD goes beyond contributing to knowledge about development. We conceive of and encourage discussion about practical policy innovations in areas such as trade, aid, health, education, climate change, labor mobility, private investment, access to finance, and global governance to foster shared prosperity in an increasingly interdependent world.

As a nimble, independent, nonpartisan, and nonprofit think tank, we leverage modest resources to combine world-class scholarly research with policy analysis and innovative outreach and communications to turn ideas into action.